Applying Enterprise JavaBeans™
Second Edition

The Java™ Series

Lisa Friendly, Series Editor
Tim Lindholm, Technical Editor
Ken Arnold, Technical Editor of The Jini™ Technology Series
Jim Inscore, Technical Editor of The Java™ Series, Enterprise Edition   **http://www.javaseries.com**

Eric Armstrong, Stephanie Bodoff, Debbie Carson, Maydene Fisher, Dale Green, Kim Haase
The Java™ Web Services Tutorial

Ken Arnold, James Gosling, David Holmes
The Java™ Programming Language, Third Edition

Joshua Bloch
Effective Java™ Programming Language Guide

Mary Campione, Kathy Walrath, Alison Huml
The Java™ Tutorial, Third Edition: A Short Course on the Basics

Mary Campione, Kathy Walrath, Alison Huml,Tutorial Team
The Java™ Tutorial Continued: The Rest of the JDK™

Patrick Chan
The Java™ Developers Almanac 1.4, Volume 1

Patrick Chan
The Java™ Developers Almanac 1.4, Volume 2

Patrick Chan, Rosanna Lee
The Java™ Class Libraries, Second Edition, Volume 2: java.applet, java.awt, java.beans

Patrick Chan, Rosanna Lee, Doug Kramer
The Java™ Class Libraries, Second Edition, Volume 1: java.io, java.lang, java.math, java.net, java.text, java.util

Patrick Chan, Rosanna Lee, Doug Kramer
The Java™ Class Libraries, Second Edition, Volume 1: Supplement for the Java™ 2 Platform, Standard Edition, v1.2

Kirk Chen, Li Gong
Programming Open Service Gateways with Java™ Embedded Server

Zhiqun Chen
Java Card™ Technology for Smart Cards: Architecture and Programmer's Guide

Maydene Fisher, Jon Ellis, Jonathan Bruce
JDBC™ API Tutorial and Reference, Third Edition

Li Gong, Gary Ellison, Mary Dageforde
Inside Java™ 2 Platform Security, Second Edition: Architecture, API Design, and Implementation

James Gosling, Bill Joy, Guy Steele, Gilad Bracha
The Java™ Language Specification, Second Edition

Doug Lea
Concurrent Programming in Java™, Second Edition: Design Principles and Patterns

Rosanna Lee, Scott Seligman
JNDI API Tutorial and Reference: Building Directory-Enabled Java™ Applications

Sheng Liang
The Java™ Native Interface: Programmer's Guide and Specification

Tim Lindholm, Frank Yellin
The Java™ Virtual Machine Specification, Second Edition

Roger Riggs, Antero Taivalsaari, Mark VandenBrink
Programming Wireless Devices with the Java™ 2 Platform, Micro Edition

Henry Sowizral, Kevin Rushforth, Michael Deering
The Java 3D™ API Specification, Second Edition

Sun Microsystems, Inc.
Java™ Look and Feel Design Guidelines: Advanced Topics

Kathy Walrath, Mary Campione
The JFC Swing Tutorial: A Guide to Constructing GUIs

Seth White, Maydene Fisher, Rick Cattell, Graham Hamilton, Mark Hapner
JDBC™ API Tutorial and Reference, Second Edition: Universal Data Access for the Java™ 2 Platform

Steve Wilson, Jeff Kesselman
Java™ Platform Performance: Strategies and Tactics

The Jini™ Technology Series

Eric Freeman, Susanne Hupfer, Ken Arnold
JavaSpaces™ Principles, Patterns, and Practice

The Java™ Series, Enterprise Edition

Stephanie Bodoff, Dale Green, Kim Haase, Eric Jendrock, Monica Pawlan, Beth Stearns
The J2EE™ Tutorial

Rick Cattell, Jim Inscore, Enterprise Partners
J2EE™ Technology in Practice: Building Business Applications with the Java™ 2 Platform, Enterprise Edition

Mark Hapner, Rich Burridge, Rahul Sharma, Joseph Fialli, Kim Haase
Java™ Message Service API Tutorial and Reference: Messaging for the J2EE™ Platform

Inderjeet Singh, Beth Stearns, Mark Johnson, Enterprise Team
Designing Enterprise Applications with the Java™ 2 Platform, Enterprise Edition

Vlada Matena, Sanjeev Krishnan, Beth Stearns
Applying Enterprise JavaBeans™ 2.1, Second Edition: Component-Based Development for the J2EE™ Platform

Bill Shannon, Mark Hapner, Vlada Matena, James Davidson, Eduardo Pelegri-Llopart, Larry Cable, Enterprise Team
Java™ 2 Platform, Enterprise Edition: Platform and Component Specifications

Rahul Sharma, Beth Stearns, Tony Ng
J2EE™ Connector Architecture and Enterprise Application Integration

Applying Enterprise JavaBeans™
Second Edition

Component-Based Development for the J2EE™ Platform

Vlada Matena

Sanjeev Krishnan

Linda DeMichiel

Beth Stearns

✦Addison-Wesley

Boston • San Francisco • New York • Toronto • Montreal
London • Munich • Paris • Madrid
Capetown • Sydney • Tokyo • Singapore • Mexico City

To my family
—Vlada Matena

To my parents and Kavitha
—Sanjeev Krishnan

To Jim and Caroline
—Linda DeMichiel

To two very special women: Edith Aujame and Jeanne Ashe
—Beth Stearns

Contents

Foreword

THE server-side landscape has changed considerably in the short time since the first edition of this book. Adoption of the Java™ 2 Platform, Enterprise Edition (J2EE™ platform) has been rampant; J2EE has taken over the mainstream of enterprise computing; and the J2EE technology is coming of age. The Enterprise JavaBeans™ (EJB) architecture—the core component technology of the J2EE platform—has evolved significantly from the model originally released as the EJB 1.1 specification, and this evolution has been driven largely by the needs of the J2EE community.

The evolution of the Enterprise JavaBeans architecture in the 2.0 and 2.1 releases reflects recent changes in distributed computing along with changes in the use of component technology.

The major forces driving the evolution of the EJB technology are the change in the way distributed applications are now structured and how EJB components are used to implement these applications.

Although the Enterprise JavaBeans architecture was originally conceived as providing a distributed business component facility, developers tend to use enterprise beans more for their ability to encapsulate business logic rather than to achieve distribution. To meet developer demand for light-weight, high-performance access to enterprise beans in applications where multitier distribution is not desired, the EJB 2.0 architecture introduced the concept of local enterprise beans. Local enterprise beans provide the benefit of EJB encapsulation coupled with the benefits of container services (such as transactions, security, and persistence), but without the additional complexity and overhead associated with distribution. Local EJB interfaces avoid the performance overhead of remote method invocation, and enable the developer to pass objects between enterprise beans using call-by-reference semantics. In the J2EE 1.3 platform, distribution in applications occurs primarily at the Web layer, and enterprise beans are used primarily for their benefits in structuring an application's business logic.

Another factor that has impacted the evolution of the Enterprise JavaBeans architecture is the experience that has been gained by both developers and vendors using EJB 2.0 container-managed persistence (CMP). This experience demonstrated the popularity of the concept, but it also uncovered limitations with the original EJB 1.1 design. The early CMP architecture, by necessity, was somewhat limited in scope. Experience showed that this early CMP architecture did not fully address the needs of EJB product vendors in ensuring a high level of scalability and performance, nor the needs of developers in facilitating more sophisticated modeling and portability.

The architects of the EJB 2.0 architecture therefore completely revamped the architecture's CMP model. The new architecture enables vendors to provide implementations with high performance and added features for ease of use. Such features include container-managed relationships—with support for automatic referential integrity management—and a portable query language, which allows developers to specify queries over related sets of entity beans using a convenient and portable SQL-like language. The EJB 2.0 CMP architecture allows EJB developers to more rapidly develop sophisticated applications that fully leverage the benefits provided by the EJB architecture. This new architecture retains the original EJB benefits while adding much richer persistence support and better container control of CMP entity bean state.

A third trend that has influenced the EJB architecture's evolution is the interest in more loosely-coupled, asynchronous applications. This led to the introduction of a third enterprise bean type in EJB 2.0—the message-driven bean. Message-driven beans enable the EJB technology—and with it the J2EE platform—to enter the world of asynchronous computing. Message-driven beans enable enterprise beans to receive asynchronous messages, thus allowing EJB components to integrate with legacy systems that use messaging to provide loosely-coupled application integration. Because the core messaging technology of the J2EE platform is the Java™ Message Service (JMS), EJB 2.0 message-driven beans were initially directly targeted at support for the use of JMS messaging. The EJB 2.1 architecture continues this support for asynchronicity. The EJB 2.1 architecture further generalizes message-driven beans to support the integration of arbitrary messaging types, and the 2.1 architecture also extends the technology by including the EJB timer service.

The evolution of the EJB architecture takes another exciting shift in direction with the EJB 2.1 release. A major new Web distribution model called Web services has emerged in the industry. This is a model for offering services designed to be accessed via programs rather than a browser. The central focus of the new EJB 2.1 architecture is Web services. Web services support in the EJB 2.1 architecture allows the functionality of EJB applications to be exposed over the Web, where they can be dynamically discovered and accessed over HTTP. Most importantly,

Web services allow service consumers and providers to be loosely and flexibly coupled; Web services support use from heterogeneous systems and enable integration of non-J2EE systems.

Initially, developers thought that implementing a Web service was equivalent to stripping the browser-support layer from an existing application and directly exposing its business logic. As experience with Web services has grown, it has become clear that Web service applications still require a non-browser *service* presentation layer to decouple Web services clients from the complexity of business logic. With the Web service support it now provides, the EJB 2.1 architecture is an excellent facility for implementing a Web service's presentation layer.

The EJB 2.1 architecture also enables enterprise beans to be clients of Web services, making it possible for application developers to compose EJB applications from aggregations of such services. The implementation of Web services with the EJB 2.1 architecture is easy and straightforward, and leverages the familiar stateless session bean model.

The global access and interoperability currently provided by the Simple Object Access Protocol (SOAP) and Web Services Description Language (WSDL) Web services standards adds significant value to enterprise bean components and the EJB architecture. With Web services, the EJB architecture gains global reach. Access to a service implemented with enterprise bean components is no longer restricted to EJB-aware clients; this service can now be accessed with the same global, heterogeneous model that empowered browser-based services. In addition to its new role in implementing the service presentation layer for Web services, the EJB 2.1 architecture continues to deliver a robust business component model for implementing the business logic and domain models of both Web sites and Web services.

The Enterprise JavaBeans architecture, at the core of the J2EE platform, has played a key role in its evolution—expanding its scope in providing scalable and reliable enterprise computing, and adding new features to promote more rapid development of enterprise applications. In addition to fulfilling its original goals of providing *the* portable component model for enterprise applications, the EJB architecture has expanded to encompass the key technological underpinnings to support integration with legacy systems, asynchronous communication, and the infrastructure for Web services technologies.

The EJB architecture and its components have thus matured to support today's style of applications—applications that focus on the Web for distribution, require loosely-coupled messaging for integrating business flows, and desire formal components for better encapsulation of business logic within multiple service tiers.

The EJB architecture team and expert group have done a great job shepherding the EJB technology through this process of evolution. They have ensured that the EJB architecture has retained all of its original essential benefits while at the same time keeping it closely in tune with today's evolving needs.

Mark Hapner
Lead Architect, J2EE platform
Sun Microsystems

Preface

THIS book, now in its second edition, provides in-depth coverage of the Enterprise JavaBeans™ (EJB) 2.1 architecture, explaining how to develop and deploy enterprise applications by using the latest EJB component architecture. This second edition covers the new 2.0 and 2.1 features of the EJB architecture, including message-driven beans and asynchronous communication, enhanced container-managed persistence, support for Web services, and the EJB™ Query Language (EJB QL).

This book is part of the successful Java BluePrints program created by Sun Microsystems with the introduction of the Java™ 2 Platform, Enterprise Edition (J2EE™ platform). The Java BluePrints program has been used by thousands of application architects, developers, and students to attain a better understanding of the programming model inherent in the J2EE platform.

This book and the Java BluePrints program do not provide information on how to use individual Java technologies to write applications—that's the role of the companion Java Tutorial program. Instead, Java BluePrints focuses on guidelines for application architecture.

Readers of this book should be familiar with the Java™ programming language, should have a basic knowledge of the J2EE platform, and should have had some exposure to enterprise beans and the EJB architecture. Although we briefly cover the basics of the EJB architecture, this book is not meant to be a tutorial for those just getting started with enterprise beans. Instead, the book provides in-depth coverage of the EJB 2.0 and 2.1 architectures for information technology (IT) personnel implementing applications in-house and for independent software vendors (ISVs) developing generic applications for sale to enterprises.

The EJB architecture defines a component model for enterprise applications, focusing on the following:

- How to design an application as a set of components

- How the components interact with each other

- How the components interact with their EJB container

The EJB architecture defines these interactions as *contracts*, which enable applications to use components from different sources. Because EJB components must adhere to these contracts, an application can consist of software components from multiple vendors.

The EJB specification defines the architecture contracts mainly from the point of view of the container vendor. In contrast, this book presents the EJB architecture from the point of view of the application developer—that is, the person who develops EJB applications.

A detailed description of the development of two enterprise applications forms the backbone of the book. Although the example applications are relatively simple, they illustrate many of the typical problems encountered in enterprise application development. We use these examples to show how the EJB architecture helps developers solve these problems.

The first example is a benefits enrollment application developed in-house by an IT department. This application works well for explaining how a session bean works and for illustrating how developers use session beans.

The second example turns the benefits application from the first example into an application developed by an ISV. An ISV's design goals differ from those of an in-house IT department. The ISV must design the application so that it can be easily deployed in many different customers' operational environments. Because each customer has a unique operational environment, the ISV must address a number of challenges. In addition, an ISV typically needs to design the application so that it can be extended by a customer or integrator. We illustrate how the entity bean architecture helps ISVs to overcome these challenges.

The EJB 2.1 architecture makes it possible to implement applications as Web services. This updated edition of the book includes a chapter that describes how to incorporate and use enterprise beans in a Web service.

These annotated examples illustrate many of the techniques for applying the EJB architecture to specific problems in enterprise application development. In addition, we describe the individual features of the EJB architecture and discuss when and how they should be used in applications.

Although the typical application developer does not need to know how the EJB container works, we illustrate some of the inner workings of the EJB container. We do this mainly to give the reader an appreciation of how much work the container performs on behalf of the application.

Conventions Used in This Book

The following are the conventions used in this book.

Graphics

Many of the graphics in this book depict Unified Modeling Language (UML) diagrams. The conventions used in these diagrams follow the UML standard. Briefly, Figure P.1 illustrates the arrows and connectors used in standard UML diagrams.

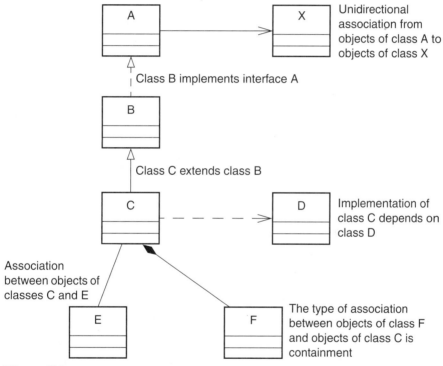

Figure P.1 UML Symbols

Typographic Conventions

Table P.1 describes the typographic conventions used in this book.

Table P.1 Typographic Conventions

Typeface or Symbol	Meaning	Example
AaBbCc123	The names of commands, files, and directories; interface, class, method, variable, and deployment descriptor element names; programming language keywords	Edit the file AccountBean.java. Uses an AccountHome object. Invokes the method ejbCreate.
AaBcCc123	Book titles, new words or terms, or words to be emphasized	Read Chapter 2 in *EJB 1.1 Specification.* This is a *stateless session bean.* You *must* be careful when using this option.

Other Sources of Information

You should refer to other publications related to the Java 2 Platform, Enterprise Edition (J2EE) application architecture. The following books and specifications are of particular interest to developers of application components other than enterprise beans.

- "Enterprise JavaBeans™ 2.1 Specification, Final Release," Sun Microsystems, 2002. Available at http://java.sun.com/j2ee.

- "Java™ 2 Platform, Enterprise Edition Specification, Version 1.4," Sun Microsystems, 2002. Available at http://java.sun.com/j2ee.

- "Java™ 2 Platform, Enterprise Edition, Connector Specification, Version 1.5," Sun Microsystems, 2002. Available at http://java.sun.com/j2ee.

- "Java™ API for XML-Based RPC Specification Version 1.0," Sun Microsystems, 2002. Available at http://java.sun.com/j2ee.

- *J2EE™ Connector Architecture and Enterprise Application Integration* by Rahul Sharma, Beth Stearns, and Tony Ng (Addison-Wesley, 2001).

- *Java™ Message Service API Tutorial and Reference: Messaging for the J2EE™ Platform* by Mark Hapner, Rich Burridge, Rahul Sharma, Joseph Fialli, and Kim Haase (Addison-Wesley, 2001).

- *Designing Enterprise Applications with the J2EE™ Platform, Second Edition* by Inderjeet Singh, Beth Stearns, Mark Johnson, and Enterprise Team (Addison-Wesley, 2002).

- *The J2EE™ Tutorial* by Stephanie Bodoff, Dale Green, Kim Haase, Eric Jendrock, Monica Pawlan, and Beth Stearns (Addison-Wesley, 2002). Also available at `http://java.sun.com/j2ee/tutorial`.

Note about the Example Applications

It is important to note that the example applications described in the book are written *without* the use of an interactive development environment (IDE). Normally, enterprise developers use a commercial IDE when developing EJB applications. An IDE generates much of the JDBC™ and other database access code—code that is often tedious to write by hand. However, we wanted our examples to illustrate how the EJB architecture works; had we used an IDE, the code it generated would obscure the discussion of the EJB architecture. Therefore, we chose to write all the code manually. Keep this in mind and realize that because in practice, a lot of the code is generated automatically by the IDE, developing with the EJB architecture is easier than some of our code samples may indicate.

Because our goal is to illustrate the use of the EJB architecture, we wanted to keep the code relatively simple. As a result, we don't always show what some developers would consider to be the best coding practices for enterprise applications. By including code to show such practices, we would have obscured the EJB discussion. For the sake of simplicity of the code examples, we sometimes do not handle properly all exceptions thrown by the code.

The example application for this second edition is available for download at `http://java.sun.com/docs/books/applyingejb/2ed/download`.

Contents of the Book

The book begins by describing the advantages of the EJB architecture. Chapter 1, Advantages of the Enterprise JavaBeans™ Architecture, discusses the various enterprise application architectures and how they have evolved, especially with the growth of the Web. The chapter describes the current state-of-the-art EJB, J2EE, and Web services architectures and explains how they are well suited to meet today's enterprise computing needs.

Chapter 2, Enterprise JavaBeans Architecture Overview, provides a concise overview of the EJB architecture. For someone not so familiar with the EJB architecture, this chapter is a good starting point because it defines the EJB terminology and the structure of enterprise beans. The chapter defines and describes EJB applications and such basic concepts as business entities and business processes. It provides an overview of the various enterprise bean types, the parts that comprise an enterprise bean, and how to use enterprise beans to model business logic of enterprise applications.

The development of an EJB application can be thought of in terms of the tasks that need to be performed. To that end, Chapter 3, Enterprise JavaBeans Roles, delineates the roles and tasks involved during the application development process.

Once the stage has been set and the introductory material explained, the book focuses on session beans, entity beans, and message-driven beans. Two chapters focus on session beans and two chapters focus on entity beans. Chapter 4, Working with Session Beans, discusses typical programming styles for applications using session beans. This chapter is of interest to bean developers implementing session beans and to application programmers developing session bean clients. For bean developers, the chapter describes how best to implement the methods of a session bean. For application programmers developing session bean clients, the chapter shows how to use the session bean home, remote, and local interfaces properly. An extensive benefits enrollment application example illustrates the key points about session beans.

Chapter 5, Session Bean in Its Container, describes the support and services that an EJB container provides for a session bean. Containers typically provide services to session beans when they are deployed and customized for a particular operational environment and at runtime, when a client application invokes the session bean. Although the container services are hidden from the bean developer and the client programmer, these services go a long way in simplifying bean and application development. This chapter describes much of what goes on behind the scenes.

After completing the discussion of session beans, Chapter 6, Using Message-Driven Beans and Connectors, presents message-driven beans and their use in enterprise application integration (EAI). A message-driven bean, a new type of enterprise bean introduced in the EJB 2.0 architecture, enables asynchronous message-oriented communication with enterprise beans. This chapter presents the basic concepts of the Java™ Message Service (JMS) and then explains how to develop message-driven beans. The benefits enrollment application from Chapter 4 is extended to show how to integrate it with a payroll application in a loosely coupled manner using message-driven beans.

The book then shifts its focus to entity beans. Entity beans differ significantly from session beans. Chapter 7, Understanding Entity Beans, combines a presentation of the basic concepts regarding programming with entity beans, from both the client and bean developer points of view, with a discussion of the services that the container provides to entity beans. This chapter is analogous to Chapter 5 for session beans. The chapter also provides a detailed description of strategies for managing entity object state: bean-managed and container-managed persistence, including the EJB QL query language. Chapter 8, Entity Bean Application Example, takes the benefits enrollment application example used for session beans and shows how to write the same application using entity beans. The example illustrates many of the techniques for working with entity beans and using container-managed persistence, as well as how entity beans can be used by ISVs to make their applications reusable across many customers' operational environments.

Web services technologies have become prominent in the last few years as a means to integrate applications across enterprises using interoperable, standards-based protocols and service description formats. Chapter 9, Using Enterprise JavaBeans in Web Services, introduces Web services technologies. It discusses how to use the EJB architecture to build and access Web services using new Java standard APIs that are being developed.

Virtually all applications using enterprise beans rely on transactions. Chapter 10, Understanding Transactions, describes the EJB architecture approach to transaction demarcation. The chapter covers the essential aspects of transactions necessary for application developers.

Security is another area of critical importance to enterprise applications. The EJB architecture provides declarative support for security management. Chapter 11, Managing Security, describes the EJB security environment, particularly from the point of view of the application developer.

The book also includes an appendix and a glossary. Appendix A contains code samples of supporting classes. The complete, up-to-date EJB API reference can be found at `http://java.sun.com/apis.html`.

Acknowledgments

WE would like to thank the following individuals who, on short notice, took the time to review the early draft of the book and provided us with invaluable feedback: Mark Hapner, Bill Shannon, Rahul Sharma, Rick Cattell, George Copeland, Susan Cheung, Liane Acker, Jim Frentress, Moshe Sambol, and John Stearns. We also want to thank the following individuals for reviewing the final draft of the book and for providing feedback: Liane Acker, Ken Nordby, Jorgen Thelin, Marc Fleury , Jim Healy, and Jim Frentress.

We especially want to thank Walter Jenny and Rahul Sharma. Walter's programming brought the entity bean example application to life at the JavaOne show in June 2001. Rahul not only reviewed both drafts of the book but also developed the PayrollBean to use the J2EE™ Connector specification to access a mainframe application.

We want to thank Ken Saks and Inderjeet Singh for reviewing the new material added in this second edition. In addition, Ken was particularly helpful answering questions related to the latest specifications and making sure that the text and sample code reflect those specifications.

We want to thank Christine Stearns for her ideas and sketches for the second-edition cover art, and the Addison-Wesley artists for its implementation.

We also want to acknowledge the following people who helped us accomplish all the tasks necessary to publish this book: Jeff Jackson, for enthusiastically encouraging us to do this book; Lisa Friendly and Jim Inscore, for assisting us with publication details; and Mike Hendrickson, Ross Venables, Ann Sellers, Jacquelyn Doucette, and Marcy Barnes-Henrie, among others at Addison-Wesley, who had the flexibility to adapt their schedules to ours.

CHAPTER 1

Advantages of the Enterprise JavaBeans™ Architecture

ENTERPRISE JavaBeans (EJB) is a state-of-the-art architecture for developing, deploying, and managing reliable enterprise applications in production environments. This chapter illustrates the benefits of using the EJB architecture for enterprise applications.

This chapter discusses the evolution of enterprise application architectures. Such architectures inevitably must evolve because the underlying computer support and delivery systems have changed enormously and will continue to change in the future. With the growth of the Web and the Internet, more and more enterprise applications, including intranet and extranet applications, are now Web based. Together, the Java™ 2 Platform, Enterprise Edition (J2EE™) and the EJB architectures provide superior support for Web-based enterprise applications.

Using the EJB architecture has many benefits. This chapter describes the advantages of the EJB architecture and its benefits to application developers and customers.

1.1 From a Two-Tier to a J2EE Architecture

Enterprise application architectures have undergone an extensive evolution. The first generation of enterprise applications consisted of centralized mainframe applications. In the late 1980s and early 1990s, most new enterprise applications followed a two-tier, or *client/server*, architecture. Later, the enterprise architecture evolved to a three-tier architecture and then to a Web-based architecture. The current evolutionary state is now represented by the J2EE application architecture. The J2EE architecture provides comprehensive support for two- and three-tier applications, as well as Web-based and Web services applications.

This section discusses the evolution of enterprise application architectures, starting with the two-tier architecture. Because it has little relevance to the material in this book, we do not describe how the architectures evolved from the centralized mainframe architecture to the two-tier architecture.

1.1.1   Two-Tier Application Architecture

With a two-tier application, a business system is structured as a collection of operating system–level application processes that execute on the client machine: typically, a PC in a corporation. Each such application implements one or several business processes, as well as the GUI (graphical user interface) presentation logic for the interactions between the business processes and the user. (A business process is an encapsulation of a user's interactions with some enterprise information.) The application running on the client PC communicates over the network with a database server storing the corporate databases. The database server stores the corporate data, and the client application typically accesses the data via Structured Query Language (SQL) statements (Figure 1.1).

Before the existence of the Web, the two-tier architecture worked well for most applications. Its main advantage is that it is easy to develop two-tier applications, particularly because the presentation logic and the business logic reside in the same process, and the developer does not have to deal with the complexity of a distributed application.

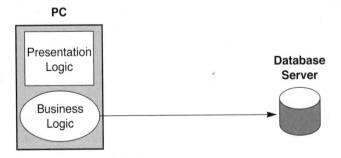

Figure 1.1   Two-Tier Application Architecture

However, its disadvantages outweigh its advantages. The main disadvantage of the two-tier architecture is that programmers cannot cleanly separate business logic from presentation logic. This results in a number of problems: easily compromised database integrity, difficulties in administration and maintenance, exposure to security violations, limited scalability, restricted client architecture requirements, and limitation to one presentation type.

- **It is easy to compromise database integrity.** Because each client program embeds the business logic, an error or bug in the client program can easily compromise the integrity of the corporate database.

- **It is difficult to administer in a large enterprise.** In this architecture, the application is deployed on the client machines, and the information technology (IT) department of the corporation must maintain the application. If a business process changes, the IT department must replace all copies of the old version of the application with a new version of the application. This is a difficult task in a corporation with tens of thousands of PCs, especially when many of them may be "unmanaged" laptop machines.

- **It is difficult to maintain the code.** The two-tier architecture does not support modular programming, making it difficult to maintain application code. Maintenance difficulty increases exponentially for larger organizations, which typically use more programmers to code and maintain applications.

- **It exposes the applications to security violations.** A skillful programmer may "hack" the application installed on the PC to alter the business process that the application implements.

- **Its scalability is limited; it is difficult to scale to a large number of users.** Each running application typically needs a connection to the corporate database. Because the number of open connections is typically limited by the database product, it may not be possible for all users to run the application at the same time.

- **It requires a homogeneous client architecture.** Before the advent of the Java language, the two-tier architecture typically required the client machines to be homogeneous. For example, it typically required all client machines to be PCs running the same type of operating system.

- **It ties the application to one particular presentation type.** Because the same application implements not only the business processes but also the presentation, it may not be possible to reuse the implementation of the business process with a different presentation type, such as a browser or intelligent cell phone.

The onset and growth of the Web changed all the rules. Although the corporation could live with the limitations of the two-tier architecture before the Web, these limitations essentially make the two-tier architecture completely incompatible with the Web, chiefly because Web clients inherently lack intelligence, and because there are so many such clients. In addition, the limitations of the two-tier architecture make it impossible for an enterprise to integrate its business applications with applications from partners, customers, and suppliers. As a result, application developers and their customers have been seeking alternative application architectures.

1.1.2   Traditional Three-Tier Application Architecture

The traditional three-tier architecture overcomes some of the limitations of the two-tier architecture. The three-tier architecture splits the presentation logic from the business logic, placing the business logic on a server; only the presentation logic is deployed on the client PCs (Figure 1.2).

The three-tier architecture brings about a number of improvements. The middle-tier server improves scalability by reusing expensive resources, such as database connections, across multiple clients. Improved scalability results in improved performance. This architecture also improves security and application management. The three-tier architecture has been used in most enterprise resource planning (ERP) systems and in the systems specialized for high-volume transaction processing (CICS, Tuxedo, and others).

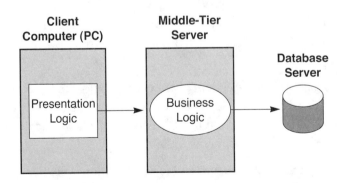

Figure 1.2   Three-Tier Application Architecture

Although it eliminates some of the flaws of the two-tier architecture, the three-tier architecture too has certain disadvantages: complexity, lack of application portability, vendor incompatibility, limited adoption, and Web incompatibility.

- **Complexity**—Developing a three-tier application is more complex than developing a two-tier application. For example, the programmer must deal with distribution, multithreading, security, and so forth. Distributed applications introduce substantial system-level programming complexities with which the developer must deal. Also, distributed applications require the customer IT department to compensate for the lack of application deployment and administration support. In an attempt to reduce the complexity of distributed applications, vendors resorted to using application frameworks, such as transaction processing (TP) monitors. ERP vendors used the concept of an application server. The intention of the application frameworks was to free the application programmer from having to deal with these complexities. Today, *application server* is the most frequently used term for a distributed application framework.

- **Lack of application portability**—Because each vendor of an application framework for the three-tier platform uses different application program interfaces (APIs) in its framework, it is not possible for independent software vendors (ISVs) to write applications that are deployable on application servers provided by other vendors.

- **Vendor incompatibility**—It is difficult to integrate applications from multiple vendors, because each vendor uses a different set of protocols, and there is no standard interoperability among protocols.

- **Limited adoption**—ISVs have no incentive to write applications for multiple competing frameworks that are not widely adopted. Although tools exist to support distributed applications, these tools work only on the frameworks for which they were developed. Many tools do not work across most frameworks. As a result, there is limited support for a consistent set of tools. Likewise, programmers' knowledge of tools and frameworks is also limited.

- **Incompatibility with the Web**—The traditional three-tier architecture does not work directly with the Web. The three-tier architecture uses a proprietary protocol for the communication between the client and the application running on the server, and this proprietary protocol does not work with the Web. Although many application framework vendors have added support for Web clients as a front end to their existing products, the resultant architecture still suffers from the other drawbacks listed here.

1.1.3 Early Web-Based Application Architecture

The introduction and growth of the Web changed everything. Because neither the two-tier nor the traditional three-tier architecture supports the development of Web applications, early Web application developers had to devise another approach. They used various plug-in extensions to Web servers. These extensions invoke on the server programs that dynamically construct HTML (HyperText Markup Language) documents from the information stored in corporate databases. Likewise, the Web server extensions enter information submitted in HTML forms into the corporate database.

An example of such an extension is cgi-bin scripts. (CGI, or Common Gateway Interface, is an interface for developing HTML pages and Web applications. CGI applications are commonly referred to as *cgi-bin scripts*.) Although cgi-bin scripts and similar mechanisms allowed a corporate developer to build simple Web applications, the cgi-bin approach does not scale to more complex enterprise applications, for the following reasons:

- Cgi-bin scripts do not provide well-structured encapsulation of the underlying business process or of a business entity.

- Cgi-bin scripts are difficult to develop, maintain, and manage. High-level application development tools do not provide good support for the development of cgi-bin scripts.

- Cgi-bin scripts intertwine the implementation of business processes with the implementation of the presentation logic. When it is necessary to change one part of the implementation, such as a business process, the other part may be changed inadvertently.

- Cgi-bin script implementations do not foster the maintenance of the integrity of business rules. The implementation of an enterprise's business rules is scattered across the cgi-bin scripts deployed on numerous Web servers in the enterprise. Therefore, it is difficult for the enterprise to maintain the integrity of its business rules.

1.1.4   J2EE Application Architecture

J2EE is a standard architecture specifically oriented to the development and deployment of enterprise Web-oriented applications using the Java programming language.
ISVs and enterprises can use the J2EE architecture for not only the development and
deployment of intranet applications, thus effectively replacing the two-tier and
three-tier models, but also for the development of Internet applications, effectively
replacing the cgi-bin-based approach. The J2EE architecture provides a flexible distribution and tiering model that allows enterprises to construct their applications in
the most suitable manner. This model encompasses all the generations of application
architectures and supports the latest Web services architectures, as shown in the following diagrams.

Figure 1.3 illustrates the J2EE application programming model for Web-based
applications. This programming model is typically used for e-commerce applications, in which the client is a customer's computer or device on the Internet, as
well as for enterprise applications, in which the client is an employee's computer.
The figure shows how the EJB and Web tiers may be either colocated in the same
application server or distributed across servers.

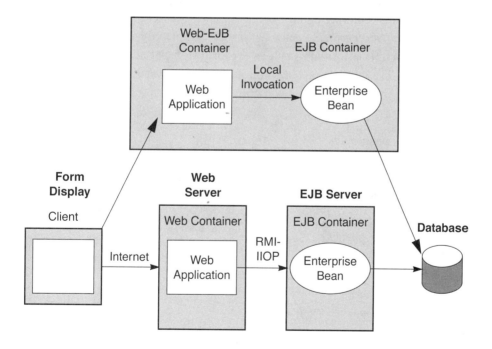

Figure 1.3   J2EE Application Programming Model for Web-Based Applications

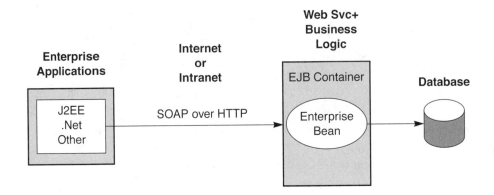

Figure 1.4   J2EE Application Programming Model for Web Service Applications

Figure 1.4 shows how the J2EE architecture may be used for Web service interactions between two enterprises or between two applications within an enterprise. In this scenario, the EJB tier directly provides a Web service view that applications in another enterprise may use over the Internet. Because it supports standard Web service protocols, such as SOAP (Simple Object Access Protocol), and service description formats, such as WSDL (Web Services Description Language), the J2EE architecture can interoperate with non-J2EE applications in other enterprises or within the same enterprise.

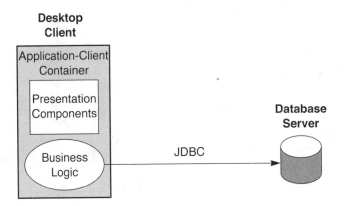

Figure 1.5   J2EE Application Programming Model for Two-Tier Applications

J2EE also provides support for two-tier and three-tier applications. Figure 1.5 illustrates the support for two-tier applications. (Note that *Application-Client Container* refers to the Java 2, Standard Edition [J2SE] programming environment.)

Figure 1.6 illustrates the support for three-tier applications. Presentation components are kept separate from business logic on two different tiers, whereas a third tier holds the persistent data.

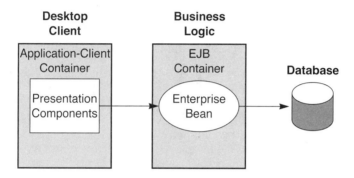

Figure 1.6   J2EE Application Programming Model for Three-Tier Applications

The J2EE platform also provides supports for Java applets, small programs loaded from the Web container to the browser, where they reside in an applet container. The Web container hosts the Web application, and the EJB container hosts the business logic. Figure 1.7 illustrates this application programming model.

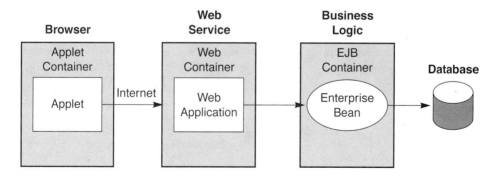

Figure 1.7   J2EE Application Programming Model for Web-Based Applets

The J2EE platform consists of four programming environments, called *containers*:

1. **EJB container** — Provides the environment for the development, deployment, and runtime management of enterprise beans. Enterprise beans are components that implement business logic, which consists of business processes and entities.

2. **Web container** — Provides the environment for the development, deployment, and runtime management of servlets and JavaServer Pages™ (JSP). The servlets and JSP are grouped into deployable units called *Web applications*. A Web application implements the presentation logic of an enterprise application.

3. **Application-client container** — Provides the environment for executing J2EE application clients. This environment is essentially J2SE.

4. **Applet container** — Provides the environment for executing Java applets. This environment is typically embedded in a Web browser.

This book focuses mainly on the development and deployment of enterprise beans rather than on the development of the other application parts. We demonstrate fragments of the other parts (Web applications) only to illustrate the interactions between enterprise beans and their clients. Refer to *Designing Enterprise Applications with the J2EE™ Platform, Second Edition* by Inderjeet Singh, Beth Stearns, Mark Johnson, and the Enterprise Team (Addison-Wesley, 2002) for a more complete description of how to develop these other parts of a J2EE application.

Note also that the J2EE platform embraces the Common Object Request Broker Architecture (CORBA). All J2EE containers include a CORBA-compliant Object Request Broker (ORB). The interoperability protocol between EJB containers from multiple vendors is based on CORBA standards, such as remote method invocation over Internet Inter-ORB Protocol (RMI-IIOP) and other CORBA standards for transactions, security, and name services. These interoperable protocols allow application servers from different vendors to interoperate within an enterprise.

1.2   Advantages of the Architecture

The EJB component architecture is the backbone of the J2EE platform. The core of a J2EE application is comprised of one or several enterprise beans that perform the application's business operations and encapsulate the business logic of an application. Other parts of the J2EE platform, such as the JSP, complement the EJB architecture to provide such functions as presentation logic and client interaction control logic.

ISVs, integrators, and customers can develop and customize EJB applications. As we explain how EJB applications overcome the limitations of the two- and three-tier architectures and the early Web application architectures and enjoy additional advantages not found in these architectures, keep in mind that the EJB architecture defines the following major roles, which Chapter 3, Enterprise Java-Beans Roles, discusses in detail:

- **Bean developer**—Develops the enterprise bean component

- **Application assembler**—Composes the enterprise bean component into larger, deployable units

- **Deployer**—Deploys the application within a particular operational environment

- **System administrator**—Configures and administers the enterprise computing and networking infrastructure

- **EJB container provider** and **EJB server provider**—A vendor (or vendors) specializing in transaction and application management and other low-level services

The EJB architecture provides benefits to all these roles. Here we focus on the benefits to application developers and customers.

1.2.1   Benefits to the Application Developer

The EJB architecture provides the following benefits to the application developer: simplicity, application portability, component reusability, ability to build complex applications, separation of business logic from presentation logic, easy development of Web services, deployment in many operating environments, distributed deployment, application interoperability, integration with non-Java systems, and educational resources and development tools.

- **Simplicity**—It is easier to develop an enterprise application with the EJB architecture than without it. Because the EJB architecture helps the application developer access and use enterprise services with minimal effort and time, writing an enterprise bean is almost as simple as writing a Java class. The application developer does not have to be concerned with system-level issues, such as security, transactions, multithreading, security protocols, distributed programming, connection resource pooling, and so forth. As a result, the application developer can concentrate on the business logic for the domain-specific application.

- **Application portability**—An EJB application can be deployed on any J2EE-compliant server. This means that the application developer can sell the application to any customers who use a J2EE-compliant server. This also means that enterprises are not locked in to a particular application server vendor. Instead, they can choose the "best-of-breed" application server that meets their requirements.

- **Component reusability**—An EJB application consists of enterprise bean components. Each enterprise bean is a reusable building block. There are two essential ways to reuse an enterprise bean:

    1. An enterprise bean not yet deployed can be reused at application development time by being included in several applications. The bean can be customized for each application without requiring changes, or even access, to its source code.

    2. Other applications can reuse an enterprise bean that is already deployed in a customer's operational environment, by making calls to its client-view interfaces. Multiple applications can make calls to the deployed bean.

    In addition, the business logic of enterprise beans can be reused through Java subclassing of the enterprise bean class.

- **Ability to build complex applications**—The EJB architecture simplifies building complex enterprise applications. These EJB applications are built by a team of developers and evolve over time. The component-based EJB architecture is well suited to the development and maintenance of complex enterprise applications. With its clear definition of roles and well-defined interfaces, the EJB architecture promotes and supports team-based development and lessens the demands on individual developers.

- **Separation of business logic from presentation logic** — An enterprise bean typically encapsulates a business process or a business entity (an object representing enterprise business data), making it independent of the presentation logic. The business programmer need not worry about formatting the output; the Web page designer developing the Web page need be concerned only with the output data that will be passed to the Web page. In addition, this separation makes it possible to develop multiple presentation logic for the same business process or to change the presentation logic of a business process without needing to modify the code that implements the business process.

- **Easy development of Web services** — The Web services features of the EJB architecture provide an easy way for Java developers to develop and access Web services. Java developers do not need to bother about the complex details of Web services description formats and XML-based wire protocols but instead can program at the familiar level of enterprise bean components and Java interfaces and data types. The tools provided by the container manage the mapping to the Web services standards.

- **Deployment in many operating environments** — The goal of an ISV is to sell an application to many customers. Because each customer has a unique operational environment, the application typically needs to be customized at deployment time to each operational environment, including different database schemas.

  - The EJB architecture allows the bean developer to separate the common application business logic from the customization logic performed at deployment.

  - The EJB architecture allows an entity bean to be bound to different database schemas. This persistence binding is done at deployment. The application developer can write code that is not limited to a single type of database management system (DBMS) or database schema.

  - The EJB architecture facilitates the deployment of an application by establishing deployment standards, such as those for data source lookup, other application dependencies, security configuration, and so forth. The standards enable the use of deployment tools. The standards and tools remove much of the possibility of miscommunication between the developer and the deployer.

- **Distributed deployment** — The EJB architecture makes it possible for applications to be deployed in a distributed manner across multiple servers on a network. The bean developer does not have to be aware of the deployment topology when developing enterprise beans but rather writes the same code whether the client of an enterprise bean is on the same machine or a different one.

*   **Application interoperability**—The EJB architecture makes it easier to integrate applications from different vendors. The enterprise bean's client-view interface serves as a well-defined integration point between applications.

*   **Integration with non-Java systems**—The related J2EE APIs, such as the J2EE Connector specification and the Java™ Message Service (JMS) specification, and J2EE Web services technologies, such as the Java™ API for XML-based RPC (JAX-RPC), make it possible to integrate enterprise bean applications with various non-Java applications, such as ERP systems or mainframe applications, in a standard way.

*   **Educational resources and development tools**—Because the EJB architecture is an industrywide standard, the EJB application developer benefits from a growing body of educational resources on how to build EJB applications. More important, the powerful application development tools available from the leading tool vendors simplify the development and maintenance of EJB applications.

1.2.2   Benefits to Customers

A customer's perspective on the EJB architecture is different from that of the application developer. The EJB architecture provides the following benefits to the customer: choice of application server, facilitation of application management, integration with the customer's existing applications and data, integration with enterprise applications of customers, partners, and suppliers, and application security.

*   **Choice of server**—Because the EJB architecture is an industrywide standard and is part of the J2EE platform, customer organizations have a wide choice of J2EE-compliant servers. Customers can select a product that meets their needs in terms of scalability, integration capabilities with other systems, security protocols, price, and so forth. Customers are not locked in to a specific vendor's product. Should their needs change, customers can easily redeploy an EJB application in a server from a different vendor.

- **Facilitation of application management** — Because the EJB architecture provides a standardized environment, server vendors have had the motivation to develop application management tools to enhance their products. As a result, sophisticated application management tools provided with the EJB container allow the customer's IT department to perform such functions as starting and stopping the application, allocating system resources to the application, and monitoring security violations, among others.

- **Integration with a customer's existing applications and data** — The EJB architecture and the other related J2EE APIs simplify and standardize the integration of EJB applications with any non-Java applications and systems at the customer operational environment. For example, a customer does not have to change an existing database schema to fit an application. Instead, an EJB application can be made to fit the existing database schema when it is deployed.

- **Integration with enterprise applications of customers, partners, and suppliers** — The interoperability and Web services features of the EJB architecture allow EJB-based applications to be exposed as Web services to other enterprises. This means that enterprises have a single, consistent technology for developing intranet, Internet, and e-business applications.

- **Application security** — The EJB architecture shifts most of the responsibility for an application's security from the application developer to the server vendor, system administrator, and the deployer. The people performing these roles are more qualified than the application developer to secure the application. This leads to better security of the operational applications.

1.3   Conclusion

This chapter's high-level discussion of the various enterprise application architectures described their advantages and disadvantages. It showed how these architectures have evolved to the EJB architecture and highlighted its unique benefits from the perspective of both the developer and the customer, or client.

The chapter also introduced the terms *bean developer, deployer,* and *system administrator* — three of the six major roles defined by the EJB architecture. These roles are described further in Chapter 3, Enterprise JavaBeans Roles.

From here, we focus on the EJB architecture in greater detail. Chapter 2 provides an overview of that architecture.

Enterprise JavaBeans
Architecture Overview

THIS chapter provides an overview of the EJB architecture, the backbone of the J2EE platform. The EJB architecture specifies how to develop and deploy server-side application business logic components written in the Java programming language.

Enterprise beans serve as the building blocks of distributed enterprise applications. This chapter discusses the structure of enterprise beans: the enterprise bean class, its business interfaces (the home interface, the component interface, the Web service interface), the deployment descriptor, and so forth. This chapter introduces the session, entity, and message-driven enterprise bean types and explains how the three enterprise bean types model and implement different types of business logic. Finally, the chapter discusses the EJB container environment in which EJB applications run and the services and functions provided by the container.

2.1   Enterprise JavaBeans Applications

Enterprise beans are components that are used as parts of distributed enterprise applications. Each enterprise bean encapsulates a part of the business logic of the application. An enterprise bean typically communicates with resource managers (such as database management systems), other enterprise beans, and other enterprise applications.

At the same time, various types of clients access enterprise beans. The clients of an enterprise bean can be other enterprise beans, Web service and enterprise applications, servlets, or application clients.

At runtime, an enterprise bean resides in an *EJB container.* An EJB container provides the deployment and runtime environment for enterprise beans, including such services as remote access using standard distributed protocols, security, transaction, deployment, and concurrency and instance life-cycle management. (Refer to Section 2.4, Container Tools and Services, on page 44 for a complete discussion of the EJB container and its services.) The process of installing an enterprise bean in an EJB container is called *enterprise bean deployment.*

An enterprise application can include one or more enterprise beans. When an application includes multiple enterprise beans, they can be deployed in one or more containers located on the enterprise's network.

Figure 2.1 illustrates an enterprise application that includes seven enterprise beans—EJB1 through EJB7—as well as components that are not enterprise beans: a Web service (WebService1), a Web application (WebApp1) comprised of several JavaServer Pages, and an application-client program (Client1). The figure illustrates how an enterprise bean can function as a client of another enterprise bean. Each enterprise bean that invokes a method on another enterprise bean is considered a client of the second enterprise bean. For example, EJB3 is a client of EJB5 and EJB6, whereas EJB2 is a client of EJB3 and EJB4.

An enterprise can deploy the enterprise beans of the application illustrated in Figure 2.1 in either a single EJB container or multiple EJB containers. Figure 2.2 illustrates the deployment across three EJB containers that reside on multiple machines on a network.

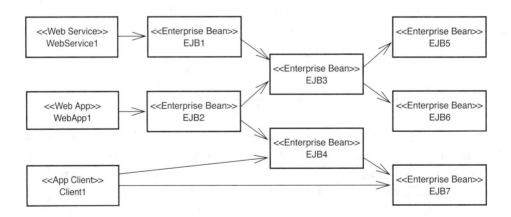

Figure 2.1   Enterprise Application with Multiple Enterprise Beans

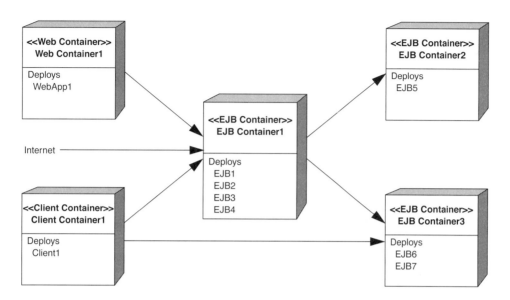

Figure 2.2   Deployment Across Multiple EJB Containers

A client accesses an enterprise bean through the enterprise bean's *client-view API*. An enterprise bean can provide a remote client-view API, a local client-view API, or a Web service client-view API.

The remote client-view API is location transparent. This means that a client, regardless of whether it executes in the same Java™ virtual machine (JVM) as the enterprise bean or in a different JVM, can use the same API to invoke an enterprise bean. If the JVMs are in different containers, the client communicates with the enterprise bean over the network to perform the invocation. The remote client-view API consists of the bean's remote component and remote home interfaces.

If the client and the enterprise beans are intended to be in the same JVM, the developer may use a local client view, which allows the container to use an optimized internal path to perform the invocation without the overheads of remote calls. Furthermore, the local client-view API has more capabilities than the remote client-view API. The local client-view API consists of the local component and local home interfaces.

If the enterprise bean needs to expose its functionality as a Web service to other Java or non-Java clients, then the developer may use a Web service client view. Like the remote client view, a Web service client view is location transparent. However, it includes specific features that allow the methods of the enterprise bean to be exposed as Web service operations and accessed using XML-based Web service protocols. In the EJB 2.1 architecture, the Web service client view is available to only a specific kind of bean: stateless session beans.

The client-view API is independent of the type of the client using the API. This means that a client that is itself an enterprise bean uses the same API to invoke another enterprise bean as, for example, a Web application and a stand-alone Java client program. While it is possible for an application developer to provide more than one client-view API for an enterprise bean, the developer typically designs an enterprise bean with a single client view in mind. (Refer to Section 2.3, Structure of Enterprise Beans, on page 27 for more information on the client-view API.)

To succeed in the marketplace, all enterprise applications must quickly adapt to rapidly changing requirements; at the same time, enterprises need to evolve their businesses. It is essential that an application environment allow for this evolution, and the EJB architecture and the client-view API do allow for this. The organization of an application's business logic into components that communicate with one another via a well-defined client-view API enables application evolution to be accomplished with a minimum of overhead and disruption or downtime. If business rules change, an enterprise needs to upgrade only the enterprise bean that implements the changed business rules. If the upgraded enterprise bean preserves the original client-view API or provides a backward-compatible client-view API, an enterprise does not need to change the rest of the application to accommodate the changed business rules.

2.2   Business Entities and Processes, and Enterprise Bean Types

As already noted, EJB applications organize the application's business rules into components. Each component typically represents a business entity or a business process. Some EJB components implement business entities, whereas others implement business processes.

2.2.1   Business Entities

A *business entity* is a business object representing some information maintained by an enterprise. A business entity has state, or data values, and this state is kept persistently, typically in a database. Business processes can change the state of a business entity. However, the business entity and its state exist independently of the business processes that change the entity state.

For example, you might have a business entity, such as Customer, that represents your customer data and the business rules associated with the data. You might also have an Order entity that encapsulates customer order data with its associated business rules. Other examples of business entities are Account, Employee, and so forth.

Each business entity maintains state about itself. For example, the Customer entity keeps the customer's shipping and billing address as part of its state. The business rules associated with a business entity constrain the values of the entity state. For example, a business rule may dictate that the ZIP code field in the customer billing address field must be a valid five- or nine-digit ZIP code. It is desirable to enforce this business rule when changes are attempted to the ZIP code field, regardless of the business process that makes the changes to the ZIP code.

Often, relationships are defined between business entities. For example, the Customer entity and the Order entities have a one-to-many association relationship. The business rules for the entities involved in a relationship include the maintenance of the relationship. The rules for the maintenance of relationships involve deciding under what conditions one entity becomes associated with another entity, what conditions may change that association, and how the deletion of one entity impacts associated entities. For example, the designer of an application needs to ask such questions as, Does an Order have to be associated with a Customer? If a Customer is deleted, should all Orders associated with the Customer be deleted as well?

2.2.2   Business Processes

A *business process* is a business object that typically encapsulates an interaction of a user with business entities. A business process typically updates or changes the state of the business entities. A business process may also have its own state. If a business process has its own state, the state exists only for the duration of the business process; when the business process completes, the state ceases to exist.

Although some business processes require that the state of a business process be persistent, the state of other business processes may be transient. Persistent state is usually required when a business process has multiple steps, each possibly performed by different actors. A business process with multiple actors is called a *collaborative business process*. This need for multiple steps performed by multiple actors may occur, for example, when processing a loan application or an expense report.

Transient state is usually sufficient if one actor in one conversation can complete the business process. In this book, we refer to a business process with one actor as a *conversational business process*: One actor engages in a conversation with the system. (An actor can be a user or another program.) A good example of a conversational business process is an individual withdrawing money at an automated teller machine (ATM) or an employee enrolling into a company's benefits program.

Other examples of business processes are such actions as fulfilling an order, promoting an employee, scheduling a meeting among multiple participants, closing a bank account, processing a loan application, electing members to the board of directors, scheduling a payment via an online banking application, and so forth. Most business-to-customer Web applications can be considered business processes. These processes are typically conversational business processes.

2.2.3   Business Rules

After identifying the business entities and the business processes, the application architect needs to formulate the business rules. The business rules are organized according to the components that implement the business entities and processes.

The business rules that apply to the state of a business entity should be implemented in the component that represents the business entity. The idea is to keep rules that pertain to an entity's state independent of any business process that acts on the business entity. Certainly, the business rules should be independent of the component representing the business process. For example, the business rule that an account balance must not be allowed to become negative should be implemented in the component that represents the Account entity, because this rule is independent of the business processes that cause the account balance to change.

Likewise, the business rules that apply to a specific business process should be implemented in the component that represents the business process. For example, the business rule that the dollar amount of an ATM withdrawal transaction must be a multiple of $20 should be implemented in the component that implements the ATM withdrawal business process, not in the Account entity.

2.2.4   Enterprise Bean Types

In EJB applications, the business entities and processes are implemented as enterprise beans. The EJB architecture defines three types of enterprise beans: *session beans*, *entity beans*, and *message-driven beans*. Session beans may be stateful or stateless. Entity beans may manage their state themselves—bean-managed persistence—or let the container do it for them—container-managed persistence. Message-driven beans are always stateless: Their life cycle is similar to that of stateless session beans.

The syntax of the session bean and that of the entity bean client-view API are almost identical. However, the two enterprise bean types have different life cycles and different persistence management and provide different programming styles to their clients. Message-driven beans do not have a client-view API; instead, clients communicate asynchronously with message-driven beans in a message-oriented manner. In general, a developer must know the type of the enterprise bean when writing a client application. However, in the case of message-driven beans, the bean's existence is hidden behind the message destination to which the client sends messages.

Stateless Bean Types: Message-Driven Beans and Stateless Session Beans

Message-driven beans and stateless session beans are stateless, which means they retain no client state between method invocations. As a result, stateless beans are typically used to model business processes rather than business entities. Because they are stateless, these bean types are lightweight and provide a high degree of scalability. In addition, because they retain no client state, stateless session beans and message-driven beans can be used across multiple clients.

Stateful Bean Types: Differentiating Session Beans and Entity Beans

To understand whether a business process or business entity should be implemented as a stateful session bean or an entity bean, it is important to understand the life-cycle and programming differences between them. These differences pertain principally to object sharing, object state, transactions, and container failure and object recovery. (See Table 2.1.)

Object sharing pertains to entity objects. Only a single client can use a stateful session bean, but multiple clients can share an entity object among themselves.

The container typically maintains a stateful session bean's object state in main memory, even across transactions, although the container may swap that state to secondary storage when deactivating the session bean.

The object state of an entity bean is typically maintained in a database, although the container may cache the state in memory during a transaction or even across transactions. Other, possibly non-EJB-based, programs can access the state of an entity object that is externalized in the database. For example, a program can run an SQL query directly against the database storing the state of entity objects. In contrast, the state of a stateful session object is accessible only to the session object itself and the container.

The state of an entity object typically changes from within a transaction. Because its state changes transactionally, the container can recover the state of an entity bean should the transaction fail. The container does not maintain the state of a session object transactionally. However, the bean developer may instruct the container to notify the stateful session objects of the transaction boundaries and transaction outcome. These notifications allow the session bean developer to synchronize manually the session object's state with the transactions. For example, the stateful session bean object that caches changed data in its instance variables may use the notification to write the cached data to a database before the transaction manager commits the transaction.

Session objects are not recoverable; that is, they are not guaranteed to survive a container failure and restart. If a client has held a reference to a session object, that reference becomes invalid after a container failure. (Some containers implement session beans as recoverable objects, but this is not an EJB specification requirement.) An entity object, on the other hand, survives a failure and restart of its container. If a client holds a reference to the entity object prior to the container failure, the client can continue to use this reference after the container restarts.

Table 2.1 depicts the significant differences in the life cycles of a stateful session bean and an entity bean.

Table 2.1   Entity Beans and Stateful Session Beans: Life-Cycle Differences

Functional Area	Stateful Session Bean	Entity Bean
Object state	Maintained by the container in main memory across transactions. Swapped to secondary storage when deactivated.	Maintained in database or other resource manager. Typically cached in memory in a transaction.
Object sharing	A session object can be used by only one client.	An entity object can be shared by multiple clients. A client may pass an object reference to another client.

Table 2.1 Entity Beans and Stateful Session Beans: Life-Cycle Differences *(Continued)*

Functional Area	Stateful Session Bean	Entity Bean
State externalization	The container internally maintains the session object's state. The state is inaccessible to other programs.	The entity object's state is typically stored in a database. Other programs, such as an SQL query, can access the state in the database.
Transactions	The state of a session object can be synchronized with a transaction but is not recoverable.	The state of an entity object is typically changed transactionally and is recoverable.
Failure recovery	A session object is not guaranteed to survive failure and restart of its container.[a] The references to session objects held by a client become invalid after the failure.	An entity object survives the failure and the restart of its container. A client can continue using the references to the entity objects after the container restarts.

[a.] Some containers may implement session objects as recoverable objects, but this is not required by the EJB specification.

Choosing Entity Beans or Stateful Session Beans

The architect of the application chooses how to map the business entities and processes to enterprise beans. No prescriptive rules dictate whether to use a stateful session bean or an entity bean for a component: Different designers may map business entities and processes to enterprise beans differently.

You can also combine the use of session beans and entity beans to accomplish a business task. For example, you may have a session bean represent an ATM withdrawal that invokes an entity bean to represent the account.

The following guidelines outline the recommended mapping of business entities and processes to entity and session beans. The guidelines reflect the life-cycle differences between the session and entity objects.

- A bean developer typically implements a business entity as an entity bean.

- A bean developer typically implements a conversational business process as a stateful session bean. For example, developers implement the logic of most Web application sessions as session beans.

- A bean developer typically implements as an entity bean a collaborative business process: a business process with multiple actors. The entity object's state represents the intermediate steps of a business process that consists of multiple steps. For example, an entity object's state may record the changing information—state—on a loan application as it moves through the steps of the loan-approval process. The object's state may record that the account representative entered the information on the loan application, the loan officer reviewed the application, and application approval is still waiting on a credit report.

- If it is necessary for any reason to save the intermediate state of a business process in a database, a bean developer implements the business process as an entity bean. Often, the saved state itself can be considered a business entity. For example, many e-commerce Web applications use the concept of a shopping cart, which stores the items that the customer has selected but not yet checked out. The state of the shopping cart can be considered to be the state of the customer shopping business process. If it is desirable that the shopping process span extended time periods and multiple Web sessions, the bean developer should implement the shopping cart as an entity bean. In contrast, if the shopping process is limited to a single Web session, the bean developer can implement the shopping cart as a stateful session bean.

2.2.5   Message-Driven Beans

Message-driven beans are asynchronously invoked enterprise beans. Message-driven beans are designed for integrating EJB applications with message-oriented enterprise applications.

Message-driven beans do not have a client-view API; that is, they do not define home or component interfaces. Clients access message-driven beans by sending them messages.

Unlike session or entity beans, message-driven beans do not have business methods. Message-driven beans define a message listener method, which the EJB container invokes to deliver messages. Furthermore, message-driven beans also do not hold any state between invocations of the message listener method. Their life cycle is very similar to that of stateless session beans.

Message-driven beans are generally used to implement business processes rather than business entities. Designers should consider implementing a business process as a message-driven bean if that process needs to execute as a result of an external application sending a message. Message-driven beans thus allow a loosely coupled form of integration with other enterprise applications. (Chapter 6 explores message-driven beans in depth.)

2.3   Structure of Enterprise Beans

A main goal of the EJB architecture is to free the enterprise application developer from having to deal with the system-level aspects of an application. That allows the bean developer to focus solely on the business aspects of an application.

The bean developer produces the application as a set of enterprise beans. Each enterprise bean consists of the enterprise bean class, the enterprise bean client-view API, and the deployment descriptor.

- **The enterprise bean class** is a Java class that implements the business methods and the enterprise bean object life-cycle methods. The enterprise bean class may use other helper classes or entire class libraries to implement the business methods.

- **The enterprise bean client-view API** consists of the enterprise bean *home interface*, the enterprise bean *component interface*, and the enterprise bean *Web service endpoint interface*. The enterprise bean home interface defines the create and remove methods that control the life cycle of the enterprise bean objects, as well as find methods and home methods that perform aggregate operations that are not specific to an individual bean object. The enterprise bean component interface and the Web service interface define the business methods that a client can invoke on the individual enterprise bean objects. The methods in the component and Web service interfaces and the create, find, and home methods in the home interface reflect the needs of each particular bean and thus vary from bean to bean.

  Enterprise beans can now have three types of client views: local, remote, and Web service. The EJB 2.1 specification introduces a local client view for session and entity beans. A session or entity bean not distributed across multiple platforms can benefit from the performance advantages of using a local client view. Such a bean must be located on the same Java virtual machine as its clients. For a local view, the bean defines a local component interface and a local home interface. Colocated enterprise beans can use these local interfaces to make direct, local method calls on the methods of other beans and avoid the remote invocation overhead. It's possible to implement fine-grained access between beans using a local client view. A bean uses a local interface to provide tight coupling with its clients and to use pass-by-reference semantics for parameters of method invocations.

  The EJB architecture retains its support for a remote client view for beans intended for use in a distributed environment. For a remote view, the session or entity bean defines a remote component interface and a remote home interface. An enterprise bean defines a remote client view when its clients may reside in a JVM different from the bean. Each method call on a bean's remote home or component interface results in a remote method invocation, which, although necessary for distributed systems, adds a certain amount of network overhead and performance limitations. The overhead of a remote invocation occurs even if the client and the bean are located on the same JVM. See Section 2.3.1, Local and Remote Client Views, on page 31 for more information.

EJB 2.1 architects a third type of client view for enterprise beans that are exposed as Web services. This Web service client view consists of a *Web service endpoint interface*, which is an interface similar to a remote interface. There is no home interface in this Web service client view. Chapter 9 describes the Web service client view in more detail.

Note that an enterprise bean can have one or more local, remote, or Web service client views. Typically, however, a bean has only one of these views.

- **The deployment descriptor** is an XML document that contains the declarative information about the enterprise bean. (*XML* is the *Extensible Markup Language*, a markup language that lets you define tags to identify data and text in documents.) This information is intended for the enterprise bean consumer: the application assembler and deployer. The deployment descriptor also contains the declaration of the enterprise bean's environment entries. These entries are used for customizing the enterprise bean to the operational environment. The XML deployment descriptor is usually generated by the same tool you use to develop your enterprise beans. The XML document conforms to a schema or grammar that defines the structure of the document and the data types of its elements.

The method names declared in the enterprise bean class correspond to the method names declared in the home, component, and Web service interfaces. A naming convention correlates the method names in the enterprise bean class with the corresponding names in the home, component, and Web service interfaces. See Section 2.3.4, Enterprise Bean Class, on page 38 for more details on this naming convention.

A naming convention is also recommended for the enterprise bean class, Web service interface, component interface, and home interface, although you are not required to adhere to this convention.

- The enterprise bean class name is typically a descriptive name of the business entity or process with the word `Bean` appended.

- The Web service interface or component interface name, whether remote or local, is simply the business entity name.

- The home interface is the same business entity name with the word `Home` appended. Because most enterprise beans will not simultaneously have both a remote and a local view, it is sufficient to append `Home` to the entity name for the home interface. However, if a bean does have a remote and local view, ambiguities can be resolved in two ways.

  - With the EJB 2.0 and 2.1 architectures, most code is developed using local interfaces, and remote interfaces are used less frequently. To keep the code of these tightly coupled beans concise, leave the names of the local interfaces as is, and prepend `Remote` to the remote home and component interfaces.

  - When migrating from earlier versions of the EJB architecture, particularly if retaining the use of remote interfaces, to resolve ambiguities, the local home interface is the business entity name with `LocalHome` appended. (The local component interface is the business entity name with `Local` added to it.) The remote home interface remains the entity name with `Home` appended.

- The name of the enterprise bean as a whole is the same business entity name with `EJB` appended.

For example, if you have an Account business entity, you might name the enterprise bean class `AccountBean`. Following the convention, you would name its home interface `AccountHome` and the component interface `Account`. You would refer to the entire enterprise bean as AccountEJB (see Figure 2.3).

If the bean implements both a local view and a remote view and if most of your beans use local interfaces, you might name its remote home interface `RemoteAccountHome` to differentiate it from the local home interface, `AccountHome`. Similarly, you might name the remote component interface `RemoteAccount`. Conversely, if you are migrating your beans from earlier EJB architectures, for the same bean you might name its local home interface `AccountLocalHome` to differentiate it from the remote home interface, `AccountHome`, and you might name the local interface `AccountLocal`. Because the client works mostly with the component interface, this convention provides the most natural name for the component interface type.

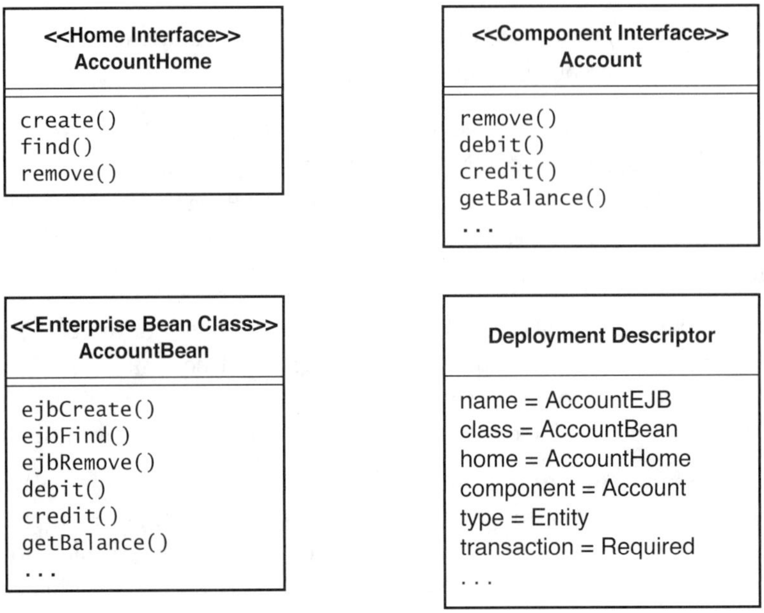

```
┌─────────────────────────────┐          ┌─────────────────────────────┐
│      <<Home Interface>>      │          │    <<Component Interface>>   │
│        AccountHome           │          │          Account             │
├─────────────────────────────┤          ├─────────────────────────────┤
│  create()                    │          │  remove()                    │
│  find()                      │          │  debit()                     │
│  remove()                    │          │  credit()                    │
│                              │          │  getBalance()                │
│                              │          │  . . .                       │
└─────────────────────────────┘          └─────────────────────────────┘


┌─────────────────────────────┐          ┌─────────────────────────────┐
│   <<Enterprise Bean Class>>  │          │                              │
│        AccountBean           │          │     Deployment Descriptor    │
├─────────────────────────────┤          ├─────────────────────────────┤
│  ejbCreate()                 │          │  name = AccountEJB           │
│  ejbFind()                   │          │  class = AccountBean         │
│  ejbRemove()                 │          │  home = AccountHome          │
│  debit()                     │          │  component = Account         │
│  credit()                    │          │  type = Entity               │
│  getBalance()                │          │  transaction = Required      │
│  . . .                       │          │  . . .                       │
└─────────────────────────────┘          └─────────────────────────────┘
```

Figure 2.3   Enterprise Bean Parts

The `AccountHome` interface, the enterprise bean home interface, defines the `create`, `find`, and `remove` methods that control the life cycle of the `Account` objects. The client of an enterprise bean uses these home interface methods to create, find, and remove Account objects.

The `Account` interface, the enterprise bean component interface, defines the business methods that the client of an enterprise bean can invoke on the individual Account objects.

The `AccountBean` class, the enterprise bean class, defines the implementation of the life-cycle methods defined in the home interface and the implementation of the business methods defined in the component interface. As noted previously, the bean developer follows a naming convention that ensures a match between the names of the methods of the home and component interfaces and the names of the methods of the enterprise bean class.

The deployment descriptor for the enterprise bean is an XML document. The deployment descriptor specifies the following:

- The enterprise bean name

- The names of the home and component interfaces

- The name of the enterprise bean class

- The enterprise bean type

- Information describing the services, such as transactions, that the enterprise bean expects from its container

- The enterprise bean environment entries, which provide, for example, information about dependencies on other enterprise beans and resource managers

A single deployment descriptor typically provides information about multiple enterprise beans. For enterprise beans that have been assembled into an application, the deployment descriptor also captures the application assembly information.

2.3.1 Local and Remote Client Views

Both session and entity beans can implement local and remote client views. The choice of whether to implement an enterprise bean with a local or a remote client view depends on a number of considerations, most of which apply to both session and entity beans. However, when developing entity beans, you should also consider persistence and relationship handling. Entity beans that are targets of container-managed relationships must use a local client view. Chapter 7 addresses issues specific to entity beans.

Generally, session and entity beans use local interfaces when they are located in the same container as their clients. The EJB 2.1 specification requires that a session or entity bean using a local interface be deployed in the same JVM as the client. When the bean and its clients are guaranteed to be located on the same JVM, there is no need to use a remote interface and incur a remote invocation overhead. (As noted previously, this remote invocation overhead occurs even if the components are located on the same JVM.) However, enterprise beans whose distribution must ensure location independence should continue to use remote interfaces.

Local interfaces also allow a client and a bean to be tightly coupled. Entity beans using local interfaces can, in addition, use fine-grained access to underlying data objects and not suffer performance consequences. An entity bean with a remote interface should be restricted to providing coarse-grained access to underlying data objects.

Parameter-passing mechanisms differ for beans using local or remote interfaces. Use of local interfaces makes it possible to pass parameters between clients and beans by using pass-by-reference semantics. With remote interfaces, on the other hand, parameters are passed between a bean and a client by using pass-by-value semantics. Passing parameters by value prevents the bean from inadvertently modifying the client data, as the bean gets its own copy of the data separate from the client's copy.

Pass-by-reference parameter passing achieves higher performance because it avoids the overhead of object copying. At the same time, because clients and beans share a reference to the same copy of data, care must be taken because variable values may change in unintended ways. Both the client and the bean view and act on the same single copy of the data. Any actions the bean performs on the data affect the client's view of the data. Developers migrating an enterprise bean from a remote interface to a local interface should pay particular attention to the effect that these parameter-passing semantics may have on their application.

Local interfaces provide the EJB and client developers with an easier programming model that is identical to the normal Java class invocation model. Programming with remote interfaces, on the other hand, requires that the developers carefully design their interfaces to take into account the higher performance overheads of remote calls. The remote-client developer also needs to be more careful about handling `RemoteExceptions` that may occur during the remote call, owing to network problems. Thus remote interfaces result in a more heavyweight programming model based on Java RMI semantics, whereas local interfaces provide a lighter-weight programming model akin to normal Java classes. Table 2.2 summarizes the differences between local and remote client views.

Table 2.2 Comparison of Local and Remote Client Views

Functional Area	Local Client View	Remote Client View
Parameter passing	By reference	By copy
Client colocation requirements	Must be colocated	Can be in different JVM
Invocation overhead	Small	Large
Relationship support	Via entity container-managed relationships	None

2.3.2   Enterprise Bean Home Interfaces

An enterprise bean defines a home interface that corresponds to its client view. As explained earlier, a bean can define a remote client view, a local client view, a Web service client view, or all three. (However, a Web service client view does not define a home interface.)

A bean that implements a remote client view implements a home interface that extends the EJBHome interface. Similarly, a bean that implements a local client view implements a home interface that extends the EJBLocalHome interface. The enterprise bean home interface, whether local or remote, controls the life cycle of the enterprise bean objects, defining the methods that create, find, and remove enterprise bean objects, as well as home methods that perform aggregate operations not specific to a bean instance.

The create, find, and home methods are implemented in the enterprise bean class. The remove methods are inherited from the EJBHome interface if the home interface is for a remote client view or from the EJBLocalHome interface if the home interface is for a local client view.

Code Example 2.1 shows the code for the remote client view AccountHome home interface:

```java
import java.rmi.RemoteException;
import javax.ejb.CreateException;
import javax.ejb.FinderException;
import java.util.Collection;

public interface AccountHome extends javax.ejb.EJBHome {
    // create methods
    Account create(String lastName, String firstName)
        throws RemoteException, CreateException, BadNameException;
    Account createBusinessAcct(String businessName)
        throws RemoteException, CreateException;
    ...

    // find methods
    Account findByPrimaryKey(AccountKey primaryKey)
        throws RemoteException, FinderException;
    Collection findInactive(Date sinceWhen)
        throws RemoteException, FinderException, BadDateException;
    ...
```

```
    // home methods
    public void debitAcctFee(float fee_amt)
        throws RemoteException, OutofRangeException;

    ...

}
```

Code Example 2.1 AccountHome Interface

The home interface—local or remote—may define multiple create and find methods. In the previous example, the AccountHome interface defines two create methods and two find methods. Although the bean developer must name all create methods by beginning with the word create, the name can be followed by a descriptive word. The AccountHome interface defines a create method and a createBusinessAcct method.

In addition, the bean developer can arbitrarily define the type and the number of arguments for the create methods. For example, the AccountHome create method takes two arguments—lastName and firstName. The createBusinessAcct method takes only one argument: businessName. These arguments are all String types. Another developer could just as easily have defined a create method to take three arguments: a String type, a Date type, and a Double type. Note that the remote home interface create methods all return the enterprise bean remote interface, which in our example is Account, and throw javax.ejb.CreateException. The local home interface create methods, in contrast, return the enterprise bean local interface.

The names of the find methods always begin with find followed by a descriptive word. The AccountHome interface defines two find methods: findByPrimarykey and findInactive. As with the create methods, the bean developer arbitrarily defines the arguments for the find methods. The find methods return either the enterprise bean remote interface or a collection of such interfaces, and they throw javax.ejb.FinderException. For example, the findInactive method has one argument—sinceWhen—and returns a Collection of Account remote interfaces. The findByPrimaryKey method has one argument—primaryKey—and returns one Account remote interface.

Note that the bean developer may define the create and find methods to throw additional application-specific exceptions. In our example, the create method throws BadNameException, and the findInactive method throws BadDateException.

Keep in mind that not all enterprise beans have create and find methods. Session beans do not have find methods. Some entity beans may choose not to define a create method. See Chapter 7, Understanding Entity Beans, for more information on these exceptions.

Both the local and the remote home interfaces may define business methods that work across all bean instances. These methods, called *home methods*, contain logic that is not specific to a particular bean instance. A bean developer is free to give a home method any name as long as it does not start with `create`, `find`, or `remove`. When it is part of a remote home interface, a home method's arguments and return types must be valid RMI types, and the method must throw `RemoteException`.

The method can also throw additional application exceptions. For example, `AccountHome` includes a home method, `debitAcctFee`, that is run once per month to subtract a monthly maintenance fee from every account. Home methods are applicable only to entity beans; they do not apply to session beans.

Home methods on a local home interface are not constrained by RMI limitations for arguments and return types. Although they do not throw `RemoteException`, these methods may throw application-specific exceptions.

Remote Home Interface

The remote and local home interfaces share many commonalities but also have some key differences. The remote home interface is a valid remote interface for the Java RMI-IIOP. (RMI-IIOP, a version of RMI implemented to use the CORBA IIOP protocol, provides interoperability with CORBA objects, regardless of their implementation language if all remote interfaces are originally defined as RMI interfaces.) By *valid for RMI-IIOP*, we mean that the remote home interface methods throw the exception `java.rmi.RemoteException` and that the arguments and return values for all remote home interface methods are legal types for RMI-IIOP.

Finally, note that every enterprise bean remote home interface extends the `javax.ejb.EJBHome` interface. The `EJBHome` interface defines the methods supported by all enterprise bean home interfaces (see Code Example 2.2):

```
import java.rmi.RemoteException;
public interface EJBHome extends java.rmi.Remote {
    void remove(Handle handle)
            throws RemoteException, RemoveException;
    void remove(Object primaryKey)
            throws RemoteException, RemoveException;
```

```
        EJBMetaData getEJBMetaData() throws RemoteException;
        HomeHandle getHomeHandle() throws RemoteException;
    }
```

Code Example 2.2 EJBHome Interface

The EJBHome interface defines two remove methods. The first method removes an enterprise bean object identified by a handle, an object that provides a reference to an enterprise bean object and that can be stored in persistent storage. The second method, which pertains only to entity beans, removes an enterprise bean object identified by a primary key.

The method getEJBMetaData returns the metadata interface for the enterprise bean. Clients that use dynamic invocation—that is, clients written using a scripting language—use the EJBMetaData interface; its use is not discussed in this book. The getHomeHandle method is used to obtain a handle for the enterprise bean home object. See the section Use of Object Handles on page 118 in Chapter 4 for more information on using session object handles.

Local Home Interface

Every enterprise bean local home interface extends the javax.ejb.EJBLocalHome interface, which defines the one local home interface method: the remove method. A local home interface is not valid for RMI-IIOP; nor do any local home interface methods throw the exception java.rmi.RemoteException. Otherwise, the local home interface follows the same rules as the remote home interface. See Code Example 2.3:

```
    public interface EJBLocalHome {
        void remove(Object primaryKey)
            throws RemoveException;
    }
```

Code Example 2.3 EJBLocalHome Interface

2.3.3   Enterprise Bean Component Interface

The enterprise bean component interface defines the business methods that a client can invoke on the individual enterprise bean objects. An enterprise bean may have a local interface and/or a remote interface. For both component interfaces, the bean developer defines the types of the method arguments, the return value type, and the exceptions thrown by the methods.

Enterprise Bean Remote Interface

An enterprise bean may have a remote interface. A remote interface is an RMI interface that can be invoked by clients residing on any machine on the network. Code Example 2.4 shows the Account remote interface:

```
import java.rmi.RemoteException;
public interface Account extends javax.ejb.EJBObject {
    BigDecimal getBalance() throws RemoteException;
    void credit(BigDecimal amount) throws RemoteException;
    void debit(BigDecimal amount)
        throws RemoteException, InsufficientFundsException;
    ...
}
```

Code Example 2.4 Account Interface

Like the remote home interface, the enterprise bean remote interface is a valid remote interface for RMI-IIOP. The bean developer must declare the remote interface methods to throw the exception java.rmi.RemoteException, along with the other exceptions that the methods throw. In addition, the arguments and return values for all remote interface methods must be legal types for RMI-IIOP.

Every enterprise bean remote interface extends the javax.ejb.EJBObject interface, which defines the methods supported by all enterprise bean remote interfaces. Code Example 2.5 shows the code for this interface:

```
import java.rmi.RemoteException;
public interface EJBObject extends java.rmi.Remote {
  public EJBHome getEJBHome() throws RemoteException;
  public Object getPrimaryKey() throws RemoteException;
```

```
    public void remove() throws RemoteException, RemoveException;
    public Handle getHandle() throws RemoteException;
    boolean isIdentical (EJBObject obj2) throws RemoteException;
}
```

Code Example 2.5 EJBObject Interface

The method getEJBHome allows the client to get the enterprise bean object's home interface. The getPrimaryKey method pertains only to entity bean remote interfaces and enables a client to get the primary key of the entity object. The remove method deletes the enterprise bean object. The getHandle method returns a handle to the enterprise bean object, whereas the isIdentical method allows the client to determine whether two enterprise bean object references refer to the same enterprise bean object.

Enterprise Bean Local Interface

A bean's local interface defines the business methods that a local client, which is a client residing in the same JVM as the bean instance, may invoke on the individual bean objects. Every enterprise bean local interface extends the javax.ejb.EJB-LocalObject interface, which defines the methods supported by all local interfaces. Although it does not throw java.rmi.RemoteException, a local interface may throw an arbitrary number of application-defined exceptions. See Code Example 2.6:

```
    public interface EJBLocalObject {
        public EJBLocalHome getEJBLocalHome();
        public Object getPrimaryKey();
        public void remove() throws RemoveException;
        boolean isIdentical(EJBLocalObject obj);
    }
```

Code Example 2.6 EJBLocalObject Interface

2.3.4   Enterprise Bean Class

The enterprise bean class provides both the implementation of the life-cycle methods defined in the home interface and the implementation of the business methods defined in the component interface. The enterprise bean class also defines the implementation of the container callback methods defined in the `javax.ejb.SessionBean`, `javax.ejb.EntityBean`, and `javax.ejb.MessageDrivenBean` interfaces. Furthermore, an enterprise bean class for an entity bean must provide the implementation for any home methods in its home interface.

A client does not directly invoke methods on the enterprise bean class instances. Rather, the client invokes the methods of the home and component interfaces. The implementation classes of these interfaces delegate to the enterprise bean class instances. Code Example 2.7 shows the `AccountBean` enterprise bean class:

```
import java.rmi.RemoteException;
public class AccountBean implements javax.ejb.EntityBean {
    // life cycle methods from home interface
    public AccountKey ejbCreate(String lastName, String firstName)
        throws CreateException, BadNameException { ... }
    public AccountKey ejbCreateBusinessAcct(String businessName)
        throws CreateException { ... }
    public void ejbPostCreate(String lastName, firstName)
        throws CreateException, BadNameException { ... };
    public void ejbPostCreateBusinessAcct(String businessName)
        throws CreateException { ... }
    public AccountKey ejbFindByPrimaryKey(AccountKey primaryKey)
        throws FinderException { ... }
    public Collection ejbFindInActive(Date sinceWhen)
        throws FinderException, BadDateException { ... }

    // business methods from remote interface
    public BigDecimal getBalance() { ... }
    public void credit(BigDecimal amount) { ... }
    public void debit(BigDecimal amount)
        throws InsufficientFundsException { ... }
    ...

    // container callbacks from EntityBean interface
    public ejbRemove() throws RemoveException { ... }
    public void setEntityContext(EntityContext ec) { ... }
    public void unsetEntityContext(EntityContext ec) { ... }
    public void ejbActivate() { ... }
```

```
      public void ejbPassivate() { ... }
      public void ejbLoad() { ... }
      public void ejbStore() { ... }
   }
```

Code Example 2.7 AccountBean Class

The enterprise bean class begins by implementing the ejbCreate, ejbPost-Create, and ejbFind methods. These methods correspond to the create and find methods defined in the home interface. In the enterprise bean class, these method names are prefixed with ejb. This naming convention prevents name collisions with the names of the business methods. Chapter 4, Working with Session Beans, and Chapter 7, Understanding Entity Beans, explain how the method arguments, return values, and exceptions of the ejbCreate, ejbPostCreate, and ejbFind methods correspond to the method arguments, return values, and exceptions for the create and find methods defined in the home interface.

Next, the enterprise bean class implements the business methods defined in the component and Web service endpoint interfaces. The business methods implement the business rules for the business entity or process that the enterprise bean represents. Entity beans also provide the implementation for any home methods defined in the home interface. The home method signatures match those in the home interface but include the prefix ejbHome. For example, if an entity bean's home interface included a home method called debitAcctFee, the entity bean's class would implement the corresponding method ejbHomeDebitAcctFee.

Finally, the enterprise bean class implements certain container callback methods. An entity bean class implements the container callbacks defined in the javax.ejb.EntityBean interface. A session bean class implements the callbacks defined in the javax.ejb.SessionBean interface. A message-driven bean implements the callbacks defined in the javax.ejb.MessageDrivenBean interface. The container invokes these callback methods as part of its life-cycle management of an instance.

Note that the javax.ejb.EntityBean interface defines the ejbRemove method. The ejbRemove method corresponds to the remove methods defined in the enterprise bean home and component interfaces.

Why do the parent interfaces define the signatures for the remove and ejb-Remove methods, whereas the bean developer defines the create, ejbCreate, ejb-PostCreate, find, and ejbFind methods? The reason for this asymmetry is that the signatures of the `remove` and `ejbRemove` methods are the same for all enterprise beans. However, the bean developer defines the signatures of the create, `ejb-Create`, `ejbPostCreate`, find, and `ejbFind` methods, and thus they can vary from one bean to another.

Furthermore, you implement an enterprise bean class differently when it is for an entity bean that uses container-managed persistence. The section Container-Managed Persistence on page 178 in Chapter 7 explains these differences.

Implementation of Select Methods

The select methods apply only to entity beans with container-managed persistence. Although select methods are not defined in the bean's component or home interfaces, entity beans provide implementations for these methods in the bean class. These methods are implemented as `public`, `abstract` methods whose names have the prefix `ejbSelect`. The select methods, which must also throw `javax.ejb.FinderException`, are closely associated to EJB QL queries, in that each select method is associated with a query defined in the deployment descriptor. The select methods can return local objects, and they can return the value of a container-managed persistent field.

Implementing Component Interfaces within the Bean Class

Developers should be careful if implementing a component interface within the enterprise bean class. Note that the `AccountBean` class in our example does not implement, in the sense of the Java language, the `Account` interface. The EJB architecture allows the enterprise bean class to implement the enterprise bean's component interface but does not require the enterprise bean class to do so.

If the enterprise bean class implements the component interface, the bean developer must be careful not to pass `this` inadvertently as a method argument or result. Instead, the bean developer must call the `getEJBObject` or `getEJBLocal-Object` method on the instance's `EntityContext` or `SessionContext` interface. The `getEJBObject` or `getEJBLocalObject` method returns an object reference to the associated enterprise bean object. (For more information, see the section Session Object Creation on page 93 in Chapter 4.) This is illustrated in Code Example 2.8:

```
public class AccountBean implements javax.ejb.EntityBean, Account {
    ...
    public Account returnSelfWrong() {
        ...
```

```
            return this;  // THIS WOULD CAUSE A RUNTIME ERROR
      }

      public Account returnSelfCorrect() {
          ...
          return (Account)entityContext.getEJBObject(); // CORRECT
      }
  }
```

Code Example 2.8   Obtaining an Object Reference to an Associated Bean Object

What could happen with the preceding code? If the `AccountBean` class implements the `Account` interface, as Code Example 2.8 illustrates, the programming error is detected at runtime, not at compile time. To put it another way, the application has a programming error that is detected only at runtime, not before.

If the `AccountBean` class does not implement the `Account` interface, the Java compiler detects the programming error when compiling the `returnSelfWrong` method. It is always better to catch errors at compile time rather than at runtime. Therefore, it is recommended that the enterprise bean class not implement the component interface.

The EJB architecture allows the enterprise bean class to implement the component interface so that the EJB architecture can support higher-level business-object frameworks layered on top of itself. The use of such business object frameworks may lead to a situation in which the component interface and the enterprise bean class implement a common application-specific interface. For this reason, the EJB specification does not prohibit the enterprise bean from inheriting the component interface or a superinterface of the component interface.

2.3.5   Deployment Descriptor

The deployment descriptor is an XML document that contains the declarative information about one or more enterprise beans. The deployment descriptor ships with the enterprise beans in an ejb-jar file, a Java archive (JAR) file that contains enterprise beans with their deployment descriptors.

The main role of the deployment descriptor is to define certain bean behavior declaratively rather than programmatically in the bean class. This allows the application assembler or deployer to change how the enterprise bean works, such as its transaction demarcation behavior or its database schema, without modifying the bean's code. The bean developer typically uses application development tools to produce the deployment descriptor. As noted previously, the deployment descriptor describes

- The enterprise bean parts: the home and component interfaces, the enterprise bean class, the Web service interface, and the Web service deployment descriptor

- The services that the enterprise bean expects from its container; for example, transaction demarcation instructions for the enterprise bean methods

- The dependencies that the enterprise bean has on other enterprise beans and resource managers

The deployment descriptor is used by the application assembler and deployer. When assemblying multiple enterprise beans into an application, an application assembler uses tools to read the deployment descriptors of multiple enterprise beans. Using these tools, the application assembler adds information explaining how to assemble the enterprise beans in an application. The application assembler may also describe in the deployment descriptor additional information intended for the deployer, such as the intended security model for the application.

Finally, the deployment tools process the deployment descriptor. For example, the deployment tools tell the deployer about the dependencies on other enterprise beans and resource managers. This serves as a prompt to the deployer to resolve the dependencies. Code Example 2.9 is a fragment of a deployment descriptor:

```
...
<entity-bean>
    <ejb-name>AccountEJB</ejb-name>
    <home>com.wombat.AccountHome</home>
    <remote>com.wombat.Account</remote>
    <ejb-class>com.wombat.AccountBean</ejb-class>
    <persistence-type>Bean</persistence-type>
    <prim-key-class>com.wombat.AccountKey</prim-key-class>
    ...
</entity-bean>
...
<container-transaction>
    <method>
```

```
            <ejb-name>AccountEJB</ejb-name>
            <method-name>*</method-name>
        </method>
        <trans-attribute>Required</trans-attribute>
    </container-transaction>
    ...
```

Code Example 2.9 Deployment Descriptor Fragment

Code Example 2.9 shows only a portion of a typical deployment descriptor and is not meant to be a complete list of all deployment descriptor elements. Rather, it is intended to give you an idea of the information contained in the descriptor. For example, the ejb-name element specifies the name that the bean developer gives to the enterprise bean. The home and remote elements specify the fully qualified names of the enterprise bean home and remote interfaces. (If the bean implemented a local client view, the local element would specify the fully qualified name of the bean's local interface.) The ejb-class element specifies the fully qualified name of the enterprise bean class. The persistence-type element specifies that the enterprise bean uses bean-managed persistence. The prim-key-class element specifies the Java class of the entity bean's primary key. (See Chapter 7, Understanding Entity Beans, for more information on persistence management and entity bean primary keys.) The container-transaction element specifies that the container must invoke the enterprise bean methods in a transaction context.

The deployment descriptor is an XML file and is usually produced by application development tools, although one could create a deployment descriptor by hand, using a text editor. Note that the deployment descriptor is intended to be processed by application assembly and deployment tools, not by humans.

2.4   Container Tools and Services

Enterprise beans implement the business logic of an application. By themselves, however, they are not a complete operational application. You must first deploy an enterprise bean in a container so that it becomes part of a runnable application.

Deployment tools, provided by the container vendor—note that the commercial term for an EJB container is *application server*—read the deployment descriptor for the enterprise beans and generate additional classes, called *con-*

tainer artifacts. The complete application consists of the enterprise beans, the generated container artifacts, and the container.

Recall that the container includes the implementation of the system-level services that are required by the application. The container artifacts enable the container to inject these system-level services into the application. In other words, the container uses the generated artifacts to interpose on the client calls to the enterprise beans so that the container can inject its services into the application.

2.4.1 Container Artifacts

Container artifacts are the additional classes generated by container tools at deployment. These classes are necessary to bind the enterprise beans with the container runtime. At a minimum, the container tools generate the classes that implement the enterprise bean home and component interfaces. Because the goal of the EJB architecture is to allow clients to invoke the enterprise bean via the home, remote, and Web service interfaces over the network, the objects that implement these interfaces cannot be simple Java objects. The home and remote objects are distributed Java RMI objects that implement the communication between a remote client and the enterprise bean deployed in the container. The Web service endpoint object is a JAX-RPC (Java API for XML-based RPC) endpoint object. These objects also communicate internally with the container at runtime to inject container services into the client method invocation path. Although the services provided by the container must meet the requirements of the EJB specification, container vendors still have a great deal of latitude in how they implement these services.

The EJB architecture allows any distributed object protocol to be used between the clients and the container for invocations to a remote interface. However, compliant container implementations must support at least the RMI-over-IIOP protocol for enterprise bean invocations, along with the CORBA transaction, security, and name service mechanisms. This allows clients and enterprise beans to interoperate even when they are running in containers built by different vendors. Of course, containers may support additional protocols, which could be used when both the client and the EJB container are running in the same vendor's environment. When the container is using RMI-IIOP, the container tools typically generate two RMI-IIOP object types (Figure 2.4). Each RMI-IIOP object type consists of multiple Java classes.

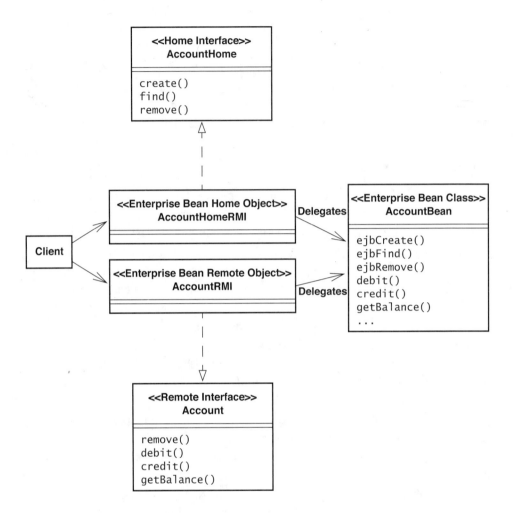

Figure 2.4   Container Artifacts

AccountRMI and AccountHomeRMI are RMI-IIOP object types. Their instances are distributed CORBA objects that implement the communication between the clients and the enterprise beans in the container. The AccountHomeRMI object type provides the implementation of the enterprise bean home interface, AccountHome. The AccountRMI object type provides the implementation of the enterprise bean remote interface, Account.

The instances of the `AccountRMI` object type are referred to as *enterprise bean objects*. The instances of the `AccountHomeRMI` object type are referred to as *enterprise bean home objects*. Most container implementations create only one instance of the enterprise bean home object type. This one instance is shared among all clients.

The client communicates with the enterprise bean objects—`AccountRMI`—and the enterprise bean home object—`AccountHomeRMI`. The client never communicates directly with the instances of the enterprise bean class. Because the container vendor defines the implementation of the `AccountRMI` and `AccountHomeRMI` objects, these objects can inject or add the container services when delegating the client-invoked methods to the enterprise bean instances.

For the local home and local interfaces, too, the container needs to similarly generate implementation classes that implement all the methods in these interfaces and delegate to the actual enterprise bean class after injecting container services. However, because they are accessed only by clients in the same JVM, both the local and local home objects are not distributed Java RMI objects. The local and local home objects follow a similar inheritance hierarchy as for remote interfaces but implement the local interface and local home interface, respectively.

For the Web service interface, the container again needs to generate the appropriate skeleton classes to communicate with the Web services protocol layer in the application server. The Web services protocol is typically Simple Object Access Protocol (SOAP), so the container-generated artifacts extract the EJB invocation request from the SOAP message and perform the invocation. See Chapter 9 for more information. Figure 2.5 illustrates the instances of the RMI-IIOP objects, local objects, and Web service objects that exist at runtime in our AccountEJB example.

2.4.2   Container Runtime Services

As discussed in Section 2.4.1, Container Artifacts, the EJB architecture uses a method-call interposition protocol to invoke the methods of the enterprise bean. Rather than invoking the methods of the enterprise bean directly, the client invokes them indirectly via the runtime objects generated by the container tools. This method-call interposition allows the container to inject its services transparently to the enterprise bean and client application code. The deployer specifies the services that the container adds to a method call. The deployer bases this specification on the information in the enterprise bean's deployment descriptor.

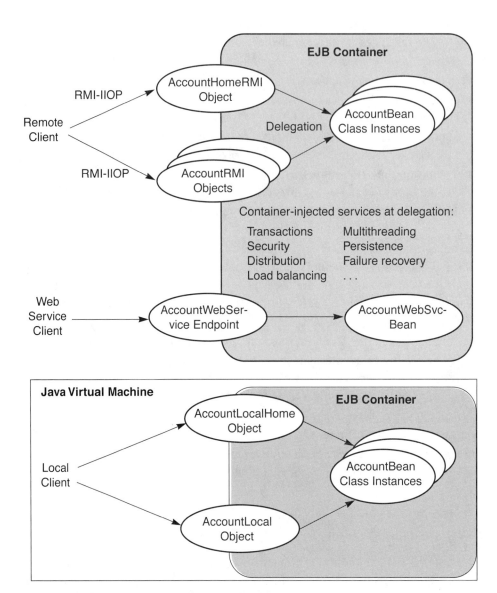

Figure 2.5   AccountEJB Example Runtime Objects

The container provides the following services to enterprise beans deployed in the container: distributed object protocol, thread management and synchronization, process management, transactions, security, state management, resource pooling, data access, system administration support, failure recovery, high availability, and clustering.

- **Distributed object protocol**—The container implements the distributed object protocol used for communication between the enterprise beans and their clients. For example, if the container uses RMI-IIOP for the communication with clients, the container includes an ORB and RMI-IIOP runtime library. The container tools automatically generate the RMI-IIOP stubs and skeletons for the enterprise beans' home and remote interfaces at deployment. This service allows the bean developer to write only local Java code. The developer does not have to implement distributed programming.

- **Thread management and synchronization**—The container starts and stops threads as needed to serve multiple client requests. The container synchronizes the threads to avoid concurrent method invocations of an enterprise bean instance. This relieves the bean developer from having to do complex multithreaded programming. Instead, the bean developer codes the business methods as if the enterprise bean instances were used by only one user.

- **Process management**—The container may use as many operating system processes as is optimal on the target server machine and/or as set by the system administrator. Because the container handles system process usage, the bean developer does not have to learn how to manage operating system processes.

- **Transactions**—The container manages transactions according to the information in the deployment descriptor. Based on the deployment descriptor instructions, the container may

  - Wrap a method invocation in a transaction
  - Import a transaction from the client
  - Run the method without a transaction

  If a method executes in a transaction, the container propagates the transaction to resource managers and to other enterprise beans called by the enterprise bean. The container also performs the transaction-commit protocol. Having the container handle transactions means that the bean developer does not have to implement the complex management of transactions in a distributed system.

- **Security**—The container performs security checks before permitting a client to access an enterprise bean business method. The container checks whether a client is authorized to invoke a business method before it delegates a client call. This authorization service means that security policies do not have to be hard-coded into the enterprise beans. The deployer and system administrator can set security policies to meet the needs of the enterprise by using administration and deployment tools.

- **State management**—The container performs state management and optimizes resource usage. When it needs to free resources, the container can deactivate an enterprise bean object. Later, the container activates the object when the object is invoked by a client. State management by the container means that the container can achieve scalability to a high number of users with minimal burden on the bean developer.

- **Resource pooling**—The container can efficiently reuse resources, such as database connections, to achieve better performance. As a result, the bean developer does not have to develop complex pooling logic as part of the application code.

- **Data access**—The container generates the data access logic for entity beans with container-managed persistence. This not only makes the development of the bean easier but also makes it possible to adapt an enterprise bean at deployment time to work with existing customer databases.

- **System administration support**—The container provides system administration tools to manage deployed applications. These tools enable the management of enterprise bean applications at runtime. This support also relieves the bean developer from having to develop the administration support as part of the application. For example, the container may allow the system administrator to classify applications by priority and to set limits on the resources used by low-priority applications.

- **Failure recovery**—The container can provide automatic restart of a failed transaction or application. This means that the bean developer does not code failure recovery or restart logic into the application.

- **High availability**—Containers may provide sophisticated high-availability strategies to mask various server errors from the clients. It is important to note that the support for high availability is transparent to the bean developer. Thus, most well-formed EJB applications can be made highly available simply by deploying them in a container that implements the support for high availability.

- **Clustering**—A high-end container may be distributed across multiple nodes of a clustered server. Clustering is transparent to the bean developer. This transparency enables all EJB applications to run on a clustered system.

Table 2.3 summarizes the services that the container provides to the enterprise beans at runtime.

Table 2.3   Container Runtime Services

Service	Description	Benefit
Distributed object protocol	The container implements the distributed object protocol used for communication between the enterprise beans and their clients.	The bean developer writes only local Java code and does not have to implement distributed programming.
Thread management and synchronization	The container starts and stops threads as they are needed to serve multiple client requests. The container synchronizes the threads to avoid concurrent method invocations of an enterprise bean instance.	The bean developer does not have to implement the complexity of multithreaded programs but instead codes the business methods as if the enterprise bean were used by only one user.
Process management	The container may use as many operating system processes as is optimal on the target server machine and/or as set by the system administrator.	The bean developer does not have to learn how to manage operating system processes.
Transactions	Based on the information in the deployment descriptor, the container may wrap a method invocation in a transaction, import a transaction from the client, and propagate a transaction into resource managers and other enterprise beans used by the enterprise bean. The container also performs the transaction-commit protocol.	The bean developer does not have to implement complex management of transactions in a distributed system.

Table 2.3   Container Runtime Services *(Continued)*

Service	Description	Benefit
Security	The container checks whether the client is authorized to invoke a business method before delegating a client call.	Security policies do not have to be hard-coded into the enterprise beans but rather can be set by the deployer and system administrator to meet the needs of the enterprise.
State management	When it needs to free resources, the container can deactivate an enterprise bean object. Later, the container activates the object when it is invoked by a client.	The container can achieve scalability to a high number of users with minimal effort by the bean developer.
Resource pooling	The container can efficiently reuse resources, such as database connections, to achieve better performance.	The bean developer is not burdened with developing any complex pooling logic.
Data access	For entity beans with container-managed persistence, the container generates the data access logic.	An enterprise bean can be adapted at deployment to work with existing customers' databases.
System administration support	The container provides administration tools to manage deployed applications.	Enterprise bean applications are manageable at runtime. The bean developer does not have to develop the administration support as part of the application.
Failure recovery	The container can provide automatic restart of a failed transaction or application.	The bean developer does not code any failure recovery or restart logic into the application.
High availability	Containers may provide sophisticated high-availability strategies to mask various server errors to the client.	Because the support for high availability is transparent to the bean developer, any EJB application can be made highly available by deploying it in a container that supports high availability.

Table 2.3   Container Runtime Services *(Continued)*

Service	Description	Benefit
Clustering	A high-end container may be distributed across multiple nodes of a clustered server.	Because clustering is transparent to the bean developer, all EJB applications are enabled to run on a clustered system.

2.5   Conclusion

This chapter presented a detailed discussion of EJB applications and enterprise bean types. It defined business entities and processes and showed how architects can implement business rules. It also showed how the various enterprise bean types correlate with the business entities and business processes and how enterprise beans implement the business logic of an application.

Enterprise beans have a defined structure consisting of the enterprise bean class, the client-view API, and the deployment descriptor. Using simple code examples, the chapter explained the home and component interfaces of the client-view API and a typical enterprise bean implementation class. Another example demonstrated the key parts of the deployment descriptor, particularly the information that it contains about each enterprise bean.

Beneath these enterprise beans and applications is the container. It is the container's services and tools that complete the operational environment. The chapter explained the runtime services provided by the container and summarized their benefits.

Chapter 4, Working with Session Beans, brings this theoretical discussion to life, using a real-world enterprise application example.

CHAPTER 3

Enterprise JavaBeans Roles

THE EJB architecture simplifies the development of complex business applications by viewing the development process in terms of the tasks that need to be performed. The architecture divides the EJB application development and deployment processes into distinct roles and gives each role a specific set of tasks. These roles address application development, infrastructure services, application assembly and integration, and deployment and administration issues.

We group these tasks by functionality, identifying six major functional areas, each responsible for a separate portion of the application development and deployment processes. To simplify things further, we can think of each functional area as a role. An individual can perform one or more roles within an enterprise or EJB application development environment. However, it is highly unlikely that one person would perform all six roles. More often, one or more individuals together may be responsible for just one role.

This chapter describes the six roles involved in the EJB application development and deployment processes:

- Bean developer

- Application assembler

- Deployer

- System administrator

- EJB container provider

- EJB server provider

In addition, this chapter describes the tool vendor roles that frequently come into play in an EJB enterprise environment.

3.1   EJB Roles

The EJB architecture defines six distinct roles in the application development and deployment life cycle. A role may be fulfilled by a single individual or by an organization. The opposite may also occur, depending on the environment; a single party may perform several EJB roles. For example, the EJB container provider and the EJB server provider are typically the same vendor. Or one programmer may perform the two EJB roles of enterprise bean developer and application assembler. Figure 3.1 illustrates how the six roles defined by the EJB architecture may interact when developing and deploying an EJB application in a typical enterprise environment.

Usually, at least several distinct parties are responsible for these six roles, and these roles—or the functional areas they represent—are interdependent. Therefore, the EJB architecture specifies a contract, or set of requirements, for each role. These requirements ensure that the product of one EJB role is compatible with the product of the other EJB roles.

How do typical enterprise software people fit in with the EJB architecture roles? That is, how do "traditional" information systems individuals and ISVs fit into EJB roles? In the EJB environment, a "traditional" application programmer becomes an enterprise bean developer and, possibly, an application assembler. Both are responsible for focusing on the business problem of their enterprise environment and for developing the business logic solutions. The EJB tasks defined for a bean developer and an assembler allow that person to focus on the business problem and business logic.

The EJB container and server providers focus on the development of a scalable, secure, and manageable infrastructure used for the deployment of the applications created by the bean developers and application assemblers. In this book, the term *EJB container* often refers collectively to both the EJB container and the EJB server. The system administrator takes the container product from the EJB container provider and installs it in the enterprise's operational environment.

The deployer defines and sets the deployment policies for individual enterprise applications. The deployer also integrates the applications with the existing operational environment.

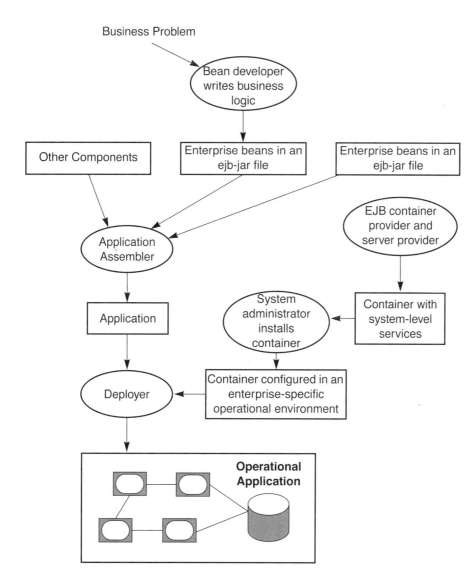

Figure 3.1   EJB Roles in an Enterprise Environment

3.1.1 Bean Developer

The bean developer is the programmer who writes and produces enterprise beans. The bean developer may

- Work for an ISV that produces enterprise beans components or applications that are comprised of enterprise beans

- Work within a corporate enterprise environment

- Be an application integrator

The bean developer starts with a perceived or existing business problem requiring a solution. For example, an ISV may perceive a need for a generic application to view and modify employee benefits, or an enterprise may want to implement its own application for managing benefits. It is the bean developer who develops reusable enterprise beans that implement business processes or business entities and that provide a solution to the business problem. A bean developer of multiple enterprise beans often performs the role of the application assembler (Section 3.1.2) by specifying how the enterprise beans are assembled—that is, how they should work together.

Typically, a bean developer is an expert in the application domain, such as finance or manufacturing. The bean developer implements the business processes and entities. Essentially, the bean developer is responsible for writing the enterprise beans that implement the business processes and entities. The business processes and entities are implemented in the Java language in the form of the enterprise bean classes.

The bean developer also defines the bean's client-view interfaces and the bean's deployment descriptor. The deployment descriptor includes enterprise bean structural information, such as the name of the enterprise bean class. The deployment descriptor also declares all the enterprise bean's external dependencies, which are the names and types of the resource managers used by the enterprise bean. The bean developer outputs an ejb-jar file that contains one or more enterprise beans. An ejb-jar file is a JAR file that contains enterprise beans with their deployment descriptors.

Because the EJB container manages system-level tasks, the bean developer need not be concerned about the distribution, transaction, security, and other non-business-specific aspects of the application. This means that the bean developer is neither required to be an expert at system-level programming nor to program into the enterprise bean such services as transactions, concurrency, security, and remote distribution. The bean developer relies on the EJB container to handle or provide these services.

3.1.2   Application Assembler

The application assembler combines enterprise beans into larger, deployable application units. In a sense, the application assembler composes the application, identifying an application's required pieces and specifying how they fit together so that the application runs successfully.

Applications typically consist of numerous pieces and components. Often, an application requires multiple enterprise beans to carry out its business logic. In our example, one enterprise bean handles the logic for accessing employee data, and another enterprise bean focuses on the logic for benefits information. The application often requires other non–enterprise bean pieces, in addition to the enterprise beans components. The application assembler must identify these pieces and combine them with the enterprise beans into the application.

Like the bean developer, the application assembler is also an application domain expert. However, the application assembler focuses on the enterprise bean's deployment descriptor and the enterprise bean's client-view contract. Although the application assembler must be familiar with the functionality provided by the enterprise beans, an intimate knowledge of the implementation of the enterprise beans is not needed.

The application assembler takes as input one or more ejb-jar files produced by the bean developer or developers. The application assembler adds the assembly instructions and outputs one or more ejb-jar files that contain the enterprise beans and their application assembly instructions. For example, the application assembler may take an ejb-jar file that contains the TransferEJB session bean and another ejb-jar file that contains the AccountEJB entity bean and may produce a new ejb-jar file that contains both enterprise beans. The deployment descriptor of the new ejb-jar file includes the linkage between the TransferEJB bean and the AccountEJB bean.

When composing an application, the application assembler can also combine enterprise beans with other types of application components, such as Web applications. For more information on using other types of application components, refer to the J2EE publications listed in the preface.

If you are familiar with the EJB specification, you may have noted that it describes the case in which the application assembly step occurs *before* the deployment of the enterprise beans. However, the application assembler can assemble the application *after* the deployment of all the enterprise beans or the deployment of some of the beans. The EJB architecture does not preclude the case of performing application assembly after the deployment of all or some of the enterprise beans.

3.1.3   Deployer

The deployer's job is to deploy enterprise beans in a specific operational environment that includes a specific EJB server and container. The deployer receives enterprise beans in one or more ejb-jar files produced by a bean developer or application assembler. The deployer, who has expert knowledge of the specific EJB container and operational environment, then customizes these beans for the target operational environment. Finally, the deployer deploys these customized enterprise beans—or an entire assembled application that includes enterprise beans—in a specific EJB container or in multiple containers on the enterprise network.

As part of the deployment process, the deployer must resolve all the external dependencies declared by the bean developer. For example, the deployer must ensure that all resource manager connection factories are present in the operational environment and must bind them to the resource manager connection factory references declared in the deployment descriptor. (A resource manager connection factory is an object that produces connections. For example, a JDBC DataSource object is a factory of JDBC Connection objects.) The deployer must also follow the application assembly instructions defined by the application assembler. The deployer also sets up the security environment for an application by mapping the security roles defined by the application assembler to the user groups and accounts that exist in the operational environment in which the enterprise beans are deployed.

To perform these tasks, the deployer uses tools provided by the EJB container provider. The deployment process typically has two stages:

1. The deployer first generates the additional artifacts that enable the container to manage the enterprise beans at runtime. These artifacts are container specific.

2. The deployer installs the enterprise beans and the additional artifacts into the EJB container.

A qualified deployer may take on some tasks of the roles of the application assembler or bean developer by customizing the enterprise beans when deploying them. For example, a deployer may subclass the enterprise bean class and insert additional business rules into the subclass.

3.1.4   System Administrator

The system administrator configures and administers the enterprise computing and networking infrastructure, which includes the EJB server and the container. The system administrator is also responsible for administering security at the enterprise. For example, the system administrator adds user accounts, groups users into user groups, and manages the various mappings of security information necessary when the enterprise uses multiple systems. In large organizations, the system administrator may have multiple security-based roles. For example, there could be a security officer, separate from the system administrator, who oversees the mapping of users to roles.

The system administrator is also concerned with deployed applications. The administrator oversees the well-being of the deployed enterprise bean applications at runtime. This means that the administrator monitors the running application and takes appropriate actions if the application behaves abnormally.

The EJB architecture does not define the requirements for system management and administration. The system administrator typically uses runtime monitoring and enterprise management tools provided by the EJB server and container providers to accomplish these tasks.

3.1.5   EJB Container Provider

The EJB container provider, or simply *container provider*, provides

- The deployment tools necessary for the deployment of enterprise beans

- The runtime support for instances of the deployed enterprise beans

From the perspective of the enterprise beans, the container is part of the target operational environment. The container runtime library provides the deployed enterprise beans with transaction and security management, network distribution of clients, scalable management of such resources as connections and threads, and other services generally required as part of a manageable server platform.

The container provider implements an EJB container that meets the functionality requirements set forth by the EJB specification. The container provider vendor may also implement the EJB server. The EJB specification does not dictate the interface between the server and the container; nor does it define how the provider is to devise the required functionality. As a result, the container provider vendor is free to split the implementation of the required functionality between the EJB container and server as needed. Typically, container providers market the EJB container and EJB server in a single product under the name application server.

For the most part, a container provider's expertise is system-level programming. The container provider focuses on the development of a scalable, secure, transaction-enabled container that is integrated with an EJB server. The container provider insulates the enterprise bean from the specifics of an underlying EJB server by providing the simple, standard EJB API between the enterprise bean and the container.

In addition to an API, the container provider provides various tools for system administration. These tools permit a system administrator to monitor and manage the container and its enterprise beans, particularly during runtime. There also may be tools for version control of installed enterprise bean components. For example, the container provider may provide tools to allow an administrator to upgrade enterprise bean classes without invalidating existing clients or losing the state of the existing enterprise bean objects.

The container provider also manages the persistence issues for its entity beans that use container-managed persistence. The container provider's tools generate code that moves data between the enterprise bean's container-managed fields and a database or an existing application. This code generation typically takes place at deployment time.

3.1.6   EJB Server Provider

The EJB server provider is a specialist in the area of distributed transaction management, distributed objects, and other lower-level system services. A typical EJB server provider is an operating system vendor, middleware vendor, or database vendor.

The EJB architecture assumes that the EJB server provider and the EJB container provider roles are the same vendor and therefore does not define any interface requirements for the EJB server provider. The EJB specification draws the separation between the EJB container and the EJB server to illustrate that an EJB container can be developed on top of a preexisting transaction processing system. (The latter would be referred to as the EJB server.)

3.2   Tools

Tools are very important to the EJB application environment. The container provider or other third-party vendors may provide tools to support the EJB application
development, assembly, integration, and deployment tasks, simplifying everyone's
job. The diversity of the EJB environment leaves room for a variety of tools, such as
interactive development environment (IDE) tools, data access tools, Unified Modeling Language (UML) tools, Web page authoring tools, non-EJB application integration tools, deployment tools, and container and server management tools.

- **IDE tools**—An IDE tool supports the EJB architecture and simplifies enterprise bean development. In an EJB-aware IDE, the bean developer does not
  need to learn the low-level details of the EJB specification. For example, a
  good IDE can generate template code for the enterprise bean class and its associated home and component interfaces. An IDE can also simplify the debug-
  ging process and provide an easy-to-use environment for application
  assembly.

- **Data access tools**—Most enterprise beans need to access data in databases.
  Good data access tools can greatly simplify the bean developer's efforts. The
  most important are data access tools that implement the data access for entity
  bean container-managed persistence. See the section Container-Managed Persistence on page 178 in Chapter 7.

- **UML tools**—A UML modeling tool facilitates the high-level design of enterprise applications, providing a graphical view of the business entities and processes and their interactions. An EJB-aware modeling tool allows architects
  and bean developers to specify the mapping of a design model to a set of enterprise beans that implement the model, and it may generate the skeleton code
  for the enterprise beans.

- **Web page authoring tools**—Most recent enterprise applications have a Web
  component, which means that they display Web pages to their users. Web
  pages can be complex to design and develop, and these tools simplify this task.
  EJB-aware Web page authoring allows the components implementing the Web
  pages to invoke enterprise beans.

- **Non-EJB application integration tools**—Many enterprise bean applications
  will be added to environments that include preexisting enterprise information
  systems, such as ERP systems, mainframe applications, and so forth. It is es-

sential that enterprises be able to integrate their existing systems with these newly developed enterprise bean applications. Although such integration can be a major task, it can be made easier with tools that address specific legacy systems. The J2EE platform includes the J2EE Connector specification, which simplifies and standardizes the task of integrating EJB and non-EJB applications.

- **Deployment tools**—The container vendors typically bundle deployment tools with their EJB products. Vendors other than the container provider may provide deployment tools. If so, these tools are typically specific for a particular container. Deployment tools help with such tasks as processing the information in the XML deployment descriptor file and resolving the application's dependencies on the operational environment.

- **Container and server management tools**—These tools monitor the state of the EJB container within the system. They also monitor the state of deployed beans.

3.3   Conclusion

By now, you should have a good understanding of the major functional areas of the EJB architecture. This chapter introduced and explained the six major functional areas, or roles, encompassed by the EJB architecture. These roles correlate with real-life enterprise positions—jobs that must be carried out to develop and implement an enterprise application. Subsequent chapters view the various parts of the EJB architecture from the perspective of these roles.

Keep the six roles in mind as you read the following chapters. In particular, the chapters illustrating the session bean (Chapter 4) and entity bean (Chapter 8) example applications discuss the roles that implement or are responsible for various parts of these applications. In some cases, these views may differ greatly from one another because each role sees different facets of an enterprise application according to its own functional responsibilities.

CHAPTER 4

Working with Session Beans

THIS chapter describes the typical programming style for applications using session beans, focusing on the essential information you need to use session beans in Web-based enterprise applications. The chapter describes a session bean from two points of view: the session bean developer, who implements a session bean; and the client application programmer, who uses the session bean.

Some sections discuss how the bean developer should implement the session bean methods, including the business methods, create methods, and the remove method. These sections also describe how the bean developer defines the home and component interfaces for a session bean.

The chapter also illustrates how the client creates and uses a session object. In particular, the chapter shows the client programmer how to use the session bean's home interface to create a session object and how to use the component interfaces—either a local interface or a remote interface—to invoke business methods on the session object. (Session objects are explained later in Section 5.1, Container Artifacts, on page 128.) Chapter 9 explains in detail the Web service client view for session beans.

The example application illustrated in this chapter uses only session beans. For simplicity, we assume that a single organization developed the application. Chapter 6, Using Message-Driven Beans and Connectors, shows an alternative way of constructing the example application using a message-driven bean. Chapter 8, Entity Bean Application Example, extends the example application to incorporate entity beans. Chapter 9, Using Enterprise JavaBeans in Web Services, illustrates how to use enterprise beans and Web services technology to integrate applications built by multiple organizations.

4.1   When to Use Session Beans

A session bean is a particular type of enterprise bean used to implement a communication session between a client and a server. A session object lasts for the duration of the client's session. This means that a session is defined as the time between the creation of the session bean and its removal. A *stateful* session object stores the state information, or conversational state, for the client that creates and uses the session bean. A *stateless* session bean does not store any conversational state on behalf of a client. Section 4.2.1, Stateful versus Stateless Session Beans, on page 69 discusses the differences between stateless and stateful session beans.

A session bean typically implements a business process performed from start to end by a single actor in a single session, the scope of which is referred to as a *conversation*. (For an in-depth discussion of conversational state, refer to Section 4.2.2, Understanding Conversational State, on page 71.) For example, session beans are suitable in the following two situations:

1. To implement the session logic of Web applications. One or more session beans can usually implement the business process that drives the conversation with a user. For example, a session bean can implement the business process to enter a customer's shipping and billing information.

2. To implement the session logic of traditional (non-Web-based) three-tier applications. For example, a session bean can implement the business process performed by a bank teller when entering multiple checks on behalf of a customer.

These two cases are discussed in more detail in the following sections. In addition, stateless session beans are used when an enterprise application needs to expose itself as a Web service. This is discussed in Chapter 9.

4.1.1   Session Beans in Web Applications

A session bean is well suited for the implementation of a business process that drives the conversation between a Web application and a user accessing the application through a browser. Figure 4.1 illustrates the segments of a Web application and shows the session bean's position within the business logic segment.

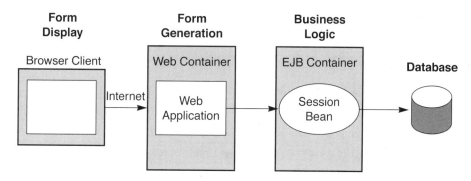

Figure 4.1   Session Beans in a Web Application

The user's browser exchanges information with the Web application in the HTML format by using the HyperText Transfer Protocol (HTTP). The Web application, which is a collection of JSPs and servlets deployed in the Web container, processes the HTTP requests. The Web application is responsible for processing the requests sent by the user's browser and for generating the HTML pages that are sent back to the browser in reply. To accomplish this, the Web application invokes one or more session beans, which process the data sent by the user and generate the data that is formatted—usually by the JSP or servlet—into the HTML page sent as the reply.

The Web application architecture—that is, the servlet and JSP specifications—define the concept of an HTTP session. An HTTP session spans multiple HTTP requests from the user; the Web application controls the start and end of an HTTP session. The Web container supports the HTTP session concept to allow the Web application to retain session-specific state across multiple requests from the same user.

Although it is possible to embed the implementation of a business process directly into the Web application, it is preferable to encapsulate the business process into a session bean. The encapsulation of the business process makes it possible to reuse the business process with a different presentation interface, such as a Palm Pilot or touch-tone phone interface. See Section 2.2, Business Entities and Processes, and Enterprise Bean Types, on page 20, for more information about business processes.

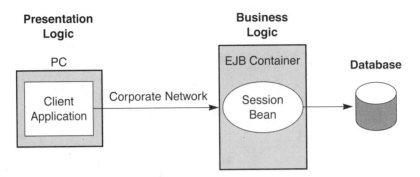

Figure 4.2   Session Beans in a Traditional Three-Tier Application

4.1.2   Session Beans in Traditional Three-Tier Applications

The traditional three-tier application implements the presentation logic of the application as a Java client application that runs directly on the user's PC. The client application implements the GUI for the business process. Driven by the user's input, the client application interacts over the corporate network with the session bean that implements the business processes. Figure 4.2 illustrates how session beans fit within a three-tier application.

Session beans simplify the design and implementation of the three-tier application by shifting to the EJB container most of the complexities resulting from the distributed application design. Session beans often enable an existing two-tier application to be easily converted to a three-tier architecture by allowing the designer to separate the code that implements the business process from the code that implements the GUI. The application designer packages the code that implements the business process as a session bean. The client application implementing the presentation logic can be implemented, for example, as a Swing application. (A Swing application uses the GUI components provided by J2SE.)

4.2   Understanding the State of a Session Object

Before delving into the details of the example application, it is important to understand the state of a session object. Section 4.2.1 explains how a session bean maintains its state. In particular, it explains the differences between stateful and stateless session beans. Section 4.2.2 describes the conversational state of a stateful session bean.

4.2.1   Stateful versus Stateless Session Beans

You can design a session bean to be either *stateful* or *stateless*. An instance of a stateful session bean class is associated with one client. The instance retains state on behalf of the client across multiple method invocations.

Session objects and the stateful instances of the session bean class have a one-to-one correspondence. The EJB container always delegates the method invocations from a given client to the same stateful session bean instance. The instance variables of the stateful session bean class provide a convenient mechanism for the application developer to retain client-specific state on the server.

A stateful session bean typically implements a conversational business process. A stateful instance of a session bean class is associated with an object identity and is bound to a specific client.

In contrast, a stateless session object does not retain any client-specific state between client-invoked methods. The EJB container maintains a pool of instances of the session bean class and delegates a client method invocation to any available instance. It is important to note that the instance variables of a stateless session bean class may not contain any client-specific state when a method invocation completes. The reason is that the EJB container may reuse the instance of the stateless session bean class to service method invocations from a different client.

A stateless session bean typically implements a procedural service on top of a database or legacy application. The service is implemented as a collection of procedures that are bundled into a stateless session bean class. An instance of a stateless session bean class is not associated with any object identity and can be used by any client.

Our example, which we present in detail later in this chapter, uses a session bean, called *EnrollmentEJB*, to implement a conversational business process. The session bean is implemented as a stateful session bean. The same example uses a different session bean, called *PayrollEJB*, to implement a procedural service on top of a database called `PayrollDatabase`. PayrollEJB is implemented as a stateless session bean.

Figures 4.3 and 4.4 illustrate the differences between a stateful and a stateless session bean. In Figure 4.3, `obj1`, `obj2`, and `obj3` are distributed session objects. Their object type, the `EnrollmentRMI` type, implements the `Enrollment` remote interface. The instances `inst1`, `inst2`, and `inst3` are instances of the `Enrollment-Bean` stateful session bean class. Each session object always delegates to the same instance of the `EnrollmentBean` bean class.

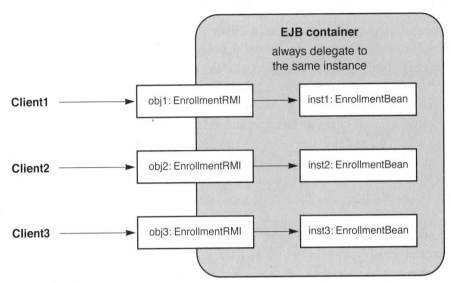

Figure 4.3   Stateful Session Bean

In Figure 4.4, by contrast, the session object `obj` is a distributed object. Its object type, the `PayrollRMI` type, implements the `Payroll` remote interface. The instances `inst1` and `inst2` are instances of the `Payroll` stateless session bean class, and the container keeps them in a pool. The object `obj` delegates to any available instance of the `PayrollBean` class. This is in contrast to the Figure 4.3 stateful session bean object, which always delegates to the same instance.

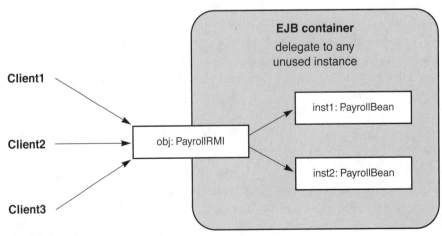

Figure 4.4   Stateless Session Bean

4.2.2   Understanding Conversational State

As noted earlier, a stateful session bean instance keeps the server-side state on behalf of a single client. The instance retains the state across multiple client-invoked methods. Keep in mind that the state consists of

- The instance variables defined in the session bean class

- All the objects reachable from the instance variables

If multiple clients use the same session bean, each client creates and uses its own session object. The session objects do *not* share state across multiple clients, thus ensuring that each client has its own private application-specific state on the server. The bean developer does not have to synchronize the access to the instance variables of the session bean class.

Because the session bean typically implements a conversation between the user of the application and the application itself, the state retained in the session object is often referred to as *conversational state*. What information is usually kept in the conversational state? The conversational state typically consists of the following two types of information:

1. **Data read from databases**—The session object reads client-specific data from the database at the beginning of the business process, or the data is read for it by another session or entity object. The session object caches this data in its instance variables for the duration of the business process to avoid multiple database operations. Two examples of client-specific data in our sample application are the employee information and the current employee benefits information. The Enrollment bean reads the employee information—first name, last name, department, and so forth—and the current benefits information from the respective databases at the beginning of the business process and caches both sets of information for the duration of the user conversation. The Enrollment bean uses the employee information in various steps of the business process and also reads the current benefits information to set the default selections for the multiple-choice options presented to the user.

2. **Information entered by the user**—The session object may keep information entered by the user in a previous step if a subsequent step of the business process requires that information. For example, the Enrollment bean retains the coverage option selected by the user in step 1 and the smoker status entered in step 2, because it must use this information in later steps to calculate the cost

of the medical and dental insurance choices.

Why is it important for an application to retain the client-specific conversational state in the session bean instance variables? If the session object could not store a client's conversational state in its instance variables, each client-invoked method on the session object would have to retrieve the state from the underlying database. Fetching data from the database can be expensive, especially if the database is located on a different network node than the application server or if the data requires a complicated database query to retrieve it.

Retaining client-specific state across client-invoked methods is not unique to the session bean or the EJB architecture. For example, Web containers support the concept of *session state* in which a Web application is allowed to save client-specific state in the Web container. For example, the servlet API supports the `ServletContext.setAttribute(String name, Object value)` and `ServletContext.getAttribute(String name)` methods for saving and retrieving client-specific values.

However, using a session bean to implement a conversational business process offers distinct advantages over other approaches.

- A single Java class—the session bean class—implements a session bean. The same Java class implements both the conversational state and the business methods that access the state. The application developer uses an intuitive paradigm—writing a Java class—to implement the business process. The instance variables of the Java class hold the conversational state, and the methods of the class are the business methods that can be called by the client.

- The business process is encapsulated in a well-formed session bean component. Both humans and application assembly tools can easily understand the client view of the session bean. Multiple applications can easily reuse the session bean.

- When implemented as a session bean, the business process can be customized at application assembly or deployment, using the enterprise bean environment mechanism. For example, an environment entry could be used to specify whether an Account bean converts local currency amounts to euros.

- The bean developer does not have to be concerned with system-level issues, such as thread management, scalability, transaction management, error recovery, security, and so on. The bean developer codes the session bean as a security-unaware, single-thread, single-user application. The container transparently adds these services to the session bean code at runtime.

The EnrollmentWeb Web application delegates the maintenance of the conversational state to the `Enrollment` session object. EnrollmentWeb creates this session object at the beginning of the user's conversation with the EnrollmentWeb application and stores its reference in the HTTP session state:

```
...
EnrollmentHome enrollmentHome = ...; // get home object from JNDI
Enrollment enrollment = enrollmentHome.create(emplNumber);
session.setAttribute("EnrollmentBean", enrollment);
...
```

EnrollmentWeb keeps the object reference of the `Enrollment` session object in its HTTP session state.

4.3 Overview of the Example Application

We now delve into an example application that uses session beans. This application uses the concepts discussed in previous sections, including stateful and stateless session beans and their local and remote interfaces. Chapter 9 looks at a session bean example that has a Web service client view.

Our example application, called *Benefits Enrollment*, is an employee self-service Web application through which an employee manages his or her benefits enrollment selections. The application lets employees enter, review, and change their employer-provided benefits selections.

The Star Enterprise IT department developed the Benefits Enrollment application. The IT department relied on its knowledge of the human resources–related databases—payroll, employee, and benefits databases— and their schemas when developing the application.

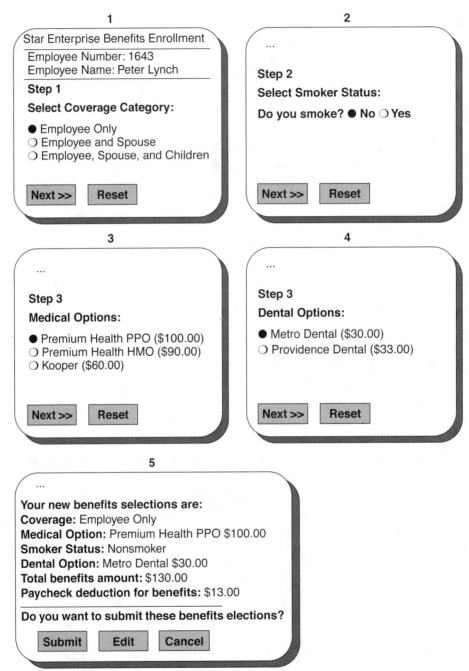

Figure 4.5   Benefits Enrollment HTML Page Sequence

4.3.1 User View of the Application

An employee invokes the application by pointing his or her browser at a specific Uniform Resource Locator (URL). The application displays a sequence of HTML pages that contain the various benefits choices available to the employee. On each page, the employee can select from one of the displayed choices. After the employee makes a selection, the application displays the next page. After the employee makes all applicable selections, the application displays a summary of the employee's selections and prompts the employee to confirm them. If the employee confirms the selections, the application updates the user's benefits record in the benefits database.

When the application displays choices to the user, it also indicates the most recent benefits selection, which it obtains from the user's benefits record. Before confirming selections, the employee may click the browser's Back button to return to previous pages and change previous selections. The application updates the user's benefits record only if the user successfully completes all the pages and confirms the selections at the end of the page sequence. Otherwise, the application leaves unmodified the previous selections stored in the benefits database.

Figure 4.5 illustrates the sequence of pages displayed by the application. The figure does not show two pages: the initial login page and the final page, which confirms that the user's changes have been accepted and that they become effective as of the next paycheck.

4.3.2 Main Parts of the Application

Figure 4.6 illustrates the main parts of the Benefits Enrollment application. The EnrollmentEJB session bean implements the business rules of the benefits enrollment business process. The business process consists of a conversation between one user and the server. Therefore, we implement it as a stateful session bean. The EnrollmentWeb Web application is a set of JSPs that implements the presentation logic of the Benefits Enrollment application.

The Enrollment bean accesses a number of corporate databases: `EmployeeDatabase`, `PayrollDatabase`, and `BenefitsDatabase`.

- **`EmployeeDatabase`**—`EmployeeDatabase` contains information about employees, such as first name, last name, birth date, department, manager, and so on. `EmployeeDatabase` also maintains information about how the enterprise is organized into various departments.

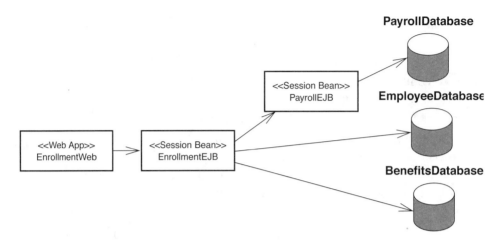

Figure 4.6   Parts of the Benefits Enrollment Application

- **PayrollDatabase**—`PayrollDatabase` keeps payroll data for each employee, such as salary and various paycheck-related information. Employees are responsible for a portion of their benefit costs, which is handled by a payroll deduction. The payroll information includes the amount deducted from each employee's paycheck to cover the employee's portion of the premium paid by the company to the benefits providers.

- **BenefitsDatabase**—The `BenefitsDatabase` includes the information about available benefits and providers. It also contains the employee's current benefits selections.

Because of the sensitivity of the payroll information, the payroll department does not allow applications outside of the payroll system to access `PayrollDatabase` directly. Applications, including the Benefits Enrollment application, must go through the PayrollEJB stateless session bean to access payroll information. The Payroll bean allows client applications to access only those parts of the payroll information to which they have been authorized by the payroll department.

The application is deployed as a distributed application across multiple servers. Figure 4.7 illustrates the application deployment.

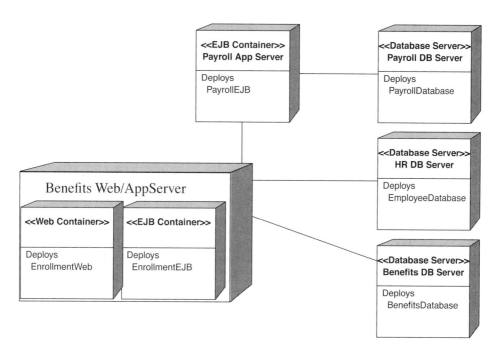

Figure 4.7   Deployment of the Benefits Enrollment Application

The EnrollmentWeb Web application is deployed in a Web container on an application server maintained by the benefits department. The EnrollmentEJB enterprise bean is deployed in an EJB container on the same application server owned by the benefits department. The Benefits application server provides an integrated environment for the deployment of both Web applications and enterprise beans. (Because they use local interfaces, our session beans must be colocated on the same server. If the beans used remote component interfaces, the Web and application servers could be two different servers or the same server.)

The PayrollEJB enterprise bean is deployed on an application server owned by the payroll department. The three databases accessed by the benefits enrollment process may reside on three different database servers, as illustrated in Figure 4.7.

4.3.3   The Benefits Enrollment Business Process

Figures 4.8 and 4.9 illustrate the interactions that occur among the parts of the application during the benefits enrollment business process. Note how the interactions correspond to the sequence of pages shown in Figure 4.5 on page 74. (The numbers to the left of the interactions correspond to the page numbers in Figure 4.5, as well as to steps in the business process.) A step-by-step explanation of these interactions follows the diagrams.

- **Login Screen**—From a browser, the user starts by entering the URL of the EnrollmentWeb's starting JSP. Before invoking the EnrollmentWeb Web application, the Web container displays a login page to the user. The user logs in by entering his or her ID and password, and the Web container authenticates the user. (Note that the authentication logic is implemented by the Web container, not by the EnrollmentWeb Web application.) Then the Web container invokes the EnrollmentWeb Web application. EnrollmentWeb invokes the `create` method on the `EnrollmentHome` interface, the home interface for the EnrollmentEJB enterprise bean, which creates a new `Enrollment` bean session object and a corresponding instance of the `EnrollmentBean` class, which sets up its initial state by reading the information from the corporate databases. The `EnrollmentBean` instance also creates a `PayrollEJB` object so that it can later update the payroll information. EnrollmentWeb invokes the Enrollment bean's `getEmployeeInfo` method, which uses the helper type `EmployeeInfo` to return the pertinent employee identification information. In a similar fashion, EnrollmentWeb next invokes the bean's `getCoverageOptions` method, which uses the helper type `Options` to return the available coverage options to EnrollmentWeb.

- **Step 1: Coverage Categories**—EnrollmentWeb displays the first HTML page of the benefits enrollment process. This page displays available coverage categories and asks the user to select a particular category. The employee makes a selection and clicks the Next button to send the selection to EnrollmentWeb. EnrollmentWeb calls Enrollment bean's `setCoverageOption`, passing it the coverage category, so that the bean keeps the selected coverage category. EnrollmentWeb then invokes the bean's `getSmokerStatus` method, formats the returned data into an HTML page, and displays the next page to the user.

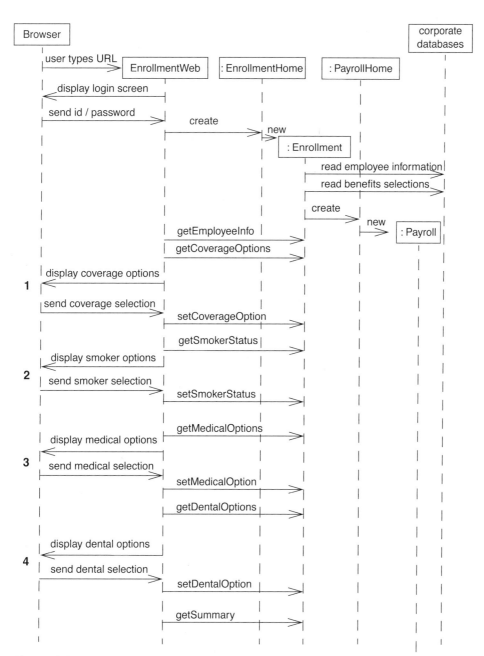

Figure 4.8 Benefits Enrollment Process Interactions, Part 1

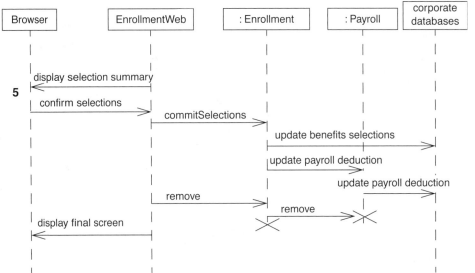

Figure 4.9   Benefits Enrollment Process Interactions, Part 2

- **Step 2: Smoker Status**—The user indicates whether he or she smokes, clicking the Next button to send the smoker status to EnrollmentWeb, which in turn invokes the setSmokerStatus method to store the status. Then, EnrollmentWeb invokes the bean's getMedicalOptions method, which uses the helper object Options to return the available medical insurance options to EnrollmentWeb. EnrollmentWeb formats the returned data into an HTML page for display to the user.

- **Step 3: Medical Options**—After the user selects from the displayed list of medical options and clicks the Next button to send the selection, EnrollmentWeb calls the setMedicalOption bean method to store the selection. EnrollmentWeb next invokes the bean's getDentalOptions method, which returns to EnrollmentWeb the helper object Options with available dental options. EnrollmentWeb formats the returned data into an HTML page for display to the user.

- **Step 4: Dental Options**—The user selects one of the dental options and clicks the Next button to send the selection to EnrollmentWeb. EnrollmentWeb calls the setDentalOption bean method, passing it the selected option, and stores the selection. EnrollmentWeb calls the bean's getSummary method, which returns all selections and their total costs in the Summary helper object. EnrollmentWeb formats the data into an HTML page and displays the selection summary page.

- **Step 5: Selection Summary and Confirmation** — After the user confirms his or her selections and sends the confirmation to EnrollmentWeb, it in turn calls the bean's `commitSelections` method, which updates the benefits record and the payroll deduction in the respective databases.

- **Acknowledgment Page** (not shown in Figure 4.5) — EnrollmentWeb sends an HTML page to the user's browser with a message acknowledging that the user's changes have been permanently recorded in the corporate databases. EnrollmentWeb also calls the `remove` method on the `Enrollment` object to end the enrollment business process. As part of processing the `remove` method, the `Enrollment` object invokes the `remove` method on the `Payroll` object.

4.4 EnrollmentEJB Stateful Session Bean in Detail

Let's now look at how the Benefits Enrollment example application uses the EnrollmentEJB stateful session bean. EnrollmentEJB illustrates the design of a typical stateful session bean. We start with a description of the EnrollmentEJB session bean implementation. Then we discuss how the client — that is, EnrollmentWeb in our example — uses the EnrollmentEJB's client-view interfaces.

4.4.1 EnrollmentEJB Session Bean Parts

Our example follows the recommended naming convention for an enterprise bean and its interfaces. Because this is a session bean implementing the enrollment business process, we name the session bean class `EnrollmentBean`. The component interface for `EnrollmentBean` is `Enrollment`. The home interface is `EnrollmentHome`. We refer to the session bean as a whole by using the name *EnrollmentEJB*.

Because EnrollmentEJB has only local interfaces, it can be accessed only by clients in the same Java virtual machine as the bean itself. The `Enrollment` interface is a local interface that extends the `javax.ejb.EJBLocalObject` interface. The `EnrollmentHome` interface is a local home interface that extends the `javax.ejb.EJBLocalHome` interface.

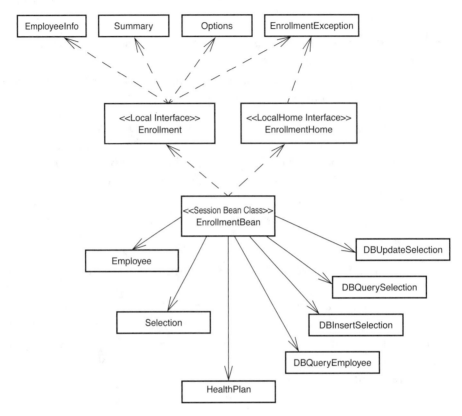

Figure 4.10 Main Parts of the EnrollmentEJB Session Bean

Figure 4.10 illustrates the Java classes and interfaces that make up the Enroll-mentEJB session bean. (Refer to Graphics, on page xvii, for an explanation of the UML symbols used in this diagram.) In addition to the local interface, local home interface, and the session bean class, EnrollmentEJB uses a number of helper classes.

The `Options`, `Summary`, `EmployeeInfo`, and `EnrollmentException` helper classes are visible to the client view because they are used by the `Enrollment` and `EnrollmentHome` interfaces to pass information between the client and the session bean. The `EmployeeInfo` helper class passes employee information; the `Options` class passes a list of available benefits options to the client. The `Summary` helper class passes a summary of the user's benefits selections; the `EnrollmentException` class is the application-defined exception.

The `DBQueryEmployee`, `DBInsertSelection`, `DBQuerySelection`, and `DBUpda-teSelection` classes are internal helper classes that implement data access operations. These classes follow the command bean design pattern explained in the section Data Access Command Beans on page 100.

The `Employee` and `Selection` classes are used internally by the `Enrollment-Bean` class. They hold the information about employee and selection benefits in their conversational state. The `EnrollmentBean` class also uses one or more classes that implement the `HealthPlan` interface and encapsulate the plan-specific information, such as the calculation of the plan premium.

Session Bean Component Interface

Session beans can have a local or remote component interface. Session beans may have a local interface that defines the business methods that a local client, residing in the same JVM as the bean instance, may invoke on the individual session objects. Session beans may also have a remote interface: an RMI interface that can be invoked by clients residing on any machine on the network. The local and remote interfaces are together referred to as the *component interface*. The bean developer defines the local interface and/or the remote interface, and the EJB container provides its implementation. The implementation delegates to the session bean class instances.

Code Example 4.1 shows the `Enrollment` local interface for the Enrollment-Bean session bean:

```
package com.star.benefits;

import javax.ejb.*;

public interface Enrollment extends EJBLocalObject {
    EmployeeInfo getEmployeeInfo() throws EnrollmentException;
    Options getCoverageOptions() throws EnrollmentException;
    void setCoverageOption(int choice) throws EnrollmentException;
    Options getMedicalOptions() throws EnrollmentException;
    void setMedicalOption(int choice) throws EnrollmentException;
    Options getDentalOptions() throws EnrollmentException;
    void setDentalOption(int choice) throws EnrollmentException;
    boolean getSmokerStatus() throws EnrollmentException;
    void setSmokerStatus(boolean status) throws EnrollmentException;
    Summary getSummary() throws EnrollmentException;
```

```
    void commitSelections() throws EnrollmentException;
}
```

Code Example 4.1   Enrollment Local Interface

Note that our example Enrollment local interface follows the EJB rules for all enterprise bean local interfaces (see the section Enterprise Bean Local Interface on page 38).

The local interface methods can throw an arbitrary number of application-defined exceptions. We have declared the Enrollment local interface methods to throw the application-defined exception EnrollmentException, which defines the individual error codes thrown by the session bean to its clients.

Session Bean Home Interface

Session beans may have a local home interface that allows a local client to control the life cycle of the session objects. Session beans may also have a remote home interface that can be accessed by clients on any machine on the network. The bean developer defines the local home and/or remote home interface, and the EJB container provides its implementation.

Code Example 4.2 shows the EnrollmentHome local home interface for the EnrollmentBean session bean:

```
package com.star.benefits;

import javax.ejb.*;

public interface EnrollmentHome extends EJBLocalHome {
    Enrollment create(int emplnum) throws CreateException,
    EnrollmentException;
}
```

Code Example 4.2   EnrollmentHome Local Home Interface

The EnrollmentHome local home interface follows the EJB rules for defining a session bean local home interface (see Section 2.3.2, Enterprise Bean Home Interfaces, on page 33 for these rules).

Unlike the local interface, a session bean's local home interface cannot define arbitrary methods. It can define only methods whose name starts with `create`. Although these create methods can have an arbitrary number of arguments and argument types, every create method must return the session bean's local interface. Every session bean's local home interface must define at least one `create` method. Further, the `throws` clause of every create method must define the `javax.ejb.CreateException` exception and may define additional application-specific exceptions.

Client-View Helper Classes

The client-view interfaces for the session bean—that is, the local interface and the local home interface—use several helper Java classes to pass information between the client and the session bean. The Enrollment bean's client-view interfaces use four helper classes:

1. The `EmployeeInfo` class passes employee information, such as the employee's first name and last name.

2. The `Options` class passes a list of available options to the client. An `Options` object contains the description and cost of each option and the currently selected option.

3. The `Summary` class passes a summary of the user's selections, enabling the user to confirm the selections before they are committed to the corporate databases.

4. The `EnrollmentException` class is an application-defined exception. The methods of `EnrollmentBean` throw this exception to the client to indicate various application-level errors, such as when invalid values are passed to the methods' input parameters.

Section A.1, Session Bean Helper Classes, on page 361 gives the definition of the four helper classes.

Session Bean Class

A session bean class is a Java class that defines the implementation of certain specific methods. The session bean class implements the session bean's business methods, which are defined in the component interface. This class also defines implementations of the `ejbCreate` methods that correspond to the create methods defined in the home interface and implementations of the methods defined in the javax.ejb.SessionBean interface. A session bean class may also implement additional helper methods invoked internally by the previous methods.

In our example, the EnrollmentBean class is the session bean class. Code Example 4.3 shows the skeleton of the EnrollmentBean class:

```
public class EnrollmentBean implements SessionBean
{
    // public no-arg constructor
    public EnrollmentBean() { }

    // Implementation of business methods defined in the
    // session bean's local interface.
    public EmployeeInfo getEmployeeInfo() { ... }
    public Options getCoverageOptions() { ... }
    public void setCoverageOption(int choice) throws
            EnrollmentException { ... }
    public Options getMedicalOptions() { ... }
    public void setMedicalOption(int choice) throws
            EnrollmentException { ... }
    public Options getDentalOptions() { ... }
    public void setDentalOption(int choice) throws
            EnrollmentException { ... }
    public boolean getSmokerStatus() { ... }
    public void setSmokerStatus(boolean status) { ... }
    public Summary getSummary() { ... }
    public void commitSelections() { ... }

    // Implementation of the create(...) methods defined in
    // the session bean's home interface.
    public void ejbCreate(int emplNum) throws
            EnrollmentException { ... }

    // Implementation of the methods defined in the
    // javax.ejb.SessionBean interface.
    public void ejbRemove() { ... }
    public void ejbPassivate() { ... }
    public void ejbActivate() { ... }
    public void setSessionContext(SessionContext sc) { ... }

    // Various helper methods that are used internally by
    // the session bean implementation.
```

```
    private void calculateTotalCostAndPayrollDeduction() { ... }
    private void readEnvironmentEntries() { ... }
    private static String[] parseClassNames(String list) { ... }
    private static void trace(String s) { ... }
}
```

Code Example 4.3 EnrollmentBean Class

The EnrollmentBean class is a typical example of a session bean class implementation. Note that we have defined the EnrollmentBean class as public; we cannot define it to be final or abstract. Note also that it has a public constructor that takes no arguments and that it has no finalize method. (In fact, according to the specification, a session bean class must define a public constructor with no arguments, and it cannot define a finalize method.)

The EnrollmentBean class implements four kinds of methods:

1. The business methods that were declared in the bean's remote interface—the getEmployeeInfo, getSummary, and commitSelections methods and the methods to get and set various benefits options.

2. An ejbCreate method that matches the create method of the home interface (see the section Session Bean Create Methods on page 88 for more information on how these methods are related).

3. Implementations of the javax.ejb.SessionBean interface methods.

4. Helper methods that are invoked only internally by its business methods. Note that these methods are declared as private.

Session Bean Business Methods

The session bean class implements the business methods declared by its local interface. The method name, number and types of parameters, and return value type for these business methods must match those defined in the local interface. In addition, the throws clauses for the session bean class business methods must not include more checked exceptions than the throws clauses of the corresponding local interface methods. (Note that the methods in the session bean class can define fewer exceptions than the methods in the local interface.)

Note, too, that the business methods must be declared public. They must not be declared final or static. For example, the EnrollmentBean class defines a number of business methods, including the following:

```
public EmployeeInfo getEmployeeInfo() { ... }
public Options getCoverageOptions() { ... }
public void setCoverageOption(int choice)
        throws EnrollmentException { ... }
```

These methods match the following methods of the Enrollment local interface:

```
EmployeeInfo getEmployeeInfo() throws EnrollmentException;
Options getCoverageOptions() throws EnrollmentException;
void setCoverageOption(int choice) throws EnrollmentException;
```

Session Bean Create Methods

The session bean class defines ejbCreate<Method> methods that correspond to the create<Method> methods defined in the home interface. Each create method in the local home or remote home interface of a stateful session bean must have a corresponding ejbCreate method in the session bean class. For example, if the local home interface has a method named createEnrollmentBean, a method named ejbCreateEnrollmentBean must be in the session bean class.

The ejbCreate method has the same number of parameters, and each parameter must be of the same type as those defined in the home interface's corresponding create method. However, unlike the create methods, the ejbCreate methods define void as the return value type. (The return value is void because the container does not need any information from the bean to create the object reference that will be returned to the client as the result of the create method.) The throws clause for each ejbCreate method must not include more checked exceptions than the throws clause of the corresponding create method. However, the throws clause for the ejbCreate method can have fewer exceptions than the corresponding create method.

Like the business methods, the ejbCreate methods must be declared public and must not be declared final or static. For example, the EnrollmentBean class declares the following ejbCreate method:

```
public void ejbCreate(int emplnum) throws
        EnrollmentException { ... }
```

This method corresponds to the create method defined in the EnrollmentHome local home interface:

```
Enrollment create(int emplnum) throws
        CreateException, EnrollmentException;
```

SessionBean Interface Methods

A session bean class is required to implement the four methods defined by the `javax.ejb.SessionBean` interface. The EJB container invokes these methods on the bean instance at specific points in a session bean instance's life cycle. Code Example 4.4 shows the definition of the `SessionBean` interface:

```
public interface SessionBean extends EnterpriseBean {
    void setSessionContext(SessionContext sessionContext) throws
            EJBException, RemoteException;
    void ejbRemove() throws EJBException, RemoteException;
    void ejbActivate() throws EJBException, RemoteException;
    void ejbPassivate() throws EJBException, RemoteException;
}
```

Code Example 4.4 `SessionBean` Interface

The container invokes the `setSessionContext` method before invoking any other methods on the bean instance. The container passes the instance a reference to the `SessionContext` object. The instance can save the reference and use it during its lifetime to invoke methods on the `SessionContext` object.

When it is about to remove the instance, the container invokes the `ejbRemove` method. This happens either in response to a client's invoking the `remove` method or when a session timeout expires (see the section Session Object Removal on page 99).

The container invokes the `ejbPassivate` method when passivating an instance and the `ejbActivate` method when activating the instance. The container can passivate an instance to reclaim the resources held by the instance. Passivation and activation are described in the section Session Object Passivation and Activation on page 102.

4.4.2   `EnrollmentBean` Session Bean Class Details

In this section, we focus in detail on the `EnrollmentBean` stateful session bean class to understand how a bean developer implements a session bean class. We start by discussing the individual methods that implement the session bean's functions. We also suggest that you first refer to the full listing of the source code for Enrollment-Bean, which you can find in Section A.2, EnrollmentBean Source Code, on page 366.

Section 4.4.3, Client Developer's Perspective, on page 104 explains how a client uses the EnrollmentBean. The EnrollmentBean class uses several command beans for database access. The section Data Access Command Beans on page 100 describes these command beans.

Plugging in Multiple Insurance Providers by Using Environment Entries

The EnrollmentBean class does not hard-code into the bean class either the set of insurance providers or the calculation of the insurance premium. To facilitate changes to the set of insurance providers and to the algorithm to calculate the premium, the IT department of Star Enterprise defined an extensible mechanism for "plugging" the insurance information into the EnrollmentEJB bean. The IT department uses the EJB environment mechanism to configure the set of available plans without the need to recompile the EnrollmentEJB bean.

The IT department of Star Enterprise defined the HealthPlan interface to keep insurance-related logic separate from the session bean code. Developers can change the insurance portion of the business logic and not have to change the session bean code. By keeping the insurance premium logic encapsulated within this HealthPlan interface, developers not only can change the algorithm that calculates the insurance cost without having to change the session bean code but also can add insurance providers without having to change the session bean code.

Code Example 4.5 shows the definition of the HealthPlan interface:

```
public interface HealthPlan {
    String getPlanId();
    String getDescription();
    double getCost(int coverage, int age, boolean smokerStatus);
}
```

Code Example 4.5 HealthPlan Interface

Each insurance plan Star Enterprise offers its employees is represented by a class that implements the HealthPlan interface. Each such insurance plan class provides its own implementation for the `HealthPlan` interface's `getCost` method, which calculates the insurance cost or premium, based on the employee's selected coverage category, age, and smoker status. Each insurance plan class also implements the `getPlanID` and `getDescription` methods, which are used by the Enrollment session bean. Code Example 4.6 provides an example of a class that implements the `HealthPlan` interface:

```
package com.star.plans;
import com.star.benefits.HeathPlan;

public class PremiumHealthPPOPlan implements HealthPlan {
    public PremiumHealthPPOPlan() { super(); }

    public String getPlanId() { return "PHPPO"; }
    public String getDescription() { return "PremiumHealth PPO"; }
    public double getCost(int coverage, int age,
        boolean smokerStatus) {
            // Calculate the insurance premium based on the
            // coverage category, age, and smoking status.
            ...
            return premium;
        }
    }
}
```

Code Example 4.6   Insurance Plan Class Implementing the `HealthPlan` Interface

Premium Health Care, the insurance provider in our example, implements this class. By providing its own implementation, the insurance company has the flexibility to use Java code to describe the algorithm that determines the insurance premium, based on the employee's coverage category, age, and smoking status. Other insurance providers chosen by Star Enterprise would provide their own implementations of the `HealthPlan` interface.

The IT department at Star Enterprise uses the EnrollmentEJB bean's environment entries to configure the list of medical and dental plans available to employees. In our example, the deployer sets the `medicalPlans` and `dentalPlans` environment entries to a colon-separated list of Java classes that implement the `HealthPlan` interface (see Code Example 4.7):

```
...
<enterprise-beans>
   <session>
      <display-name>Enrollment Bean</display-name>
      <ejb-name>EnrollmentEJB</ejb-name>
      ...
      <env-entry>
         <env-entry-name>medicalPlans</env-entry-name>
         <env-entry-type>java.lang.String</env-entry-type>
         <env-entry-value>com.star.benefits.plans.PremiumHealth
         PPOPlan:com.star.benefits.plans.PremiumHealthHMOPlan:
         com.star.benefits.plans.Kooper</env-entry-value>
      </env-entry>
      <env-entry>
         <env-entry-name>dentalPlans</env-entry-name>
         <env-entry-type>java.lang.String</env-entry-type>
         <env-entry-value>com.star.benefits.plans.MetroDental:
         com.star.benefits.plans.ProvidenceDental</env-entry-value>
      </env-entry>
      ..
   </session>
   ...
```

Code Example 4.7   Deployment Descriptor Environment Entries

The EnrollmentEJB bean uses the `readEnvironmentEntries` method to construct a list of medical plans. The method looks up the value of the `medicalPlans` environment entry as shown in Code Example 4.8:

```
...
Context ictx = new InitialContext();
String medicalPlanList = (String) ictx.lookup("java:comp/env/medi-
calPlans");
String[] medicalPlanClassNames = parseClassNames(medicalPlanList);
medicalPlans = new HealthPlan[medicalPlanClassNames.length];
for (int i = 0; i < medicalPlanClassNames.length; i++) {
   medicalPlans[i] = (HealthPlan)Class.forName(
      medicalPlanClassNames[i]).newInstance();
```

```
}
. . .
```

Code Example 4.8 Constructing a List of Medical Plans

Stateful Session Bean Conversational State

The EnrollmentEJB session object's conversational state consists of the contents of
the `EnrollmentBean` instance variables, including the Java objects reachable from
these variables. The `ejbCreate` method initializes the conversational state, the business methods update the state, and the `ejbRemove` method destroys the conversational state.

The conversational state of the `Enrollment` session object consists of a number
of objects; some are primitives, such as `int`, `boolean`, and `double` types, and some
are Java classes. The `EnrollmentBean` class declares these objects at the beginning,
prior to defining the business methods. The following objects comprise the bean's
conversational state: `medicalPlans`, `dentalPlans`, `employeeNumber`, `employee`,
`selection`, `age`, `medicalSelection`, `dentalSelection`, `totalCost`, `payrollDeduc-
tion`, `employeeDS`, `benefitsDS`, and `payroll`.

If it passivates a session object during the object's lifetime, the container
moves the conversational state to secondary storage. The container restores the
state when the object is later activated. The section Session Object Passivation and
Activation on page 102 describes how a bean developer deals with session object
passivation and activation.

Session Object Creation

How is a stateful session object created? The container creates a session object and
an instance of the session bean class when the client invokes one of the create
methods defined in the bean's home interface. The container performs the following
steps:

1. Creates an instance of the session bean class, using the constructor that takes
   no arguments

2. Invokes the `setSessionContext` method on the instance

3. Invokes the `ejbCreate` method on the instance

For `EnrollmentBean`, the container uses the following constructor to create a
session bean class instance:

```
public EnrollmentBean() { }
```

The container calls the `setSessionContext` method to associate the bean instance with its `SessionContext` interface, which provides methods to access runtime properties of the context in which a session bean instance runs. If, during its life cycle, the bean instance needs to invoke the methods of the `SessionContext` interface, the instance should retain the `SessionContext` reference in an instance variable as part of its conversational state.

In our example, the `setSessionContext` method implementation is empty:

```
public void setSessionContext(SessionContext sc) { }
```

The method implementation is empty because the `EnrollmentBean` instances do not need to access the `SessionContext` interface during their lifetime. If, however, it wants access to the `SessionContext` reference at a later time, an instance needs to save this reference, and it does so from within the `setSessionContext` method. Rather than implementing an empty method, the developer includes code in `setSessionContext` to save the `SessionContext` reference. Section 11.3.7, Programmatic Security API, on page 355 illustrates the use of the `SessionContext` interface.

Finally, the container invokes the `ejbCreate` method on the instance. If the session bean has multiple `ejbCreate` methods, the container invokes the one with the same name and arguments corresponding to the create method invoked by the client. The `EnrollmentBean` class has only a single `create` method:

```
public void ejbCreate(int emplNum) throws EnrollmentException {
    ...
}
```

The session bean instance uses the `ejbCreate` method to initialize its conversational state: the session class instance variables. The instance may retrieve the session bean environment entries, read information from the corporate databases, and initialize the instance variables for later use by the business methods.

In the `ejbCreate` method, the `EnrollmentBean` instance stores the employee number, reads the environment entries, reads and caches the employee record, reads the current benefits selections, and sets up instance variables, as follows:

- **Stores the employee number**—The instance stores the employee number passed from the client in the instance variable `employeeNumber`.

- **Reads the environment entries**—The instance reads the session bean environment entries, using the method `readEnvironmentEntries`. The environment entries are defined in the deployment descriptor. The deployer configured the values of the `java:comp/env/jdbc/EmployeeDB` and `java:comp/env/jdbc/BenefitsDB` environment entries so that the session bean used the appropriate corporate databases. The deployer also configured the value of the `java:comp/env/ejb/PayrollEJB` environment entry to the home interface of the dependent enterprise beans (the PayrollEJB bean, in our example). The instance also obtains from the environment entries the names of the classes for the configured medical and dental plans offered by Star Enterprise to its employees. With this information, the instance builds the `medicalPlans` and `dentalPlans` tables used later by the business methods.

- **Reads and caches the employee record**—Using the DBQueryEmployee command bean, the instance reads the employee record from the database and caches this data in the `employee` variable. The business methods use this data in their subsequent operations. If the employee record does not exist, the instance throws `EJBException`, a system-level exception indicating to the container that the instance ran into an unexpected error condition from which it cannot recover. When it catches an `EJBException` from an instance, the container invokes no other method on the instance and instead destroys the instance.

- **Reads current benefits selections**—The instance next uses the DBQuery-Selection command bean to read the user's current benefits selection record from the database into the `selection` object. If the record does not exist, the instance initializes the `selection` object with some default values.

- **Sets up instance variables**—The instance sets up various other instance variables used later by the business methods. It calculates the user's age, stores the value in the age variable, and builds the `medicalPlans` and `dentalPlans` tables that are used to present benefit plan choices to the user.

(See the code listing for `ejbCreate` in Section A.2, EnrollmentBean Source Code, on page 366.)

It is important to note that the work the instance performs in the `ejbCreate` method cannot be moved to the constructor or to the `setSessionContext` method. The reason is that the container might not have the full execution context for the instance when invoking the constructor and `setSessionContext` methods. If a session bean developer incorrectly attempts to implement the functionality performed by the `ejbCreate` method in the constructor or the `setSessionContext` method, the execution of either of these latter methods would likely result in a thrown exception.

Session Bean Business Methods

The `EnrollmentBean` class implements all the business methods defined in the `Enrollment` remote interface. This section describes the implementation of the `get-MedicalOptions`, `setMedicalOption`, and `commitSelections` business methods, which are illustrative implementations of a typical session bean's business methods.

Code Example 4.9 illustrates the implementation of the `getMedicalOptions` method:

```
public Options getMedicalOptions() {
    Options opt = new Options(medicalPlans.length);
    for (int i = 0; i < medicalPlans.length; i++) {
        HealthPlan plan = medicalPlans[i];
        opt.setOptionDescription(i, plan.getDescription());
        opt.setOptionCost(i,
            plan.getCost(selection.coverage,
                age, selection.smokerStatus));
    }
    opt.setSelectedOption(medicalSelection);
    return opt;
}
```

Code Example 4.9   The `getMedicalOptions` Method Implementation

The `getMedicalOptions` method creates an `Options` object and initializes it with the descriptions and costs of the available medical plans. The method also sets an indicator to the current medical plan selection and finishes by returning the initialized `Options` object to the client. Note that the `getMedicalOptions` method uses the information stored in the instance's conversational state from the execution of the `ejbCreate` method. (For example, the `ejbCreate` method stored the table of the available medical plans in the `medicalPlan` variable.) This illustrates that the instance's conversational state holds the information across client-invoked methods.

Code Example 4.10 shows the implementation for the `setMedicalOption` method:

```
public void setMedicalOption(int choice) throws EnrollmentException
{
    if (choice >= 0 && choice < medicalPlans.length) {
        medicalSelection = choice;
        selection.medicalPlanId = medicalPlans[choice].getPlanId();
    } else {
        throw new EnrollmentException(
                EnrollmentException.INVAL_PARAM);
    }
}
```

Code Example 4.10 The `setMedicalOption` Method Implementation

The `setMedicalOption` method takes a single input argument: an index number into the list of medical plans in the `Options` object. (This index number was returned by the previously invoked `getMedicalPlans` method.) The `setMedicalPlan` method first checks the validity of the input argument. If the argument is valid, `setMedicalPlan` updates the session bean conversational state to reflect the selected medical plan: It updates the `selection` object, the `medicalSelection` variable, and the `totalCost` and `payrollDeduction` variables.

If the argument is invalid, the method throws `EnrollmentException` to the client. Because `EnrollmentException` is an application-defined exception, it does not cause the container to remove the session object or to roll back the transaction, unlike the system-level exception `EJBException`. The client can continue the enrollment business process by invoking the `setMedicalOption` method with a valid choice.

The `commitSelections` method updates the corporate databases to reflect the user's selection of benefits. Code Example 4.11 shows its implementation:

```
public void commitSelections() {
    // Insert new or update existing benefits selection record.
    if (createSelection) {
        DBInsertSelection cmd1 = null;
```

```
          try {
             cmd1 = new DBInsertSelection(benefitsDS);
             cmd1.setEmplNumber(employeeNumber);
             cmd1.setCoverage(selection.coverage);
             cmd1.setMedicalPlanId(selection.medicalPlanId);
             cmd1.setDentalPlanId(selection.dentalPlanId);
             cmd1.setSmokerStatus(selection.smokerStatus);
             createSelection = false;
          } catch (SQLException ex) {
             throw new EJBException(ex);
          } finally {
             if (cmd1 != null)
                cmd1.release();
          }
       } else {
          DBUpdateSelection cmd2 = null;
          try {
             cmd2 = new DBUpdateSelection(benefitsDS);
             cmd2.setEmplNumber(employeeNumber);
             cmd2.setCoverage(selection.coverage);
             cmd2.setMedicalPlanId(selection.medicalPlanId);
             cmd2.setDentalPlanId(selection.dentalPlanId);
             cmd2.setSmokerStatus(selection.smokerStatus);
             cmd2.execute();
          } catch (SQLException ex) {
             throw new EJBException(ex);
          } finally {
             if (cmd2 != null)
                cmd2.release();
          }
       }
       // Update information in the payroll system.
       DeductionUpdateBean cmd = null;
       try {
          cmd = new DeductionUpdateBean(payroll);
          cmd.setEmployee(employeeNumber);
          cmd.setDeduction(payrollDeduction);
          cmd.execute();
       } catch (Exception ex) {
```

```
        throw new EJBException();
    } finally {
        if (cmd != null) cmd.release();
    }
}
```

Code Example 4.11 The `commitSelections` Method Implementation

The `commitSelections` method updates two databases: the `selections` table in `BenefitsDatabase` and, via the DeductionUpdateBean command bean and PayrollEJB enterprise bean, the `paycheck` table in `PayrollDatabase`. The EJB container ensures that the update of the multiple databases is performed as a transaction. As you can see, the bean developer does not have to write any code to manage the transaction.

The bean developer used the deployment descriptor to specify that the `commitSelections` method must run in a transaction. See Chapter 10, Understanding Transactions, for more information on how the transaction attributes specified in the deployment descriptor instruct the container to manage transactions on behalf of the enterprise bean.

Session Object Removal

When finished using a session object, a client removes the object by calling the `remove` method of the remote interface or home interface. The client's invocation of the `remove` method on the session object or home object causes the container to invoke the `ejbRemove` method on the session bean instance. The instance uses the `ejbRemove` method to release any resources that it has accumulated. For example, the EnrollmentBean bean instance uses the `ejbRemove` method to remove the `Payroll` session object, as shown in Code Example 4.12:

```
public void ejbRemove() {
    try {
        payroll.remove();
    } catch (Exception ex) { }
}
```

Code Example 4.12 Using the `ejbRemove` Method

The client invocation of the `remove` method is the normal way of removing a session object. In our application, EnrollmentWeb invokes the `remove` method. However, there are other ways to remove a session object.

When a deployer deploys the session bean in an EJB container, the container typically allows the deployer to specify a client inactivity timeout for the session bean. The client inactivity timeout is a specified period of time. If the client does not invoke a session object for the amount of time specified by the timeout value, the container automatically removes the session object. When this happens, the container *may* invoke the `ejbRemove` method on the session bean instance before removing the session object. The container is not obligated to invoke the `ejbRemove` method when the client inactivity timeout occurs.

Under what circumstances might the container *not* invoke the `ejbRemove` method? If the session bean object is in the passivated state at the time of the removal, the container is not required to activate a passivated session bean instance for the sole purpose of removing the instance. The EJB specification allows the container to skip invoking the `ejbActivate` method to activate a passivated session bean instance solely to invoke the `ejbRemove` method on the instance. This enables the container to avoid the overhead of activating the session bean instance. If the session bean objects allocate resources other than Java objects, such as records in a database, and these objects are normally released in `ejbRemove`, the application should provide a cleanup mechanism to avoid resource leakage because of the missed `ejbRemove` calls. For example, the application can include a program that periodically cleans up the resources that have not been released by the missed `ejbRemove` calls.

Note that the bean developer does not have to release resource manager connections, such as JDBC connections, in the `ejbRemove` method. The EJB container tracks all resource manager connections held by a session bean instance; the container automatically releases the connections when the instance is removed. This automatic release of JDBC connections is not shown in our example, because the EnrollmentEJB bean does not retain open database connections across business methods.

Data Access Command Beans

The EJB specification does not prescribe any specific data access strategy for a session bean. In our example application, the `EnrollmentBean` class delegates all database operations to *command beans*.

A command bean is a design pattern used frequently in enterprise applications. An application uses a command bean to encapsulate a call to another application or a database call. Note that a command bean is a regular JavaBean, not an enterprise bean. Code Example 4.11 on page 99 illustrates the use of a command bean.

The application creates a command bean instance and then invokes zero or more set methods to pass the input parameters to the intended application or database call. The application then invokes the `execute` method, which makes the call to the target application or database. Finally, the application invokes zero or more get methods to obtain the values of the output arguments.

The command bean design pattern ensures uniformity with the interface in calling an application or a database. That is, the calling sequence looks the same, regardless of the type of the called application or database. This uniformity makes it possible to use command beans in application development tools.

The `EnrollmentBean` class uses five command beans for its data access. Descriptions of these command beans and their code can be found in the Code Examples A.17 through A.21.

The DBQueryEmployee command bean reads employee information for an employee with a given employee number from a database (Code Example A.17). The DBQuerySelection command bean reads the benefits selections for an employee with a given employee number from a database (Code Example A.18). The DBInsertSelection command bean inserts benefits selections into the database (Code Example A.19). The DBUpdateSelection command bean updates benefits selections in the database (Code Example A.20). Code Example A.21 illustrates the database-related command beans' superclasses.

The DeductionUpdateBean command bean encapsulates the invocation of the `setBenefitsDeduction` method on the Payroll enterprise bean (see Code Example 4.11). In Chapter 6, Using Message-Driven Beans and Connectors, we show an alternative implementation of the DeductionUpdateBean, one that uses a message-driven bean to update the payroll database.

Database Connections

It is usually good practice to acquire JDBC connections just before they are needed and to release them as soon as they are not needed. The command beans follow this practice for JDBC connections:

- Each command bean acquires a JDBC connection prior to executing a JDBC statement.

- Once it has established the JDBC connection, each command bean object creates and executes a particular JDBC statement.

- After the statement executes, each command bean releases the JDBC connection.

Adhering to this practice—establishing a JDBC connection, executing the JDBC statement, and then releasing the connection—allows the EJB container to maximize the reuse of the physical database connections by multiple session bean instances. Thus, a small number of physical database connections can be serially reused by a large number of session bean instances. This sharing of physical database connections is transparent to the session bean code. The EJB container provides the ability to reuse connections as a service to the enterprise bean applications. This service is usually called *JDBC connection pooling*.

What happens if an instance opens a JDBC connection and holds it across multiple client calls? In that case, the number of open JDBC connections would equal the number of active session bean instances, which in turn is equal to the number of users. When many users simultaneously access the application, the number of open JDBC connections could exceed a system-defined resource limit and potentially cause the application to fail. To avoid application failures resulting from open connection failures, the EJB container would have to passivate some instances so that they would release their connections. The application would run correctly, but its performance might be lower because of the overhead of excessive instance passivation and activation.

Session Object Passivation and Activation

A stateful session object lasts for the duration of the business process implemented by the session object. The business process typically spans multiple client-invoked business methods and may last for several minutes, hours, or even days. For example, an employee may start the Benefits Enrollment application, fill in the first two screens, leave for several hours, and, on returning, complete the remaining steps.

The state of a stateful session object often may occupy a nontrivial amount of main memory on the server. In addition, the state may include expensive resources such as TCP/IP (Transmission Control Protocol/Internet Protocol) or database connections. (Our example does not show these types of resources.) Therefore, it is important that the EJB container be able to reclaim the resources by having the capability to save the state of a stateful session object in some form of secondary memory, such as a database. Later, when the state of the session object is once again needed for the invocation of a business method, the EJB container can restore the state from the saved image.

The process of saving the session object's state to secondary memory is called *passivation*; the process of restoring the state, *activation*. The container typically passivates a session object when resources need to be freed to process requests from other clients or when the session bean instance needs to be transferred to a different process for load balancing. For example, the container passivates the instance by invoking the `ejbPassivate` method in the instance, then serializing it and moving it to secondary storage. When it activates the session object, the container restores the session bean instance's state by deserializing the saved image of the passivated instance and then invoking the `ejbActivate` method on the instance.

Recall from the discussion in Section 4.2.2, Understanding Conversational State, that the instance variables of the session bean class maintain the state of a stateful session object. To passivate a session object, the EJB container uses the Java serialization protocol—or another functionally equivalent mechanism—to serialize the state of the instance and save it in secondary storage.

For many session beans, including our example EnrollmentEJB bean, the passivation and activation processes do not require any programming effort from the bean developer. The bean developer has to ensure only that the objects held in the session bean instance variables are serializable at passivation.

In addition to serializable objects, the instance's state may include references to several objects that do not need to be serializable at passivation. These objects are

- References to other enterprise beans' local and remote home and component interfaces

- References to the `SessionContext` interface

- References to the Java Naming and Dictionary Interface (JNDI) context `java:comp/env` and its subcontexts

- References to resource manager connection factories, such as JDBC `DataSource` objects

- References to the `UserTransaction` interface

The EJB container recognizes these objects during passivation; therefore, they do not have to be serializable.

Although not prohibited by the EJB specification, the session bean class should not declare fields as transient, because the EJB specification does not specify how the EJB container handles transient fields across instance passivation. Although some containers may preserve the values of transient fields across passivation, others may reset the transient fields to their Java language initial default value.

The EJB container allows the session bean class to participate in the session object passivation and activation protocol. For this purpose, the SessionBean interface defines the ejbPassivate and ejbActivate methods. The EJB container invokes the ejbPassivate method just before passivating the instance. The EJB container invokes the ejbActivate method just after activating the instance.

The session bean instance uses the ejbPassivate method to release any expensive resources that can be easily reconstructed at activation and to ensure that the instance fields contain only serializable objects. For example, an instance must close any open database connections or TCP/IP connections because these objects are not serializable.

The session bean instance uses the ejbActivate method to reacquire the resources released by the ejbPassivate method so that the instance is ready to accept a client-invoked business method. For example, the instance would reopen the database or TCP/IP connections closed in the ejbPassivate method.

The container can invoke the ejbPassivate method on a session bean instance while the instance is not involved in a transaction. Because the bean developer cannot prevent the container from invoking ejbPassivate, the bean must be coded to accept ejbPassivate at any time between transactions.

The EnrollmentEJB class leaves the ejbPassivate and ejbActivate methods empty. The reason is that all the instance variables either are serializable or refer to objects that do not require serialization, as indicated by the previously listed categories.

4.4.3   Client Developer's Perspective

This section describes the EnrollmentEJB session bean from the perspective of the client developer—that is, how the client application uses the EnrollmentEJB session bean. In our example, the client is the EnrollmentWeb Web application, which consists of several JSPs.

In this section, we focus on the segments of the EnrollmentWeb code relevant to using a session bean. (The examples show only the relevant portions of the code.) We neither show nor explain EnrollmentWeb's functions outside of its interaction with the session bean. We do not show how the EnrollmentWeb application generates the HTML pages that are sent to the user's browser; nor do we show how the EnrollmentWeb application processes the user input that the browser sends as HTTP post requests.

Session Object Creation

The application process begins when a user visits the Benefits Web site. The Web container logs in the user and invokes the EnrollmentWeb application, which is the client of the EnrollmentSession bean. The EnrollmentWeb application executes the code segment shown in Code Example 4.13 to create an Enrollment session object, which drives the conversation with the user and stores the user-specific information from one HTTP request to the next:

```
...
import javax.naming.*;
import com.star.benefits.*;
...
String loginID = request.getUserPrincipal().getName();
int emplNumber = Integer.parseInt(loginID);

InitialContext ictx = new InitialContext();
EnrollmentHome enrollmentHome = (EnrollmentHome)
            ictx.lookup("java:comp/env/ejb/EnrollmentEJB");
enrollment = enrollmentHome.create(emplNumber);

session.setAttribute("EnrollmentBean", enrollment);
...
```

Code Example 4.13 Creating a Session Object from a JSP

The getUserPrincipal method is a servlet API method that obtains the user's login identifier, which is a unique number assigned to each employee. The method returns the login ID that the user entered in the login page displayed to the user by the Web container. EnrollmentWeb then uses the Integer.parseInt method to convert the `loginID` string to an integer value representing the user's unique employee number.

Next, EnrollmentWeb must locate the bean's local home interface. To do so, EnrollmentWeb first needs to obtain a JNDI initial naming context. The code instantiates a new `javax.naming.InitialContext` object, which our example calls `ictx`. EnrollmentWeb then uses the context `lookup` method to obtain the Enrollment bean's home interface. Note that the deployer has previously configured the EnrollmentWeb's initial naming context such that the name `java:comp/env/ejb/EnrollmentEJB` resolves to the Enrollment bean's local home object.

The `lookup` method returns an object that the code must then cast to the expected type. Our example casts it to `EnrollmentHome` using the Java `cast` operator because the `EnrollmentHome` object is a local home reference.

In contrast, we use a remote home reference to access the Payroll bean. For remote home references, such as the one for the Payroll bean, you should use the `javax.rmi.PortableRemoteObject.narrow` method to perform type narrowing of the client-side representations of the remote home and remote interfaces. This method makes a remote client program interoperable with all compliant EJB container implementations. Note that it is not sufficient simply to use the Java `cast` operator for remote references; in fact, using the cast operator may not work in some container implementations. (Note that the EJB specification requires that applications use the `javax.rmi.PortableRemoteObject.narrow` method to perform type conversion of references of the EJB remote home and remote interfaces.)

Once it obtains a reference to the home interface, EnrollmentWeb can call a create method on that home interface to create a session object. In Code Example 4.13, EnrollmentWeb invokes the home interface `create` method and passes the user's employee number for the method argument. The `create` method returns a reference to the session object that implements the `Enrollment` local interface. At this point, EnrollmentWeb can use the session object reference to invoke the bean's business methods. See the next section, Business Method Invocation, for further details.

Finally, the EnrollmentWeb application stores the session object reference of the `Enrollment` session object in its HTTP session state. The application does this by using the servlet API `setAttribute` method. The session object represents the HTTP session for the current user.

Business Method Invocation

The local client—the EnrollmentWeb application—invokes the `Enrollment` object's business methods to accomplish the tasks of the Benefit Enrollment application. This is the business logic of a session bean, and each session bean has its own unique logic.

Code Example 4.14 shows the business logic portion of the EnrollmentWeb code for our example:

```
// Get EmployeeInfo.
EmployeeInfo employeeInfo = enrollment.getEmployeeInfo();
...
Options coverageOptions = enrollment.getCoverageOptions();
// Display coverageOptions and let the user make a selection.
enrollment.setCoverageOption(selection);
...
boolean smokerStatus = enrollment.getSmokerStatus();
// Display smoker status screen and let the user make a selection.
enrollment.setSmokerStatus(smokerStatus);
...
Options medicalOptions = enrollment.getMedicalOptions();
..
// Display medicalOptions and let the user make a selection.
enrollment.setMedicalOption(selection);
...
Options dentalOptions = enrollment.getDentalOptions();
// Display dentalOptions and let the user make a selection.
enrollment.setDentalOption(selection);
...
Summary summary = enrollment.getSummary();
// Display summary of selected choices, and prompt user to confirm.
enrollment.commitSelections();
...
```

Code Example 4.14 Client Business Method Invocation

The logic in the code mirrors the sequence of the Benefit Enrollment application's HTML screens (see Figure 4.3 on page 70). EnrollmentWeb starts by gathering the necessary data—in this case, the employee data and available coverage options. To accomplish this, EnrollmentWeb first invokes the Enrollment object's getEmployeeInfo method to gather employee information—first and last names—based on the employee's identifier. The getEmployeeInfo method uses the EmployeeInfo helper class to pass this information.

Next, EnrollmentWeb invokes the getCoverageOptions method, which uses the Options helper class to return the available benefits coverage options. The method returns the various coverage options and their descriptions and the employee's current benefits selection, if any. When it receives all the information, EnrollmentWeb formats the data into an HTML page, with the employee's current coverage option highlighted, and displays the first screen of the Benefits Enrollment application to the user. (This is the Step 1: Select Coverage Category screen.)

The user makes a benefits selection and clicks the Next button. EnrollmentWeb calls the setCoverageOption method to test the validity of the selection. If the user makes an invalid selection, the setCoverageOption method throws EnrollmentException, which displays that the error is the result of an invalid parameter. (Recall that because EnrollmentException is an application-defined exception, it does not cause the container to remove the session object.) The setCoverageOption method saves the selection.

EnrollmentWeb then displays the smoker-status screen and invokes the getSmokerStatus method. This method returns a Boolean type to EnrollmentWeb, indicating the user's smoker status. EnrollmentWeb invokes the setSmokerStatus method to save the user's indicated smoker status. The setSmokerStatus method in turn stores the smoker selection.

Before displaying the third screen in the sequence—the medical options screen—EnrollmentWeb invokes the getMedicalOptions method to extract and return the available medical coverage options. This method uses the Options helper class to return the medical options, with their descriptions and appropriate costs given the user's smoker status. EnrollmentWeb receives the medical coverage information and formats the data into an HTML page, which is returned to the user's browser as the Step 3: Medical Options screen.

The user selects the desired medical coverage, and EnrollmentWeb uses the setMedicalOption method to transmit the selection to the benefits application, which saves the selection. The method first checks that the selection is valid; if it is not, the method throws the EnrollmentException application exception.

Next, EnrollmentWeb retrieves the available dental options by invoking the `getDentalOptions` method, formatting the data into an HTML page, and returning the page to the user's browser for display. The user selects a dental option, which EnrollmentWeb saves by invoking the `setDentalOption` method.

Finally, EnrollmentWeb invokes the `getSummary` method to retrieve the individual data for the user's previously entered coverage selections and to calculate the total cost of all the options. EnrollmentWeb formats the data into an HTML page and returns it to the user's browser. The user can view his or her selections, see what each selection costs, and verify the total payroll deduction amount for these benefits. The user can modify the selections at this point or accept them. When they are accepted, EnrollmentWeb commits the user's coverage selections by invoking the `commitSelections` method.

Session Object Removal

The local client—the EnrollmentWeb application—removes the session object at the completion of the enrollment business process after processing the user's confirmation response—that is, after it invokes the `enrollment.commitSelections` method on the `Enrollment` session object. This is illustrated as follows:

```
...
enrollment.remove();
session.removeAttribute("EnrollmentBean");
...
```

Note that once it removes the stateful session bean, EnrollmentWeb cannot make additional invocations of the bean's business methods. If EnrollmentWeb attempted to invoke a business method on a stateful session object after removing the object, the application would receive the `java.rmi.NoSuchObjectException` error.

Session Object Identity

A stateful session object has a unique identity. The EJB container assigns the identity to the object at the object's creation. Each invocation of a create method on the session bean home interface results in the generation of a new unique identifier.

Unlike an entity object's object identity, which is visible to the client, the object identifier of a session bean is not available to the client. However, a client may use the `isIdentical` method of the `EJBObject` interface to determine whether two session object references refer to the same session object. Code Example 4.15 illustrates this:

```
...
Enrollment obj1 = ...;
Enrollment obj2 = ...;
if (obj1.isIdentical(obj2)) {
    // obj1 and obj2 refer to the same session object.
    ...
} else {
    // obj1 and obj2 refer to different session objects.
    ...
}
```

Code Example 4.15 Comparing Session Object References

Most session bean client applications, including our EnrollmentWeb application example, typically do not need to compare the references of session objects for identity purposes. Generally, only entity bean applications need to use comparisons for object identity.

4.5   PayrollEJB Stateless Session Bean

The PayrollEJB session bean provides remote access to `PayrollDatabase`. Because payroll data is sensitive information, most, if not all, enterprises set up their environments to restrict access to payroll data. The PayrollEJB session bean exists principally to provide applications, such as the Benefits Enrollment application, with restrictive access to `PayrollDatabase`. In addition, PayrollEJB may implement an audit trail.

An application that wants to access the payroll information cannot access `PayrollDatabase` directly, such as by using JDBC. Instead, an application must use the PayrollEJB session bean to access the information indirectly. By requiring applications to use the PayrollEJB session bean to access `PayrollDatabase`, the payroll department restricts the access to the payroll information to the functions defined in the PayrollEJB session bean. In addition, the payroll department can use the EJB declarative security mechanism enforced by the EJB container to restrict access to the individual methods of PayrollEJB to specific applications.

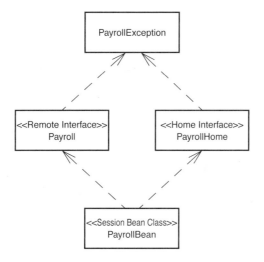

Figure 4.11 PayrollEJB Session Bean Parts

4.5.1   PayrollEJB Stateless Session Bean Parts

Figure 4.11 illustrates the main parts of the PayrollEJB stateless session bean.

The remote interface is called `Payroll`. The home interface is called `Payroll-Home`. The session bean class is called `PayrollBean`. The methods of the remote and home interfaces throw the application exception `PayrollException`.

PayrollEJB Session Bean Remote Interface

The `Payroll` remote interface defines the business methods that a client may invoke on the individual session objects. Code Example 4.16 shows the definition of the `Payroll` remote interface:

```
package com.star.payroll;

import javax.ejb.*;
import java.rmi.RemoteException;

public interface Payroll extends EJBObject {
   void setBenefitsDeduction(int emplNumber, double deduction)
      throws RemoteException, PayrollException;
```

```
double getBenefitsDeduction(int emplNumber)
    throws RemoteException, PayrollException;
double getSalary(int emplNumber)
    throws RemoteException, PayrollException;
void setSalary(int emplNumber, double salary)
    throws RemoteException, PayrollException;
}
```

Code Example 4.16 `Payroll` Remote Interface

The `Payroll` interface follows the same EJB rules for all enterprise bean remote interfaces.

PayrollEJB Session Bean Home Interface

The `PayrollHome` home interface defines the `create` method used by the client to create a session object. Code Example 4.17 shows the definition of this interface:

```
import javax.ejb.*;
import java.rmi.RemoteException;

public interface PayrollHome extends EJBHome {
    Payroll create() throws RemoteException, CreateException;
}
```

Code Example 4.17 `PayrollHome` Home Interface

Note that `PayrollHome` defines only one `create` method and that this method takes no arguments. Note also that `PayrollHome` defines no other methods. According to the EJB specification, the home interface of a stateless session bean must have a single `create` method that takes no arguments. The home interface cannot define any other methods.

PayrollEJB Helper Classes

The PayrollEJB session bean uses only one helper class, `PayrollException`, which defines the payroll-specific exceptions. The `Payroll` and `PayrollHome` interfaces are defined to throw the exception PayrollException. Code Example 4.18 shows the definition of the PayrollException class:

```
package com.star.payroll;

public class PayrollException extends Exception {
    // error codes
    public static int UNKNOWN = 0;
    public static int INVAL_EMPL_NUMBER = 1;

    static String[] defaultMessage = {
        "unknown error code",
        "invalid employee number"
    };

    int errorCode;

    public PayrollException() { super(); }
    public PayrollException(String s) { super(s); }
    public PayrollException(int errorCode, String s) {
        super(s);
        this.errorCode = errorCode;
    }
    public PayrollException(int errorCode) {
        super(errorCode >= 0 && errorCode < defaultMessage.length ?
            defaultMessage[errorCode] : "");
        this.errorCode = errorCode;
    }
}
```

Code Example 4.18 PayrollException Helper Class

PayrollEJB Session Bean Class

The PayrollBean class, the PayrollEJB's session bean class, is defined as shown in Code Example A.3 on page 378. The PayrollBean session bean class is a Java class that defines the implementation of the PayrollEJB session bean. Specifically, this class defines

- The business methods that are defined in the `Payroll` remote interface

- The `ejbCreate` method, which corresponds to the `create` method defined in the `PayrollHome` interface

- The methods defined in the `javax.ejb.SessionBean` interface

PayrollEJB Business Methods Implementation

The PayrollEJB session bean defines four business methods. The implementations of these business methods—`setSalary`, `getSalary`, `setBenefitsDeduction`, and `getBenefitsDeduction`—use JDBC to read or update the underlying `PayrollData-base`.

The PayrollBean bean instance acquires a database connection at the start of each business method and releases the connection at the end of the business method. In this example, the bean developer chose not to hold the database connection across business method invocations; the developer did this to allow the application server's connection pooling mechanism to maximize the reuse of database connections. However, it is also legal to hold the database connection across all business method invocations—that is, to acquire the database connection in the `ejbCreate` method, use it in the business methods, and then release it in the `ejbRemove` method.

Recall that a stateless session bean instance does not maintain state for a specific client. The `PayrollBean` class does not keep any state that is specific to a client: conversational state. The EJB container can use a stateless session bean instance to process serially the requests from multiple clients. The container can also route each request occurrence from a given client to a different instance, even if that client is running within the context of a transaction. Therefore, instances of a stateless session bean class must not hold any conversational state. (However, they can contain objects that are not specific to a client, such as JDBC data sources, as illustrated in our example.) The client must pass all the state necessary to process a request in the business method arguments.

As the example code illustrates, the paradigm provided by a stateless session bean is essentially procedural programming. This is in contrast to a stateful session bean and an entity bean, both of which provide the object-oriented programming paradigm.

The `ejbCreate` Method Implementation

Note that the `PayrollBean` class leaves the implementation of the `ejbCreate` method empty. The container invokes the `ejbCreate` method after creating the instance of the `PayrollBean` class and invoking the `setSessionContext` method on the instance. The bean developer needs to keep in mind that the container may create instances of a stateless session bean class in no direct relationship to the client-invoked create methods. This differs from a stateful session bean, in which the container creates the instance when a client invokes a create method through the session bean's home interface.

For example, the container may choose to create a fixed number of instances of the stateless session bean when the container starts and then use these instances to handle all subsequent client-invoked methods. Therefore, the `ejbCreate` method does not execute in a client context. Therefore, it would be an error for the `ejbCreate` method to invoke, for example, the `getCallerPrincipal` method on the associated `SessionContext` interface.

A stateless session bean typically uses the `ejbCreate` method to acquire various resources that will be used across subsequently invoked business methods. An example of such a resource would be a TCP/IP connection or a JDBC data source.

The `SessionBean` Method Implementation

The `PayrollBean` class defines empty implementations of the `setSessionContext`, `ejbRemove`, `ejbActivate`, and `ejbPassivate` `SessionBean` interface methods. PayrollBean is really a simple, uncomplicated bean, and as such does not need the functionality provided by the `setSessionContext` and `ejbRemove` container-invoked methods. (The `ejbActivate` and `ejbPassivate` methods are not called on stateless session beans.)

The container calls the `setSessionContext` method after creating the PayrollBean instance and before invoking the `ejbCreate` method on the instance. If it needs to invoke any of the methods that relate to `SessionContext` during its lifetime, the instance should save the passed `SessionContext` reference in an instance variable and should do this from within the `setSessionContext` method.

The `ejbRemove` Method Implementation

The container invokes the `ejbRemove` method before discarding the instance. Once it invokes the `ejbRemove` method on an instance, the container does not invoke any further business methods in the instance. The `ejbRemove` method is typically used to release any resources acquired in the `ejbCreate` method.

Note the comments in the `PayrollBean` code for the `ejbActivate` and `ejbPassivate` methods, which indicate that the container never calls the `ejbActivate` and `ejbPassivate` methods. The concept of passivation and activation applies only to stateful session beans; the container thus never calls these methods on a stateless session bean.

Data Access

The `PayrollBean` class makes direct use of JDBC in its business methods to access the database. Some application developers may prefer encapsulating the data access by using command beans (see the section Data Access Command Beans on page 100).

If a JDBC call throws an exception, the `PayrollBean` instance catches the exception and throws `EJBException`. You may notice that the instance does not close the JDBC connection before throwing `EJBException`, even though closing the connection is considered good programming practice. (For example, we always close the JDBC connection in the command beans used by Enrollment-Bean. We do so by calling the `release` method in the `finally` clause.) However, because the container manages resources for bean instances, not closing the JDBC connection does not result in a leak of resources. The container catches `EJBException` and closes all the resources, including JDBC connections, that are held by the instance. Management of resources is one of the services that the EJB container provides on behalf of the enterprise bean instances. The JDBC driver collaborates with the container to achieve the management of resources.

4.5.2   Client Developer's Perspective

In our example application, the EnrollmentEJB session bean is the client of the PayrollEJB session bean. EnrollmentEJB creates a stateless session object as follows:

```
...
PayrollHome payrollHome = (PayrollHome)
PortableRemoteObject.narrow(
    ictx.lookup("java:comp/env/ejb/PayrollEJB"),
    PayrollHome.class);
payroll = (Payroll)payrollHome.create();
...
```

A client uses the same API to create a stateless session bean as it does to create a stateful session bean. However, as discussed in the section The ejbCreate Method Implementation on page 115, invoking the `create` method on the home interface of a stateless session bean does not necessarily create a new instance of the session bean class. The implementation of the session bean's home interface `create` method may simply produce an object reference to the existing distributed object that implements the session bean's remote interface and then may return the reference to the client.

After it creates a stateless session object, the client can invoke the object's business methods through the remote interface. For example, EnrollmentBean invokes the `setBenefitsDeduction` method through the DeductionUpdateBean command bean as follows:

```
...
// Update information in the payroll system.
try {
    payroll.setBenefitsDeduction(employeeNumber, payrollDeduction);
} catch (PayrollException ex) {
    ...
} catch (RemoteException ex) {
    ...
}
...
```

Finally, when finished using the `Payroll` object, the client releases it by invoking the `remove` method, as follows:

```
...
try {
    payroll.remove();
} catch (Exception ex) {
}
...
```

Note that all stateless session objects within the same home interface have the same object identity. (However, objects from different home interfaces have different identities.) The following code example shows that two `Payroll` bean objects have the same identity, with the `isIdentical` method returning `true`:

```
Payroll payroll = (Payroll)payrollHome.create();
Payroll payroll2 = (Payroll)payrollHome.create();
if (payroll.isIdentical(payroll2)) {// this test returns true
    ...
} else {
    ...
}
```

This is in contrast to a stateful session bean. Every stateful session object has a unique identity.

Use of Object Handles

The EJB architecture allows a session bean client to store an object reference of a session bean's home or remote interface in persistent storage. To do this, a client uses the object's *handle*. The handle is needed because the home or remote interface references are not guaranteed to be serializable. The EJB specification defines two interfaces for working with handles:

1. The javax.ejb.Handle interface for the handles of enterprise bean objects

2. The javax.ejb.HomeHandle interface for the handles of the enterprise bean home objects

Code Example 4.19 illustrates the use of a session object handle:

```
...
ObjectOutputStream outputStream = ...;
...
Handle handle = payroll.getHandle();
outputStream.writeObject(handle);
...
```

Code Example 4.19 Using a Session Bean Handle

Note in this example that the client first obtains the handle by invoking the getHandle method on the session object. The client then serializes the handle into ObjectOutputStream.

At a later point, another client program running in the same client environment can deserialize the handle and create an object from the session object reference. Code Example 4.20 shows how this is done:

```
...
ObjectInputStream inputStream = ...;
...
Handle handle = (Handle)inputStream.readObject();
Payroll payroll = (Payroll)
        PortableRemoteObject.narrow(handle.getEJBObject(),
                Payroll.class);
// invoke business methods on payroll session object
payroll.setBenefitsDeduction();
```

Code Example 4.20 Deserializing a Handle

Note that the `PortableRemoteObject.narrow` mechanism, although complicated to use, ensures that the client code works with all EJB containers.

The Benefits Enrollment application does not use handles directly. Clients, such as application clients and Web applications, however, may use the handle mechanism in several ways, as follows:

- **Maintain a reference to the session object**—A Web application may maintain a reference to the session object in its HTTP session state. If it needs to swap the HTTP session state to secondary storage, the Web container may use the handle mechanism to retain the reference to the session object.

- **Migrate the HTTP session to another process**—The Web container may choose to migrate the HTTP session to another process on the same or a different machine. The Web container may use the handle mechanism to migrate the session object reference from one process to another.

- **Store HTTP session data**—The Web container may choose to implement the Web application as stateless by storing all the HTTP session data in an HTTP cookie. The Web container may use the handle to externalize the session object reference and store it in the cookie.

Note that a container crash invalidates any session handles for session objects that were stored in persistent storage.

4.6 Database Schemas

The Benefits Enrollment application uses three databases. In order for you to understand the example application, this section describes the schemas for these databases.

4.6.1 The Employee Database

The Star Enterprise human resources department maintains information about employees, company departments, and department positions in EmployeeDatabase. The information is stored in three tables. The Employees table within the database holds employee identifying information. Code Example 4.21 shows the SQL CREATE statement defining this table:

```
CREATE TABLE Employees (
    empl_id INT,
    empl_first_name VARCHAR(32),
    empl_last_name VARCHAR(32),
    empl_addr_street VARCHAR(32),
    empl_addr_city VARCHAR(32),
    empl_addr_zip VARCHAR(10),
    empl_addr_state VARCHAR(2),
    empl_dept_id VARCHAR(10),
    empl_start_date DATE,
    empl_position VARCHAR(5),
    empl_birth_date DATE,
    PRIMARY_KEY (empl_id)
)
```

Code Example 4.21 The Employees Table Schema

The Employees table contains the following columns:

- **empl_id**—The employee identifier number, which uniquely identifies each employee and is the primary key for these records

- **empl_first_name and empl_last_name**—The employee's first and last names

- **empl_addr_street, empl_addr_city, empl_addr_zip, and**

`empl_addr_state`—The employee's complete address

- `empl_dept_id`—The identifier—a foreign key reference to a row in the De-partments table—for the department in which the employee works

- `empl_start_date`—The employee's start date with the company

- `empl_position`—The identifier—a foreign key reference to a `Positions` table record—for the employee's current job or position

- `empl_birth_date`—The employee's date of birth

`EmployeeDatabase` includes two other tables that pertain to the Benefits Enrollment application. The `Positions` table keeps, in the `pos_desc` column, a description of each job position within the company. The primary key of this table is the `pos_id` column, which contains the position identifier. Code Example 4.22 shows the schema for this table:

```
create table Positions (
    pos_id VARCHAR(5),
    pos_desc VARCHAR(32),
    PRIMARY_KEY (pos_id)
)
```

Code Example 4.22 The `Positions` Table Schema

The third relevant table in `EmployeeDatabase` is the `Departments` table, which keeps information about each department within the company. Code Example 4.23 shows the schema for this table:

```
create table Departments (
    dept_id VARCHAR(10),
    dept_desc VARCHAR(32),
    dept_mgr INT,
    PRIMARY_KEY (dept_id)
)
```

Code Example 4.23 The `Departments` Table Schema

The `Departments` table contains the following columns:

- **`dept_id`**—The unique department identifier, the primary key for the table

- **`dept_desc`**—A description of the department

- **`dept_mgr`**—The `empl_id` of the current manager of the department

4.6.2   The Benefits Database

The `BenefitsDatabase` schema defines one table, `Selections`, pertaining to the Benefits Enrollment application. Code Example 4.24 shows the schema defining the `Selections` table:

```
create table Selections (
    sel_empl INT,
    sel_coverage INT,
    sel_medical_plan VARCHAR(10),
    sel_dental_plan VARCHAR(10),
    sel_smoker CHAR(1),
    PRIMARY_KEY (sel_empl)
)
```

Code Example 4.24 The `Selections` Table Schema

The `Selections` table contains the following columns:

- **`sel_empl`**—The identifier number of the employee for whom the benefits selections pertain

- **`sel_coverage`**—The type of coverage selected by the employee

- **`sel_medical_plan`**—The plan identifier of the employee's selected medical plan

- **`sel_dental_plan`**—The plan identifier of the employee's selected dental plan

- **`sel_smoker`**—An indicator, Y or N, of whether the employee is a smoker

4.6.3 The Payroll Database

The `PayrollDatabase` schema defines one table relevant to the Benefits Enrollment application—the `Paychecks` table. Code Example 4.25 shows its definition:

```
create table Paychecks (
    pay_empl INT,
    pay_salary FLOAT,
    pay_ded_benefits FLOAT,
    PRIMARY_KEY (pay_empl)
)
```

Code Example 4.25 The `Paychecks` Table Schema

This table maintains two columns: the employee's payroll amount, or salary (`pay_salary`), and the benefits deduction amount (`pay_ded_benefits`). The table's primary key is the employee identifier number, which is held in the `pay_empl` column.

4.7 Container-Provided Benefits

The previous sections described the tasks required of the session bean developers when developing the Enrollment and Payroll session beans. It is equally interesting to examine the tasks that the bean developers do *not* have to do because of the services provided by the EJB container. These services are distributed programming, concurrency and multithreading, transaction management, security management, resource pooling and other scalability issues, system administration, and high availability.

* **Distributed programming**—Because the EJB container handles distributed programming, the session bean developer doesn't have to deal with the complexity of writing a distributed application. To the developer, the session bean classes are Java classes that require no distributed programming knowledge. The EJB container provides the implementation of the session beans' home and remote interfaces by creating distributed RMI-IIOP objects. This allows the Payroll application to be written in the same way, regardless of whether its

client (EnrollmentEJB) is deployed on the same machine or on a different machine.

- **Concurrency and multithreading**—The developer can write the session bean classes as if they were used by one user. The EJB container makes it possible for multiple users to execute the benefits application concurrently. How does the container accomplish this? For the EnrollmentEJB stateful session bean, the container creates a `private` instance of the `EnrollmentBean` class for each connected user. In the case of the PayrollEJB stateless session bean, the container multiplexes the requests from multiple users across one or more instances of the `PayrollBean` class. The bean developer does not have to write any thread synchronization code into the application, because the EJB container does not allow conflicts resulting from multithreading to arise in the enterprise bean code.

- **Transaction management**—The bean developer does not have to write transaction management code. Note that the `EnrollmentBean` and `PayrollBean` classes contain no transaction management–related code. The EJB container automatically wraps the business methods into transactions, based on the deployment descriptor information for the bean. For example, the container does the following:

  - Starts a transaction before the execution of the `EnrollmentBean.commitSelections` method

  - Propagates the transaction to `BenefitsDatabase`, the `PayrollBean.setBenefitsDeduction` method, and `PayrollDatabase`

  - Performs a two-phase commit protocol across the two databases when the `EnrollmentBean.commitSelections` method has completed

- **Security management**—The session bean developer does not have to include security-related code in the respective bean implementations. The `EnrollmentBean` and `PayrollBean` classes contain no security-related code. The deployer and the system administrator set the security management policies by using facilities provided by the container, which enforces these security policies.

- **Resource pooling and other scalability issues**—The session bean developer does not have to deal with scalability issues in the bean's code. In our benefits example, the programmer did not have to deal directly with the issue of simultaneous access by a great number of users. That is, What happens if 10,000 employees all logged in to the benefits application and tried to use it at the same time? If such an event did occur, the EJB container would pool expensive server resources, such as JDBC connections, and this pooling would be transparent to the session bean code. Similarly, if the system happened to be low on memory, the EJB container would passivate some session objects and move them temporarily to secondary storage. In addition to being transparent to the bean, this avoids thrashing and achieves optimal throughput and response time.

- **System administration**—The EJB container provides tools for system administration so that the bean developer does not have to include such code in the application. In the benefits example, the session bean developer didn't have to write code to make the application capable of system administration. The EJB container provides application administration tools that are used by the Star Enterprise IT staff to manage the application at runtime.

- **High availability**—If it is concerned about the availability aspects of the application, Star Enterprise should deploy the application in an EJB container that provides high availability. The session bean developer does not have to do anything different in the bean's code to make the application highly available.

4.8 Conclusion

This chapter provided an in-depth discussion of session beans. It explained the different types of session beans and their states and showed how session beans fit into a multitiered architecture and how they model business logic.

An extensive employee benefits enrollment example illustrated the various parts of session beans and how to use them effectively. The example showed how to use the home, remote, and local interfaces; create and remove session bean instances; use command beans to encapsulate database access; and use session bean activation and passivation.

The chapter also provided views of session beans from both the application and client developers' perspectives and summarized the tasks that the container performs for an EJB application. By managing such tasks as distributed programming, concurrency, transaction and security handling, and so forth, the bean developer can focus on the application's business logic. The next chapter goes into greater detail about the services provided by the EJB container.

CHAPTER 5

Session Bean in Its Container

SESSION beans, like all enterprise beans, reside at runtime within an EJB container. The EJB container manages the session beans and provides numerous system-level services to support its session beans.

This chapter describes the support that an EJB container implements for session beans. Typically, a container provides services to session beans on two occasions: at deployment and later, when the session bean is used by a client. These built-in container services simplify application development because the application programmer does not have to develop this portion of the logic as part of the application.

This chapter also describes how the EJB container manages session beans. The chapter explains how the container facilitates locating a session bean's home interface and creating a session object, how it handles a client's invocation of the business methods of the bean, how it handles a session bean that has timed out or is removed, and so forth. This chapter also discusses the special classes that support the distributed object protocol, which the container generates for the bean at runtime.

Although a bean developer will likely find the material in this chapter informative and interesting, this knowledge is not necessary to develop session beans. The container services are present in all EJB containers; they exist "under the covers," and the developer can assume that they are there and can treat them like a black box. In most cases, the services are transparent to the bean code; in other cases, the container exposes them as a simple API to the bean. We present a description of the services that the container performs for session beans, merely to give the reader an appreciation of the container's work.

Certain things happen in the EJB environment when a session bean is deployed in a container and subsequently invoked by a client. We focus on how the EJB container handles and manages container artifacts, home interface lookup, session object creation, business method invocation, transaction management, passivation and activation, session object removal and timeout, and invocation of other session beans.

- **Container artifacts**—These are the additional classes that the EJB container generates to manage the session bean at runtime and to support the distributed object protocol.

- **Home interface lookup**—A client performs a JNDI lookup of the session bean's home interface.

- **Session object creation**—A client program creates a new session object when invoking a create method on a session bean home object.

- **Business method invocation**—A client program invokes the business methods on the session object.

- **Transaction management**—The container creates and manages a transaction transparently to the session bean class.

- **Passivation and activation**—The container reclaims resources by moving the session object state to secondary memory: passivation. Later, the container restores the session object state—activation—when the session object is needed to handle a client-invoked business method.

- **Session object removal and timeout**—The container removes a session object when the client invokes the `remove` method or when the bean's timeout limit is reached.

- **Invocation of other session beans**—One session bean may be a client of another session bean.

5.1   Container Artifacts

Recall from Section 2.4.1, Container Artifacts, on page 45 that when a session bean is deployed in an EJB container, the tools provided by the container vendor generate additional classes, called *container artifacts*. The container uses container artifacts to manage the session bean at runtime and to support the distributed object protocol between the client program and the EJB container.

For session beans having a local interface and a local home interface, such as EnrollmentEJB in the previous chapter, the container generates the classes `EnrollmentLocalObject` and `EnrollmentLocalHome`—these names are illustrative for a typical container—which implement the `Enrollment` and `EnrollmentHome` interfaces, respectively.

For session beans having a remote interface and a remote home interface, the container tools generate the `PayrollRMI` and `PayrollHomeRMI` distributed object types (Figure 5.1).

`PayrollRMI` and `PayrollHomeRMI` are typically RMI-IIOP object types. Their instances are distributed CORBA objects that implement the communication between the client and the container. The `PayrollRMI` type provides the implementation of the session bean's remote interface, `Payroll`. The `PayrollHomeRMI` type provides the implementation of the session bean's home interface, `Payroll-Home`.

We refer to the instances of the `PayrollRMI` object type as *session objects,* and we refer to the instances of the `PayrollHomeRMI` object type as *session bean home objects*. Most containers create a single session bean home object that is shared among all clients, but some containers may use multiple instances of the session bean home object.

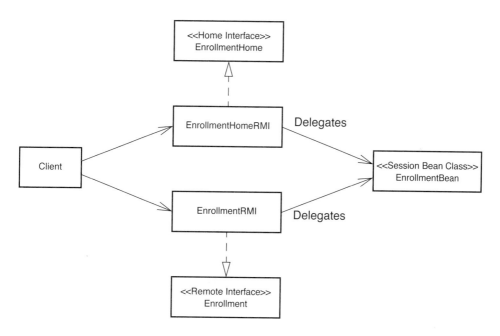

Figure 5.1 `Enrollment` Class Diagram

The implementation of each RMI-IIOP type consists of multiple Java classes. Although you do not need to know RMI-IIOP details to write an enterprise bean, you may be interested to see the RMI-IIOP specification, which details how to implement RMI-IIOP objects; see the section Other Sources of Information in the preface on page xviii to locate the specification.

5.2   How the Container Manages Session Beans at Runtime

This section explains how the EJB container manages the session bean at runtime. We use object interaction diagrams (OIDs) to illustrate the interactions among the client, the distributed objects implemented by the container, and the instances of the session bean class. Some of the examples that follow use the remote interface and the remote home interface to illustrate the interactions. Keep in mind that similar interactions happen for local interfaces, too, except that local objects have no distributed objects and hence no network activity.

5.2.1   EJB Home Interface Lookup

Recall that a client program uses the following code to locate a session bean's home interface:

```
...
Context ictx = new InitialContext();
Object h = ictx.lookup("java:comp/env/ejb/PayrollEJB");
PayrollHome payrollHome = (payrollHome)
    PortableRemoteObject.narrow(h, PayrollHome.class);
...
```

This code performs a JNDI lookup operation and casts the found object to the PayrollHome home interface type.

The OID in Figure 5.2 illustrates the EJB container actions that occur "under the covers" when the client initiates a lookup operation.

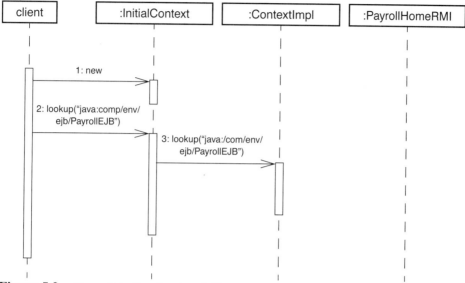

Figure 5.2   Home Interface Lookup OID

1. The client application creates an instance of the `InitialContext` class, which, because it is part of the JNDI, is defined in the `javax.naming` package.

2. The client invokes the `lookup` operation and passes to the method the string `java:comp/env/ejb/PayrollEJB` as the parameter.

3. The `InitialContext` object delegates the `lookup` operation to a `ContextImpl` class provided by the EJB container. What causes this to happen? At deployment, the deployer must configure the JNDI namespace for the client application. In our example, the deployer configured the JNDI `InitialContext` object to delegate all JNDI operations for names beginning with the prefix `java:` to a `ContextImpl` class provided by the EJB container. If the client resides on a different machine from the container, this operation may result in a network trip to the container.

The container returns the `PayrollHomeRMI` home object to the client. The client program obtains a reference to the RMI stub for the `PayrollHomeRMI` object. The stub implements the `PayrollHome` interface, which allows the client to subsequently invoke the methods defined in the `PayrollHome` interface on the stub.

Note that the EJB specification requires the client to convert the result of the `lookup` operation by using the `PortableRemoteObject.narrow` method. The reason is that the home object is a remote object. If the client uses a simple Java cast to convert the result of the `lookup` operation, the `cast` operation could fail with some EJB container implementations.

5.2.2   Session Object Creation

Let's look at what happens when the client program invokes the `create` method on the session bean home object with the following line of code:

```
payroll = payrollHome.create();
```

The OID diagram (Figure 5.3) illustrates how the container performs this operation.

1. The client program invokes the `create` operation on `PayrollHome`, which is the RMI stub for the `PayrollHomeRMI` object. The stub forwards the request over RMI-IIOP to the implementation of the `PayrollHomeRMI` object residing in the EJB container. (The figure does not show the forwarding operation.)

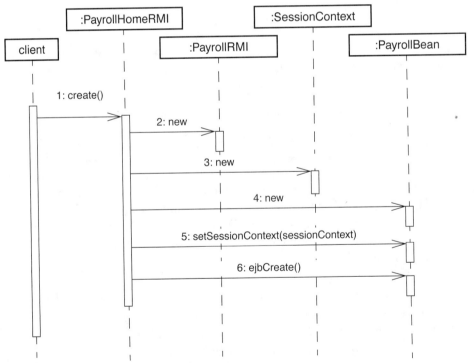

Figure 5.3   Create a Session Object OID

2. The implementation of the `PayrollHomeRMI` object creates a new `PayrollRMI` object. Note that this is a distributed RMI-IIOP object, not a simple Java object.

3. The implementation of the `PayrollHomeRMI` object creates a `SessionContext` object. The container uses the `SessionContext` object internally to manage information about the associated `PayrollBean` instance.

4. The implementation of the `PayrollHomeRMI` object also creates an instance of the `PayrollBean` class, using the `public` constructor, which takes no arguments.

5. The implementation of the `PayrollHomeRMI` object then invokes the `setSessionContext` method on the `PayrollBean` instance to pass the `SessionContext` object to the instance. The instance may save the reference to the `SessionContext` object and use it later to communicate with the container.

6. The implementation of the `PayrollHomeRMI` object invokes the matching `ejbCreate` method on the `PayrollBean` instance. The parameters to the `ejbCreate` method are the parameters of the client-invoked `create` method. The session bean instance may perform the initialization of its conversational state — for stateful session beans — in the `ejbCreate` method.

When these operations are complete, the container returns a remote object reference of the `PayrollRMI` distributed object to the client program. The stub implements the `Payroll` remote interface.

The `create` operation does not run in the client's transaction context. Therefore, if a client's transaction rolls back after the client creates a session object, the container does not remove the new session object, such as `PayrollRMI`, in our example; nor does it undo the work of the `ejbCreate` method. The client can use the session object.

5.2.3 Business Method Invocation

This section discusses how the container manages the execution of the client-invoked business methods. This is probably the heart of an EJB application.

The OID for the business method invocations is the most complex of the OIDs. It is important to keep in mind that these diagrams illustrate what the container is doing for the application. Because the container is responsible for these actions, the application developer's job is greatly simplified. To put it another way, the application developer merely invokes one business method, but the container must manage this with approximately 14 separate operations. Without the EJB container and environment, the application developer would have to write the code for these 14 operations, a far-from-easy task.

In addition, the case we are examining here is rather simple. Two session beans use two databases in a transaction. Although one session bean does call another enterprise bean within a transaction, the session bean does not import a client's transactions; nor does it use the SessionSynchronization interface. Many real situations are much more complex, involving multiple databases, other enterprise beans, multiple transactions, transaction synchronization, and so forth. In these cases, the container's job is even more complex and involves many more steps.

For our example, let's consider the case when the client, the EnrollmentWeb application, invokes the following business method on the Enrollment object:

```
enrollment.commitSelections(selection);
```

The OID diagram in Figure 5.4 illustrates the sequence of actions the container takes.

1. The client invokes the commitSelections business operation on the Enroll-mentLocalObject instance.

2. The container initiates a new transaction. This happens because the bean developer specified the EnrollmentEJB session bean to be a bean with container-managed transaction demarcation and assigned the Requires transaction attribute to the commitSelections method. When a bean uses container-managed transaction demarcation, the container evaluates the bean's transaction attribute and determines how to handle the transaction demarcation. If a container-managed bean has the Requires transaction attribute, the container initiates a new transaction if the client is not already participating in a transaction. Note that if the client is already participating in a transaction, the client's invocation of the EnrollmentLocalObject object propagates the client's transaction to the container, and the container performs the work done by the session bean in the client's current transaction. See Chapter 10, Understanding Transactions, for more information. The container also checks whether the client is allowed to invoke the business method. If the client is not allowed to invoke the business method, the container throws RemoteException to the client. See Chapter 11, Managing Security, for information on security management.

3. The EnrollmentLocalObject object delegates the object invocation to the En-rollmentBean instance.

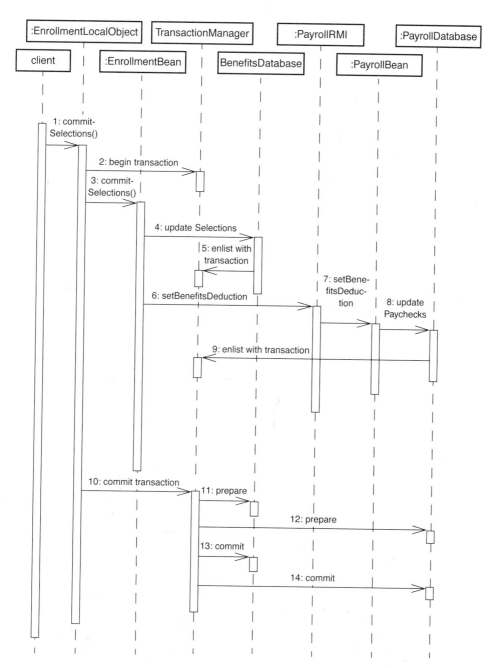

Figure 5.4 Business Method Invocation OID

4. The `EnrollmentBean` instance—the DBUpdateBenefits command bean used by `EnrollmentBean`—performs a database operation to update the record in the `Selections` table in `BenefitsDatabase`.

5. The DBMS that stores `BenefitsDatabase` enlists itself with the transaction started in step 2. This is to ensure that the update to the `Selections` table is included as part of the transaction.

6. The `EnrollmentBean` instance—through the DeductionUpdateBean command bean—invokes the `PayrollRMI` session object via its RMI stub. The container propagates the transaction with the invocation to the `PayrollRMI` object.

7. The `PayrollRMI` object delegates the object invocation to the `PayrollBean` instance.

8. The `PayrollBean` instance updates the record in the `Paychecks` table in `PayrollDatabase`.

9. The DBMS that stores `PayrollDatabase` enlists itself with the transaction to ensure that the update to the `Paychecks` table is included as part of the transaction.

10. Before sending a reply to the client, the `EnrollmentLocalObject` object commits the transaction.

11.–14. The transaction manager coordinates the two-phase commit protocol across the two databases enlisted in the transaction.

After the transaction manager commits the transaction, the `EnrollmentLocalObject` object sends the reply to the client. If the commit fails for any reason, the `EnrollmentLocalObject` object throws `javax.ejb.EJBException` to the client.

5.2.4 Session Bean Passivation and Activation

Let's assume that the user invoked a business method, such as the `getMedicalOptions` method, and then decided to interrupt the session with the EnrollmentWeb application. For example, the user starts the enrollment process, gets to the page displaying the available medical options, and then, realizing that it is time to go to lunch, locks the workstation screen, leaving the application where it is to resume it later. Shortly thereafter, the container detects that the `Enrollment` session object—recall that the Enrollment session bean is stateful—has been idle for a while. At that point, the container may decide to reclaim the memory resources by passivating the session object.

The OID diagram in Figure 5.5 illustrates the actions that the container takes to passivate the session object.

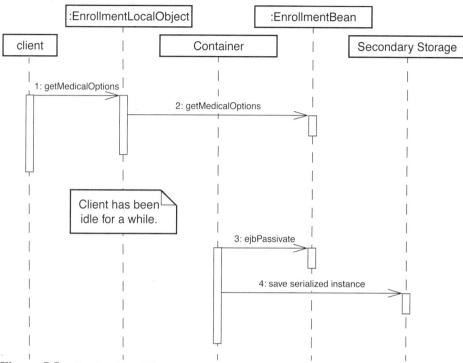

Figure 5.5 Passivation OID

1. The client invokes the `getMedicalOptions` business operation on `Enrollment-LocalObject`.

2. The `EnrollmentLocalObject` object delegates the object invocation to the `EnrollmentBean` instance. At this point, the user leaves for lunch.

3. The container detects that the client has not invoked a method on the session bean object for a while. If the container needs to reclaim the resources held by the session bean object, the container may choose to passivate the session bean object. The container invokes the `ejbPassivate` method on the `EnrollmentBean` instance. The `ejbPassivate` method gives the instance a chance to prepare its conversational state for passivation.

4. The container saves the serialized instance of `EnrollmentBean`'s state to secondary storage.

Later, when the user comes back from lunch and resumes the session with the EnrollmentWeb application, the container activates the passivated object. It does this by taking the actions illustrated in Figure 5.6.

1. The user returns from lunch and resumes the EnrollmentWeb application from the point at which the getMedicalOptions business operation on the EnrollmentLocalObject object was invoked. Now the user submits the form that results in the invocation of the setMedicalOption method on the session object.

2. The EnrollmentLocalObject object tells the container—this is an internal communication within the container—to activate the object invocation and the state of the EnrollmentBean instance.

3. The container loads into main memory the serialized instance of EnrollmentBean that it had previously stored in secondary storage.

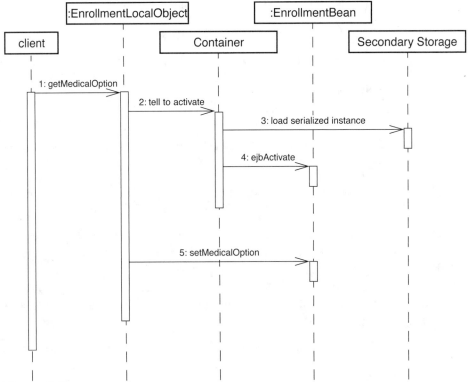

Figure 5.6   Activation OID

4. The container invokes the `ejbActivate` method on the `EnrollmentBean` instance, which at this point has been notified that it has been activated and can perform whatever operations are necessary to transfer itself to a state in which it can accept the invocation of a business method.

5. The `EnrollmentLocalObject` object delegates the `setMedicalOption` object invocation to the `EnrollmentBean` instance.

5.2.5   Session Object Removal

The client invokes the `remove` method on the `EnrollmentLocalObject` object to remove the session bean instance. This is shown in the following code segment:

```
enrollment.remove();
```

The client call to the `remove` method causes the container to invoke the following sequence of actions, as illustrated in Figure 5.7.

1. The client invokes the `remove` operation on the `EnrollmentLocalObject` object that implements the `Enrollment` interface.

2. The `EnrollmentLocalObject` object invokes the `ejbRemove` method in the `EnrollmentBean` instance to give the instance a chance to release the resources held in its conversational state. The JVM will eventually garbage collect the `EnrollmentBean` instance and all objects reachable from the instance.

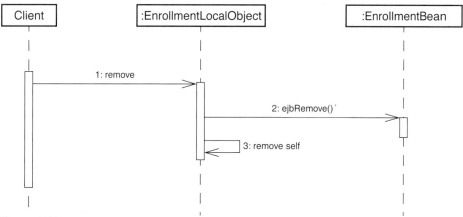

Figure 5.7   Session Bean Removal OID

3. The `EnrollmentLocalObject` object removes itself. At that point, a client is no longer able to use the `EnrollmentLocalObject` object.

If a client attempts to invoke a business method on a local session object after the object has been removed, the client receives `javax.ejb.NoSuchObjectLocal-Exception`. (For remote objects, the client receives `java.rmi.NoSuchObjectEx-ception`.)

A client cannot remove a session object while the object is participating in a transaction. That is, the `remove` method cannot be called when the object is participating in a transaction; this throws `javax.ejb.RemoveException` to the client. For session objects having a remote interface, a client may also remove the session object, using the `EJBHome.remove(Handle handle)` method. Handles are discussed in Chapter 4.

The container has the option of invoking the `ejbRemove` method on an instance after the life of the session bean instance has expired, even without a prior `remove` method call from the client. See Section 5.2.6, Session Bean Timeout, which follows.

Finally, the `remove` operation does not run in the client's transaction context. Therefore, if a client's transaction rolls back after the client removed a session object, the container does not restore the removed session object, such as `Enrollment-LocalObject` in our example; nor does it undo the work of the `ejbRemove` method.

5.2.6 Session Bean Timeout

In some cases, a client may create a session object but then never call the `remove` method on this object. To handle these occurrences, the container typically uses a timeout mechanism to automatically remove session objects that are no longer used by clients. The deployer usually sets the timeout.

The container must be able to remove a session bean without waiting for the `remove` method invocation, because it needs, eventually, to deallocate the resources that it allocated for the session object, such as the space on secondary storage, to store the serialized image of the session bean instance. Essentially, if a client has not invoked the session object for a specified period of time, the container implicitly removes the session object. Keep in mind, however, that a session bean timeout never occurs while a session object is in a transaction.

When it removes the session object because of the timeout, the container may or may not choose to call the `ejbRemove` method on the session bean instance. The state of the session object determines whether the container invokes the `ejbRemove` method. If a session object is not in the "passive" state, the container invokes the `ejbRemove` method. If the session object has been passivated by the container, the container may simply reclaim the secondary storage allocated for the session object and not call the `ejbRemove` method. Therefore, the developer must design the application to tolerate the case in which the `ejbRemove` method is not called when a session object is removed.

5.3 Conclusion

This chapter explained how an EJB container manages a session bean during runtime. The chapter discussed the container artifacts and covered the container's handling of session bean creation, business method invocation, session bean activation and passivation, session bean removal, and session bean timeout.

This completes the discussion on session beans. The next chapter focuses on message-driven beans and asynchronous communication between applications.

CHAPTER **6**

Using Message-Driven Beans and Connectors

ENTERPRISE applications must be able to use data from existing legacy systems and a wide variety of databases. Processes within applications must be able to not only communicate with one another but also send and receive data to and from other applications. This communication within and between enterprise applications and data stores is essential in business operations. J2EE-distributed applications rely on messaging systems, such as Java Message Service (JMS), for highly reliable and scalable communications and on J2EE connectors to facilitate integrating with underlying data stores and legacy systems. The EJB architecture introduces a new enterprise bean type specifically designed to handle asynchronous communication. Whereas earlier releases of the EJB architecture supported only a synchronous mode of communication, the EJB 2.0 and 2.1 architectures use a message-driven bean to support asynchronous communication. Message-driven beans make it easy for J2EE applications to process asynchronous messages.

Messaging systems, such as JMS, allow separate, uncoupled applications to communicate asynchronously and reliably, based on an architecture in which individual components communicate on a peer-to-peer basis. Messaging systems not only promote loose coupling between sending and receiving components but also allow a high degree of anonymity between senders and receivers. To the message receiver, or consumer, it doesn't matter who produced the message, when it was produced, and from where it was sent.

Message-driven beans serve as router processes that operate on incoming enterprise messages from a message service provider. A bean developer might use a message-driven bean to integrate an EJB-based system with a legacy system or to enable business-to-business interactions. The message-driven bean's sole responsibility is to process messages, because its container automatically manages the component's entire environment.

This chapter provides background information on the communication modes available to enterprise applications, including an overview of JMS and how it facilitates enterprise application integration. The chapter describes concepts of message-driven beans and extends the benefits enrollment example from the previous chapters to illustrate effective use of message-driven beans.

This chapter also demonstrates how applications can communicate using the J2EE Connector architecture and connectors. In brief, the J2EE Connector architecture is a standard API for connecting the J2EE platform to enterprise information systems, such as enterprise resource planning, mainframe transaction processing, and database systems. The Connector architecture defines a set of scalable, secure, and transactional mechanisms, adherence to which facilitates integrating an enterprise information system with a J2EE platform. Refer to the section Other Sources of Information on page xviii for more information on the J2EE Connector architecture.

6.1   JMS and Communication Modes

An integral part of the J2EE platform, JMS is a standard Java API that can be used across various types of enterprise messaging systems. A Java application uses the JMS API to connect to an enterprise messaging system. Once connected, the application through the API uses the facilities of the underlying messaging system to create messages and to communicate asynchronously with one or more peer applications.

6.1.1   Synchronous and Asynchronous Communication

Communication between applications or components can be either synchronous or asynchronous. Synchronous communication follows a request/response interaction model. A component sends a request to another component and then suspends, or blocks, its processing while it waits for the other component to act on the request and send its response. The component thread continues its processing only after it receives the response.

A synchronous request/response interaction model is typical for most remote function call–based APIs, whereby the caller application or component invokes a function on another component. This communication is considered synchronous because the caller waits synchronously while the function executes on the other component. The caller thread continues only when the function returns.

Generally, for synchronous communication to work properly, the sender must have knowledge of both the receiver's availability and its methods. In particular, the sender must know the receiver's methods well enough to send its requests in the proper form. Such shared knowledge required between senders and receivers is considered tightly coupled communication. Synchronous communication results in tight coupling, or increased dependency, between applications and components, a situation that is not always desirable.

Asynchronous messaging, by contrast, is a loosely coupled distributed mode of communication that allows applications to communicate by exchanging messages in a way that leaves senders independent of receivers. The sender sends its message and does not have to wait for the receiver to receive or process that message. In addition, the communication mechanism itself is separate from the sending and receiving components. An application or component sends a request to a destination other than the receiving process, regardless of the receiver's availability. The recipient retrieves the request from this destination. The only requirement is that both processes know the message format and the intermediate destination.

Asynchronous messaging communication using JMS can be either queue-based communication or publish/subscribe messaging. Queue-based communication, also referred to as *point-to-point messaging*, entails sending messages to a message queue that is independent of both the sender and the receiver. The sender process sends a message to this message queue, and the receiver process receives its messages from the queue. The message queue acts as a message buffer between two communicating processes.

The publish/subscribe messaging mechanism enables a sender to broadcast its message to multiple receivers. Publish/subscribe messaging systems support an event-driven model whereby information producers and consumers participate in the message transmission. A publisher application publishes messages on a specific topic. Any number of applications, called *subscribers*, can subscribe to this topic and receive the messages published by the publisher. The publish/subscribe facility delivers the published messages to the subscribing applications, based on the subscribed topic. In other words, a publishing application publishes its message to a well-known node, called a *topic*, within a content-based hierarchy. You can think of a publish/subscribe system as a message broker that gathers and distributes messages. The topic serves as the intermediary between message publishers and message subscribers.

6.1.2   JMS Overview

JMS is a standard Java API that allows applications to send and receive messages asynchronously. JMS has been designed so that messaging systems vendors can easily integrate their products with the Java platform. A Java application uses the set of interfaces and semantics defined by the JMS API to connect to an enterprise messaging-oriented middleware (MOM) system. Once connected, the application, through the JMS API, can use the facilities of the underlying messaging system to create messages and to communicate asynchronously with one or more peer applications. JMS provides a consistent set of interfaces that its clients can use to send and receive messages independently of the underlying messaging system.

Because the JMS API is an integral part of the J2EE platform, any J2EE or Web component can synchronously send or receive a JMS message. By using a message-driven enterprise bean, a J2EE component can asynchronously consume JMS messages. Message sending and receiving can also be made part of a transaction. In addition, JMS providers may implement message-driven beans such that they process messages concurrently.

The JMS API architecture consists of the following:

- **JMS provider**—The implementation of the JMS API for a messaging system. An application uses the JMS provider to access the services of the underlying messaging system.

- **JMS client**—A Java application, either an application client or a J2EE component, that produces and consumes messages. A JMS client application uses the JMS API to access the messaging system's asynchronous messaging services. JMS supports peer-to-peer messaging, so both producer and consumer applications are clients of the JMS provider.

- **JMS domain**—The type of asynchronous message-based communication supported by the JMS provider and messaging system. JMS supports two domain types: queue-based point-to-point messaging and publish/subscribe messaging. Applications use different JMS interfaces, depending on the domain.

- **JMS message**—A JMS message consists of a header, properties, and a body. The message *header* identifies the message. For example, it might identify the type of subscriber that is interested in the message. The *properties* of a message are specific to an application and provider. They often provide further identification information. The message *body* is the content of the message. A message may be one of several formats. A `TextMessage` format contains only string data and is ideal for XML-based messages. An `ObjectMessage` format wraps a single arbitrary serializable Java object or a collection of such objects. (JMS supports additional formats to these commonly used formats.)

Clients use JMS to connect to the messaging system provider and send and receive messages. Clients create JMS sessions, or objects, which provide a context, or environment, to produce or receive messages. From within a session, a client can create a `MessageProducer` object to send messages and a `MessageConsumer` object to receive messages.

Refer to the section Other Sources of Information on page xviii for additional JMS references.

6.2   Message-Driven Bean Concepts

Message-driven beans are EJB components that process asynchronous messages. These messages may be delivered via JMS or by using any other messaging system, such as the Java™ API for XML Messaging (JAX-M). Message-driven beans asynchronously consume messages from a message destination, such as a JMS queue or topic.

Message-driven beans are components that receive incoming enterprise messages from a messaging provider. The primary responsibility of a message-driven bean is to process messages, because the bean's container automatically manages other aspects of the message-driven bean's environment. Message-driven beans contain business logic for handling received messages. A message-driven bean's business logic may key off the contents of the received message or may be driven by the mere fact of receiving the message. Its business logic may include such operations as initiating a step in a workflow, doing some computation, or sending a message.

A message-driven bean is essentially application code that is invoked when a message arrives at a particular destination. With this type of messaging, an application—either a J2EE component or an external enterprise messaging client—acts as a message producer and sends a message that is delivered to a message destination. The container activates an instance of the correct type of message-driven bean from its pool of message-driven beans, and the bean instance consumes the message from the message destination. Because a message-driven bean is stateless, any instance of the matching type of message-driven bean can process any message. Thus, message-driven beans are programmed in a similar manner as stateless session beans.

The advantage of message-driven beans is that they allow a loose coupling between the message producer and the message consumer, thus reducing the dependencies between separate components. In addition, the EJB container handles the setup tasks required for asynchronous messaging, such as registering the bean as a message listener, acknowledging message delivery, handling re-deliveries in case of exceptions, and so forth. A component other than a message-driven bean would otherwise have to perform these low-level tasks.

6.2.1   Implementing a Message-Driven Bean

To a bean developer, message-driven beans are much like stateless session beans, having the same life cycle as stateless session beans but not having a component or home interface. The implementation class for a message-driven bean must implement the `javax.ejb.MessageDrivenBean` interface. A message-driven bean class must also implement an `ejbCreate` method, even though the bean has no home interface. Because they do not expose a component or home interface, clients cannot directly access message-driven beans. Like session beans, message-driven beans may be used to drive workflow processes. However, the arrival of a particular message initiates the process.

Implementing a message-driven bean is fairly straightforward. A message-driven bean extends two interfaces: `javax.ejb.MessageDrivenBean` and a message listener interface corresponding to the specific messaging system. (For example, when using the JMS messaging system, the bean extends the `javax.jms.Message-Listener` interface.) The container uses the `MessageDrivenBean` methods `ejbCreate`, `ejbRemove`, and `setMessageDrivenContext` to control the life cycle of the message-driven bean.

You can provide an empty implementation of the `ejbCreate` and `setMessageDrivenContext` methods. These methods are typically used to look up objects from the bean's JNDI environment, such as references to other beans and resource references. If the message-driven bean sends messages or receives synchronous communication from another destination, you use the `ejbCreate` method to look up the JMS connection factories and destinations and to create the JMS connection. The implementation of the `ejbRemove` method can also be left empty. However, if the `ejbCreate` method obtained any resources, such as a JMS connection, you should use the `ejbRemove` method to close those resources.

The methods of the message listener interface are the principal methods of interest to the developer. These methods contain the business logic that the bean executes upon receipt of a message. The EJB container invokes these methods defined on the message-driven bean class when a message arrives for the bean to service.

A developer decides how a message-driven bean should handle a particular message and codes this logic into the listener methods. For example, the message-driven bean might simply pass the message to another enterprise bean component via a synchronous method invocation, send the message to another message destination, or perform some business logic to handle the message itself and update a database.

A message-driven bean can be associated with configuration properties that are specific to the messaging system it uses. A developer can use the bean's XML deployment descriptor to include the property names and values that the container can use when connecting the bean with its messaging system.

6.2.2   JMS and Message-Driven Beans

The EJB architecture requires the container to support message-driven beans that can receive JMS messages. You can think of message-driven beans as message listeners that consume messages from a JMS destination. A JMS destination may be a queue or a topic. When the destination is a queue, there is only one message producer, or sender, and one message consumer. When the destination is a topic, a message producer publishes messages to the topic, and any number of consumers may consume the topic's messages.

A message-driven bean that consumes JMS messages needs to implement the javax.jms.MessageListener interface, which contains the single method onMessage that takes a JMS message as a parameter. When a message arrives for the bean to service, the container invokes the onMessage method defined on the message-driven bean class. The onMessage method contains the business logic that the message-driven bean executes upon receipt of a message. The bean typically examines the message and executes the actions necessary to process it. This may include invoking other components.

The onMessage method has one parameter, the JMS message itself, and this parameter may be any valid JMS message type. The method tests whether the message is the expected type, such as a JMS TextMessage type, and then casts the message to that type and extracts from the message the information it needs.

Because the method does not include a `throws` clause, no application exceptions may be thrown during processing.

The EJB architecture defines several configuration properties for JMS-based message-driven beans. These properties allow the container to appropriately configure the bean and link it to the JMS message provider during deployment. These properties include the following:

- `destinationType`—Either a `javax.jms.Queue` if the bean is to receive messages from a JMS queue, or a `javax.jms.Topic` if the bean is to receive messages from a JMS topic.

- `subscriptionDurability`—Used for JMS topics to indicate whether the bean is to receive messages from a durable or a nondurable subscription. A durable subscription has the advantage of receiving a message even if the EJB server is temporarily offline.

- `acknowledgeMode`—When message-driven beans use bean-managed transactions, this property indicates to the container how to acknowledge the delivery of JMS messages. (When beans use container-managed transactions, the message is acknowledged when the transaction commits.) Its values may be `Auto-acknowledge`, which is the default, or `Dups-ok-acknowledge`. The `Auto-acknowledge` mode indicates that the container should acknowledge messages as soon as the onMessage method returns. The `Dups-ok-acknowledge` mode indicates that the container may lazily acknowledge messages, which could cause duplicate messages to be delivered.

- `messageSelector`—Allows a developer to provide a JMS message selector expression to filter messages in the queue or topic. Using a message selector expression ensures that only messages that satisfy the selector are delivered to the bean.

6.2.3   Message-Driven Beans and Transactions

Because messaging systems often have full-fledged transactional capabilities, message consumption can be grouped into a single transaction with such other transactional work as database access. This means that a bean developer can choose to make a message-driven bean invocation part of a transaction. Keep in mind, however, that if the message-driven bean participates in a transaction, you must also be using container-managed transaction demarcation. The deployment descriptor transaction attribute, which for a message-driven bean can be either `Required` or `NotSupported`, determines whether the bean participates in a transaction.

When a message-driven bean's transaction attribute is set to `Required`, the message delivery from the message destination to the message-driven bean is part of the subsequent transactional work undertaken by the bean. By having the message-driven bean be part of a transaction, you ensure that message delivery takes place. If the subsequent transaction fails, the message delivery is rolled back along with the other transactional work. The message remains available in the message destination until picked up by another message-driven bean instance. Note that the message sender and the message receiver, which is the message-driven bean, do not share the same transaction. Thus, the sender and the receiver communicate in a loosely coupled but reliable manner.

If the message-driven bean's transactional attribute is `NotSupported`, it consumes the message outside of any subsequent transactional work. Should that transaction not complete, the message is still considered consumed and will be lost.

It is also possible to use bean-managed transaction demarcation with a message-driven bean. With bean-managed transaction demarcation, however, the message delivery is not part of the transaction, because the transaction starts within the `onMessage` method.

6.2.4   Message-Driven Bean Usage

Bean developers should consider using message-driven beans under certain circumstances:

- To have messages automatically delivered

- To implement asynchronous messaging

- To integrate applications in a loosely coupled but reliable manner

- To have message delivery drive other events in the system workflow

- To create message selectors, whereby specific messages serve as triggers for subsequent actions

6.3   Using a Message-Driven Bean in the Benefits Application

Let's look at how the same benefits application described in Chapter 4 might look using a message-driven bean to replace the PayrollEJB session bean. See Figure 6.1.

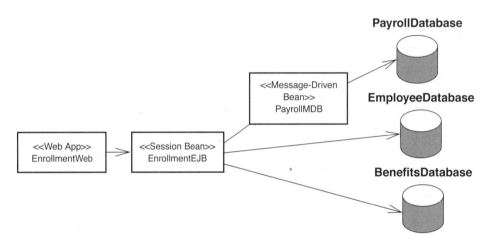

Figure 6.1   Parts of the Benefits Enrollment Application

Star Enterprise wants to use a loosely coupled integration model between the Benefits Enrollment and other enterprise applications and its own internal payroll system maintained by the payroll department. Star Enterprise needs to implement a loosely coupled integration model for several reasons:

- The payroll department and application may be geographically distributed.

- The payroll application may be based on a different hardware or software configuration at different payroll sites, and these configurations may differ from the configurations for the enterprise and Benefits Enrollment applications.

- The enterprise applications may need to update payroll information without being dependent on the payroll system's availability to process requests.

Star Enterprise can achieve such loose integration by using an enterprise messaging system. After an enterprise messaging system has been implemented, its enterprise applications, including the Benefits Enrollment application, send payroll updates to the PayrollQueue reliable message queue maintained by the payroll department. At some point, unrelated to when updates are sent to the queue, the payroll application receives the payroll-update messages from `PayrollQueue` asynchronously and processes them.

Chapter 4 discussed Star Enterprise's payroll system organization. In that context, it consists of two principal parts:

- The PayrollEJB stateless session bean deployed in the payroll department's application server

- `PayrollDatabase`, located in the payroll department's database server, for storing payroll information for all Star Enterprise employees

We now add a message-driven bean called *PayrollMDB*, which enables the payroll application to receive messages from the `PayrollQueue` message queue.

6.3.1 PayrollMDB Message-Driven Bean

PayrollMDB, a message-driven bean that follows the requirements of the EJB 2.1 architecture, consists of the `PayrollMDB` class and associated deployment descriptors. Code Example 6.1 shows the complete code for the `PayrollMDB` implementation class:

```
public class PayrollMDB implements MessageDrivenBean,
        MessageListener {

    private PayrollLocal payroll;

    public void setMessageDrivenContext(MessageDrivenContext mdc) {
        try {
            InitialContext ictx = new InitialContext();
            PayrollLocalHome payrollHome = (PayrollLocalHome)
                    ictx.lookup("java:comp/env/ejb/PayrollEJB");
            payroll = payrollHome.create();
        } catch ( Exception ex ) {
            throw new EJBException("Unable to get Payroll bean", ex);
        }
    }

    public void ejbCreate() { }
```

```
    public void ejbRemove() { }

    public void onMessage(Message msg) {
        MapMessage map = (MapMessage)msg;
        try {
            int emplNumber = map.getInt("Employee");
            double deduction = map.getDouble("PayrollDeduction");

            payroll.setBenefitsDeduction(emplNumber, deduction);
        } catch ( Exception ex ) {
            throw new EJBException(ex);
        }
    }
}
```

Code Example 6.1   PayrollMDB Implementation Class

The PayrollMDB class implements two interfaces: javax.ejb.MessageDriven-Bean and javax.jms.MessageListener. The JMS MessageListener interface allows the bean to receive JMS messages with the onMessage method. The MessageDrivenBean interface defines a message-driven bean's life-cycle methods called by the EJB container.

Of the three such life-cycle methods, only one is of interest to PayrollMDB—setMessageDrivenContext. The container calls setMessageDrivenContext immediately after the PayrollMDB bean instance is created. PayrollMDB uses this method to obtain a local reference to the Payroll stateless session bean, first looking up the PayrollLocalHome local home object and then invoking its create method. The setMessageDrivenContext method then stores the local reference to the stateless bean in the instance variable payroll for later use in the onMessage method.

The ejbCreate and ejbRemove life-cycle methods are empty. They can be used for any initialization and cleanup that the bean needs to do.

The real work of the PayrollMDB bean is done in the onMessage method. The container calls the onMessage method when a JMS message is received in the PayrollQueue queue. The msg parameter is a JMS message that contains the message sent by the Benefits Enrollment application or other enterprise application. The method typecasts the received message to a JMS `MapMessage` message type, which is a special JMS message type that contains property-value pairs and is particularly useful when receiving messages sent by non-Java applications. The EJB container's JMS provider may convert a message of `MapMessage` type either from or to a messaging product–specific format.

Once the message is in the proper type or format, the `onMessage` method retrieves the message data: the employee number and payroll deduction amount, using the `Employee` and `PayrollDeduction` properties, respectively. The method then invokes the local business method `setBenefitsDeduction` on the Payroll stateless session bean method to perform the update of the employee's payroll information in `PayrollDatabase`.

The PayrollMDB bean's deployment descriptor declares its transaction attribute as `Required`, indicating that the container starts a transaction before invoking the `onMessage` method and to make the message delivery part of the transaction. This ensures that the Payroll stateless session bean performs its database update as part of the same transaction and that message delivery and database update are atomic. If an exception occurs, the transaction is rolled back, and the message will be delivered again. By using the `Required` transaction attribute for the message-driven bean, the developer can be confident that the database update will eventually happen.

6.3.2   PayrollEJB Local Interfaces

In the previous section, PayrollMDB used the local interfaces of the PayrollEJB stateless session bean. These interfaces provide the same functionality as the remote interfaces described in Chapter 4. Because these interfaces are local, they can be accessed only by local clients deployed in the same JVM as the PayrollEJB bean. As a result, the PayrollMDB bean can use these local interfaces because it is deployed together with the PayrollEJB bean in the payroll department's application server. See Code Example 6.2:

```
public interface PayrollLocal extends EJBLocalObject {
    void setBenefitsDeduction(int emplNumber, double deduction)
        throws PayrollException;
    double getBenefitsDeduction(int emplNumber)
        throws PayrollException;
    double getSalary(int emplNumber)
        throws PayrollException;
    void setSalary(int emplNumber, double salary)
```

```
            throws PayrollException;
    }


    public interface PayrollLocalHome extends EJBLocalHome {
        PayrollLocal create() throws CreateException;
    }
```

Code Example 6.2   Payroll Class

6.4   Using JMS and Connectors for Communication

We have seen how message-driven beans can be used to implement incoming communication from an enterprise application to EJB components. We now illustrate two approaches for outgoing communication from EJB applications to enterprise information systems. Both approaches focus on the communication between enterprise bean components and enterprise information systems. One approach emphasizes the use of JMS; the other uses the J2EE Connector technology. Application server products that support the J2EE (1.3 or 1.4) platform provide both JMS and J2EE Connector technologies.

6.4.1   Using JMS to Communicate with Messaging Systems

JMS provides APIs that allow an enterprise bean component to send and receive messages that flow through enterprise messaging systems. We have already seen how a message-driven bean, such as PayrollMDB can be used to receive JMS messages from a messaging system. Here, we explain how an enterprise bean sends JMS messages to an enterprise messaging system message queue.

Recall from Chapter 4 the communication requirements for the Benefits Enrollment application, especially the need to keep Star Enterprise's payroll database updated with payroll changes. In a loosely coupled model, the Benefits Enrollment application needs to send payroll-update notifications to the `Payroll-Queue` reliable queue in Star Enterprise. To accomplish this, the Benefits Enrollment application uses a DeductionUpdateBeanJMS command bean. The EnrollmentEJB stateful session bean component of the application invokes this command bean. Code Example 6.3 shows the complete code for the DeductionUpdateBeanJMS command bean:

```
public class DeductionUpdateBeanJMS implements
        DeductionUpdateBean {

    private Queue payrollQueue;
    private QueueConnectionFactory factory;
    private int emplNumber;
    private double deduction;

    public DeductionUpdateBeanJMS() {
        try {
            InitialContext ictx = new InitialContext();
            payrollQueue = (Queue)ictx.lookup(
                    "java:comp/env/jms/PayrollQueue");
            factory = (QueueConnectionFactory)ictx.lookup(
                    "java:comp/env/jms/QueueConnectionFactory");
        } catch ( Exception ex ) {
            throw new EJBException("Unable to get Payroll bean", ex);
        }
    }

    public void setBenefitsDeduction(int emplNumber,
            double deduction) {
        this.emplNumber = emplNumber;
        this.deduction = deduction;
    }

    public void execute() {
        QueueConnection connection=null;
        try {
            // Create a connection
            connection = factory.createQueueConnection();

            // Create a transactional session
            QueueSession session =
                    connection.createQueueSession(true, 0);

            // Create a sender
            QueueSender sender = session.createSender(payrollQueue);
```

```
            // Send the message
            MapMessage message = session.createMapMessage();
            message.setInt("Employee", emplNumber);
            message.setDouble("PayrollDeduction", deduction);

            sender.send(message);

        } catch (Exception ex) {
            throw new EJBException(ex);
        } finally {
            try {
                if( connection != null ) {
                    connection.close();
                }
            } catch(Exception e) {}
        }
    }
    public void release() {
    payrollQueue = null;
        factory = null;
    }
}
```

Code Example 6.3 DeductionUpdateBeanJMS Class

Note that the DeductionUpdateBeanJMS class implements the DeductionUp-dateBean interface. EnrollmentEJB uses the DeductionUpdateBean command bean interface. Chapter 4 shows how EnrollmentEJB uses this command bean; DeductionUpdateBean directly invokes the Payroll session bean, thus providing a tightly coupled interaction between the Benefits Enrollment and payroll applications.

Here, we show how to accomplish the same interaction in a loosely coupled fashion. The DeductionUpdateBeanJMS class uses JMS to communicate with the PayrollMDB bean through PayrollQueue. Using the message queue provides a loosely coupled interaction between the Benefits Enrollment and payroll applications.

To initiate a connection to PayrollQueue, the command bean needs two JMS objects: one representing the JMS queue and the other representing a connection factory to a queue. In its constructor, `DeductionUpdateBeanJMS` uses JNDI to look up the JMS `PayrollQueue` queue object and the JMS `QueueConnectionFactory` object.

`PayrollQueue` and `QueueConnectionFactory` need to be declared in the JNDI environment of the sender bean, which in this case is EnrollmentEJB. This is done by including two reference elements in EnrollmentEJB's XML deployment descriptor. The `PayrollQueue` reference is declared using a `message-destination-ref` element. This element includes the JNDI name at which the bean looks up `PayrollQueue` and the `PayrollQueue`'s expected Java type—in this case, `javax.jms.Queue`. This element also declares that the message destination is used for sending or consuming messages—in this example, for sending messages. The `QueueConnectionFactory` is declared using a `resource-ref` element, which again includes the JNDI name and expected Java type (`javax.jms.QueueConnection-Factory`).

The `setBenefitsDeduction` method stores the employee number and payroll-deduction amount. These two fields are later inserted into the JMS message before the message is sent.

`DeductionUpdateBeanJMS`'s execute method does the actual work of connecting to the queue and sending the JMS message. This method first obtains a `Queue-Connection` object from `QueueConnectionFactory` and then creates a `QueueSession` object, which represents a single-threaded interaction between the command bean and the JMS provider. Next, `execute` creates a `QueueSender` object, using the `PayrollQueue` queue, and then instantiates a `MapMessage` object for the message to be sent, filling it with the employee number and payroll-deduction information. Finally, the method uses the `QueueSender` object to send the message to `PayrollQueue`.

It is important to note that the message send operation is transactional in nature. This means that the message is not sent if the transaction in which the command bean is called should be rolled back because of an error. Making the message send operation transactional ensures that the payroll deduction is applied only if an employee's benefits enrollment procedure completes successfully.

In addition, the `PayrollQueue` object enforces security access control to ensure that only authorized users can send payroll-deduction messages to it. The EJB container and the JMS provider perform the security-related interactions with the `PayrollQueue` object at the time the JMS connection to `PayrollQueue` is created.

6.4.2   Setting Up Messaging Flow within Applications

Sometimes an EJB application contains message senders and message receivers, and it is necessary to link them together. This can be done using XML deployment descriptor elements in the application. This facility is necessary when an application requires asynchronous message-based communication between its parts. For example, if the EnrollmentEJB session bean and the PayrollMDB message-driven bean were packaged in the same J2EE application, we would need to make sure that messages sent by EnrollmentEJB were routed to PayrollMDB through `PayrollQueue`.

Senders and receivers can be linked using a destination object, which is a queue or a topic for JMS. First, declare this destination object using the `message-destination` deployment descriptor element, which contains the name of the destination (for example, `PayrollQueue`). Next, link the message destination reference from the sending EJB component to this message destination using a `message-destination-link` element in the sending EJB component's deployment descriptor. Finally, using a similar link element, link the receiving message-driven bean to the destination as a consumer of messages. This completes the routing of messages between sender and receiver in the same application.

6.4.3   Using Connectors to Communicate with Enterprise Information Systems

Enterprise beans can use the J2EE Connector technology to communicate to legacy applications. Here, we illustrate how communication using a connector, or resource adapter, might take place between an enterprise bean and a mainframe application.

In this scenario, Star Enterprise's Payroll System is a mainframe application consisting of a collection of CICS transaction processing (TP) programs. Prior to deploying the Benefits Enrollment application, Star Enterprise needed to give its nonmainframe applications access to payroll information. To accomplish this, Star Enterprise purchased a mainframe connectivity product from vendor Aardvark. With its product, Aardvark included a resource adapter enabling communication with the mainframe system. Because it complies with the requirements of the J2EE Connector architecture, the resource adapter can be plugged into any J2EE-compliant application server.

After it deployed Aardvark's mainframe connectivity product into its Payroll application server, Star Enterprise developed an implementation of the PayrollEJB stateless session bean that uses Aardvark's resource adapter to access the Payroll mainframe system. The resource adapter has two functions:

1. It integrates with the EJB container, using the system-level contracts defined in the Connector architecture.

2. It communicates with the Payroll System CICS TP programs on the mainframe.

Refer to the section Other Sources of Information on page xviii for more information on the J2EE Connector architecture. For the source code for the `PayrollBean` class, see `PayrollBean` Implementation Class Using Connectors, on page 410.

The implementation of the `setBenefitsDeduction` method in `PayrollBean` uses the Common Client Interface (CCI) APIs defined in the J2EE Connector architecture. The CCI APIs provide a standard way for enterprise beans and other J2EE components to access enterprise information systems. The `setBenefitsDeduction` method begins with setup work to establish a connection to the underlying database and to define the parameters for its execution. The method first obtains a `Connection` object to use for its communication with the mainframe application. The method uses this object to create an `Interaction` object, which it will subsequently use for a single interaction with the mainframe application.

The `setBenefitsDeduction` method next creates an `InteractionSpecImpl` object. The method passes to the `InteractionSpecImpl` object the name of the target TP mainframe program and the direction of the interaction. In our example, the `SYNC_SEND` verb indicates that arguments pass only to the mainframe. For the last setup step, the `setBenefitsDeduction` method creates a `MappedRecord` object and uses the `put` methods to set the values of input arguments to be sent to the target mainframe program.

Finally, setup is completed and the `setBenefitsDeduction` method invokes the `execute` method on the `Interaction` object. The `execute` method causes the resource adapter to send the input arguments to the `SETPAYROLL_DEDUCTION` program on the mainframe. "Under the covers," the EJB container and the mainframe resource adapter propagate the transaction from the `PayrollBean` instance to the mainframe TP program. The developer of `PayrollBean` did not have to write any transaction-related code to enable this propagation of the transaction.

The preceeding example provides a brief introduction to using the J2EE Connector technology for accessing enterprise information systems from an enterprise bean. For a more detailed discussion, refer to the book *J2EE™ Connector Architecture and Enterprise Application Integration*, by Rahul Sharma, Beth Stearns, and Tony Ng (Addison-Wesley, 2001).

6.5   Conclusion

This chapter presented a brief overview of the communication mechanisms used by J2EE applications, particularly focusing on asynchronous messaging and JMS. These technologies form the foundation for understanding message-driven beans. The chapter introduced and described the basic concepts of message-driven beans. The chapter included sections on how developers can implement and use message-driven beans in their applications. This discussion illustrated how J2EE applications can use message-driven beans to simplify using the JMS API and to facilitate receiving messages asynchronously.

To illustrate how to use asynchronous messaging and message-driven beans effectively, the Benefits Enrollment application was changed in this chapter to show how to use a message-driven bean instead of a session bean to handle payroll updates. Using a message-driven bean facilitated a looser coupling between the Benefits Enrollment and payroll applications.

The chapter also discussed how an EJB application can use the J2EE Connector technology to integrate with enterprise information systems. The next chapter begins the discussion of entity beans.

CHAPTER 7

Understanding Entity Beans

AN entity bean is a component that encapsulates the implementation of a business entity or a business process. The encapsulation of a business entity or process is typically independent of the client application that uses the entity bean. As a result, an entity bean can be reused by many client applications.

This chapter focuses on the basics of entity beans from a programming point of view. The chapter describes the client view of an entity bean—the view of the application developer who uses an entity bean—and the view of the developer of the entity bean itself. We also describe the life cycle of entity bean class instances and show how the container manages the instances at runtime.

Clients of entity beans, similar to session bean clients, use the methods of the home and component interfaces. However, because the life cycles of an entity object and a session object differ, an entity bean client takes a different approach to using the home interface methods for creating and removing entity objects. In addition, each entity object has a unique identity, which allows the home interface to define find methods for locating entity bean instances.

A bean developer must write the implementation of the entity bean's business logic in addition to the life-cycle-related methods. The bean developer is also concerned about entity object persistence. The state of an entity object is stored in a resource manager, such as a database or other persistent storage. The entity bean methods access the state in the resource manager, using either container-managed persistence (CMP) or bean-managed persistence (BMP).

This chapter also explains how the container manages entity bean instances. Although not all developers need to know this information, it is interesting to see what happens beneath the surface during the various method invocations, passivation and activation, and transactions.

7.1   Client View of an Entity Bean

We begin by describing the client view of an entity bean: the view seen by an application developer who uses an entity bean in a client application. Note that the client application developer is typically different from the developer—or company—that developed the bean.

An entity bean is a component that gives its client a true object-oriented abstraction of a business entity or a business process. For example, a real-life business entity may be an account, employee, customer, and so forth. A business process, on the other hand, can be the sequence involved in granting a loan approval, opening a bank account, scheduling a meeting, and so forth. When an entity bean is used to implement a business entity or a process, each individual business entity or process is represented by an entity object.

In most cases, entity beans are used with a local client view. Such entity beans are developed with local interfaces, which enable the bean to take advantage of the complete range of the EJB 2.0 and 2.1 architectural features. For example, an entity bean implemented with container-managed persistence can participate in container-managed relationships with other entity beans. With container-managed relationships, the EJB container manages the persistent relationships between entity beans much like it manages a bean's persistence.

Entity beans with local interfaces make the most use of the resources of the EJB environment. However, the beans are restricted to being colocated on the same JVM as their clients. When an entity bean's application is such that the bean must provide a remote client view, the developer can take steps to use the local-view advantages and still retain distributed capabilities. Principally, the developer can provide a session bean with a remote client view as a facade to entity beans with local views. Or, the developer can provide the entity bean itself with a remote interface in addition to its local interface.

Four concepts define the client view of an entity bean:

1. Home interface

2. Component interface: local and remote interfaces

3. Primary key and object identity

4. Life cycle of an entity object

In the following sections, we explain and illustrate how a client uses the home and component interfaces to manipulate entity objects. We also discuss the role of the primary key in the client view and explain the life cycle of an entity bean.

7.1.1   Home Interface

A client uses the home interface to manage the life cycle of individual entity objects. Life-cycle operations involve creating, finding, and removing entity objects. Specifically, the client uses the home interface methods to create new entity objects and to find and remove existing ones.

A client can also use business methods on the home interface to perform aggregate operations on entity objects. Keep in mind that these aggregate operations are not specific to any particular entity object.

In addition, a client can use the home interface to obtain the `javax.ejb.EJB-MetaData` interface for the entity bean and to obtain a handle for the home interface. These functions apply only to entity beans implementing a remote home interface.

Although the signatures of the create and find methods may be different for each entity bean, the life-cycle operations are uniform across all entity beans. This uniformity makes it easier for a client developer to use entity beans supplied by other developers.

Let's look at the example `AccountHome` interface, which was used in Chapter 2. Code Example 7.1 shows the `AccountHome` interface with a local client view:

```
import javax.ejb.CreateException;
import javax.ejb.FinderException;
public interface AccountHome extends javax.ejb.EJBLocalHome {
    // create methods
    Account create(String lastName, String firstName)
       throws CreateException, BadNameException;
    Account createBusinessAcct(String businessName)
       throws CreateException;
    ...


    // find methods
    Account findByPrimaryKey(AccountKey primaryKey)
       throws FinderException;
    Collection findInactive(Date sinceWhen)
       throws FinderException, BadDateException;
```

```
    ...
    // home methods
    public void debitAcctFee(float fee_amt)
        throws OutofRangeException;

    ...
}
```

Code Example 7.1 AccountHome Interface

Recall that the AccountHome interface previously implemented a remote client view and thus extended the javax.ejb.EJBHome interface. A home interface for an entity bean that implements a local client view extends the javax.ejb.EJBLocalHome interface. See Section 2.3.2, Enterprise Bean Home Interfaces, on page 33. The next sections explain the client's use of the home interface.

Locating the Home Interface

The client must first obtain the home interface to use it. A client obtains the local home interface for the AccountEJB entity bean from the client's environment, using the JNDI API, casting the returned value to the home interface type. The deployer has configured the home interface in the JNDI namespace (Code Example 7.2):

```
Context initCtx = new InitialContext();
AccountHome accountHome = (AccountHome) initCtx.lookup(
    "java:comp/env/ejb/CheckingAccountEJB");
```

Code Example 7.2 Obtaining a Local Home Interface

If the AccountEJB entity bean uses a remote client view, a client also obtains the remote home interface for the bean from the client's environment, using JNDI. However, the client must use the PortableRemoteObject.narrow method to cast the value returned from JNDI to the home interface type (Code Example 7.3):

```
Context initCtx = new InitialContext();
AccountHome accountHome = (AccountHome)PortableRemoteObject.narrow(
```

```
initCtx.lookup("java:comp/env/ejb/CheckingAccountEJB"),
    AccountHome.class);
```

Code Example 7.3 Obtaining a Home Interface for a Bean with a Remote View

Using Create Methods

An entity bean home interface defines zero or more create methods, each representing a different way to create a new entity object. Each create method must begin with the word `create` and may be followed by a descriptive word. The number and types of the input parameters of the create methods are entity bean specific. The return value type for all create methods is always the entity bean's component interface.

Returning to our example, the client can use the `AccountHome` interface to create new `Account` objects, as follows:

```
Account account1 = accountHome.create("Matena", "Vlada");
Account account2 = accountHome.create("Stearns", "Beth");
Account businessAcct = accountHome.createBusinessAcct(
        "ComputerEase Publishing");
```

It is important to understand that when the client invokes a create operation, the entity bean creates the representation of the entity object's state in a persistent store, such as a relational database. This is in contrast to invoking a create method on a session bean. Invoking a create method on a session bean results only in the creation of a session bean instance; it does not result in the creation of persistent state in a persistent store.

It is possible for a home interface to define no create methods, and sometimes this approach is useful and preferable. Because the entity object's state exists in the resource manager independently from the entity bean and its container, it is possible to create or remove an entity object directly in the resource manager. (The section Entity Object State and Persistence on page 176 explains how a resource manager manages the state of an entity object.)

An application is not limited to going through the entity bean and its container to create or remove the object. For example, an application can use SQL statements to create or remove an `Account` object in a relational database. In some situations, the bean developer does not want to allow the entity bean clients to create entity objects and instead wants to ensure that the entity objects are created solely by other means. In such a case, the entity bean's home interface would have zero create methods. This is discussed in more detail in Section 7.2.7, Using Entity Beans with Preexisting Data, on page 235.

Using Find Methods

The home interface defines one or more find methods. A client uses the find methods to look up entity objects that meet given criteria.

All entity bean home interfaces define a `findByPrimaryKey` method to allow the client to find an entity object by its primary key. The `findByPrimaryKey` method takes a single input parameter with a type that is the entity bean's primary-key type. The return value type is the entity bean's component interface.

Our example AccountEJB client may use the `findByPrimaryKey` method, as follows:

```
AccountKey pk = new AccountKey();
pk.setAccountNumber("100-300-423");

try {
    Account account = accountHome.findByPrimaryKey(pk);
} catch (ObjectNotFoundException ex) {
    // account with the given primary key does not exist
}
```

If the `findByPrimaryKey` method completes successfully, the client knows that the entity object with the given primary key exists. If the entity object does not exist when the client invokes the `findByPrimaryKey` method, the method throws `javax.ejb.ObjectNotFoundException` to the client.

In addition to the required `findByPrimaryKey` method, the home interface may include additional find methods. The number and types of the input arguments of these additional find methods are entity bean specific. A find method's return value type is either the entity bean's component interface or `java.util.Collec-tion`. Any find methods that can potentially find more than one entity object should define the return value type as `java.util.Collection`; those that can return at most one entity object should define the return value type as the component interface type.

The following example illustrates using a find method, `findInactive`, that may return more than one entity object:

```
Date sinceDate = ...;
Collection inactiveAccounts = accountHome.findInactive(sinceDate);
Iterator it = inactiveAccounts.iterator();
while (it.hasNext()) {
    Account acct = (Account) it.next(),
    // do something with acct
    acct.debit(100.00);
}
```

The findInactive method returns a collection of accounts that have been inactive since a given date. The client uses an iterator to obtain the individual entity objects returned in Collection.

Note that, had the bean used a remote client view, the client must use the PortableRemoteObject.narrow operation to cast an object retrieved from the collection to the entity bean's remote interface type. The client cannot simply retrieve the next object in Collection:

```
Account acct = (Account) it.next();
```

Instead, the client performs the retrieval as follows:

```
Account acct = (Account)PortableRemoteObject.narrow(it.next(),
                  Account.class);
```

Using remove **Methods**

As noted earlier, all entity bean local home interfaces extend the javax.ejb.EJBLocalHome interface, and all entity bean remote home interfaces extend the javax.ejb.EJBHome interface. The EJBLocalHome interface defines one remove method, whereas the EJBHome interface defines two remove methods. A client uses the EJBHome or EJBLocalHome remove methods to remove the entity objects specified by the method's input parameter.

The void remove(Object primaryKey) method is defined by the EJBHome and EJBLocalHome interfaces. This method is used to remove an entity object by a given primary key. The void remove(Handle handle) method, defined by the EJBHome interface only for remote home interfaces, is used to remove an entity object identified by a given handle. The following code illustrates using a remove method:

```
AccountKey pk = new AccountKey();
pk.setAccountNumber("100-300-423");
accountHome.remove(pk);
```

It is important to understand that successful execution of a `remove` method results in the removal of the representation of the entity object's state from the resource manager that stores the state. In the previous example, the `remove` method results in the removal of the specified account record from the database.

Using Home Business Methods

The home interface may also define business methods that operate across all bean instances. Suppose that a client wants to periodically subtract a set fee from all account records. Rather than having to write code to retrieve all `Account` instances and subtract a set amount from each account's balance, a client might use `AccountHome`'s `debitAcctFee` method to accomplish this same operation across all `Account` instances. For example:

```
if (monthlyUpdate) {
    accountHome.debitAcctFee(acctFee);
}
```

7.1.2   Component Interface

To get a reference to an existing entity object's component interface—either its remote interface or its local interface—the client can

- Receive the reference as a result of a create method
- Find the entity object by using a find method defined in the entity bean's home interface
- Receive the reference as an input parameter or a method result in a method call

Once it obtains the reference to the entity bean's component interface, the client can do a number of things with that reference:

- Invoke business methods on the entity object through the component interface
- Obtain a reference to the entity bean's home interface

- Pass the reference in a parameter or as a result of a remote or local method call

- Obtain the entity object's primary key

- Remove the entity object

Code Example 7.4 shows the definition of the `Account` component interface, which is a local interface:

```
public interface Account extends javax.ejb.EJBLocalObject {
    double getBalance();
    void credit(double amount);
    void debit(double amount) throws InsufficientFundsException;
    ...
}
```

Code Example 7.4 Account Interface

Had the AccountEJB bean implemented a remote client view, each of the `Account` component interface methods would throw `java.rmi.RemoteException` in addition to its other exceptions.

Code Example 7.5 illustrates using the component interface for a bean with a local client view:

```
// Somehow obtain a reference to an Account object.
Account acct = ...;

// Invoke business methods.
double balance = acct.getBalance();
acct.debit(200.00);
acct.credit(300.00);

// Obtain the primary key.
AccountKey pk = (AccountKey)acct.getPrimaryKey();

// Obtain the home interface.
AccountHome home = (AccountHome) acct.getEJBHome();

// Pass the entity object as a parameter in a method call.
```

```
// (Foo is an enterprise bean's local home or component interface.)
Foo foo = ...;    // Foo
foo.someMethod(acct, ...);


// Remove the entity object.
acct.remove();
```

Code Example 7.5   Using the Component Interface

7.1.3   Primary Key and Object Identity

Every entity object has an identity unique within the scope of its home interface.
The primary key determines this identity. If two entity objects with the same home
interface have the same primary key, they are considered identical entity objects. If
they have a different primary key, they are considered different entity objects.

A client can test whether two entity object references refer to the same entity
object by using the isIdentical method. The following code segment illustrates
using the isIdentical method to compare two object references to determine
whether they are identical:

```
Account acct1 = ...;
Account acct2 = ...;

if (acct1.isIdentical(acct2)) {
      // acct1 and acct2 refer to the same entity object
} else {
      // acct1 and acct2 refer to different entity objects
}
```

Alternatively, if it obtains two entity object references from the same home
interface, the client can determine if these objects are identical by comparing their
primary keys:

```
AccountHome accountHome = ...;
Account acct1 = accountHome.findOneWay(...);
Account acct2 = accountHome.findAnotherWay(...);

if (acct1.getPrimaryKey().equals(acct2.getPrimaryKey())) {
      // acct1 and acct2 refer to the same entity object
```

```
} else {
    // acct1 and acct2 refer to different entity objects
}
```

Note that comparing primary keys is valid only when comparing objects obtained from the same home interface. When objects are obtained from different home interfaces, the client must use the `isIdentical` method on one of the objects to perform the comparison.

7.1.4   Entity Object Life Cycle

Figure 7.1 illustrates an entity object's life cycle, as seen from the perspective of a client. In the diagram, the term *referenced* means that the client holds an object reference for the entity object. The figure illustrates the following points about an entity object's life cycle:

- **Creating an entity object**

  - A client can create an entity object by invoking a create method defined in the entity bean's home interface.

  - It is possible to create an entity object without involving the entity bean or its container. For example, using a direct database insert can create the representation of the entity object's state in the resource manager—that is, in the database.

- **Finding an entity object**—A client can look up an existing entity object by using a find method defined in the home interface.

- **Invoking business methods**—A client that has an object reference for the entity object can invoke business methods on the entity object.

- **Understanding the life cycle**—The life cycle of the entity object is independent of the life cycle of the client-held object references. This means that an entity object is not removed when it is no longer referenced by a client. Likewise, the existence of an object reference does not ensure the existence of the entity object.

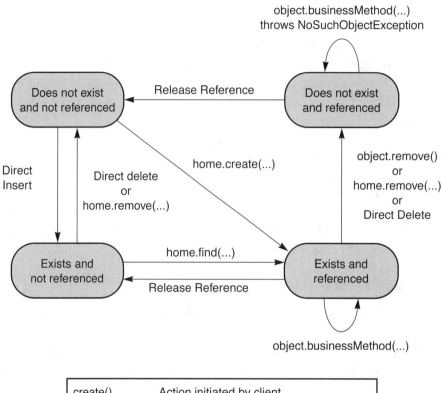

Figure 7.1 Client View of an Entity Object Life Cycle

- **Removing an entity object**

  - A client can remove an entity object by using one of the remove methods defined in the home and component interfaces. If a client attempts to invoke a business method on an entity object after the object has been removed, the client receives NoSuchObjectException.

  - It is possible to remove an entity object without involving the entity bean or its container. For example, using a direct database delete can remove the representation of the entity object's state from the resource manager: the database. If a client attempts to invoke a business method on an entity object after its state has been removed from the database, the client receives NoSuchObjectLocalException (or NoSuchObjectException if a remote client).

Entity objects are considered to be, in general, persistent objects. An entity object can be accessed concurrently through multiple JVMs. The lifetime of an entity object is not limited by the lifetime of the JVM process in which the entity bean instances execute.

Although the crash of the JVM may result in the rollback of current transactions, it does not destroy previously created entity objects; nor does it invalidate the references to the component and home interfaces held by clients.

An entity object remains accessible to its clients as long as the representation of its state is maintained in the resource manager or until a reconfiguration of the bean or container invalidates the object references and handles held by the clients. This can happen, for example, when the entity bean is uninstalled from the container or if the container is reconfigured to listen on a different network address.

Multiple clients can access the same entity object concurrently. If so, the container uses transactions to isolate the clients' work from one another. This is explained in Section 7.2.6, Concurrent Invocation of an Entity Object, on page 233.

7.2 Bean Developer View of an Entity Bean

The bean developer's view of an entity bean differs from that of the client. Essentially, the bean developer is responsible for the implementation of the methods defined in the bean's component and home interfaces, as well as the callback methods of the `EntityBean` interface. The developer needs to know how to implement correctly the methods defined by the home interface—the find, create, and home methods—the business methods, and the methods defined by the `EntityBean` interface. These method implementations access the state of the entity objects maintained in a resource manager. As a result, the bean developer needs to understand entity object state and persistence to implement the entity bean methods optimally.

We begin this section by describing entity object state and persistence. The entity object state is managed by a resource manager. Management of state is separate from the container's management of entity bean instances. The developer can use either the CMP or the BMP approach to access object state. Each of these two persistence approaches has advantages and drawbacks.

For entity beans using CMP, the developer can use the EJB QL query language to implement the find methods. EJB QL is an SQL-like query language. The developer can also define additional queries for use internal to the bean itself, using `ejbSelect` methods. We discuss these concepts in this section.

This section also describes various approaches to using the `ejbLoad` and `ejbStore` methods. The container invokes these methods on the bean implementation. The developer can use these methods to take advantage of the container's cache management capabilities and to maximize performance. (See Section 7.2.4, Caching Entity Bean State, on page 219.) This section ends with a discussion on how the container manages multiple client invocations on an entity object.

7.2.1 Entity Object State and Persistence

The methods of an entity bean class access the object's state in a resource manager. Most resource managers, such as relational databases, manage entity objects' state externally to the bean instances (Figure 7.2).

Separating the state of the entity objects from the instances of the entity bean class has the following advantages:

- **Facilitates persistence and transactions**

  - Separating an entity object's state from the bean class instance allows the entity object's state to be persistent. Separation permits the life cycle of the entity object's state to be independent of the life cycle of the entity bean class instances and of the life cycle of the JVMs in which the instances are created.

  - The resource manager, instead of the entity bean or the EJB container, can handle the implementation of the ACID properties—atomicity, consistency, isolation, and durability—which pertain to transactions.

- **Promotes the implementation of the EJB server**

  - Separation makes it possible to implement the entity object's state to be accessible concurrently from multiple JVMs, even when the JVMs run on different network nodes. This is essential to a high-end implementation of an EJB server.

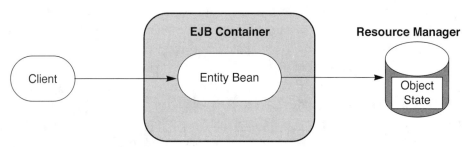

Figure 7.2 Entity Object's State Managed by Resource Manager

- It makes it possible to implement a highly available EJB server. Should a node of the JVM be unavailable, another JVM can access the entity object's state.

- **Improves accessibility between Java and non-Java applications**

  - It makes it possible to externalize an entity object's state in a representation suitable for non-Java applications. For example, if a relational database keeps the state of entity objects, the state is available to any application that can access the database via SQL statements.

  - It makes it possible to present data residing in an enterprise's databases as entity beans. Similarly, it allows the creation of an entity bean facade on top of the client interfaces of the enterprise's non-Java application. This client-view entity bean of the enterprise's preexisting data or applications makes it easier to develop and integrate new Java applications with the legacy data or applications.

The entity bean architecture is flexible about the choice of the type of resource manager in which to store an entity object's state. Examples of resource managers in which the state of an entity bean can be stored are

- A relational database system

- An application system, such as an ERP system or mainframe application

- A nonrelational database, such as a hierarchical database or an object-oriented database

- Some form of fast secondary-memory resource manager that may be provided by the EJB container as an option

The state of most entity beans is typically stored in a resource manager external to the EJB container—these are the database or application systems noted in the first three examples just presented. The fast secondary memory integrated with the EJB container is a special example. If provided, it typically is used only for storing the state of short-lived entity objects with states that are not accessed by other applications running outside the EJB container.

Because a resource manager maintains the state of an entity object, an entity bean instance must use an API to access the state of the associated entity object. (Associating an instance with an entity object is called *object activation,* and it is explained in Section 7.2.3, Entity Bean Instance Life Cycle, on page 196.) An entity bean instance can access the state of its associated entity object by using two access styles: BMP and CMP. Because CMP is the preferred approach, it is discussed first.

Container-Managed Persistence

Container-managed persistence (CMP) is a resource manager–independent data access API tailored for use by entity beans. CMP offers distinct advantages over bean-managed persistence (BMP). Probably the main advantage of CMP involves database access code. It is simpler to write database access code with CMP than to write such code with BMP. Database access with BMP usually entails coding JDBC calls. Using CMP, the developer need only describe *what* state is to be stored persistently; the container takes care of *how* the persistence is performed. With BMP, on the other hand, the developer is responsible for both what state to persist and how that state is to be persisted.

Another important advantage of CMP is that it greatly enhances an entity bean's portability. A developer uses the same API—that is, the EJB CMP methods—regardless of the underlying type of resource manager. The same entity bean can thus be used with any type of resource manager.

CMP enables the development of entity beans with implementations that can be used with multiple resource manager types and database schemas. The CMP architecture allows ISVs to develop entity beans that can be adapted at deployment to work with customers' preexisting data. Because different customers use different resource manager types and have different database schemas, the deployer needs to adapt an entity bean to each customer's resource manager type and its database schema. Most important, the entity bean developer does not have to write a different implementation of the bean for each customer.

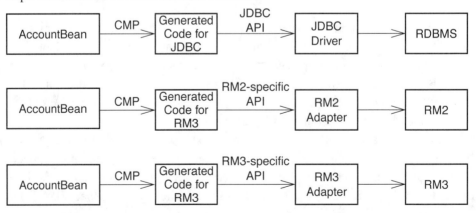

Figure 7.3   AccountBean Entity Bean Using CMP to Access Resource Managers

Figure 7.3 shows how an entity bean using CMP uses the various resource manager–specific APIs to access data in the respective resource managers. Note that the developer has to write only one entity bean class, regardless of the resource manager type. Based on the mapping done by the deployer, the container generates the appropriate data access code for the resource manager API. Therefore, the developer does not need to know or care about the actual resource manager–specific code.

The performance of CMP entity beans is also likely to be significantly better than that of BMP entity beans or session beans using JDBC. This may sound counterintuitive, because developers assume they can code database access calls in a way that is best for their application. However, obtaining good database access performance requires more than correctly coding the access calls. Rather, obtaining good performance requires such techniques as advanced knowledge of database-specific features, connection pooling, an optimized caching strategy for reducing the number of database round-trips, and more. System-level experts who build containers, persistence managers, and application servers know these advanced techniques the best. With CMP, because the container has full control over persistence management, it can optimally manage database access to achieve the highest performance. This fact has been observed with EJB-based benchmarks on several application server products.

The EJB 2.0 specification significantly extended the functionality of CMP. The persistent state of an entity bean is described by JavaBeans-like properties, which are represented in the bean class as get and set accessor methods. For example, a persistent field `foo` would be represented by the `getFoo` and `setFoo` methods in the bean class. These get and set methods allow code in the bean class to access the data items comprising the entity object's state. CMP fields are virtual fields and do not appear as instance variables in the entity bean's implementation class. The implementation class instead defines get and set methods, which are declared `public` and `abstract`, for each such `public` variable. The bean provides no implementation for these methods. Instead, the EJB container provides the method implementations. The implementation class, too, is an abstract class for entity beans that use CMP.

For example, the same `AccountBean` class coded using EJB 2.1 CMP would look as shown in Code Example 7.6:

```
public abstract class AccountBean implements EntityBean {
  // Accessor methods for container-managed fields
```

```
public abstract String getAccountNumber();     // accountNumber
public abstract void setAccountNumber(String v);

public abstract double getBalance();            // balance
public abstract void setBalance(double v);
...
// Business methods
public void debit(double amount) {
   setBalance(getBalance() - amount);
}
}
}
```

Code Example 7.6   AccountBean Entity Bean Using EJB 2.1 CMP

Note also that entity beans using CMP can implement a local or a remote client view. However, an entity bean is not required to have a local client view to use CMP. Because the local interface exposes a bean's methods only to other beans that reside within the same container, there can be fine-grained access between clients and entity beans without an undue performance overhead. Entity beans with local interfaces not only can expose their state to clients but also can use pass-by-reference semantics to pass state between related bean instances.

Applications migrating from an EJB 1.0 or 1.1 approach to the EJB 2.0 or 2.1 specification should keep in mind the change to parameter passing. The remote interface approach uses pass-by-value semantics, whereas pass-by-reference mode with local interfaces may result in unintended changes to the state of a passed value or object. With pass-by-value semantics, the invoked method's actions affect only its local copy of a value or object. With pass-by-reference semantics, there is only one copy of a particular value or object. All involved methods reference and act on the state of that one value or object.

In the EJB 1.0 and 1.1 specifications, the CMP API depended on mapping the instance variables of an entity bean class to the data items representing an entity object's state in the resource manager. For example, Code Example 7.7 shows the same AccountBean class coded using CMP:

```
public class AccountBean implements EntityBean {
   // container-managed fields
   public String accountNumber;
   public double balance;
```

```
    ...
    public void debit(double amount) {
        balance = balance - amount;
    }
}
```

Code Example 7.7   AccountBean Entity Bean Using CMP

At deployment, the deployer uses tools to generate code that implements the mapping of the instance fields to the data items in the resource manager. Although the EJB 1.1 field-based approach to CMP is still supported for applications implemented prior to the EJB 2.0 specification, this book focuses on the EJB 2.0 CMP approach.

Container-Managed Relationships

Along with an enhanced CMP approach, the EJB 2.1 specification supports container-managed relationships (CMRs) as part of the CMP architecture. Multiple entity beans are now allowed to have relationships among themselves, referred to as CMRs.

Container-managed relationships are described by CMR fields in the deployment descriptor. The EJB container supports one-to-one, one-to-many, and many-to-many relationships, automatically managing the relationships and maintaining their referential integrity. For example, consider a many-to-many bidirectional relationship, such as one between a Supplier entity bean and a Parts entity bean. If a `Supplier` instance stops providing a particular part, the container automatically removes that `Supplier` from the set of available suppliers for that `Parts` instance.

CMR fields are handled in the same way as CMP fields. CMR fields do not appear as instance variables in the entity bean's implementation. Instead, the implementation defines `public`, `abstract` get and set methods for each CMR `public` variable. The EJB container provides the method implementations, rather than the bean itself. An entity bean must provide a local client view so that it can be used as the target of a container-managed relationship.

For one-to-one and many-to-one relationships, the get and set accessors for a CMR field are defined using the related bean's local interface type. For one-to-many and many-to-many relationships, the get and set accessors use the Java `Collection` interface, as there are many instances of the related bean.

The bean provider specifies the relationships between entity beans in the deployment descriptor. At deployment, these relationship specifications become the schema definition, and the relationships may be captured in a relational database or other resource manager. For example, a relationship between two beans may appear as a foreign key relationship in a relational database.

Container-managed relationships are also key to the powerful querying features of the EJB QL query language. They allow a developer to concisely write a query that operates over several related beans.

EJB QL Query Language

The EJB 2.0 specification introduced EJB Query Language, or EJB QL, a query language that is intended to be portable across EJB containers. EJB QL is an SQL-like language for expressing queries over entity beans with container-managed persistence. EJB QL defines queries for find and select methods for entity beans with container-managed persistence.

Prior to the EJB 2.1 specification, the manner and language for forming and expressing queries for find methods were left to each individual application server. Many application server vendors let developers form queries using SQL. However, other vendors used their own proprietary language specific to their particular application server product.

In addition, each application server provided its own tool for expressing a query. Because the developer must know the database table and column names to correctly form an SQL query, application server tools that rely on SQL provided a mapping between the database names and SQL statements to help the developer.

Under the previous versions of the EJB architecture, each application server handled queries in its own manner. Migrating from one application server to another often required you to use the new server's tool to rewrite or reform your existing queries. For example, you might have to use the new server's tool to rewrite the SQL for the find methods used by the application's entity beans.

Application servers developed with early versions of the EJB architecture may also support different physical representations of the query. For example, the server may store the query in the deployment descriptor, or it may store the query someplace else. If kept in the deployment descriptor, the query may be identified with a tag unique to that particular server. These factors combined to reduce the portability of your enterprise bean application among various application servers.

EJB QL corrects many of these inconsistencies and shortcomings. EJB QL, designed to be an SQL-like language, defines find and select query methods specifically for entity beans with container-managed persistence. EJB QL's principal advantage over SQL is its portability across EJB containers and its ability to navigate entity bean relationships.

EJB QL allows querying or navigation over entity bean relationships. A query can begin with one entity bean and from there navigate to related beans. For example, the query can start with an Order bean and then navigate to the Order's line items. The query can also navigate to the products referenced by the Order's individual line items. However, this navigation requires that the bean relationships be expressed as container-managed relationships in the deployment descriptor.

With EJB QL, you can specify the query during in the application development process, and that query is kept in the deployment descriptor. Therefore, you have two options for writing the query: You can use the application server's query-related tools, or you can write the query by manually editing the deployment descriptor. The container generates the query language implementation for queries specified in the deployment descriptor.

For example, suppose that CustomerBean had a one-to-many relationship with AccountBean through the container-managed relationship field accounts. You want to form an EJB QL query to traverse from CustomerBean to Account-Bean and return all customers with large accounts. You might write the query as follows:

```
SELECT DISTINCT OBJECT(cust)
FROM Customer cust, IN(cust.accounts) acct
WHERE acct.balance > ?1
ORDER BY cust.firstName
```

In CustomerBean's home interface, a developer might define the find method associated with this query as follows:

```
public Collection findLargeCustomers(int minimumBalance)
    throws FinderException;
```

As you can see, the EJB QL query looks similar to an SQL query: The query has a SELECT clause, a FROM clause, an optional WHERE clause, and an optional ORDER BY clause.

The EJB QL query names beans using their abstract schema names. A bean's abstract schema name, which is declared in its deployment descriptor, uniquely identifies the bean in an EJB QL query. In the preceeding query, the abstract schema name of the CustomerBean is `Customer`.

The `SELECT` clause specifies the return type of the query. If the return values are to be unique—that is, no duplicates—add the `DISTINCT` keyword to the clause. You can indicate the return type by using an identification variable with the syntax `OBJECT(cust)`. This specifies that the query returns objects that are values of the identification variable `cust`. The return type may also be indicated by a path expression of the form `accounts.customer`, as long as the path expression ends in a single-valued (one-to-one or many-to-one) CMR or CMP field. You might use a path expression, for example, to implement a find method, `findLargeAccounts`, that returns a `Collection` of accounts. A path expression is the construct used to navigate from one bean to a second bean, using a CMR field of the first bean.

The return value for find methods can be only the type of the bean on whose home interface the find method is defined. There are no such restrictions on the return value for select methods defined in a bean class; their return values may be Java primitive types or bean types, or they may be collections of these types.

Similar to SQL, the return type of an EJB QL query may also be the result of an aggregate function: `AVG`, `MAX`, `MIN`, `SUM`, or `COUNT`. For example, `SELECT COUNT(cust)` returns a count of all `Customer` objects in the result of the query. The return type of the `ejbSelect` method whose query uses the `COUNT` function needs to be the Java primitive type `long`. The return type of an `ejbSelect` method using an `AVG` function needs to be `double`.

The `FROM` clause declares identification variables used in the `SELECT` and `WHERE` clauses. There are two ways to declare identification variables:

1. Declare an identification variable to be of a particular bean type—for example, `Customer cust`.

2. Use a path expression that ends in a collection-valued CMR field—that is, a one-to-many or many-to-many relationship, such as `IN(cust.accounts) acct`.

The `FROM` clause in EJB QL is similar in behavior to the `FROM` clause in SQL. With both `FROM` clauses, the effect of declaring multiple identification variables is a Cartesian product of the values of each of the identification variables. This means that if any of the clause's identification variables refers to a bean that has zero instances, the return values of the query will be empty.

The `WHERE` clause defines conditions that restrict the set of values returned from the query. The `WHERE` clause can use operators similar to SQL, including arithmetic (+, -, *, /), comparison (=, >, <, >=, <=, <>), and logical (NOT, AND, OR) operators. Like SQL, EJB QL defines additional constructs for use in the WHERE clause, including

- **BETWEEN**—For example, WHERE acct.balance BETWEEN 10000 AND 20000

- **LIKE**—For example, WHERE cust.name LIKE 'a%'

- **NULL, EMPTY comparisons**—For example, WHERE cust.name IS NULL AND cust.accounts IS EMPTY

- **IN comparisons**—For example, WHERE cust.country IN ('US', 'UK, 'France')

- **MEMBER OF comparisons**—For example, WHERE acct MEMBER OF cust.accounts

- **Built-in string functions**—CONCAT(string, string), SUBSTRING(string, start, length), LOCATE(string, string), and LENGTH(string)

- **Built-in arithmetic functions**—ABS(number), MOD(int, int), and SQRT(double)

The WHERE clause can also use input parameters, using the syntax ?1, ?2, and so forth. Parameters are numbered starting with *1* and are used in the order in which they appear in the find or select method signature. For example, consider the clause WHERE acct.balance > ?1. At runtime, the query processor substitutes the values of the parameters provided to the find or select method into the query.

The ORDER BY clause tells the query processor to order the results in a Collection by a particular CMP field or set of CMP fields. If the return type of the query is a bean type—that is, the SELECT clause has OBJECT(cust)—such as for find methods, the CMP fields used for ordering must be valid fields of the returned bean type. If the return type of the query is a CMP field type, the ORDER BY clause must use the same CMP field. Ordering can be in ascending or descending order. For example, consider the following clause:

```
ORDER BY cust.firstName ASC, cust.lastName DESC
```

This clause returns a Collection of customers in ascending order by their first names. Those customers within the Collection having the same first name are in descending order by their last names. Ascending order is the default if the ORDER BY clause specifies neither ASC nor DESC. In addition, all null values in the returned Collection either precede or follow all non-null values.

We present more EJB QL queries when we look at the entity bean example application in Chapter 8.

Although EJB QL offers certain advantages, the language itself is not quite as rich as SQL. In particular, EJB QL cannot form some of the sophisticated queries of which SQL is capable, such as nested queries. However, it is likely that application server query tools will handle these differences between the languages. Future versions of the EJB specification will enhance the richness of EJB QL.

Bean-Managed Persistence

When it uses BMP, an entity bean uses a resource manager–specific interface (API) to access state. (In the BMP approach to managing entity object state persistence, the entity bean itself manages the access to the underlying state in a resource manager.)

Figure 7.4 shows three entity bean classes (AccountBean, AccountBean2, and AccountBean3). Each class accesses a different resource manager type. For example, a bean uses JDBC to access state stored in a relational database. In Figure 7.4, AccountBean uses the JDBC API to access state stored in the relational database management system (RDBMS). If the state is stored in a different type of database, the bean uses a different API to access the state, and the API is specific to the resource manager. Thus, AccountBean2 uses an API specific to the RM2 adapter for its RM2-type database. This means that if an entity bean uses BMP, the bean code is, in general, dependent on the type of the resource manager.

For example, the AccountBean entity bean class may use JDBC to access the state of the Account entity objects in a relational database, as Code Example 7.8 illustrates.

In the example, the implementation of the debit method obtains the primary key of the Account entity object currently associated with the instance. The method uses the JDBC API to update the account balance. Note that in a real-life application development, the bean developer would likely use some data access tools, such as command beans, on top of JDBC rather than coding JDBC directly in the entity bean class.

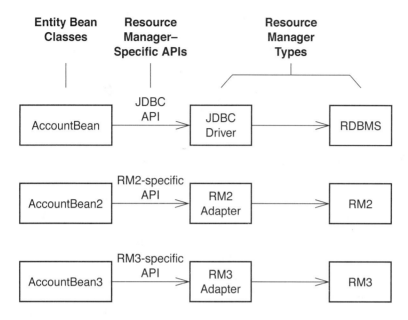

Figure 7.4 Entity Beans Using BMP to Access Different Resource Managers

```
public class AccountBean implements EntityBean {
    ...
    public void debit(double amount) {
        Connection con = ...;
        PreparedStatement pstmt = con.prepareStatement(
            "UPDATE Account SET acct_balance = acct_balance - ? " +
            "WHERE acct_number = ?"
        );
        pstmt.setDouble(1, amount);
        pstmt.setString(2, (String)ctx.getPrimaryKey());
        pstmt.execute();
        con.close();
    }
}
```

Code Example 7.8   Using the JDBC API to Access State

BMP's main advantage is that it simplifies deploying the entity bean. When an entity bean uses BMP, no deployment tasks are necessary to adapt the bean to the resource manager type or to the database schema used within the resource manager. At the same time, this is also the main disadvantage of BMP, because an entity bean using BMP is, in general, dependent on the resource manager type and the database schema. This dependency makes the entity bean less reusable across different operational environments and also means that the developer has to write much more code to do the resource manager access.

However, an entity bean using BMP can achieve some degree of independence of the entity bean code from the resource manager type and the database schema. This can be accomplished, for example, by using portable data access components when developing the BMP entity bean. Essentially, the entity bean class uses the data access components to access the entity object's state. The data access components would provide deployment interfaces for customizing the data access logic to different database schemas or even to a different resource manager type, without requiring changes to the entity bean's code.

Figure 7.5 shows the AccountBean entity bean using three APIs to access three resource manager types. This example is very much like Figure 7.4, with one significant difference. Note that instead of three separate entity beans classes (`AccountBean`, `AccountBean2`, and `AccountBean3`) implementing access to the resource manager APIs, a single entity bean class, `AccountBean`, using data access components, can access the different resource manager–specific APIs. The data access components support all three resource manager types.

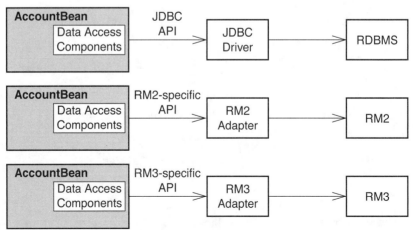

Figure 7.5   Entity Beans Using Data Access Components to Access Resource Managers

On the surface, this is similar to CMP. There is, however, a significant difference between CMP and the data access component approach. The CMP approach allows the EJB container to provide a sophisticated persistence manager that can cache the entity object's state in the container. The caching strategy implemented by the persistence manager can be tuned without making modifications to the entity bean's code. It is important to note that the CMP cache may be shared by multiple instances of the same entity bean or even by instances of different entity beans. This contrasts with the data access components approach, in which it is not possible, in general, to build a cache that can be shared by multiple instances.

7.2.2   Entity Bean Class Methods

The bean developer's primary focus is the development of the entity bean class. The bean developer is responsible for writing the implementation of the following methods:

- Business methods from the component interface

- Create methods from the home interface

- For BMP entity beans, find methods from the home interface

- Business methods from the home interface

- The container callback methods defined in the `javax.ejb.EntityBean` interface

In addition, for entity beans with CMP, the bean developer needs to write `abstract` get and set accessor methods for container-managed fields and relationships. The developer may also define `abstract` `ejbSelect` methods in the CMP bean implementation class for executing EJB QL queries internal to the bean.

The following subsections describe these methods in more detail. Section 7.2.3, Entity Bean Instance Life Cycle, on page 196 explains when and in what context the EJB container invokes these methods.

The implementation class for entity beans that use EJB 2.0 or 2.1 container-managed persistence must be an abstract class. The implementation class for entity beans that use bean-managed persistence is a concrete class.

Entity Bean Accessor Methods

Entity beans using CMP use accessor methods for the container-managed persistent fields. These accessor methods take the place of instance field declarations in the bean class. The get and set accessor methods are declared `public` and `abstract`. The bean class does not provide an implementation for these methods, because the EJB container does so. Accessor methods must be declared for both CMP and CMR fields.

We've already shown AccountBean's get and set methods for its container-managed fields `accountNumber` and `balance`. In addition, AccountBean might maintain a many-to-one relationship between accounts and customers. An account might also be involved in a one-to-many relationship, such as when a single account has a set of detail lines associated to it. If these relationships were implemented as container-managed relationships, AccountBean would include accessor methods for these CMR fields, too (Code Example 7.9):

```
public abstract class AccountBean implements EntityBean {
    // Accessor methods for container-managed fields

    public abstract String getAccountNumber();      // accountNumber
    public abstract void setAccountNumber(String v);

    public abstract double getBalance();            // balance
    public abstract void setBalance(double v);
    ...
    // Accessor methods for container-managed relationship fields
    public abstract Customer getCustomer();         // Customer
    public abstract void setCustomer(Customer customer);

    public abstract Collection getAcctDetails(); // Detail lines
    public abstract void setAcctDetails(Collection acctDetails);
}
```

Code Example 7.9 AccountBean Entity Bean

Note that the `getCustomer` accessor method returns the local entity object type `Customer`, whereas `getAcctDetails` returns a `Collection` of `Detail` objects.

Entity Bean Business Methods

The bean developer implements in the entity bean class the business methods declared by the entity bean's component interface. The rules for the business method implementations of an entity bean are similar to those for a session bean implementation. The number and types of parameters and the return value type for these business methods must match those defined in the component interface. In addition, the throws clause for the entity bean class business methods must not include more checked exceptions than the throws clause of the corresponding component interface methods. (Note that the methods in the entity bean class can define fewer exceptions than the methods in the remote interface.) Note too that the business methods must be declared public. They must not be declared final or static.

Recall that the Account component interface defines the following business methods:

```
double getBalance();
void credit(double amount);
void debit(double amount) throws InsufficientFundsException;
```

The bean developer implements these same business methods in the AccountBean class, as follows:

```
public double getBalance() { ... }
public void credit(double amount) { ... }
public void debit(double amount)
    throws InsufficientFundsException { ... }
```

Entity Bean Create Methods

The entity bean class defines ejbCreate and ejbPostCreate methods that correspond to the create methods defined in the home interface. For each create method in the home interface, the bean developer implements an ejbCreate and an ejb-PostCreate method in the entity bean class. Remember that an entity bean may choose *not* to expose the create functionality to clients, in which case the entity bean home interface defines no create methods, and, of course, the bean developer does not implement ejbCreate or ejbPostCreate methods in the bean class.

The ejbCreate and ejbPostCreate methods have the same number of parameters, each of which must be of the same type as those defined in the home interface's corresponding create method. However, the ejbCreate methods differ from the create methods, defining the bean's primary key type as their return value type. The ejbPostCreate defines the return type as void. The throws clause for each ejbCreate and ejbPostCreate method must not include more checked exceptions than the throws clause of the corresponding create method. However, the ejbCreate method throws clause can have fewer exceptions than the corresponding create method.

Like the business methods, the ejbCreate methods must be declared public. They must not be declared final or static. For example, the Account home interface declares the following create methods:

```
Account create(String lastName, String firstName)
    throws CreateException, BadNameException;
Account create(String lastName)
    throws CreateException;
Account createBusinessAcct(String businessName)
    throws CreateException;
```

Note that if Account's home interface had implemented a remote view, each of its create methods would have thrown a RemoteException in addition to the other exceptions.

The bean developer implements these corresponding ejbCreate and ejbPost-Create methods in the AccountBean class:

```
public AccountKey ejbCreate(String lastName, String firstName)
    throws BadNameException { .... }
public void ejbPostCreate(String lastName, String firstName)
    throws BadNameException { .... }

public AccountKey ejbCreate(String lastName) { .... }
public void ejbPostCreate(String lastName) { .... }

public AccountKey ejbCreate(String businessName) { .... }
public void ejbPostCreate(String businessName) { .... }
```

When creating a new entity instance, the EJB container first invokes the ejbCreate method and then invokes the matching ejbPostCreate method (see the section Invocation of Create Methods on page 199).

The ejbPostCreate method can be used for any initialization work that requires the identity of the newly created entity bean in the form of its EJBObject or EJBLocalObject reference. If it needs to pass a reference of the entity object that is being created to another enterprise bean, an instance must do so in the ejb-

PostCreate method, not in the ejbCreate method. For example, the ejbPostCre-ate-method may pass the created Account object to the Customer object as an argument in the addAccount method:

```
public class AccountBean implements EntityBean {
    EntityContext ctx;

    public ejbCreate(Customer cust) {
        // This would be an ERROR because it is illegal to
        // invoke ctx.getEJBLocalObject from an ejbCreate method.
        cust.addAccount((Account)ctx.getEJBLocalObject());
        ...
    }
    public ejbPostCreate(Customer cust) {
        // This is correct.
        cust.addAccount((Account)ctx.getEJBLocalObject());
    }
    ...
}
```

Entity Bean Find Methods

For entity beans with bean-managed persistence, the bean developer must also implement in the entity bean class ejbFind methods that correspond to the find methods defined in the home interface. Recall that an entity bean's home interface defines one or more find methods, which a client uses to locate entity objects. For CMP entity beans, the ejbFind methods are generated by the container using the EJB QL query provided by the bean developer, so the bean developer does not need to write the implementations of ejbFind methods for CMP entity beans.

At a minimum, the developer of a BMP entity bean implements an ejbFind-ByPrimaryKey method corresponding to the findByPrimaryKey method, which is defined by all entity bean home interfaces. This method looks up a single entity object, using the object's primary key. The developer also implements ejbFind methods that correspond to any additional find methods, such as those that return multiple objects, defined by the home interface. Each find method implementation has the same number of parameters, and each parameter is of the same type as the corresponding home interface find method.

The entity bean class implementations of the find methods differ in some respects from the home interface definition. In the home interface, the result type of find methods that return single objects, whether the `findByPrimaryKey` or another find method, is the entity bean's component interface. The result type of the corresponding `ejbFind` methods is the entity bean's primary key type. Similarly, in the home interface, the result type of find methods returning multiple objects is a collection (`java.util.Collection`) of objects implementing the component interface. In the implementation class, the result type of the corresponding `ejbFind` methods that return multiple objects is a collection (`java.util.Collection`) of objects of the bean's primary key type.

Finally, similar to the create methods, the `throws` clause for each `ejbFind` method must not include more checked exceptions than the `throws` clause of the corresponding find method. However, the `ejbFind` method `throws` clause can have fewer exceptions than the corresponding find method. The `ejbFind` methods must be declared `public`. They must not be declared `final` or `static`.

For example, the `AccountHome` interface defines the `findByPrimaryKey` method and an additional method, `findInactive`, which returns multiple objects:

```
import java.util.Collection;
Account findByPrimaryKey(AccountKey primaryKey)
    throws FinderException;
Collection findInactive(Date sinceWhen)
    throws FinderException, BadDateException;
```

If the AccountEJB bean is a BMP entity bean, the bean developer implements these methods in the entity bean class as follows:

```
public AccountPrimaryKey ejbFindByPrimaryKey
    (AccountPrimaryKey primkey) throws FinderException { ... };
public Collection ejbFindInactive(Date sinceWhen)
    throws BadDateException { ... };
```

Entity Bean Home Methods

Entity bean classes must also provide an implementation for each home method listed in the home interface. The bean developer implements these home methods with corresponding ejbHome methods. For example, the `AccountHome` interface includes one home method:

```
public void debitAcctFee (float fee_amt) throws OutOfRangeException;
```

The bean developer implements this method in the entity bean class as follows:

```
public void ejbHomeDebitAcctFee (float fee_amt)
    throws OutOfRangeException { ... };
```

Home methods are similar to static methods in Java classes in that they do not operate on a specific entity bean instance that has an identity. Home methods are executed by a bean instance that has not been assigned an identity. As a result, home methods cannot access the identity of the bean by using the `getPrimaryKey`, `getEJBObject`, and `getEJBLocalObject` methods of the `EntityContext` interface. This also means that home methods cannot call the get or set accessor methods for CMP and CMR fields. However, home methods can call the `ejbSelect` methods defined in the bean class. This allows home methods to execute queries and to process the results of the queries.

Select Methods

Select methods, available only for CMP entity beans, are similar to find methods in that the bean developer provides the method definitions, but the methods themselves are implemented using EJB QL queries. The bean developer defines select methods as abstract methods in the bean implementation class with a name of the form `ejbSelect<METHOD>`. The developer also provides an EJB QL query for the `ejbSelect` method in the bean's deployment descriptor. At deployment, the container's tools generate the implementation code for the `ejbSelect` method, using the EJB QL query provided by the developer.

Keep in mind that `ejbSelect` methods are not exposed through the home or component interfaces. Hence the client cannot invoke `ejbSelect` methods directly. The developer may define a home method on the home interface that delegates to the `ejbSelect` method, and then the client can invoke that home method.

However, unlike for a find method, the return value of an `ejbSelect` method is not restricted to the bean's component interface. In fact, `ejbSelect` methods can return any type, including the types of the CMP fields in the bean and the local objects of related beans. The return value may also be a single value or a `Collection` of values.

For example, an example of an `ejbSelect` method definition for the Account-Bean follows:

```
public abstract Collection ejbSelectInactiveCustomers
       (Date sinceWhen);
```

This `ejbSelectInactiveCustomers` method returns a `java.util.Collection` object containing the local entity objects for customers whose accounts have been inactive since the date provided in the parameter to the method.

EntityBean Interface Methods

An entity bean class is required to implement the methods defined by the `javax.ejb.EntityBean` interface. The EJB container invokes these methods on the bean instance at specific points in an entity bean instance's life cycle. Code Example 7.10 shows the definition of the `EntityBean` interface methods:

```
public interface EntityBean extends EnterpriseBean {
    public void setEntityContext(EntityContext ctx)
        throws EJBException, RemoteException;
    public void unsetEntityContext()
        throws EJBException, RemoteException;
    public void ejbRemove()
        throws RemoveException, EJBException, RemoteException;
    public void ejbActivate() throws EJBException, RemoteException;
    public void ejbPassivate() throws EJBException, RemoteException;
    public void ejbLoad() throws EJBException, RemoteException;
    public void ejbStore() throws EJBException, RemoteException;
}
```

Code Example 7.10 `EntityBean` Interface

Note that although the `EntityBean` interface methods throw `RemoteException`, the EJB 2.1 specification mandates that implementations of these methods must not throw `RemoteException`.

7.2.3   Entity Bean Instance Life Cycle

Every entity bean instance has a life cycle that starts from its time of creation and continues through its removal. The EJB container manages the life cycle for every instance of an entity bean class.

Bean developers who manually code the entity bean class need to know what happens during an entity bean's life cycle and how that life cycle is managed by the container. On the other hand, bean developers who use an EJB-aware application development tool do not need to know most of this information, because the application development tool may provide a simpler abstraction.

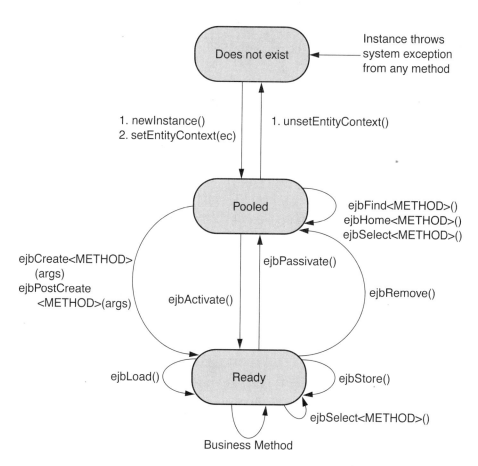

Figure 7.6   Life Cycle of an Entity Bean Instance

This section describes the various stages in the life cycle of entity bean instances, as well as the persistence and transaction management interaction details between the container and entity bean instances. These details are useful for advanced developers trying to tune the performance of their entity beans.

Figure 7.6 illustrates the life cycle of an entity bean instance. The diagram shows that an entity bean instance is in one of the following three states:

1. **Does not exist**—The container has not yet created an instance, or the container has discarded the instance.

2. **Pooled**—An instance is in the pooled state when it is not associated with a particular entity object identity.

3. **Ready**—An instance is in the ready state when the instance is associated with an entity object identity.

Each entity instance state has defined characteristics. In addition, transitions between states happen as a result of certain actions. The EJB container drives the state transition in response to client-invoked methods from the home and remote interfaces and in response to container-internal events, such as transaction commit, exceptions, or resource management.

- An instance's life begins when the container creates the instance by using `newInstance` or the `new` operator. The container then invokes the `setEntity-Context` method to pass the instance a reference to its `EntityContext` object. At this point, the instance transitions to the pooled state.

- While in the pooled state, the instance is not associated with an entity object identity. As a result, all instances in the pooled state are considered equivalent. The container can perform the following actions with an instance in the pooled state:

  - Execute an `ejbFind<METHOD>`, `ejbSelect<METHOD>`, or `ejbHome<METHOD>` method in response to a client-invoked find or home method through the home interface. Note that the instance does not move to the ready state during the execution of the `ejbFind<METHOD>`, `ejbSelect<METHOD>`, or `ejb-Home<METHOD>` method.

  - Associate the instance with an existing entity object by invoking the `ejbActivate` method on the instance. A successful execution of the `ejbActivate` method transitions the instance to the ready state.

  - Use the instance to create a new entity object by invoking the `ejbCreate` and `ejbPostCreate` methods on the instance. Successfully executing the `ejb-Create` and `ejbPostCreate` methods transitions the instance to the ready state.

  - Discard the instance by invoking the `unsetEntityContext` method on the instance. By doing so, the container notifies the instance that it will invoke no other methods on the instance.

- When the instance is in the ready state, it has an identity—that is, a primary key—and is associated with an entity object. The container can perform the following actions on an instance in the ready state:

- Invoke the `ejbLoad` method on the instance. The `ejbLoad` method instructs the instance to synchronize any cached representation it maintains of the entity object's state from the entity object's state in the resource manager. The instance remains in the ready state.

- Invoke the `ejbStore` method on the instance. The `ejbStore` method instructs the instance to synchronize the entity object's state in the resource manager with updates to the state that may have been cached in the instance. The instance remains in the ready state.

- Invoke a business method in response to a client-invoked method in the component interface. The instance remains in the ready state.

- Invoke the `ejbPassivate` method on the instance and move it to the pooled state.

- Invoke the `ejbRemove` method on the instance in response to a client-invoked `remove` method. The `ejbRemove` method transitions the instance to the pooled state.

- If an instance throws and does not catch a system exception — that is, an exception that is a subclass of `java.lang.RuntimeException` — the container catches the exception and transitions the instance to the does-not-exist state, regardless of the bean's original state.

Invocation of Create Methods

This section uses object interaction diagrams (OIDs) to illustrate what happens when an entity object is created with BMP or CMP. Figure 7.7 illustrates creating an entity object with BMP.

1. The client starts a transaction, using the `begin` method of the `UserTransaction` interface.

2. The client invokes a `create` method on the home object, which is implemented by the container. Keep in mind that the EJB container performs the diagramed operations attributed to the home object.

3. The home object invokes the matching `ejbCreate` method on the entity bean instance.

4. The bean instance creates a representation of the entity object state in the database.

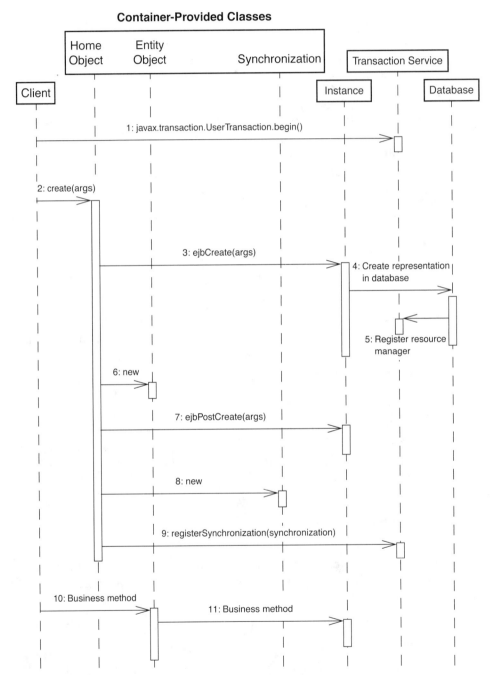

Figure 7.7   OID of Creation of Entity Object with BMP

5. The database system registers itself with the transaction service, which is a synonym for *transaction manager.*

6. The home object creates the entity object, which may be a distributed object that implements the entity bean's remote interface or a local object that implements the entity bean's local interface.

7. The home object invokes the matching `ejbPostCreate` method on the bean instance.

8. The home object creates a transaction synchronization object.

9. The home object registers the transaction synchronization object with the transaction service.

10. The client invokes a business method on the newly created entity object in the same transaction context as the `create` method.

11. The entity object delegates the invocation to the bean instance.

When the client eventually attempts to commit the transaction, the transaction service orchestrates the commit protocol, as described in the section Transaction-Commit OID on page 210.

Note that creation of the entity object is considered part of the transaction. If the transaction fails, the representation of the object's state in the database is automatically deleted, and the entity object does not exist.

Figure 7.8 shows the OID for the creation of an entity object with CMP.

1. The client starts a transaction by using the `begin` method of the `UserTransaction` interface.

2. The client invokes a `create` method on the home object. As noted earlier, the EJB container performs the diagramed operations attributed to the home object.

3. The home object invokes the matching `ejbCreate` method on the entity bean instance. The bean instance initializes itself, using the data passed in the arguments of the `ejbCreate` method.

4. The home object uses the CMP state to create the representation of the entity object state in the database.

5. The database system registers itself with the transaction service.

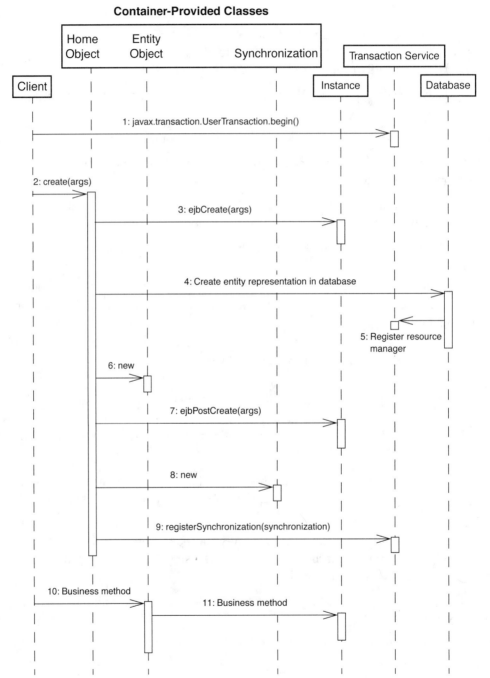

Figure 7.8 OID of Creation of Entity Object with CMP

6. The home object creates the entity object. The entity object implements the entity bean's component interface.

7. The home object invokes the matching `ejbPostCreate` method on the bean instance.

8. The home object creates a transaction synchronization object.

9. The home object registers the transaction synchronization object with the transaction service.

10. The client invokes a business method on the newly created entity object in the same transaction context as the `create` method.

11. The entity object delegates the invocation to the bean instance.

Invocation of the `remove` Method

The next two figures illustrate removing entity objects. Figure 7.9 shows the steps that take place when removing an entity object with BMP, and Figure 7.10 shows the equivalent steps for removing an entity object with CMP.

1. In Figure 7.9, the client invokes the `remove` method on the entity object.

2. The entity object invokes the `ejbRemove` method on the bean instance.

3. The instance removes the representation of the entity object state from the database.

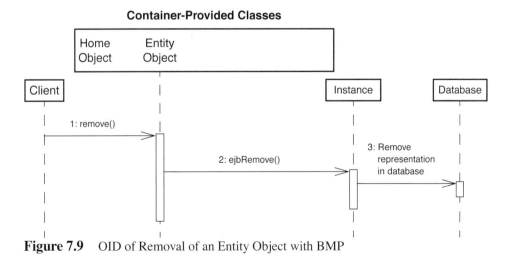

Figure 7.9 OID of Removal of an Entity Object with BMP

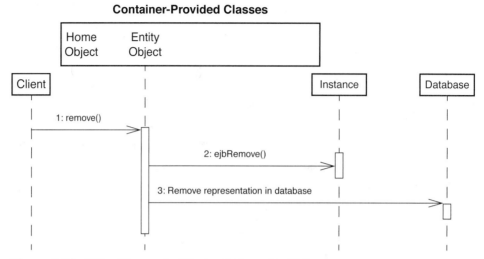

Figure 7.10 OID of Removal of Entity Object with CMP

Note that the diagram does not illustrate the transaction-related interactions among the container, transaction service, and database. The removal of the object's state representation from the database—step 3 in the diagram—is included as part of the transaction in which the remove method is executed. If the transaction fails, the object's state is not removed from the database, and the entity object continues to exist.

1. In Figure 7.10, the client invokes the remove method on the entity object.

2. The entity object invokes the ejbRemove method on the bean instance.

3. The entity object removes the representation of its state from the database.

Invocation of Find Methods

This section illustrates find method invocations on entity beans. Figure 7.11 shows the OID for a find method invocation on an entity bean instance with BMP. In contrast, Figure 7.12 shows the execution of a find method on an entity instance with CMP.

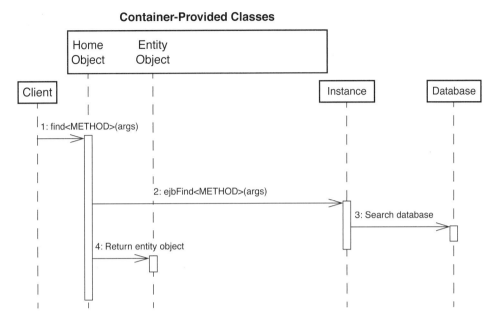

Figure 7.11 OID of Find Method Execution on a Bean-Managed Entity Instance

1. The client invokes a `find` method on the home object (Figure 7.11). As noted, the EJB container performs the diagramed operations attributed to the home object.

2. The home object invokes the matching `ejbFind` method on a bean instance.

3. The bean instance searches the database to find the object(s) that matches the find method's criteria. The instance returns the primary key—or collection of keys—from the `ejbFind` method.

4. The home object converts the returned primary key to an entity object reference—or collection of entity object references—and returns it to the client.

Note that the diagram does not illustrate the transaction-related interactions among the container, transaction service, and database. The database search—step 3 in the diagram—is included as part of the transaction in which the find method executes. Depending on the isolation level, the found objects may be protected from deletion by other transactions.

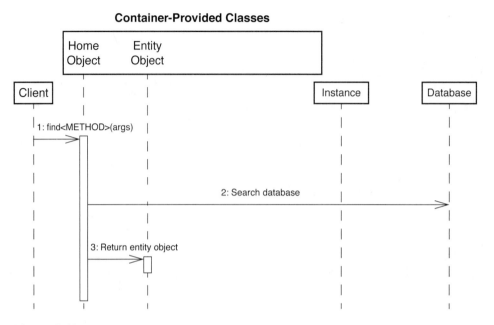

Figure 7.12 OID of Find Method Execution on a Container-Managed Entity Instance

1. The client invokes a find method on the home object (Figure 7.12). As noted, the EJB container performs the diagramed operations attributed to the home object.

2. The home object searches the database to find the object(s) that matches the find method's criteria.

3. The home object converts the primary key of the found object to an entity object reference and returns it to the client. If the find method finds more than one object, a collection of entity object references is returned to the client.

Passivation and Activation OID

The EJB architecture allows the EJB container to passivate an entity instance during a transaction. Figures 7.13 and 7.14 show the sequence of object interactions that occur for entity bean passivation and activation. Figure 7.13 is the OID for passivation and reactivation of an entity instance with BMP.

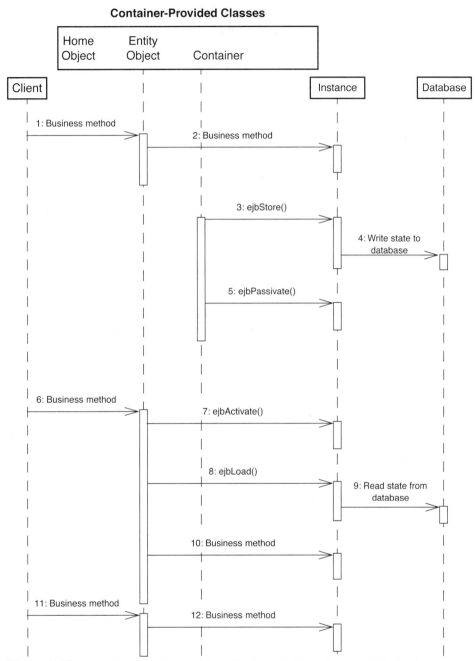

Figure 7.13 OID of Passivation and Reactivation of a Bean-Managed Entity Instance

1. The client invokes the last business method before passivation occurs.

2. The entity object delegates the business method to the bean instance.

3. The container decides to passivate the instance while it is associated with a transaction. (The reason for passivation may be, for example, that the container needs to reclaim the resources held by the instance.) The container invokes the `ejbStore` method on the instance.

4. The instance writes any cached updates made to the entity object state to the database.

5. The container invokes the `ejbPassivate` method in the instance. The instance should release into the pooled state any resources that it does not need. The instance is now in the pooled state. The container may use the instance to run find methods, activate the instance for another object identity, or release the instance through the `unsetEntityContext` method.

6. The client invokes another business method on the entity object.

7. The entity object allocates an instance from the pool. (The allocated instance could be the same instance or an instance different from the one that was associated with the object identity prior to passivation.) The container invokes the `ejbActivate` method in the instance.

8. The container invokes the `ejbLoad` method in the instance. Note that the container implements the entity object. Therefore, the `ejbActivate` and `ejbLoad` calls invoked in steps 7 and 8 are in fact invoked by the container.

9. The instance uses the `ejbLoad` method to read the object state, or parts of the object state, from the database.

10. The entity object delegates the business method to the instance.

11. The client invokes the next business method on the entity object.

12. Because the instance is in the ready state, the entity object can delegate the business method to the instance.

Figure 7.14 represents the same operations for an entity instance with CMP.

1. The client invokes the last business method before passivation occurs.

2. The entity object delegates the business method to the bean instance.

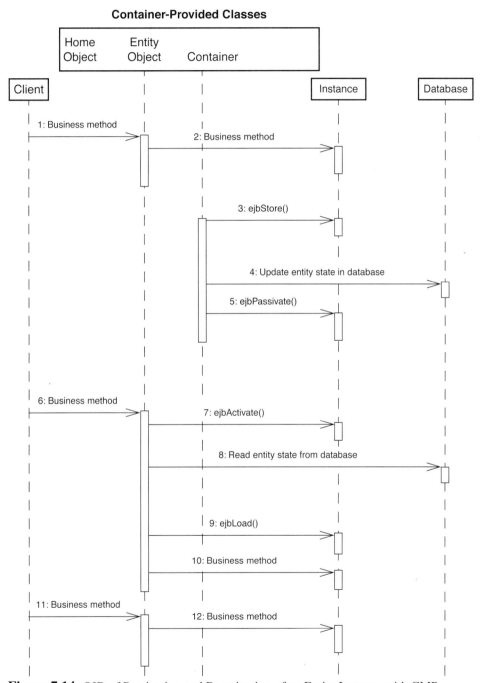

Figure 7.14 OID of Passivation and Reactivation of an Entity Instance with CMP

3. The container decides to passivate the instance while it is associated with a transaction. (The reason for passivation may be, for example, that the container needs to reclaim the resources held by the instance.) The container invokes the `ejbStore` method on the instance. The instance can use the `ejbStore` method to update its state. (See Section 7.2.4, Caching Entity Bean State, on page 219.)

4. The container updates the object state in the database with the extracted values of the CMP and CMR fields.

5. The container invokes the `ejbPassivate` method in the instance. The instance should release into the pooled state any resources that it does not need. The instance is now in the pooled state. The container may use the instance to run find methods, activate the instance for another object identity, or release the instance through the `unsetEntityContext` method.

6. The client invokes another business method on the entity object.

7. The entity object allocates an instance from the pool. (The instance could be the same instance or an instance different from the one that was associated with the object identity prior to passivation.) The container invokes the `ejbActivate` method in the instance.

8. The container reads the object state from the database.

9. The container invokes the `ejbLoad` method in the instance. Note that the container implements the entity object. Therefore, the `ejbActivate` and `ejbLoad` calls invoked in steps 7 and 9 (and the work in step 8) are in fact invoked by the container.

10. The entity object delegates the business method to the instance.

11. The client invokes the next business method on the entity object.

12. Because the instance is in the ready state, the entity object can delegate the business method to the instance.

Transaction-Commit OID

This section describes the operations that occur during transaction commit. Figure 7.15 shows the object interactions of the transaction-commit protocol for an entity instance with BMP.

1. After invoking methods on an entity bean, the client attempts to commit the transaction by invoking the `commit` method on the `UserTransaction` interface.

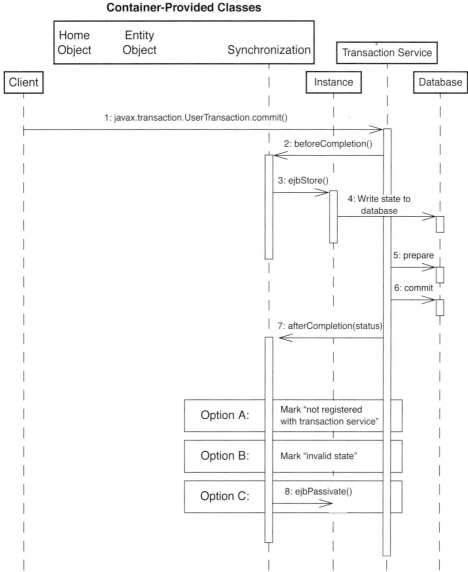

Figure 7.15 OID of Transaction Commit Protocol for a Bean-Managed Entity Instance

2. The transaction service invokes the beforeCompletion method on a transaction synchronization object implemented by the container.

3. The container invokes the `ejbStore` method on the bean instance used by the transaction.

4. The instance writes any cached updates made to the entity object state to the database.

5. The transaction service performs the prepare phase of the two-phase commit protocol. This step is skipped if the database is the only resource manager enlisted with the transaction and the transaction service implements the one-phase commit optimization.

6. The transaction service performs the commit phase of the two-phase commit protocol.

7. The transaction service invokes the `afterCompletion` method on the synchronization object.

8. If the container chooses commit option C—see the section Commit Options on page 217—the container invokes the `ejbPassivate` method in the instance.

Figure 7.16 shows the equivalent interactions of the transaction-commit protocol for an entity instance with CMP.

1. After invoking methods on an entity bean, the client attempts to commit the transaction by invoking the `commit` method on the `UserTransaction` interface.

2. The transaction service invokes the `beforeCompletion` method on a transaction synchronization object implemented by the container.

3. The container invokes the `ejbStore` method on the bean instance used by the transaction.

4. The container updates the object state in the database with the extracted values of the CMP and CMR fields.

5. The transaction service performs the prepare phase of the two-phase commit protocol. This step is skipped if the database is the only resource manager enlisted with the transaction and the transaction service implements the one-phase commit optimization.

6. The transaction service performs the commit phase of the two-phase commit protocol.

7. The transaction service invokes the `afterCompletion` method on the synchronization object.

8. If the container chooses commit option C, the container invokes the `ejbPassivate` method in the instance.

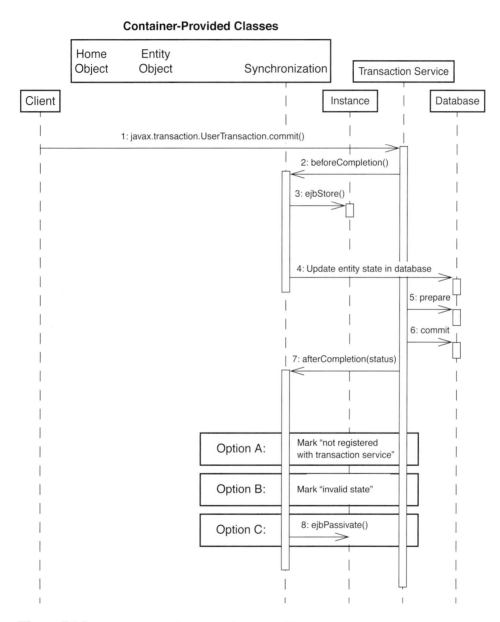

Figure 7.16 OID of Transaction Commit Protocol for CMP Entity Instance

Start of Next Transaction OID

This section describes the operations that occur at the start of the next transaction. Figure 7.17 shows the object interactions at the start of the next transaction for an entity instance with BMP.

1. The client starts the next transaction by invoking the `begin` method on the `UserTransaction` interface.

2. The client then invokes a business method on the entity object that implements the remote interface.

3. If it uses commit option C, the container allocates an instance from the pool and invokes the `ejbActivate` method on it.

4. If it uses commit option B or C, the container invokes the `ejbLoad` method on the instance.

5. The instance uses the `ejbLoad` method to read the object state, or parts of the object state, from the database. (This happens only if the container uses commit option B or C.)

6. The database system registers itself with the transaction service. (This happens only if the container uses commit option B or C.)

7. The entity object creates a `Synchronization` object.

8. The entity object registers the `Synchronization` object with the transaction service.

9. The entity object delegates the invocation of the business method to the instance.

10. The client invokes the next business method in the same transaction.

11. The entity object delegates the invocation to the instance.

Figure 7.18 shows the object interactions at the start of the next transaction for an entity instance with CMP.

1. The client starts the next transaction by invoking the `begin` method on the `UserTransaction` interface.

2. The client then invokes a business method on the entity object that implements the remote interface.

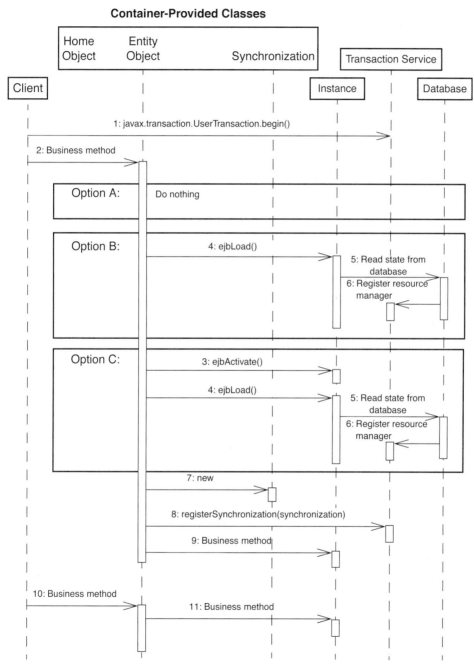

Figure 7.17 OID of Next Transaction for a Bean-Managed Entity Instance

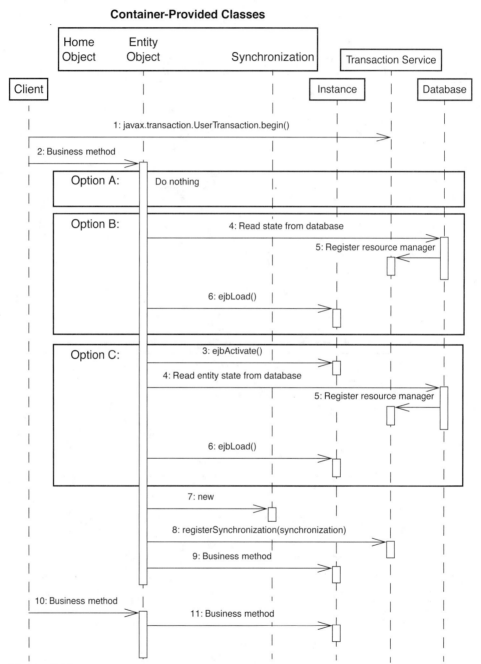

Figure 7.18 OID of Next Transaction for a Container-Managed Entity Instance

3. If it uses commit option C, the container allocates an instance from the pool and invokes the `ejbActivate` method on it.

4. If it uses commit option B or C, the container reads the values of the container-managed fields from the database.

5. The database system registers itself with the transaction service. (This happens only if the container uses commit option B or C.)

6. The container invokes the `ejbLoad` method on the instance. The implementation of the `ejbLoad` method is typically empty for instances with CMP. (This happens only if the container uses commit option B or C.)

7. The entity object creates a `Synchronization` object.

8. The entity object registers the `Synchronization` object with the transaction service.

9. The entity object delegates the invocation of the business method to the instance.

10. The client invokes the next business method in the same transaction.

11. The entity object delegates the invocation to the instance.

Commit Options

The entity bean protocol gives the container the flexibility to select the disposition of the instance state at transaction commit. This flexibility allows the container to manage optimally the caching of the entity object's state and the association of an entity object identity with the enterprise bean instances.

The container selects from the following commit options:

- **Option A**—The container caches a "ready" instance between transactions. The container ensures that the instance has exclusive access to the state of the object in the persistent storage. Because of this exclusive access, the container does not need to synchronize the instance's state from the persistent storage at the beginning of the next transaction.

- **Option B**—The container caches a "ready" instance between transactions. Unlike in option A, the container does not ensure that the instance has exclusive access to the state of the object in the persistent storage. Therefore, the container must synchronize the instance's state from the persistent storage at the beginning of the next transaction by invoking the `ejbLoad` method on the instance.

- **Option C**—The container does not cache a "ready" instance between transactions. The container returns the instance to the pool of available instances after a transaction has completed. When the entity object is reinvoked in the next transaction, the container must activate an instance from the pool to handle the invocation.

Table 7.1 summarizes the commit options. As you can see, for all three options, the container synchronizes the instance's state with the persistent storage at transaction commit.

Table 7.1   Summary of Commit Options

Option	Write Instance State to Database	Instance Stays Ready	Instance State Remains Valid
A	Yes	Yes	Yes
B	Yes	Yes	No
C	Yes	No	No

A container can implement some or all of the three commit options. If the container implements more than one option, the deployer can typically specify which option will be used for each entity bean. The optimal option depends on the expected workload.

- Given a low probability that a client will access an entity object again, using option C will result in returning the instance to the pooled state as quickly as possible. The container can immediately reuse the instance for other object identities rather than allocating new instances.

- Given a high probability that a client may access an entity object again, using option B will result in retaining the instance associated with an object identity in the ready state. Retaining the instance in the ready state saves the `ejbPassivate` and `ejbActivate` transitions on each client transaction to the same entity object.

- Option A can be used instead of option B to improve performance further by skipping the `ejbLoad` synchronization call on the next transaction. Note that option A can be used only if it can be guaranteed that no other program can modify the underlying state in the database.

The selection of the commit option is transparent to the entity bean implementation. The entity bean works correctly regardless of the commit option chosen by the container. The bean developer writes the entity bean in the same way.

The object interaction in Transaction-Commit OID on page 210 and Start of Next Transaction OID on page 214 illustrate the commit options in detail.

7.2.4 Caching Entity Bean State

In this section, we explain how an entity bean can best use the `ejbLoad` and `ejbStore` methods in the entity bean class implementation. The container invokes the `ejbLoad` and `ejbStore` methods on the instances of both BMP and CMP entity beans. However, using the `ejbLoad` and `ejbStore` methods differs between BMP and CMP entity beans.

Caching State with BMP

Recall from earlier in this chapter that the state of an entity object is kept in a resource manager. Typically, the resource manager resides on a network node different from the EJB container in which the entity bean accessing the state is deployed. Because the implementation of a business method typically accesses the entity object's state, each invocation of a business method normally results in a network trip to the resource manager. If a transaction includes multiple business method invocations, the resulting multiple calls to the resource manager over the network may increase the transaction overhead.

Figure 7.19 shows the OID for a transaction with three calls to entity bean business methods. The business methods either read or update the entity object's state stored in the resource manager. Together with the data commit at the end of the transaction, this one transaction includes a total of four network calls to the resource manager.

1. The client starts a transaction by invoking the `begin` method, which initiates the appropriate actions from the transaction manager to create a new transaction.

2. The client, working within the transaction context, invokes the `getBalance` business method on the `Account` remote interface.

3. `AccountObject`, which implements the `Account` remote interface, in turn invokes the `ejbLoad` method on the `AccountBean` instance. In our example, the instance does no work in the `ejbLoad` method.

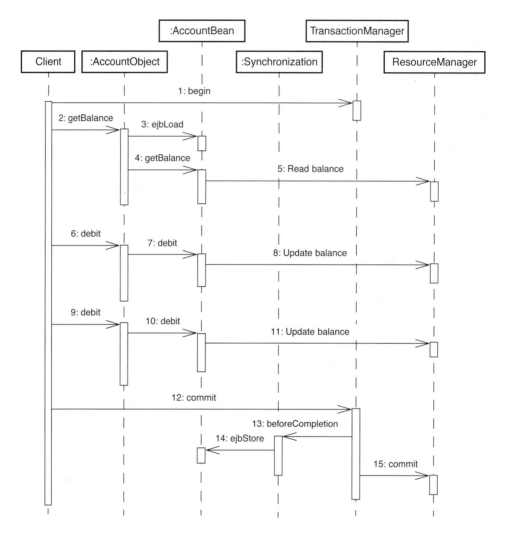

Figure 7.19 Multiple Invocations to the Resource Manager

4. `AccountObject` invokes the `getBalance` method on the `AccountBean` instance that corresponds to the `getBalance` method invoked by the client through the `Account` remote interface.

5. The `getBalance` method must access the entity object's state stored in the re-source manager—that is, it must read in the account balance information stored in the database. As a result, `AccountBean` initiates a network call to access these

values from the resource manager.

6. The client invokes the `debit` method on the `Account` remote interface.

7. The `AccountObject` invokes the `debit` method on the entity bean instance.

8. The `debit` method performs the `debit` operation by updating the account balance in the resource manager. This is the second network call to the resource manager.

9. The client invokes the `debit` method a second time.

10. The previous process (steps 6 and 7) repeats: `AccountObject` invokes the `debit` method on the entity bean instance.

11. The `debit` method performs the `debit` operation by updating the account balance in the resource manager. This is the third network call to the resource manager.

12. The work of the transaction is now complete, and the client invokes the `commit` method on the transaction manager.

13. The client's invocation causes the transaction manager first to call the `beforeCompletion` method in the `Synchronization` object implemented by the container.

14. The container invokes the `ejbStore` method on the instance. In our example, the instance does no work in the `ejbStore` method.

15. The transaction manager completes the transaction by committing the results in the resource manager. This constitutes the fourth network call.

Many bean developers will want to reduce the overhead of accessing the resource manager multiple times in a transaction. To accomplish this, the EJB architecture allows the entity bean instance to cache the entity object's state, or part of its state, within a transaction. (Some containers may allow the instance to cache the entity object's state even between transactions. Such a container would use commit option A described in the section Commit Options on page 217.) Rather than making repeated calls to the resource manager to access the object's state, the instance loads the object's state from the resource manager at the beginning of a transaction and caches it in its instance variables.

To facilitate caching, the EJB container invokes the `ejbLoad` method on the instance prior to the first business method invocation in a transaction. The instance can use the `ejbLoad` method to load the entity object's state, or part of its state, into the instance's variables. Then, subsequently invoked business methods in the instance can read and update the cached state instead of making calls to the resource manager. When the transaction ends, the EJB container invokes the `ejb-Store` method on the instance. If the previously invoked business methods updated the state cached in the instance variables, the instance uses the `ejbStore` method to synchronize the entity object's state in the resource manager with the cached state. Note that `AccountBean` in Figure 7.19 did not take advantage of the `ejbLoad` and `ejbStore` methods, although the methods were called by the container.

Figure 7.20 shows the OID diagram illustrating the use of cached state for the same account balance and debit transactions in Figure 7.19.

1. The client starts a transaction by invoking the `begin` method. This initiates the appropriate actions from the transaction manager to create a new transaction.

2. The client, working within the transaction context, invokes the `getBalance` business method on the `Account` remote interface.

3. Before any business methods execute, `AccountObject` invokes the `ejbLoad` method on the `AccountBean` instance. Recall that the `AccountObject` class was generated by the container tools.

4. From the `ejbLoad` method, `AccountBean` accesses the resource manager and reads the object's state into its instance's variables.

5. `AccountObject` then invokes the corresponding `getBalance` method on the `AccountBean` instance.

6. The client does the first invocation of the `debit` method on the `Account` remote interface.

7. `AccountObject` invokes the `debit` method on the `AccountBean` instance.

8. The client does the second invocation of the `debit` method on the `Account` remote interface.

9. `AccountObject` invokes the `debit` method on the `AccountBean` class.

10. The work of the transaction completes, and the client invokes the `commit` method on the transaction manager.

11. The transaction manager invokes the `beforeCompletion` method to signal the container (via the `Synchronization` interface) that the transaction is starting its commit process.

12. The container invokes the `ejbStore` method on the `AccountBean` instance so that it properly synchronizes the object's state in the resource manager with the updated state cached in the instance variables.

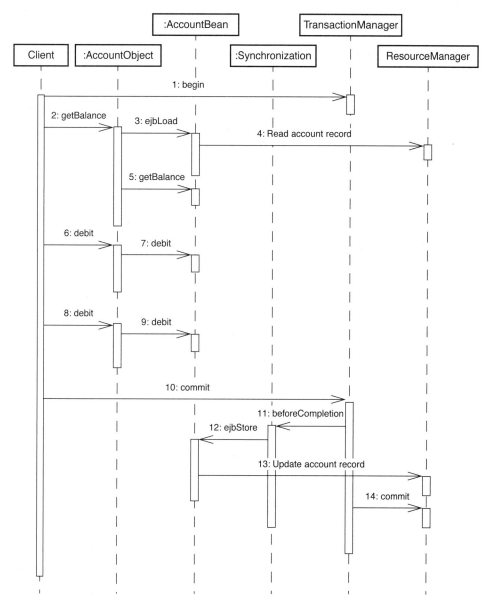

Figure 7.20 Caching State in BMP Entity Bean's Instance Variables

13. AccountBean sends changed state cached in its instance variables to the resource manager, which updates its copy of the entity object's state.

14. The transaction manager invokes the `commit` method on the resource manager to save all state changes and to end the transaction.

The container invokes the `ejbLoad` and `ejbStore` methods—as well as the business methods between the `ejbLoad` and `ejbStore` methods—in the same transaction context. When, from these methods, the entity bean instance accesses the entity object's state in the resource manager, the resource manager properly associates all the multiple resource manager accesses with the transaction; see steps 4 and 13.

Note that the container also invokes the `ejbStore` and `ejbLoad` methods during instance passivation and activation. The OIDs in the section Passivation and Activation OID on page 206 illustrate this. Because the container needs a transaction context to drive the `ejbLoad` and `ejbStore` methods on an entity bean instance, caching of the entity object's state in the instance variable works reliably only if the entity bean methods execute in a transaction context.

The `ejbLoad` and `ejbStore` methods must be used with great caution for entity beans with methods that do not execute with a defined transaction context. (These would be entity beans with methods that use the transaction attributes `NotSupported`, `Never`, and `Supports`.) If the business methods can execute without a defined transaction context, the instance should cache only the state of immutable entity objects. For these entity beans, an instance can use the `ejbLoad` method to cache the entity object's state, but the `ejbStore` method should always be a noop.

Caching State with CMP

Caching of an entity object's state works differently with CMP. An entity bean with CMP typically does not manage the caching of the entity object's state. Instead, the entity bean relies on the container. The container performs suitable cache management when it maps the CMP and CMR fields to the data items comprising the state representation in the resource manager.

Essentially, the EJB container makes it appear that the entity object's state and relationships load into the CMP and CMR fields at the beginning of a transaction and that changes to values of the CMP and CMR fields automatically propagate to the entity object's state in the resource manager at the end of the transaction. The business methods simply access the CMP and CMR fields as if the entity object's state were maintained directly by the class rather than in the resource manager.

The container performs the loading and saving of the state transparently to the entity bean's code. The container decides the following, typically using information provided by the deployer:

- The parts of the state that it "eagerly" loads at the beginning of a transaction—just before the container invokes the `ejbLoad` call on the instance

- The parts of the state that it "lazily" reads from the resource manager, according to when the business methods need these parts

The container propagates the updates made to the container-managed state to the resource manager immediately after invoking the `ejbStore` method (Figure 7.21).

1. The client starts a transaction by invoking the `begin` method. This initiates the appropriate actions from the transaction manager to create a new transaction.

2. The client, working within the transaction context, invokes the `getBalance` business method on the `Account` component interface.

3. Before any business methods execute, `AccountObject` reads the entity object state for the resource manager. Recall that the container tools generated the `AccountObject` class.

4. `AccountObject` invokes the `ejbLoad` method on the `AccountBean` instance.

5. `AccountObject` then invokes the corresponding `getBalance` method on the `AccountBean` instance.

6. The client does the first invocation of the `debit` method on the `Account` remote interface.

7. `AccountObject` invokes the `debit` method on the `AccountBean` instance.

8. The client does the second invocation of the `debit` method on the `Account` remote interface.

9. `AccountObject` invokes the `debit` method on the `AccountBean` instance.

10. The work of the transaction completes, and the client invokes the `commit` method on the transaction manager.

11. The transaction manager invokes the `beforeCompletion` method to signal the container—via the `Synchronization` interface—that the transaction is starting its commit process.

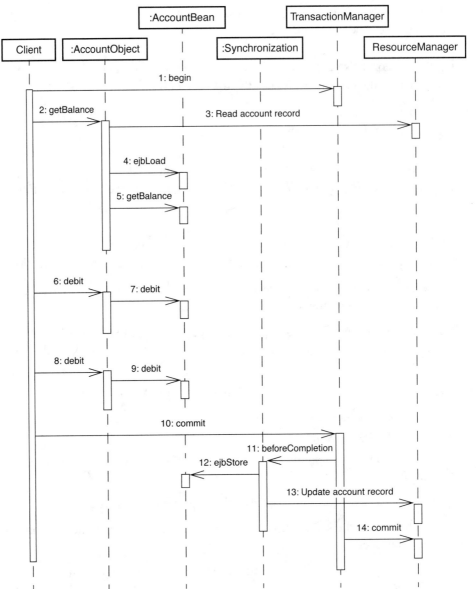

Figure 7.21 Caching with CMP Entity Beans

12. The container invokes the ejbStore method on the AccountBean instance.

13. The container updates the representation of the account state in the resource

manager with the extracted values from the CMP fields.

14. The transaction manager invokes the `commit` method on the resource manager
to save all state changes and to end the transaction.

As noted at the start of this section, an entity bean with CMP typically does
not use `ejbLoad` and `ejbStore` to manage caching of state. (This means that the
method implementations in the entity bean class are left empty.)

When and how would an entity bean with CMP use the `ejbLoad` and `ejbStore`
methods? An entity bean with CMP could use the `ejbLoad` method to compute
values derived from the CMP and CMR fields. It would then use the `ejbStore`
method to update the CMP and CMR fields with the updated derived values. The
entity bean's business methods could then directly use the derived values. In
effect, the bean instance would be caching an alternate representation of the persistent state.

Code Example 7.11 illustrates using `ejbLoad` and `ejbStore` in CMP entity
beans:

```
public abstract class AccountBean implements EntityBean {
    // container-managed fields
public abstract String getAccountNumber();    // accountNumber
    public abstract void setAccountNumber(String v);

    public abstract double getBalance();  // balance in native
                                          // currency
    public abstract void setBalance(double v);

    // fields containing values derived from CMP fields
    double balanceInEuros;
    ...

    public double getBalance() {
        return balanceInEuros;
    }

    public void debit(double amountInEuros) {
        balanceInEuros = balanceInEuros - amountInEuros;
    }

    public void credit(double amountInEuros) {
```

```
        balanceInEuros = balanceInEuros + amountInEuros;
    }

    public void ejbLoad() {
        balanceInEuros = balance * conversionFactor;
    }

    public ejbStore() {
        setBalance(balanceInEuros / conversionFactor);
    }
    }
}
```

Code Example 7.11 Using `ejbLoad` and `ejbStore` in CMP Entity Beans

`AccountBean` in Code Example 7.11 is designed for new applications that use the euro as the common currency for all currency calculations. Therefore, the methods of the `Account` component interface expect currency amounts in euros. However, the legacy account information stored in the resource manager uses the country's native currency. The CMP `AccountBean` implements the `ejbLoad` and `ejbStore` methods to perform the conversions from the native currency to euros, and vice versa.

7.2.5   Designing the Entity Bean Component Interface

The entity bean developer is responsible for the design of the bean's component interface. The entity bean developer needs to consider carefully how the bean's clients might use the methods of the component interface.

Generally, it's best to implement an entity bean with a local client view. A local client view ensures that the entity bean performs maximally and gives the bean developer the greatest latitude in designing its accessor methods. Because an entity bean with a local client view does not have the remote method invocation performance overhead, the bean developer can include individual accessor methods for each persistent attribute, regardless of the number of attributes.

If the application requires a remote view, the bean developer can use a session bean with a remote client view as a facade to entity beans with local views. This approach allows the entity bean to have the advantages of a local client view while at the same time exposing its functionality to remote clients. An entity bean can also be implemented with both a local and a remote client view.

Entity Beans with Remote and Local Client Views

A bean developer can implement an entity bean with both a local and a remote client view. Often, such a dual-purpose entity bean has one or more entity beans with local interfaces behind it. The remote entity bean interface provides a coarse-grained view of the persistent data modeled by the network of entity beans related through their local interfaces.

Clients may directly access the entity bean's remote client view. Or, the bean developer may implement a session bean with a remote interface as a facade to the entity bean with both the local and the remote view. A client may access an entity bean method exposed through both the bean's local and remote interfaces. If this occurs, the method is called with pass-by-reference semantics in the local case — when the client is located on the same JVM as the entity bean — and with pass-by-value semantics in the remote case. To avoid unintended side effects, the bean developer should keep the parameter-passing semantic differences in mind when writing the method.

Session Bean As Facade to an Entity Bean

A bean developer can implement a session bean with a remote client view and have that session bean serve as a facade to entity beans with local views. Clients use the methods of the remote session bean, which in turn accesses the functionality of the local entity beans. The session bean implements a remote view, making the functionality of the local entity beans available to its remote clients and thus freeing its clients from being restricted to the same Java virtual machine as the session bean.

By using session beans in this way, developers can manage the interaction of clients with various entity beans. In addition, the client is exposed to a single interface, which serves as a central entry point to multiple entity beans. The client interacts exclusively with the session bean and may not even be aware of the underlying entity beans in the system. This approach is useful when an application relies on multiple entity beans, as when these beans model complex business data. For particularly complex applications, the bean developer can define different session beans to serve as facades to different functional areas of the application. Generally, however, the developer should not have a session facade for each entity bean, because such an approach is not an efficient use of server resources.

Designing Accessor Methods for Entity Beans with Remote Views

Entity beans should be designed with local views, but some situations require entity beans to use a remote client view. For these situations, we describe three different approaches to the design of the entity bean's remote interface, and discuss the trade-offs with each approach.

Accessor Methods for Individual Attributes

The entity bean developer can choose to define the remote interface methods to promote individual access to each persistent attribute. With this style, the entity bean developer defines separate accessor methods in the remote interface for each individual attribute, as shown in Code Example 7.12:

```
public interface Selection extends EJBObject {
    Employee getEmployee() throws RemoteException;
    int getCoverage() throws RemoteException;
    Plan getMedicalPlan() throws RemoteException;
    Plan getDentalPlan() throws RemoteException;
    boolean getSmokerStatus() throws RemoteException;
    void setEmployee(Employee v) throws RemoteException;
    void setCoverage(int v) throws RemoteException;
    void setMedicalPlan(Plan v) throws RemoteException;
    void setDentalPlan(Plan v) throws RemoteException;
    void setSmokerStatus(boolean v) throws RemoteException;
}
```

Code Example 7.12 Accessor Methods for Individual Attributes

This style may be useful when the entity bean may have many attributes and most clients need access to only a few attributes but the set of attributes used by each client is not known beforehand. The client retrieves only the attributes needed. However, there are drawbacks to this style:

- Each client invocation of an accessor method results in a network call, reducing the performance of the application.

- If several attributes need to be updated in a transaction, the client must use client-side transaction demarcation to make the invocation of the individual set methods atomic. The transaction is also open across several network calls, further reducing overall performance by increasing lock contention on the underlying data and by adding the overhead of additional network trips for the transaction demarcation.

Unless the application requires the use of individual access methods, we recommend that the bean developer use one of the two other styles described next for the design of an entity bean's remote interface.

Accessing All Attributes in One Value Object

As an alternative to accessing attributes individually, the developer can define the remote interface methods to access all attributes in one call. This is a good approach when client applications typically need to access most or all of the attributes of the entity bean. The client makes one method call, which transfers all individual attributes in a single value object.

Accessing Separate Value Objects

In some cases, the developer may choose to apportion the individual attributes into subsets—the subsets can overlap—and then define methods that access each subset. This design approach is particularly useful when the entity bean has a large number of individual attributes but the typical client programs need to access only small subsets of these attributes. The entity bean developer defines multiple value objects, one for each subset of attributes. Each value object meets the needs of a client use case; each value object contains the attributes required by a client's use of that entity bean.

Defining the appropriate value objects and suitable business methods for the individual use case has two benefits. First, because the business method typically suggests the intended use case, it makes it easier for the client programmer to learn how to use the entity bean. Second, it optimizes the network traffic because the client is sent only the data that it needs, and the data is transferred in a single call. The `BankAccount` remote interface in Code Example 7.13 illustrates this style:

```
public interface BankAccount extends EJBObject {
    // Use case one
    Address getAddress()
        throws RemoteException, BankAccountException;
```

```
   void updateAddress(Address changedAddress)
      throws RemoteException, BankAccountException;


   // Use case two
   Summary getSummary()
      throws RemoteException, BankAccountException;


   // Use case three
   Collection getTransactionHistory(Date start, Date end)
      throws RemoteException, BankAccountException;
   void modifyTransaction(Transaction tran)
       throws RemoteException, BankAccountException;


   // Use case four
   void credit(double amount)
      throws RemoteException;
   void debit(double amount)
      throws RemoteException, InsufficientFundsException;
}
```

Code Example 7.13 Using Multiple Value Objects

The developer of this entity bean recognized three different client use cases for the bean, for which the bean defines the following value objects:

- One type of client uses the bean to obtain and update the address information.

- Another client type uses the entity bean for account summary information.

- A third client type uses the entity bean to view and possibly edit transaction history.

The design of the entity bean reflects this usage, defining the value objects Address, Summary, and Transaction for the three different client use cases. The developer has tailored the BankAccount remote methods for the three client use cases.

A fourth client type uses the entity bean to perform debit and credit transactions on the account. The fourth use case does not define any value objects.

7.2.6   Concurrent Invocation of an Entity Object

Recall that an entity object differs from a session object in terms of its client invocation. Only a single client can use a session object, and the client must ensure that it invokes the methods on the object serially. In contrast, multiple clients can concurrently invoke an entity object. However, each client must invoke the methods of the entity object serially.

Although the entity object appears as a shared object that the clients can invoke concurrently, the bean developer does not have to design the entity bean class to be multithreading safe. The EJB container synchronizes multiple threads' access to the entity object. The bean developer depends on the EJB container for appropriate synchronization to an entity object when multiple clients concurrently access the object.

This section explains how the EJB container dispatches methods invoked by multiple clients through the entity object's component interface to the entity bean instances so that the potentially concurrent execution of multiple client requests does not lead to the loss of the entity object's state integrity. If you are an advanced EJB developer interested in tuning your application server, you might find this section useful.

An EJB container may use one of two typical implementation strategies to synchronize concurrent access from multiple clients to an entity object. It is important to note that, from the bean developer's perspective, it makes no difference which strategy the container uses. The bean developer implements the same code for the entity object, regardless of the container synchronization strategy.

One implementation strategy essentially delegates the synchronization of multiple clients to the resource manager. It works as follows:

1. When a client-invoked method call reaches the container, the container first determines the target transaction context in which to invoke the business method. Chapter 10, Understanding Transactions, describes the rules for determining the transaction context for the invoked business method (see Section 10.1, Declarative Transaction Demarcation, on page 325).

2. The container attempts to locate an entity object instance that is in the ready state and already associated with the target entity object identity and the target transaction context. If such an instance exists, the container dispatches the business method on the instance.

3. If bean instances in the ready state are associated with the target entity object identity but none are in the target transaction context, the container can take an

instance not currently associated with a transaction context, invoke the `ejb-Load` method on the instance, and then dispatch the business method on it. The instance stays associated with the transaction context until the end of the transaction. Ending the transaction causes the container to invoke `ejbStore` on the instance; note that `ejbStore` executes in the transaction context.

4. If no bean instances in the ready state are suitable for dispatching the business method, the container activates an instance in the pooled state by invoking the `ejbActivate` and `ejbLoad` methods and then dispatches the business method on the instance. The instance remains associated with the transaction context, as described in the previous step.

Note that when it uses this implementation strategy, the container may concurrently dispatch multiple invocations to the same entity object by using a different instance of the entity bean class for each invocation (see Figure 7.22). In Figure 7.22, the two `Account 100` instances are associated with the same `Account 100` entity object, but each instance is in a different transaction context. Because the transaction context is associated with an instance's access to the resource manager, the resource manager performs the synchronization of the updates from the multiple bean instances to the entity object's state based on the transaction context. An EJB container using this implementation strategy uses commit option B or C described in the section Commit Options on page 217.

The second implementation strategy places a greater burden for the synchronization of client calls on the container. With this strategy, the EJB container acquires exclusive access to the entity object's state in the database. The container activates a single instance and serializes the access from multiple transactions to this instance (see Figure 7.23). The container can use any of the commit options A, B, or C if it uses this single-instance strategy.

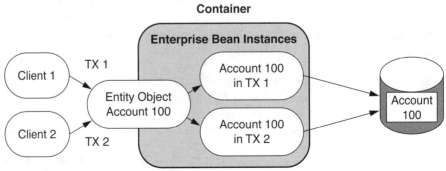

Figure 7.22 Multiple Clients Using Multiple Instances to Access an Entity Object

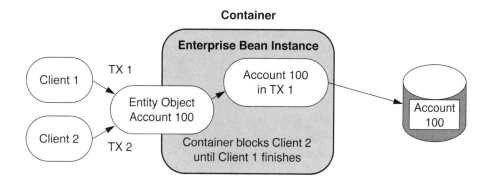

Figure 7.23 Multiple Clients Using Single Instance to Access an Entity Object

7.2.7   Using Entity Beans with Preexisting Data

It is important to understand that the representation of an entity object in the resource manager may preexist the deployment of an entity bean. For example, a bank might have been using non-object-based applications that stored account records in a database system. The bank then later developed or purchased an EJB application that included the AccountEJB entity bean, which provided the object-oriented EJB client view of the same account database records (see Figure 7.24).

The new EJB application seamlessly coexists with the legacy non-object-based application, as follows:

- An account record created by a legacy application is visible to the EJB application as an Account object. From the perspective of the EJB application, an Account object exists even if a create method of the entity bean home interface did not create it.

- Similarly, if the EJB application creates a new Account object, the legacy application can access the state of the entity object because it is a record in the database.

- If the EJB application changes the Account object by invoking methods of the Account remote interface, these changes are visible to a legacy application as changes to the account record in the database.

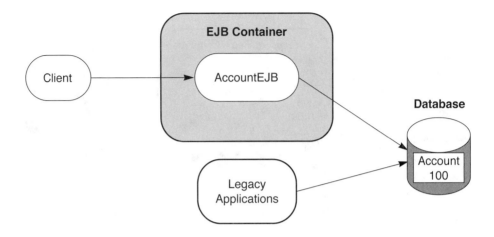

Figure 7.24   Access to Preexisting Data Shared with Legacy Applications

- Similarly, if the legacy application changes the account record in the database, the changes are visible to the EJB application as changes to the state of the Account object.

- If the legacy application deletes an account record from the database, the EJB application is no longer able to access the corresponding Account object.

- If the EJB application removes an Account object, the object-removal operation causes the deletion of the corresponding account record from the database. The legacy application is no longer able to access the record.

- The resource manager's—database system—transaction mechanism allows the EJB application to be used concurrently with the legacy application.

7.3   Timer Service

The EJB timer service is a new feature added to the EJB architecture in the EJB 2.1 specification. This feature can be used with both BMP and CMP entity beans, as well as with stateless session beans and message-driven beans. In Section 8.2, Parts Developed by Wombat, on page 249, we provide an example that illustrates use of the timer service with entity beans.

Business applications generally need a way to perform actions at specific times—for example, preparing a summary report of each day's transactions at the end of every business day—or after a certain interval of time—for example, if an acknowledgment for a business operation is not received in a certain time frame, alert an administrator. The EJB timer service can be used to provide such notifications to enterprise beans at a specific time or after specific time intervals. Notifications can be provided either once or on a recurring basis after a specified interval.

The EJB timer service is intended to be used for coarse-grained—hours, days, or longer—notifications that are usually needed for business processes. It is not designed to be accurate for fine-grained—milliseconds, seconds—time periods or for any kind of real-time processing.

7.3.1   Timer Interfaces

To set up a timer notification, an enterprise bean uses the EJB container's timer service to create a `Timer` object. The timer service is accessed using the `EJBContext.getTimerService` method. Code Example 7.14 shows the timer-related interfaces `TimerService`, `Timer`, `TimerHandle`, and `TimedObject`:

```
public interface TimerService {

    public Timer createTimer(long duration, Serializable info)
        throws java.lang.IllegalArgumentException,
        java.lang.IllegalStateException, javax.ejb.EJBException;

    public Timer createTimer(long initialDuration,
        long intervalDuration, Serializable info) throws
            java.lang.IllegalArgumentException,
            java.lang.IllegalStateException, javax.ejb.EJBException;

    public Timer createTimer(Date expiration, Serializable info)
        throws java.lang.IllegalArgumentException,
        java.lang.IllegalStateException, javax.ejb.EJBException;

    public Timer createTimer(Date initialExpiration,
        long intervalDuration, Serializable info) throws
        java.lang.IllegalArgumentException,
        java.lang.IllegalStateException, javax.ejb.EJBException;
```

```
        public Collection getTimers() throws
            java.lang.IllegalStateException, javax.ejb.EJBException;
    }

    public interface Timer {

        public void cancel() throws java.lang.IllegalStateException,
            javax.ejb.NoSuchObjectLocalException,
            javax.ejb.EJBException;

        public long getTimeRemaining() throws
            java.lang.IllegalStateException,
            javax.ejb.NoSuchObjectLocalException,
            javax.ejb.EJBException;

        public Date getNextTimeout() throws
            java.lang.IllegalStateException,
            javax.ejb.NoSuchObjectLocalException,
            javax.ejb.EJBException;

        public Serializable getInfo() throws
            java.lang.IllegalStateException,
            javax.ejb.NoSuchObjectLocalException,
            javax.ejb.EJBException;

        public TimerHandle getHandle() throws
            java.lang.IllegalStateException,
            javax.ejb.NoSuchObjectLocalException,
            javax.ejb.EJBException;
    }

    public interface TimerHandle extends Serializable {

        public Timer getTimer() throws java.lang.IllegalStateException,
            javax.ejb.NoSuchObjectLocalException,
            javax.ejb.EJBException;
    }

    public interface TimedObject {
```

```
        public void ejbTimeout(Timer timer);
    }
```

Code Example 7.14 Timer Interfaces

EJB application code uses the `createTimer` methods of `TimerService` to create `Timer` objects. There are four such methods:

- Two methods create timers that expire after a specified duration. This can be a one-time timer or a recurring timer with a specified interval between notifications.

- Two methods create timers that expire at a specified time. This, too, can be a one-time timer or a recurring timer.

A bean can create multiple timer objects. The bean can associate an information object with each timer object to help the bean differentiate between multiple timer objects.

When a timer expires, the container sends a notification to the bean that created the timer, by calling the timer's `ejbTimeout` method and providing the timer as an argument. This requires that all beans that create timers must implement the `TimedObject` interface.

Timer objects implement the `Timer` interface; which provides methods to cancel—delete—the timer; get the time remaining before the timer expires; get the time when the timer will expire; get the information object associated with the timer; and get the timer's `TimerHandle` object. A bean can get a reference to a `Timer` object in one of three ways:

1. As a return value of the `createTimer` methods on the `TimerService` interface

2. As the parameter of the `ejbTimeout` method implemented by the bean class

3. From the `TimerHandle` object for a previously created timer

The `TimerHandle` object provides a serializable handle to a `Timer` object. A bean can store this handle in a database or other persistent storage and later retrieve it. Entity beans using container-managed persistence may store the `TimerHandle` object in a CMP field.

7.3.2   Timers, Persistence, and Transactions

Timer objects are persistent objects managed by the container. This means that a timer object survives crashes of the container or process in which the enterprise bean created the timer. Typically, a container implementation would store timer objects in a database or other persistent storage, so the timer's notifications could be delivered and so the timer object could be accessed even after a container restart.

For entity beans, a timer object is associated with the bean instance—identified by a primary key—that created the timer. Thus, when a container process restarts after a crash, the container first activates an instance of that entity bean with the primary key and then, if there are any outstanding expired timer notifications for the bean, delivers these timer notifications to the bean by calling its `ejbTimeout` method. If an entity bean instance is removed, all timers associated with that bean instance are also removed.

Because there is no identity associated with instances of stateless session beans and message-driven beans, to deliver the timer notification, the container uses any bean instance of the same type as the stateless session or message-driven bean that created the timer.

Timer objects are also transactional objects. This means that timer creation, removal, and expiration typically happen within the context of a transaction. If that transaction rolls back, the timer operation is also rolled back. This results in the following semantics of timers and transactions:

- If a timer is created within a transaction and the transaction rolls back, the timer creation is rolled back—as if the timer were never created.

- If a previously created timer is deleted in a transaction and the transaction rolls back, the timer deletion is rolled back—as if the timer were never deleted. Timer notifications continue to be delivered.

- If a bean's `ejbTimeout` method has the transaction attribute `RequiresNew`, the container starts a transaction before delivering a timer notification. If that new transaction rolls back, the timer notification is also rolled back, and the container will redeliver the timer notification. Note that the `ejbTimeout` method's transaction attribute is restricted to either `RequiresNew` or `NotSupported`.

7.4 Conclusion

This chapter presented the fundamental concepts of entity beans. In particular, it described the two views of entity beans: the client view—both remote and local views—and the bean developer view. The chapter described the techniques for managing the persistent state of entity beans: container-managed persistence and the EJB QL language, and bean-managed persistence. The chapter also described how the container manages the life cycle of an entity bean instance and how the bean developer can make optimal use of the container's management of object state and persistence. Finally, it described the EJB timer service and how to use it with entity beans.

The next chapter presents the same Benefits Enrollment example that was used earlier to illustrate session beans but this time is used as an application that uses entity beans. The example application illustrates all the concepts discussed in this chapter with "real-world" code. The application illustrates many of the techniques for using entity beans to develop and integrate applications for different customers with different environments.

CHAPTER **8**

Entity Bean Application
Example

THIS chapter uses an example of a distributed application to illustrate how enterprise applications use entity beans to model business entities. The example application uses entity beans to store the persistent state of the enterprise application. The chapter also shows how organizations develop the respective components of the application and how, ultimately, the customer deploys the entire application. The example application illustrates

- **The implementation of several entity beans to highlight the various issues in managing persistence.** Entity beans use various styles to implement their persistence; thus, we illustrate the use of both CMP and BMP. We focus on the CMP programming model defined in the EJB 2.0 and 2.1 specifications. The example shows how to construct an abstract schema consisting of multiple entity beans related through their local interfaces, using container-managed relationships.

- **The use of local interfaces to develop lightweight entity beans.** The example contains several entity beans that have local interfaces. Local interfaces allow clients to access the entity beans in an efficient manner and also avoid the complexities of programming distributed objects.

- **The use of EJB QL to develop portable queries on the application's persistent state.** The example illustrates the use of EJB QL queries for find methods that can be directly invoked from clients, as well as for select methods, which are used internally by the bean.

- **The use of home business methods**. We show how home business methods are used to model aggregate operations that do not operate on a specific entity bean instance.

- **The techniques for developing applications for different customers with different operational environments.** An ISV would like to sell the application to as broad a range of customers and operational environments as possible. Our example illustrates how the ISV (1) uses entity beans with CMP to integrate its application with the customer's existing applications and database and (2) uses remote interfaces to allow flexibility in the deployment of the application with respect to client applications.

- **The design issues for remote interfaces.** The developer should design the remote interface so that its methods take into account the costs of distribution.

- **The techniques for caching an entity object's persistent state.** The example illustrates how to use the instance variables of an entity bean class, along with the `ejbLoad` and `ejbStore` methods, to cache the entity object's persistent state.

- **The correct approach that a client application, such as `EnrollmentBean`, takes to use the entity bean client-view API.**

- **The techniques for "subclassing" an entity bean with CMP to create an entity bean with BMP.** The subclass implements the data access methods.

- **The packaging of enterprise beans into J2EE standard files.** The example illustrates the packaging of enterprise beans and their dependent parts into the standard ejb-jar file and the J2EE enterprise application archive file (`.ear` file).

- **The parts of an application that do *not* have to be developed.** The example code is also interesting in what it does not include— namely, database access code in the CMP entity beans and no transaction or security management–related code. The deployment descriptors describe declaratively the transaction and security requirements for entity beans. Transaction management is described in Chapter 10, Understanding Transactions; security management, in Chapter 11, Managing Security.

This chapter begins with the description of the problem. Then, to give you a feel for the scope of the application, the application components are described from a high level, followed by detailed information on each part of the application, from the perspective of the vendor that developed the part.

8.1 Application Overview

Our example application illustrates the development and deployment of an enterprise application that consists of components developed by multiple vendors.

8.1.1 Problem Description

The example entity bean application implements a benefits self-service application. An employee uses this application to select and enroll in the benefits plans offered by the company. From the end-user perspective, the application is identical to the benefits application built using session beans, described in Chapter 4, Working with Session Beans. However, the design of the two applications differs as follows:

- The application uses entity beans with CMP to manage their persistent state. Because the entity beans use CMP, the benefits application contains no explicit database access code, and the amount of code in each entity bean is reduced drastically. Using CMP also facilitates storing the application's persistent state in a wide variety of persistence stores, including relational databases.

- Wombat Inc. developed the benefits application. Wombat is an ISV that specializes in the development of benefits applications used by enterprises. Because Wombat wants to sell its application to as many different enterprises as it can, its application must work in a myriad of operational environments. In contrast, Star Enterprise's IT department developed the application illustrated in Chapter 4. Because it was intended to be used only within Star Enterprise's own environment, that application was developed with no regard for the application's portability to other operational environments.

- The application described in this chapter allows dynamic changes to the configuration of the available medical and dental plans. For example, a benefits administrator at Star Enterprise can add and remove medical and dental plans to the benefits application. In contrast, the application in Chapter 4 requires redeployment to change the configuration of the available plans.

8.1.2 Main Parts of the Application

The example application presented here consists of multiple enterprise beans, Web applications, and databases. Typical for an application such as this, some parts already existed at Star Enterprise, whereas outside organizations developed the other parts. Figure 8.1 illustrates the logical parts of the application.

The application consists of two principal parts, which come from two sources:

1. The preexisting employee and payroll databases and PayrollEJB bean in the Star Enterprise operational environment

2. The Wombat benefits application, which consists of multiple enterprise beans and Web applications

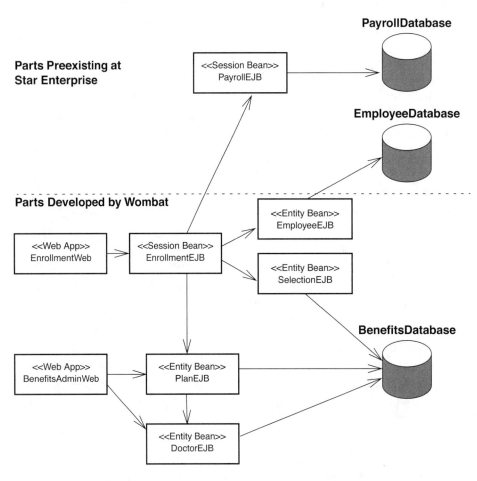

Figure 8.1   Logical Parts of the Entity Bean Benefits Application

Prior to the deployment of Wombat's benefits application, Star Enterprise used the `EmployeeDatabase`, `PayrollDatabase`, and PayrollEJB parts. These parts pertain to the following aspects of Star Enterprise's business:

- `EmployeeDatabase` contains information about Star Enterprise employees.

- `PayrollDatabase` contains payroll information about Star Enterprise.

- PayrollEJB is a stateless session bean that provides nonpayroll applications with secure access to the payroll database. Nonpayroll applications, including Wombat's benefits application, use PayrollEJB as the payroll integration interface.

Wombat, an ISV, has implemented the bulk of the benefits application. Wombat develops multiple Web applications and enterprise beans, as follows:

- EnrollmentWeb is a Web application that implements the presentation logic for the benefits enrollment process. A Wombat customer's employees, such as Star Enterprise employees when the application is deployed at Star Enterprise, access EnrollmentWeb via a browser.

- BenefitsAdminWeb is a Web application that implements the presentation logic for business processes used by the customer's benefits administration department. The benefits administration department uses BenefitsAdminWeb, for example, to customize the portfolio of plans offered to the employees.

- EnrollmentEJB, a stateful session bean that implements the benefits enrollment business process, uses several entity beans to perform its function.

- EmployeeEJB, an entity bean that encapsulates access to the customer's—Star Enterprise, in this example—employee information, uses CMP, and its main role is to allow deployment binding with the customer's employee database.

- SelectionEJB, PlanEJB, and DoctorEJB are entity beans that encapsulate the benefits selections, medical and dental plan information, and physician information, respectively.

- `BenefitsDatabase` stores the information used by the SelectionEJB, PlanEJB, and DoctorEJB entity beans.

8.1.3   Distributed Deployment

The EJB architecture provides the power and flexibility necessary to enable distributed deployment of various components in an enterprise application. Although it is possible to deploy all the Web and EJB components in a single J2EE server and to aggregate all the databases into a single database, the traditional division of "information ownership" by multiple departments within a large enterprise leads to a distributed deployment scenario illustrated in Figure 8.2. Star Enterprise has deployed the benefits application across multiple servers, including six servers within its own enterprise intranet.

The benefits department has deployed the EnrollmentWeb and BenefitsWeb Web applications on the Benefits Web server, and the enterprise beans EnrollmentEJB, SelectionEJB, EmployeeEJB, PlanEJB, and DoctorEJB on the Benefits App server. `BenefitsDatabase` is stored on the Benefits Database server. The enterprise bean PayrollEJB is deployed on the Payroll App server, which in turn provides access to the `PayrollDatabase` server. `EmployeeDatabase` is stored on the Human Resources (HR) Database server.

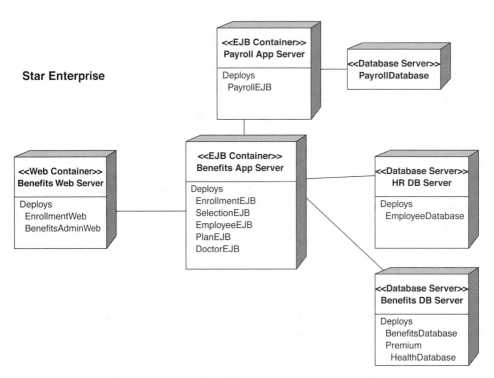

Figure 8.2   Benefits Application Deployment

8.2   Parts Developed by Wombat

Wombat Inc. is an ISV specializing in the development of applications for enterprises to use to administer benefits plans, such as medical and dental insurance plans. One Wombat application is a Web-based self-service Benefits Enrollment application. Employees of an enterprise use the application to make selections from multiple medical and dental plans offered to them by their employer.

Wombat's goal is to develop a single, generic Benefits Enrollment application and sell it to many customer enterprises. The Benefits Enrollment application is not an isolated application: It uses data provided by other applications or databases that exist in the customers' operational environment. This presents a challenge for Wombat: Every customer is likely to have a different implementation of the application or data with which the Benefits Enrollment application needs to integrate. For example, the enrollment application needs access to a database that contains information about employees, as well as access to the payroll system so that it can update benefits-related paycheck deductions. In addition, the enrollment application needs to have access to the plan-specific information provided by the insurance companies.

8.2.1   Overview of the Wombat Parts

Wombat develops the Web applications and enterprise beans, which are illustrated in Figure 8.3.

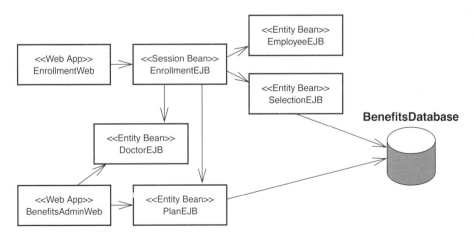

Figure 8.3   Web Applications and Enterprise Beans Developed by Wombat

Each of the following applications and enterprise beans is detailed throughout this section:

- **EnrollmentWeb**—A Web application that implements the presentation logic for the benefits enrollment process. A customer's employees use EnrollmentWeb to enroll into the offered medical and dental plans.

- **BenefitsAdminWeb**—A Web application that implements the presentation logic for business processes used by the customer's benefits administration department to configure and customize the medical and dental plans offered to the employees.

- **EnrollmentEJB**—A stateful session bean that implements the benefits enrollment business process.

- **EmployeeEJB**—An entity bean with CMP that encapsulates access to a customer's employee information so that it can accommodate the different representations of employee databases at different customer sites. CMP allows deployment binding with the customer's employee database. CMP also allows customers to implement their own database access code by writing a BMP entity bean that subclasses the CMP entity bean class.

- **SelectionEJB**—A CMP entity bean that encapsulates the benefits selections chosen by each employee.

- **PlanEJB**—A CMP entity bean that stores information about medical and dental plans and provides operations to search through plans.

- **DoctorEJB**—A CMP entity bean that stores information about physicians and dentists and provides operations to search for doctors, based on specified criteria.

The enterprise beans developed by Wombat store information in `BenefitsDatabase`. Wombat designed the `BenefitsDatabase` schema, and at deployment the customer creates the database at the customer site. Wombat also allows the customer to choose a different schema as a deployment option.

The following describe in greater detail the parts developed by Wombat.

8.2.2   EnrollmentEJB Session Bean

EnrollmentEJB is a stateful session bean that implements the benefits enrollment business process. EnrollmentEJB's home and component interfaces are the same as in the example in Chapter 4, Working with Session Beans. However, although an IT developer at Star Enterprise defined the interfaces in that chapter, Wombat defined the home and component interfaces shown in this chapter's alternative approach. Code Example 8.1 shows the EnrollmentEJB's home interface definition:

```
package com.wombat.benefits;

import javax.ejb.*;
import java.rmi.RemoteException;

public interface EnrollmentHome extends EJBHome {
    Enrollment create(int emplnum) throws RemoteException,
    CreateException, EnrollmentException;
}
```

Code Example 8.1   The EnrollmentHome Home Interface Defined by Wombat

Code Example 8.2 shows the definition of the EnrollmentEJB's remote component interface:

```
package com.wombat.benefits;

import javax.ejb.*;
import java.rmi.RemoteException;

public interface Enrollment extends EJBObject {
    EmployeeInfo getEmployeeInfo()
            throws RemoteException, EnrollmentException;
    Options getCoverageOptions()
            throws RemoteException, EnrollmentException;
    void setCoverageOption(int choice)
            throws RemoteException, EnrollmentException;
    Options getMedicalOptions()
            throws RemoteException, EnrollmentException;
    void setMedicalOption(int choice)
            throws RemoteException, EnrollmentException;
    Options getDentalOptions()
            throws RemoteException, EnrollmentException;
```

```
      void setDentalOption(int choice)
            throws RemoteException, EnrollmentException;
      boolean isSmoker()
            throws RemoteException, EnrollmentException;
      void setSmoker(boolean status)
            throws RemoteException, EnrollmentException;
      Summary getSummary()
            throws RemoteException, EnrollmentException;
      void commitSelections()
            throws RemoteException, EnrollmentException;
  }
```

Code Example 8.2   The Enrollment Remote Interface Defined by Wombat

The Enrollment and EnrollmentHome interfaces presented in this chapter are similar to those presented in Chapter 4. However, the interfaces presented here are implemented as remote interfaces, extending javax.ejb.EJBObject and javax.ejb.EJBHome, respectively. (The interfaces in Chapter 4 extended javax.ejb.EJBLocalObject and javax.ejb.EJBLocalHome.)

Wombat's developers consciously decided to make these interfaces remote instead of local when they designed the EnrollmentEJB entity bean. Wombat chose to use remote interfaces because they provide a location-independent client view. As a result, Wombat's customers, such as Star Enterprise, can deploy the EnrollmentEJB in a server other than the EnrollmentWeb application, thus allowing more flexible deployment choices. Moreover, the Benefits Enrollment application can be accessed by "rich client" applications and other enterprise applications, regardless of their location on the network. Such deployment and client access flexibility was critical for Wombat to achieve its goal of selling its benefits application to as many customers as possible.

However, the use of remote interfaces introduces new issues that need to be reflected in the design of the interfaces themselves:

- **Remote access is expensive.** Remote calls require more resources and use more overhead: They may traverse a network, they require client-side and server-side software to provide the distributed object invocation infrastructures, and they require arguments to be "deep copied" even when the client is in the same Java virtual machine. Hence, the cost of a remote call may be a hundred to a thousand times more than the cost of a local call.

Accordingly, the `Enrollment` remote interface must be designed to avoid a large number of fine-grained calls from the client and instead use a small number of large- or coarse-grained calls. Hence, the `Enrollment` interface defines the `getEmployeeInfo` method, which returns all employee information to the client in one call, using the serializable value class `EmployeeInfo`. Similarly, the `getSummary` method returns all benefits summary information in one method call, using the serializable value class `Summary`.

- **Remote access can lead to errors that are not encountered in local calls.** Because remote calls make requests on another computer over the network, any number of reasons can cause the remote call to fail, including network problems, resource/memory limits on the target computer, software errors, and so forth. The client must always be prepared to receive such exceptions and handle them if necessary. (For example, a Web component might handle an error by sending a meaningful error page to the browser.) To help identify these remote errors, the methods of the `Enrollment` and `EnrollmentHome` interface throw `java.rmi.RemoteException` as required for all remote interfaces.

- **State cannot be shared directly.** Because remote calls involve copying all arguments and return values, both the bean and the client code cannot assume that they have a reference to the actual Java object used by the other side. Thus, the bean and the client never share any state directly; they can have only copies of each other's state.

- **Remote references behave slightly differently from local references**. In particular, casting a remote reference to a derived type requires the use of the `javax.rmi.PortableRemoteObject.narrow` operation. Thus, the Enrollment-EJB's client—the EnrollmentWeb application—must use this `narrow` operation to cast `EJBHome` reference objects that are obtained through JNDI lookup to the `EnrollmentHome` interface.

`EnrollmentBean` Implementation Class

The implementation of the `EnrollmentBean` session bean class is similar to the implementation illustrated in Chapter 4. However, there are some key differences, as follows:

- EnrollmentEJB in Chapter 4 uses command beans to access the employee's database. EnrollmentEJB in this chapter uses the EmployeeEJB entity bean to encapsulate access to the employee information. Because the EmployeeEJB entity bean is implemented with CMP, the deployer can bind the EmployeeEJB bean with the customer's employee database in a standard way.

- EnrollmentEJB in Chapter 4 uses command beans to access the benefits selections in `BenefitsDatabase`. EnrollmentEJB in this chapter uses the SelectionEJB entity bean to encapsulate the access to the employees' current selections. In addition, because Wombat provides a CMP version of the SelectionEJB entity bean—the `SelectionBean` class—a customer can customize the format in which the selections are stored or even store them in a nonrelational database.

- EnrollmentEJB uses the PlanEJB entity bean to access the medical and dental plans offered to the employees. PlanEJB allows the medical and dental plan information to be dynamically updated by Wombat's customers through the BenefitsAdmin Web application. The EnrollmentEJB implementation in Chapter 4 relied on Java classes that hard-coded the plan information. This hard-coding prevented the dynamic update of plan information after the benefits application was deployed.

- EnrollmentEJB uses a command bean to update an employee's payroll with the deduction based on his or her benefits choices. Because each customer of Wombat may have a different payroll system, Wombat defines only a command bean interface: `DeductionUpdateBean`. The actual implementation class for this bean is provided by Wombat's customer, such as Star Enterprise. The class name is then set in the EnrollmentEJB's environment by the deployer.

Code Example A.4 on page 382 illustrates the source code for the `Enroll-mentBean` session bean class as it has been implemented for the example in this chapter. (Note that this implementation of `EnrollmentBean` differs from that in Chapter 4.)

Using Entity Bean Client-View Interfaces

The `EnrollmentBean` class illustrates how applications typically use the entity bean client-view interfaces. Recall that EnrollmentEJB is a client of the EmployeeEJB, SelectionEJB, and PlanEJB entity beans.

For example, let's look at how EnrollmentEJB uses the SelectionEJB entity bean. In the `ejbCreate` method, note that EnrollmentEJB uses the `findBy-PrimaryKey` method to look up an existing `Selection` object, as follows:

```
selection = selectionHome.findByPrimaryKey(
                  new Integer(employeeNumber));
```

After obtaining an object reference to the `Selection` object, EnrollmentEJB invokes a business method on the object. Here, it invokes the `Selection` object's `getCopy` method to read the current benefits selection values:

```
selCopy = selection.getCopy();
```

In the `commitSelections` method, EnrollmentEJB either creates a new `Selection` object by invoking the `create` method on the `SelectionHome` interface, or it updates the existing `Selection` object by invoking the `updateFromCopy` business method on the `Selection` object, as follows:

```
if (recordDoesNotExist) {
    selection = selectionHome.create(selCopy);
    recordDoesNotExist = false;
} else {
    selection.updateFromCopy(selCopy);
}
```

Note that EnrollmentEJB does not need to remove `Selection` objects. If it did, however, it would use the following code fragment:

```
selection.remove();
```

Alternatively, EnrollmentEJB could use the `SelectionHome` interface to remove a `Selection` object identified by its primary key:

```
selectionHome.remove(new Integer(employeeNumber));
```

EnrollmentEJB uses the other entity beans in much the same manner.

8.2.3   EmployeeEJB Entity Bean

EmployeeEJB is an entity bean that uses the container-managed persistence model defined in the EJB 2.0 and 2.1 specifications. EmployeeEJB provides an object-oriented view of the employee data used by the Benefits Enrollment application. The main role of this entity bean is to allow the integration between the benefits application and the customer's employee data.

Because Wombat does not impose rules about how a customer stores the information about its employees, customers must have the means to integrate the application with their employee data. Wombat uses the CMP mechanism to allow the deployer to bind EmployeeEJB with an existing employee database.

Wombat's customers have two choices while deploying the EmployeeEJB bean:

- **Using an object-relational mapping tool**—A customer can use an object-relational mapping tool to create a mapping from the Employee bean's abstract persistence schema—that is, its CMP and CMR fields—to the physical database schema in the preexisting employee database. In this case, the object-relational mapping tool generates the database access code.

- **Using bean-managed persistence**—Alternatively, a customer could develop a BMP entity bean that subclasses the CMP EmployeeBean class. The customer then would write the database access code.

However, Wombat designs the Employee and EmployeeHome interfaces to meet the needs of the Benefits Enrollment application.

EmployeeEJB's Primary Key

Wombat uses the employee number as the primary key for the EmployeeEJB entity bean. Its type is the class java.lang.Integer. Note that it would be an error if the employee number were the Java primitive int, because the EJB specification requires that the primary key type for an entity bean be a Java class. Furthermore, this requirement implies that primitive types that are not serializable Java classes cannot be used directly for the primary key type.

Employee Local Interface

Because EmployeeEJB is accessed only from EnrollmentEJB and both are packaged in the same benefits application, EmployeeEJB defines only local interfaces. Code Example 8.3 shows the Employee local interface definition:

```
public interface Employee extends EJBLocalObject {
    Integer getEmployeeNumber();
    String getFirstName();
    String getLastName();
    Date getBirthDate();
}
```

Code Example 8.3   The Employee Local Interface

The Employee local interface defines methods that allow its client, the EnrollmentEJB bean, to access each employee's employee number, first and last names, and date of birth. Note that these methods are fine-grained: One method returns one piece of data rather than a single method returning an aggregation of all the pieces of data. Typically, the EnrollmentEJB bean would make several calls on the Employee interface to eventually retrieve all fields for an employee. Making multiple method calls, with each method call retrieving individual data fields, is effective because local EJB calls are very efficient in typical application server implementations.

Note that the Employee local interface does not define any methods that allow clients to modify EmployeeBean's state. This implies that the EmployeeEJB is a *read-only* bean. Most EJB containers are designed to efficiently manage such read-only beans.

The EmployeeHome **Home Interface**

Code Example 8.4 shows the EmployeeHome interface definition:

```
package com.wombat.benefits;
import javax.ejb.*;

public interface EmployeeHome extends EJBLocalHome {
    // find methods
    Employee findByPrimaryKey(Integer employeeNumber)
            throws FinderException;
}
```

Code Example 8.4 The EmployeeHome Home Interface

The EmployeeHome interface defines only the mandatory findByPrimaryKey method. It defines no create methods, because the Wombat Benefits Enrollment application does not need to create new employee objects in the customer databases.

The EmployeeBean **Entity Bean Class**

The EmployeeBean class illustrates how simple it is to develop an entity bean with CMP. Note that the entity bean contains no database operations. Section 8.3.1, The Employee Database and Deployment of EmployeeEJB, on page 286 explains how the deployer binds the container-managed fields with the columns of the preexisting `EmployeeDatabase` at Star Enterprise. Note also that the entity bean class contains no implementations of any find methods, although the home interface defines the `findByPrimaryKey` method. Because EmployeeEJB is an entity bean with CMP, the EJB container supplies the implementations of its find methods. Code Example 8.5 shows the source code of the `EmployeeBean` entity bean class:

```
package com.wombat.benefits;

import javax.ejb.*;
import java.util.Date;
import com.wombat.AbstractEntityBean;

public abstract class EmployeeBean extends AbstractEntityBean {
    // Container-managed fields

    public abstract Integer getEmployeeNumber(); // primary key field
    public abstract void setEmployeeNumber(Integer n);

    public abstract String getFirstName();
    public abstract void setFirstName(String s);

    public abstract String getLastName();
    public abstract void setLastName(String s);

    public abstract Date getBirthDate();
    public abstract void setBirthDate(Date d);
}
```

Code Example 8.5   `EmployeeBean` Class Implementation

The `EmployeeBean` class, essentially a pure data object that models a business entity, is one of the simplest examples of a CMP entity bean class. The `Employee-Bean` class contains only CMP fields, and these fields define the persistent state of the employee. The class has no create methods and no relationships with other beans.

The `AbstractEntityBean` class, which `EmployeeBean` imports, is a utility class developed by Wombat. This class contains default implementations of the `javax.ejb.EntityBean` methods. The class was developed to make it easy to implement entity bean classes that do not need to use methods in the `EntityBean` interface.

There are some important things to note about the implementation of an entity bean class, particularly concerning container-managed fields and the primary key. The `employeeNumber`, `lastName`, `firstName`, and `birthDate` fields are container-managed fields of the entity bean class and are declared as such in the EmployeeEJB's deployment descriptor. These fields are also *virtual* fields. Virtual fields are represented in the `EmployeeBean` class as pairs of get and set methods. The method names are derived from the CMP field names and follow the Java-Beans design pattern. The EJB specification mandates that the get and set methods be defined as `public`, even though a client program never directly accesses them. The container uses these methods to synchronize the content of the fields they represent with the information in the database. These methods must be `public` so that the container can move the data between the fields and the database to keep them synchronized.

8.2.4   SelectionEJB Entity Bean

The SelectionEJB entity bean stores an employee's benefits selections, using CMP. By using CMP, the bean can be developed with no database dependences: Wombat's customers can use any database of their choice, including nonrelational databases, to store the persistent state of the bean.

SelectionEJB's Primary Key

Wombat uses the employee number as the primary key for the SelectionEJB entity bean. The type of the primary key is `java.lang.Integer`.

`Selection` Local Interface

Wombat designed SelectionEJB's local interface to meet the needs of its client, the EnrollmentEJB session bean. The local interface uses the `SelectionCopy` value object to pass the information between the SelectionEJB entity bean and its client, through its `getCopy` and `updateFromCopy` business methods. Code Example 8.6 shows the `Selection` interface definition:

```
package com.wombat.benefits;
```

```
import javax.ejb.*;

public interface Selection extends EJBLocalObject {
    SelectionCopy getCopy()
        throws SelectionException;
    void updateFromCopy(SelectionCopy copy)
        throws SelectionException;
}
```

Code Example 8.6   The Selection Interface Definition

The Selection interface defines methods that its clients use to obtain and update an employee's benefits selection. In the Wombat benefits application, the EnrollmentEJB session bean is the client of SelectionEJB. EnrollmentEJB uses the Selection interface's getCopy method to obtain a transient copy of the employee's benefits selection. The SelectionCopy object stores this data in memory while the employee selects the benefits options. When the employee commits those selections, EnrollmentEJB uses the updateFromCopy method to write the contents of the SelectionCopy object to the persistent fields of the SelectionEJB entity bean, thus saving the selection information to the database. Code Example 8.7 shows the code for the SelectionCopy class:

```
package com.wombat.benefits;

import com.wombat.plan.Plan;

public class SelectionCopy {
    private Employee employee;
    private int coverage;
    private Plan medicalPlan;
    private Plan dentalPlan;
    private boolean smokerStatus;

    public Employee getEmployee() { return employee; }
    public int getCoverage() { return coverage; }
    public Plan getMedicalPlan() { return medicalPlan; }
    public Plan getDentalPlan() { return dentalPlan; }
    public boolean isSmoker() { return smokerStatus; }
```

```
    public void setEmployee(Employee v) { employee = v; }
    public void setCoverage(int v) { coverage = v; }
    public void setMedicalPlan(Plan v) { medicalPlan = v; }
    public void setDentalPlan(Plan v) { dentalPlan = v; }
    public void setSmoker(boolean v) { smokerStatus = v; }
}
```

Code Example 8.7 The SelectionCopy Value Object

You might wonder why an entity bean with a local client view uses a value object such as SelectionCopy. Value objects are a useful way to avoid fine-grained data access, something you might want to consider when access is across a distributed network. A bean can also use a value object to temporarily hold information that the bean collects in the course of its processing but that the bean may not ultimately save to a database.

SelectionHome **Home Interface**

Code Example 8.8 shows the definition for the SelectionHome home interface:

```
package com.wombat.benefits;

import javax.ejb.*;

public interface SelectionHome extends EJBLocalHome {
Selection create(SelectionCopy copy)
    throws CreateException;

Selection findByPrimaryKey(Integer emplNumber)
    throws FinderException;
}
```

Code Example 8.8 The SelectionHome Home Interface

Note how the SelectionHome interface uses the SelectionCopy object as the argument of the create method. A client uses this method to create an entity object that stores an employee's benefits selections from a copy of the information passed by the client.

The SelectionHome interface also defines the mandatory findByPrimaryKey method. This method finds the Selection object by using the primary key, which is the employee number.

SelectionBean Entity Bean Class

Code Example 8.9 shows the abstract schema portion of the SelectionBean entity bean implementation:

```
public abstract class SelectionBean extends AbstractEntityBean {
    // Container-managed persistence fields
    public abstract Integer getEmployeeNumber(); // primary key field
    public abstract void setEmployeeNumber(Integer n);

    public abstract int getCoverage();
    public abstract void setCoverage(int c);

    public abstract boolean getSmokerStatus();
    public abstract void setSmokerStatus(boolean s);

    // Container-managed relationship fields
    public abstract Plan getMedicalPlan();
    public abstract void setMedicalPlan(Plan p);

    public abstract Plan getDentalPlan();
    public abstract void setDentalPlan(Plan p);
    ......
}
```

Code Example 8.9   Abstract Schema for the SelectionBean Entity Bean Class

The abstract schema defines the bean's persistent state. (For the complete listing of the source code for the SelectionBean entity bean class implementation, see Code Example A.5 on page 392.)

The `SelectionBean` class has three CMP fields: `coverage`, `smokerStatus`, and `employeeNumber`. These CMP fields are declared by using pairs of set and get methods.

The `SelectionBean` class also has two container-managed relationships, represented as CMR fields: `medicalPlan` and `dentalPlan`. Like CMP fields, CMR fields are declared by using pairs of set and get methods. The argument and return value types for CMR fields are the local interfaces of the related beans. The `medicalPlan` and `dentalPlan` CMR fields provide references to different instances of the PlanEJB bean. In the deployment descriptor, these fields are declared to be many-to-one relationships because many instances of a SelectionEJB bean are associated with a single medical plan or dental plan bean instance. Also in the deployment descriptor, the `medicalPlan` and `dentalPlan` relationships are declared to be unidirectional, implying that no corresponding CMR field in the PlanEJB bean refers to a SelectionEJB instance.

Using CMR fields to manage references to other enterprise beans has two benefits:

1. It simplifies the development of the `SelectionBean` methods because they can work directly with object references rather than having to convert object references to primary keys.

2. It avoids hard-coding into the `SelectionBean` class the database representation of the relationships to the other entity beans. As a result, a deployer is free to choose how to represent the relationships in the underlying database schema.

Note that although it could have done so, the SelectionEJB class does not define a container-managed relationship with the EmployeeEJB bean. At first glance, it seems natural to define this relationship as container managed because there is a SelectionEJB instance for each EmployeeEJB instance. In addition, SelectionEJB and EmployeeEJB use the same primary key: the employee number.

However, Wombat's developers want to give their customers the flexibility to store instances of these two beans in separate databases and not be compelled to store them together in the same database. To allow customers this flexibility, Wombat's developers chose not to define the relationship between the SelectionEJB and EmployeeEJB beans as a container-managed relationship. Generally, when two beans are related using a container-managed relationship, they must be stored in the same database. Keeping related beans in the same database allows it to manage the relationship more efficiently; for example, a relational database might use a foreign key to model the relationship. Because Wombat knows that its customers are likely to have two separate databases—an employee database managed by the human resources department and a benefits database managed by the benefits department—the developers decided to keep the EmployeeEJB and SelectionEJB beans independent. By doing so, Wombat customers can store these bean instances in separate databases or together in one database. (Although CMP allows multiple databases to be used, EJB products that permit multiple databases are still evolving.)

Let's take a closer look at the implementation of the `SelectionBean` methods. The `SelectionBeanCMP` class implements three sets of methods:

1. The business methods defined in the `Selection` local interface

2. The `ejbCreate` and `ejbPostCreate` methods that correspond to the `create` method defined in the `SelectionHome` interface

3. The container callbacks defined in the `EntityBean` interface

The `SelectionBean` class follows the EJB specification rules and does not implement the `ejbFind` methods corresponding to the find methods defined in the `SelectionHome` interface.

Business Methods

The business methods `getCopy` and `updateFromCopy` read and write the container-managed fields. The container loads and stores the contents of the container-managed fields according to the rules defined in the EJB specification. The business methods can assume that the contents of the container-managed fields are always up-to-date, even if other transactions change the underlying selection record in the database.

The code for the business methods demonstrates how an enterprise might implement simple business rules. For example, the `updateCoverage` helper method checks that the value of the coverage field is an allowed value, whereas the `updateMedicalPlan` helper method optionally checks that the value of `medicalPlan` is indeed a medical plan rather than a dental plan.

The `ejbCreate` and `ejbPostCreate` Methods

The `ejbCreate` method sets values into `SelectionBean`'s container-managed persistence fields from the values passed to it in the method parameter. In particular, the method sets the primary key by using the `setEmployeeNumber` method. Setting the primary key establishes the identity of the bean instance. After the `ejbCreate` method completes, the container extracts the values of the container-managed fields and creates a representation of the selection object in the database. Note that `ejb-Create` returns a **null** value even though the return value type is declared to be the primary key type. According to the EJB 2.1 specification, the container ignores the value returned from an `ejbCreate` method of an entity bean with container-managed persistence. However, the EJB 2.1 specification requires that the type of the `ejbCreate` method be the primary key type to allow a subclass of the `SelectionBean` class to be an entity bean with bean-managed persistence.

The `ejbPostCreate` method sets values of the CMR fields `medicalPlan` and `dentalPlan`. The EJB 2.1 specification does not allow CMR fields to be set in the `ejbCreate` method. Thus, CMR fields should be set either in the `ejbPostCreate` method or in a business method.

Life-Cycle Methods

The `SelectionBean` class inherits most of the default `EntityBean` life-cycle method implementations from the `AbstractEntityBean` class, providing an implementation only of the `setEntityContext` method. Entity bean classes typically use the `setEntityContext` method to query their environment and customize their business logic as part of their initialization. `SelectionBean`'s `setEntityContext` method calls the `readEnvironment` helper method, which accesses the environment entry available with the key `java:comp/env/checkPlanType` to do the `lookup` operation in Code Example 8.10:

```
private void readEnvironment() {
    try {
        Context ictx = new InitialContext();
        Boolean val = (Boolean)ictx.lookup(
                "java:comp/env/checkPlanType");
        checkPlanType = val.booleanValue();
        employeeHome = (EmployeeHome)ictx.lookup(
                "java:comp/env/ejb/EmployeeEJB");
    } catch (Exception ex) {
        throw new EJBException(ex);
    }
}
```

Code Example 8.10 `SelectionBean`'s `readEnvironment` Method

The value of the entry parameterizes the business logic of the bean. If the value of the environment entry is `true`, the `setMedicalPlan` and `setDentalPlan` methods check that the value of the plan to be set is indeed of the expected plan type. If the value is `false`, they do not perform these checks. The application assembler sets the value of the environment entry at application assembly. Wombat made the plan type checks optional to allow the application assembler to improve performance by omitting them if the clients of SelectionEJB are known to set the plan types correctly. We added this somewhat artificial optional check to illustrate how to use the enterprise bean environment entries to parameterize the business logic at application assembly or deployment.

8.2.5   PlanEJB Entity Bean

The PlanEJB entity bean represents medical and dental plan information that is obtained from insurance providers. This entity bean has been implemented to use container-managed persistence. PlanEJB is accessed from the EnrollmentEJB bean, as well as from the benefits administration Web application. This entity bean allows client applications to obtain details of medical and dental plans, as well as to run queries on all existing plan objects. The bean also has a facility, which uses the timer service, to e-mail to administrators on a daily basis statistics of employee enrollment in each plan.

The primary key for the PlanEJB entity bean is a unique plan identifier that is a `java.lang.String` type. The benefits department assigns unique identifiers to plan instances.

`Plan` Local Interface

Code Example 8.11 shows the methods defined by the `Plan` local interface:

```
public interface Plan extends EJBLocalObject {
    // values of planType CMP field
    public final int MEDICAL_PLAN = 1;
    public final int DENTAL_PLAN = 2;

    int getPlanType() throws PlanException;
    String getPlanId();
    String getPlanName();
    double getAgeFactor();
    void setAgeFactor(double a);
```

```
        double getCoverageFactor();
        void setCoverageFactor(double c);
        double getSmokerCost();
        void setSmokerCost(double cost);

        double getCost(int coverage, int age, boolean smokerStatus)
            throws PlanException;
        void addDoctor(Doctor doctor) throws PlanException;
        boolean removeDoctor(Doctor doctor) throws PlanException;
        Collection getAllDoctors() throws PlanException;
        Collection getDoctorsByName(Doctor template)
            throws PlanException;
        Collection getDoctorsBySpecialty(String specialty)
            throws PlanException;
    }
```

Code Example 8.11 The Plan Local Interface

The Plan local interface methods perform the following operations:

- The getPlanType method returns an integer value that indicates the type of benefits plan. The value is equal to Plan.MEDICAL_PLAN if the plan is a medical plan and to Plan.DENTAL_PLAN if the plan is a dental plan.

- The getPlanId method returns the unique identifier—the primary key—of the plan.

- The getPlanName method returns the name of the medical or dental plan.

- The getCost method returns the monthly premium charged by the plan provider. The premium is determined by the benefits enrollee's coverage category, age, and smoker status.

- The set/getSmokerCost, set/getAgeFactor, set/getCoverageFactor methods retrieve and update the smoker cost, age factor, and coverage factor of the plan.

- The addDoctor method adds a doctor to the plan.

- The removeDoctor method removes a doctor from the plan.

- The `getAllDoctors` method returns a collection of `Doctor` objects that participate in the plan. The `Doctor` class is described later.

- The `getDoctorsByName` method returns a collection of participating doctors whose names match the information in the template supplied as a method argument.

- The `getDoctorsBySpecialty` method returns all the doctors of a given specialty.

`PlanHome` Home Interface

Code Example 8.12 shows the definition of the `PlanHome` home interface:

```
public interface PlanHome extends EJBLocalHome {
    // create methods
    Plan create(String planId, String planName, int planType,
        double coverageFactor, double ageFactor, double smokerCost)
        throws CreateException;

    // find methods
    Plan findByPrimaryKey(String planID) throws FinderException;
    Collection findMedicalPlans() throws FinderException;
    Collection findDentalPlans() throws FinderException;
    Collection findByDoctor(String firstName, String lastName)
        throws FinderException;

    // home business methods
    void updateSmokerCosts(double cost) throws FinderException;
    String[] getMedicalPlanNames() throws FinderException;
    String[] getDentalPlanNames() throws FinderException;
}
```

Code Example 8.12 The `PlanHome` Home Interface

The `PlanHome` interface defines one `create` method. The benefits administration Web application uses this `create` method to add a new medical or dental plan to the benefit options provided to employees. The `PlanHome` interface also defines the find methods used by the benefits application. The find methods that can potentially return more than one object return these objects as a Java Collection and are also implemented as EJB QL queries in the deployment descriptor for PlanEJB.

- The findByPrimaryKey method returns the Plan object for a given plan identifier. The plan identifier is the primary key that uniquely identifies the plan.

- The findMedicalPlans method returns as a Collection all the medical plans configured in this home interface. Each object in the returned Collection implements the Plan interface. The EJB QL query for this method is provided in PlanEJB's deployment descriptor. The query is as follows:

```
SELECT DISTINCT OBJECT(p) FROM PlanBean p WHERE p.planType = 1
```

- The findDentalPlans method returns all the dental plans configured in this home interface. Each object in the returned Collection implements the Plan interface. The EJB QL query for this method is as follows:

```
SELECT DISTINCT OBJECT(p) FROM PlanBean p WHERE p.planType = 2
```

- The findByDoctor method returns configured in this home interface all the plans that include a specified doctor in their doctors list. This find method is implemented with an EJB QL query that navigates from the PlanEJB bean to the DoctorEJB bean. The EJB QL query for the findByDoctor method is as follows:

```
SELECT DISTINCT OBJECT(p) FROM PlanBean p, IN(p.doctors) d
    WHERE d.firstName = ?1 AND d.lastName = ?2
```

In this query, the FROM clause declares an identification variable d whose values are DoctorEJB instances belonging to PlanEJB's one-to-many CMR field doctors. The WHERE clause restricts the set of doctors to those having the requested first and last names. The SELECT clause thus returns PlanEJB instances containing doctors satisfying the condition in the WHERE clause.

In addition, the PlanHome interface defines the home business methods, whose operations are not restricted to a particular bean instance. Instead, home business methods are used to implement aggregate operations or queries on an entire set of benefits plans. The home business methods are

- **updateSmokerCost**—updates the smoker cost for all plans

- **getMedicalPlanNames**—returns an array of medical plan names

- **getDentalPlanNames**—returns an array of dental plan names

PlanBean Implementation Class

The PlanBean class is an abstract class that follows the requirements for an entity bean class with container-managed persistence. Code Example A.6 on page 396 lists the complete source code for the PlanBean entity bean class implementation.

Code Example 8.13 shows just the abstract schema for PlanBean. The abstract schema defines the bean's persistent state:

```
public abstract class PlanBean extends AbstractEntityBean implements
        TimedObject {
    // Container-managed persistence fields
    public abstract String getPlanId();
    public abstract void setPlanId(String s);

    public abstract String getPlanName();
    public abstract void setPlanName(String s);

    public abstract int getPlanType();
    public abstract void setPlanType(int s);

    public abstract double getCoverageFactor();
    public abstract void setCoverageFactor(double s);

    public abstract double getAgeFactor();
    public abstract void setAgeFactor(double s);

    public abstract double getSmokerCost();
    public abstract void setSmokerCost(double s);

    // container-managed relationships (CMR fields)
    public abstract Collection getDoctors();
```

```
    public abstract void setDoctors(Collection doctors);
      ...
}
```

Code Example 8.13 Abstract Schema for the `PlanBean` Entity Bean Class

`PlanBean` has six CMP fields that represent the persistent state of PlanEJB. These fields, declared in the deployment descriptor, are `planId`, `planName`, `planType`, `coverageFactor`, `ageFactor`, and `smokerCost`. In the `PlanBean` class, the CMP fields are represented as pairs of get and set methods.

`PlanBean` also has one CMR field, `doctors`, which represents a container-managed relationship to the DoctorEJB bean. This relationship is a many-to-many relationship: Each plan is associated with multiple doctors, and each doctor may participate in several plans. As a result, the `setDoctors` and `getDoctors` methods have argument and return types that are `java.util.Collection` types. The doctor/plan relationship is also declared as a bidirectional relationship. In a bidirectional relationship between two entity beans, each bean has a CMR field referencing the other bean. For the doctor/plan bidirectional relationship, PlanEJB declares a CMR field `doctors` that references DoctorEJB, which in turn has a CMR field referencing back to PlanEJB. Section 8.2.6, DoctorEJB Entity Bean, on page 279 discusses this in more detail.

Remember from the previous section that SelectionEJB declared two one-to-one relationships to PlanEJB. However, those were declared as unidirectional relationships from SelectionEJB to PlanEJB. Hence the `PlanBean` class does not declare a CMR field referencing back to SelectionEJB.

`PlanBean` has five types of methods:

- **Business methods**—`PlanBean` implements the business methods declared in the local interface.

- **Home business methods**—`PlanBean` implements the home business methods from the home interface.

- **Select methods**—`PlanBean` includes `ejbSelect` methods that are used to declare and invoke EJB QL queries from other methods of `PlanBean`.

- **`ejbTimeout` method**—`PlanBean` includes the `ejbTimeout` method, which is called when the bean's timer expires.

- **Life-cycle methods**—`PlanBean` includes the life-cycle methods `ejbCreate` and `ejbPostCreate`.

Business Methods

The business methods implement the operations declared in the local interface. The business methods—`getCost`, `addDoctor`, `removeDoctor`, `getAllDoctors`, `get-DoctorsByName`, and `getDoctorsBySpecialty`—are called from EnrollmentEJB and from the benefits administration Web application.

The `addDoctor` and `removeDoctor` methods operate on the `Collection` returned from the `getDoctor` method. The code for these methods is shown in Code Example 8.14:

```
public void addDoctor(Doctor doctor) throws PlanException {
    Collection doctors = getDoctors();
    doctors.add(doctor);
}

public boolean removeDoctor(Doctor doctor) throws PlanException {
    Collection doctors = getDoctors();
    return doctors.remove(doctor);
}
```

Code Example 8.14 Implementation of the `addDoctor` and `removeDoctor` Methods

The `addDoctor` method first obtains the doctors *managed* `Collection`, a live `Collection`; any changes made to the `Collection` cause the bean's persistent state to be changed. The `addDoctor` method simply adds the new DoctorEJB instance represented by the `doctor` argument to the managed `Collection`. Note that it is not necessary to add the PlanEJB instance to the corresponding plans `Collection` held by the DoctorEJB instance; the container automatically sets the other side of a bidirectional relationship when the first side is set.

The `removeDoctor` method obtains the doctors managed `Collection` and removes the `doctor` argument from the `Collection`. Again, it is not necessary to remove this PlanEJB instance from the corresponding `Collection` held by the DoctorEJB instance, because the container automatically does this for you.

The `getAllDoctors` method returns a `Collection` of all DoctorEJB instances related to a PlanEJB instance—that is, all the doctors participating in a particular insurance plan. Code Example 8.15 shows the code for `getAllDoctors`:

```
public Collection getAllDoctors() throws FinderException {
        Collection doctors = getDoctors();
        Collection doctorsCopy = new ArrayList(doctors);
    return doctorsCopy;
}
```

Code Example 8.15 Implementation of the getAllDoctors Method

You might wonder why the Plan local interface does not expose the getDoctors method. You might also wonder why the getAllDoctors method returns a new Collection rather than returning the doctors managed collection directly. The answer lies in the behavior of managed collections and transactions.

Managed collections are live collections whose state needs to be saved to the database when the transaction to which they are involved commits. Thus, managed collections are valid only in the transaction in which they were obtained. If a client of PlanEJB does not have an active transaction, the container starts a new transaction before calling the getAllDoctors method and commits the transaction immediately after the getAllDoctors method ends. In this situation, if it were given the doctors managed collection directly, the client would not be able to access the collection, as the transaction would have already committed. Operations on the collection at this point, such as obtaining an iterator, are out of the context of a transaction and would throw IllegalStateException.

To avoid such problems, Wombat's developers instead return a copy of the managed collection doctors to the client. The doctorsCopy collection is an *unmanaged* collection. A client can access an unmanaged collection at any time, without having to be within the context of a transaction, and changes to the unmanaged collection are not saved to the persistent state of the PlanEJB instance.

The getDoctorsByName method returns all doctors with the given first name and last name. To do this, the method invokes the ejbSelectDoctorsByName method. Similarly, the getDoctorsBySpecialty method returns all doctors with the given specialty. The method invokes the ejbSelectDoctorsBySpecialty method to accomplish this.

Home Business Methods

The home business methods implement the methods declared in the home interface. These methods execute on an instance that is not associated with a specific identity. As a result, they can perform only the logic that does not operate on a specific bean instance. They cannot access the identity of the bean instance that is executing the method through the `getPrimaryKey`, `getEJBObject`, and `getEJBLocalObject` methods on the `EntityContext` interface. Usually, the home business methods implement aggregate operations or queries on an entire set of beans.

The `ejbHomeUpdateSmokerCosts` method implements the `updateSmokerCosts` method declared in the `PlanHome` home interface (Code Example 8.16):

```
public void ejbHomeUpdateSmokerCosts(double cost)
        throws FinderException {
    Collection allPlans = ejbSelectAllPlans();
    Iterator itr = allPlans.iterator();
    while ( itr.hasNext() ) {
        Plan plan = (Plan)itr.next();
        plan.setSmokerCost(cost);
    }
}
```

Code Example 8.16 Implementation of the `ejbHomeUpdateSmokerCosts` Method

This method uses the `cost` argument value to set one smoker cost for all plans. The method first obtains a `Collection` of all plans, using the `ejbSelectAllPlans` method, and then iterates over all the plans, setting the cost for each plan.

Two other home business methods—the `ejbHomeGetMedicalPlanNames` and the `ejbHomeGetDentalPlanNames` methods—are shown in Code Example 8.17:

```
// get all medical plan names
public String[] ejbHomeGetMedicalPlanNames()
        throws FinderException {
    Collection names = ejbSelectPlanNames(Plan.MEDICAL_PLAN);
    return (String[])names.toArray(new String[names.size()]);
}

// get all dental plan names
public String[] ejbHomeGetDentalPlanNames()
        throws FinderException {
    Collection names = ejbSelectPlanNames(Plan.DENTAL_PLAN);
```

```
        return (String[])names.toArray(new String[names.size()]);
    }
```

Code Example 8.17 Implementation of Home Business Methods

Depending on the application's needs, it can be more efficient to use a home business method than a find method. For example, a client can use the home business method ejbHomeGetMedicalPlanNames to retrieve an array of all medical plan names in one operation. The home business method returns a Collection or array of fields of a bean. This is often more efficient than using a find method, which can return only a Collection of enterprise bean local or remote interfaces. If the client instead uses the PlanHome findMedicalPlans method, the client gets back a Collection of enterprise bean interfaces. The client then has to iterate over the Collection and extract each plan name one at a time.

Select Methods

The ejbSelect methods declare EJB QL queries that are used internally by a bean class. The queries themselves are defined in the deployment descriptor. The Plan-Bean class declares five ejbSelect methods, shown in Code Example 8.18:

```
public abstract Collection ejbSelectAllPlans()
        throws FinderException;
public abstract Collection ejbSelectPlanNames(int planType)
        throws FinderException;
public abstract Collection ejbSelectDoctorsByName
        (String planId, String fname, String lname)
        throws FinderException;
public abstract Collection ejbSelectDoctorsBySpecialty
        (String planId, String specialty) throws FinderException;
public abstract long ejbSelectNumEmployeesInPlan(Plan plan)
        throws FinderException;
```

Code Example 8.18 The ejbSelect Method Declarations in the PlanBean Class

The ejbSelectAllPlans method returns all PlanEJB instances. The EJB QL query for this select method does not have a WHERE clause:

```
SELECT DISTINCT OBJECT(p) FROM PlanBean p
```

The `ejbSelectPlanNames` method returns the names of all plans of a given plan type. The EJB QL query for this method is

```
SELECT p.planName FROM PlanBean p WHERE p.planType = ?1
```

The `ejbSelectDoctorsByName` method returns for a given plan all participating doctors whose first and last names match the specified name parameters. The EJB QL query for this method is

```
SELECT DISTINCT OBJECT(d) FROM PlanBean p, IN(p.doctors) d WHERE
p.planId = ?1 AND d.firstName = ?2 AND d.lastName = ?3
```

The `ejbSelectDoctorsBySpecialty` method returns for a given plan all participating doctors with a particular specialty. The returned `Collection` of doctors is ordered by each doctor's last name. The EJB QL query for this method is

```
SELECT DISTINCT OBJECT(d) FROM PlanBean p, IN(p.doctors) d WHERE
p.planId = ?1 AND d.specialty = ?2 ORDER BY d.lastName
```

The `ejbSelectNumEmployeesInPlan` method returns the number of employees who have chosen a given plan. The EJB QL query for this method is

```
SELECT COUNT(s) FROM SelectionBean s WHERE s.medicalPlan = ?1
OR s.dentalPlan = ?1
```

Life-Cycle Methods

There are two life-cycle methods in the PlanEJB bean. The `ejbCreate` method initializes the container-managed persistence fields of `PlanBean`, using arguments that the client passes to the method. The `ejbPostCreate` initializes the timer that provides daily statistics to plan administrators. Code Example 8.19 shows the code used to create a timer:

```
TimerService timerService = entityContext.getTimerService();
timerService.createTimer(midnight, interval, null);
```

Code Example 8.19 Creating a Timer

To create a timer, the entity bean's identity—its primary key—needs to be available, because a `Timer` object is associated with the instance of the entity bean that created it. Hence, the timer can be created in the `ejbPostCreate` method but not in the `ejbCreate` method.

The `TimerService.createTimer` method used in Code Example 8.19 takes three parameters, two of which have values:

- **midnight**—A `java.util.Date` object whose value corresponds to midnight on the day the bean instance was created

- **interval**—A `long` type whose value represents the number of milliseconds in one day

Together, these parameters indicate that the timer will first expire at midnight on the first day and then at midnight every day thereafter. Let's now look at what happens when the timer expires.

ejbTimeout Method

The `PlanBean` class has an `ejbTimeout` method. This method is defined in the `TimedObject` interface, which the `PlanBean` class implements. This method is called by the EJB container when the timer expires—at midnight every day. The code in the `ejbTimeout` method gets statistics about the `PlanBean` instances—the number of employees who have subscribed to each plan—and sends them to the administrators. It obtains these numbers by calling the select method `ejbSelectNumEmployeesInPlan`. Code Example 8.20 shows the code for the `ejbTimeout` method:

```
public void ejbTimeout(javax.ejb.Timer timer) {
    try {
        // get the number of employees who have subscribed to
        // this plan
        long numEmployeesInThisPlan = ejbSelectNumEmployeesInPlan(
                (Plan)entityContext.getEJBLocalObject());

        String emailText = "Plan " + getPlanName() + " has "
                + numEmployeesInThisPlan +" employees.";

        // email the text
        InitialContext ic = new InitialContext();
        Session session = (Session)ic.lookup(
```

```
                    "java:comp/env/MailSession");
          String toAddress = (String)ic.lookup(
                    "java:comp/env/toAddress");
          String fromAddress = (String)ic.lookup(
                    "java:comp/env/fromAddress");

          Message msg = new MimeMessage(session);
          msg.setFrom(new InternetAddress(fromAddress));
          msg.addRecipient(Message.RecipientType.TO,
                    new InternetAddress(toAddress));
          msg.setSubject("Statistics");
          msg.setText(emailText);

          Transport.send(msg);
       } catch ( Exception ex ) {
          throw new EJBException(ex);
       }
   }
}
```

Code Example 8.20 The ejbTimeout Method

The ejbTimeout method obtains the statistics by calling a select method and composing a text message string to be sent by e-mail to the plan administrator. It sends the e-mail message using the JavaMail™ APIs. Because these APIs are a standard part of the J2EE platform, they are available in all application servers that support J2EE. Typically, application servers provide an implementation of these APIs, which can send messages using SMTP (Simple Mail Transfer Protocol). The ejbTimeout method first looks up a JavaMail Session object using JNDI and then uses that object to create a JavaMail MimeMessage, which represents an e-mail message with MIME (Multipurpose Internet Mail Extensions) attachments. Next, the method sets in the MimeMessage object the sender, receiver, subject, and content text of the e-mail message. Finally, it sends the message using the default mail transport, usually SMTP. For more information about JavaMail, refer to http://java.sun.com/products/javamail.

8.2.6   DoctorEJB Entity Bean

The DoctorEJB entity bean, like PlanEJB, manages its state and relationships by using container-managed persistence. This entity bean essentially functions as a data object that stores information about physicians and dentists.

DoctorEJB Primary Key

The DoctorEJB primary key sets this bean apart from other entity beans in the benefits application. The DoctorEJB entity bean has a *composite* primary key consisting of two CMP fields—`firstName` and `lastName`—and also uses a special primary key class, `DoctorPkey`, created by Wombat's developers. Code Example 8.21 shows the code for `DoctorPkey`:

```
public class DoctorPkey implements java.io.Serializable {
    public String firstName;
    public String lastName;

    public boolean equals(Object other) {
        if ( other instanceof DoctorPkey ) {
            DoctorPkey pkey = (DoctorPkey)other;
            return (firstName.equals(pkey.firstName) &&
                    lastName.equals (pkey.lastName));
        }
        return false;
    }

    public int hashCode() {
        return (firstName.hashCode() | lastName.hashCode());
    }
}
```

Code Example 8.21 The `DoctorPkey` Primary Key Class

Because it uses a composite primary key, DoctorEJB needs to declare these two CMP fields as `public` Java fields in its `DoctorPkey` primary key class. The names of the fields in the primary key class need to be a subset of the names of the CMP fields in the bean class. In addition, the `DoctorPkey` class needs to provide implementations of the `equals` and `hashCode` methods, which allow the EJB container to use `DoctorPkey` as a key into the container's internal data structures, such as hash tables.

Doctor Local Interface

The DoctorEJB entity bean is accessed from EnrollmentEJB and from the benefits administration Web application, both of which are packaged in the same benefits application. This copackaging of the bean with its clients ensures that only local access is required. As a result, the DoctorEJB entity bean defines only local interfaces. Code Example 8.22 shows the `Doctor` local interface definition:

```
public interface Doctor extends EJBLocalObject {
    String getLastName();
    String getFirstName();
    String getSpecialty();
    String[] getHospitals();
    int getPracticeSince();
}
```

Code Example 8.22 The Doctor Local Interface

The `Doctor` local interface defines methods that allow clients to view its persistent fields but does not define any other business methods. Note that the local interface does not allow clients to modify any information in the bean. Because the DoctorEJB bean is a *read-only* bean, the EJB container can manage it more efficiently.

DoctorHome Home Interface

The `DoctorHome` interface defines a `create` method that allows the benefits administration Web application to create DoctorEJB instances when doctors are added to a plan. This interface also defines the mandatory `findByPrimaryKey` method, which takes the `DoctorPkey` primary key class as its argument. Code Example 8.23 shows the `DoctorHome` interface definition:

```
public interface DoctorHome extends EJBLocalHome {
    Doctor create(String firstName, String lastName,
            String specialty, String hospital, int practiceSince)
```

```
        throws CreateException;
    Doctor findByPrimaryKey(DoctorPkey pkey) throws FinderException;
}
```

Code Example 8.23 The DoctorHome Home Interface

DoctorBean **Entity Bean Class**

Code Example 8.24 shows the source code of the DoctorBean entity bean class:

```
public abstract class DoctorBean extends AbstractEntityBean {
    public abstract String getFirstName();
    public abstract void setFirstName(String v);

    public abstract String getLastName();
    public abstract void setLastName(String v);

    public abstract String getSpecialty();
    public abstract void setSpecialty(String v);

    public abstract String[] getHospitals();
    public abstract void setHospitals(String[] v);

    public abstract int getPracticeSince();
    public abstract void setPracticeSince(int v);

    // CMR fields
    public abstract Collection getPlans();
    public abstract void setPlans(Collection c);

    // Life-cycle methods
    public DoctorPkey ejbCreate(String firstName, String lastName,
            String specialty, String[] hospitals, int practiceSince)
            throws CreateException {
        setFirstName(firstName);
        setLastName(lastName);
        setSpecialty(specialty);
        setHospitals(hospitals);
        setPracticeSince(practiceSince);
```

```
            return null;
    }


    public void ejbPostCreate(String firstName, String lastName,
            String specialty, String[] hospitals, int practiceSince)
            throws CreateException {}
}
```

Code Example 8.24 The DoctorBean Class Implementation

The DoctorBean class is a simple entity bean class that uses container-managed persistence: CMP fields define the persistent state of each DoctorEJB instance. The CMP fields, declared in the deployment descriptor, are firstName, lastName, specialty, hospitals, and practiceSince. Each field is represented as a pair of get and set methods in the DoctorBean class.

The DoctorBean class also defines a CMR field for its relationship with the PlanEJB entity bean. This CMR field, plans, is represented by the methods set-Plans and getPlans. (Recall that the description of the PlanBean class discussed this relationship. See the section PlanBean Implementation Class on page 270.) The relationship between DoctorBean and PlanBean is bidirectional; hence, both classes have a CMR field to refer to each other. Because this relationship is many-to-many, the get and set methods in DoctorBean operate on a Collection of Plan objects.

The DoctorBean class defines an ejbCreate method that initializes the values of the CMP fields, including the two primary key fields firstName and lastName. The class also has an empty ejbPostCreate method.

8.2.7   EnrollmentWeb Web Application

The EnrollmentWeb Web application is a set of JSPs. See the example in Chapter 4, Working with Session Beans, for a description of the EnrollmentWeb Web application.

8.2.8 BenefitsAdminWeb Web Application

The BenefitsAdminWeb Web application is a set of JSPs used by the customer's benefits administration department to administer its benefits plans. The Benefits-AdminWeb Web application does the following work:

- Uses the find methods on the `PlanHome` interface to find the deployed plan beans from the respective insurance companies

- Allows the plan administrator to use the business methods on the `Plan` interface to query the doctors associated with a plan

- Uses the business methods on the `Plan` interface to allow doctors to be added and removed from a plan

- Allows the plan administrator to add or remove plans from the set of configured plans

Code Example 8.25 shows the skeleton code for adding an insurance plan to the set of configured plans. (Note that the example shows only those parts relevant to using the PlanEJB entity bean.)

```
...
// Create an entity object for the new plan.
InitialContext initialContext = new InitialContext();
PlanHome planHome = (PlanHome)initialContext.lookup
    ("java:comp/env/ejb/Plan");
Plan plan = planHome.create
    (planId, planName, planType, coverageFactor, ageFactor,
    smokerCost);
...
```

Code Example 8.25 Code for Adding a Plan

After the `create` method completes, the created plan entity object is saved to the database and becomes available to the Benefits Enrollment application. A plan administrator wanting to remove a plan from the list of configured plans invokes the `remove` method on the `PlanHome` interface and passes it the plan identifier, `planId`, which is PlanEJB's primary key:

```
...
planHome.remove(planId);
...
```

8.2.9   The Benefits Database

BenefitsDatabase stores the persistent state of the three entity beans SelectionEJB, PlanEJB, and DoctorEJB. All three beans use container-managed persistence, so Wombat does not need to specify a schema for this database. The schema is created by Wombat's customer, which in this case is Star Enterprise, using the object-relational mapping tools provided by the J2EE application server product on which these CMP entity beans are deployed.

8.2.10   Packaging of Parts

This section describes how Wombat packages its benefits application for distribution to customers.

benefits.ear File

Wombat packages the benefits application as a single J2EE enterprise application archive file, which it names benefits.ear. (An .ear file is an enterprise application archive resource file.) Figure 8.4 depicts the contents of the benefits.ear file.

The benefits.ear file contains

- The enrollment.war file with the EnrollmentWeb Web application. (A .war file is a Web archive file.) The EnrollmentWeb Web application consists of several JSPs.

- The benefits_admin.war file with the BenefitsAdminWeb Web application. The BenefitsAdminWeb Web application consists of several JSPs.

- The benefits_ejb.jar file. This is the ejb-jar file that contains the enterprise beans developed by Wombat.

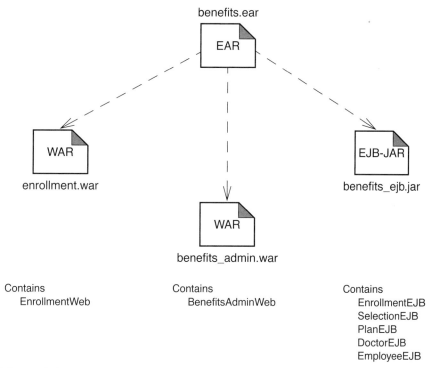

Figure 8.4 Contents of the `benefits.ear` File

`benefits_ejb.jar` File

The `benefits_ejb.jar` file contains the enterprise beans developed by Wombat. Code Example 8.26 lists the classes that the file contains:

```
com/wombat/AbstractEntityBean.class
com/wombat/benefits/DeductionUpdateBean.class
com/wombat/benefits/Employee.class
com/wombat/benefits/EmployeeBean.class
com/wombat/benefits/EmployeeHome.class
com/wombat/benefits/EmployeeInfo.class
com/wombat/benefits/Enrollment.class
com/wombat/benefits/EnrollmentBean.class
com/wombat/benefits/EnrollmentException.class
com/wombat/benefits/EnrollmentHome.class
```

```
com/wombat/benefits/Options.class
com/wombat/benefits/Selection.class
com/wombat/benefits/SelectionBean.class
com/wombat/benefits/SelectionCopy.class
com/wombat/benefits/SelectionException.class
com/wombat/benefits/SelectionHome.class
com/wombat/benefits/Summary.class
com/wombat/plan/Doctor.class
com/wombat/plan/DoctorBean.class
com/wombat/plan/DoctorHome.class
com/wombat/plan/DoctorPkey.class
com/wombat/plan/Plan.class
com/wombat/plan/PlanBean.class
com/wombat/plan/PlanException.class
com/wombat/plan/PlanHome.class
```

Code Example 8.26 Contents of the `benefits_ejb.jar` File

8.3   Parts Developed at Star Enterprise

Prior to the deployment of Wombat's benefits application, Star Enterprise already had a Benefits Enrollment application that it had developed internally. (See Chapter 4 for the description of the Benefits Enrollment application using session beans.)

With the deployment of Wombat's benefits application, Star Enterprise needs to integrate some parts of its application into Wombat's application. This section addresses these issues.

8.3.1   The Employee Database and Deployment of EmployeeEJB

The human resources department at Star Enterprise maintains the information about employees and company departments in `EmployeeDatabase`. The information is stored in multiple tables. The `Employees` table within the database is relevant to the benefits application. The schema for `EmployeeDatabase` is described in Section 4.6.1, The Employee Database, on page 120.

Note that as an ISV, Wombat had no knowledge of the schema of `EmployeeDatabase` and did not need that knowledge. Coding its benefits application as generically as possible, Wombat's primary consideration was that the application work regardless of an individual customer's schema and type of DBMS. If Wombat coded the benefits application according to the Star Enterprise schema, the application would be unusable by customers having a different schema or even a different type of DBMS.

Star Enterprise has two choices for deploying the EmployeeEJB entity bean developed by the ISV Wombat:

1. It can use an object-relational mapping tool to map the CMP fields of the EmployeeEJB to the columns of the Employees table in its relational database EmployeeDatabase. An example of such a mapping of fields follows:

CMP Field in EmployeeBean	Column Name in Employees Table
employeeNumber	empl_id
firstName	empl_first_name
lastName	empl_last_name
birthDate	empl_birth_date

2. It can develop an entity bean by using bean-managed persistence and can write the database access code in the BMP bean class. This approach is described in the next section.

8.3.2   EmployeeBeanBMP **Entity Bean Class**

The EmployeeBeanBMP bean class uses bean-managed persistence to manage the state of the EmployeeEJB entity bean. This class uses the same local interface Employee and local home interface EmployeeHome as in the EmployeeEJB entity bean. (See Section 8.2.3, EmployeeEJB Entity Bean, on page 255.) The EmployeeBeanBMP class subclasses the EmployeeBean container-managed persistence class.

This section discusses some of the important issues that need to be kept in mind when developing entity beans with bean-managed persistence. Portions of code from the EmployeeBeanBMP class are used to illustrate these points. See Section A.7, EmployeeBeanBMP Class, on page 402 for the complete code for the EmployeeBeanBMP class.

The EmployeeBeanBMP class has three types of methods:

- Get and set methods for CMP fields

- EntityBean interface life-cycle methods

- Database access helper methods

CMP Field Methods

The EmployeeBeanBMP class needs to implement all abstract methods defined in the EmployeeBean class. These methods correspond to the abstract get and set methods for the CMP fields declared in the EmployeeBean CMP class. These methods get and set concrete fields in the EmployeeBeanBMP class corresponding to the CMP fields. Code Example 8.27 shows the code for these methods:

```
public class EmployeeBeanBMP extends EmployeeBean {
    // this field holds the JDBC DataSource for the employee database
    private DataSource dataSource;
    // the following fields hold the persistent state of
    // the EmployeeBean.
    private Integer employeeNumber;
    private String firstName;
    private String lastName;
    private Date birthDate;

    // The following methods implement the abstract CMP
    // field getters/setters declared in the EmployeeBean class.
    public Integer getEmployeeNumber() {
        return employeeNumber;
    }
    public void setEmployeeNumber(Integer n) {
        employeeNumber = n;
    }

    public String getFirstName() {
        return firstName;
    }
    public void setFirstName(String s) {
        firstName = s;
    }

    public String getLastName() {
        return lastName;
    }
    public void setLastName(String s) {
        lastName = s;
    }
```

```
        public Date getBirthDate() {
            return birthDate;
        }
        public void setBirthDate(Date d) {
            birthDate = d;
        }
        ....
}
```

Code Example 8.27 Implementation of EmployeeBeanBMP Get and Set Methods

Life-Cycle Methods

The `EmployeeBeanBMP` class also implements the entity bean life-cycle methods, including `ejbCreate` and `ejbPostCreate`, and methods of the `javax.ejb.Entity-Bean` interface. Code Example 8.28 shows the code for the `ejbCreate` and `ejbPost-Create` methods:

```
public Integer ejbCreate(int emplNumber, String fname, String lname,
                Date birthDate) throws CreateException {
    // this sets all the CMP fields
    super.ejbCreate(emplNumber, fname, lname, birthDate);

    // check if the primary key exists
    if ( primaryKeyExists(emplNumber) ) {
        throw new DuplicateKeyException("Employee number " +
            emplNumber + " already exists in database");
    }

    // create a row for this bean instance
    createRow();

    // return the primary key
    return new Integer(emplNumber);
}

public void ejbPostCreate(int emplNumber, String fname,
```

```
            String lname, Date birthDate) throws CreateException
    {}
```

Code Example 8.28 EmployeeBeanBMP ejbCreate and ejbPostCreate Methods

EmployeeBeanBMP's ejbCreate method first calls its superclass Employee-Bean's ejbCreate method, which sets the values of the CMP fields by calling the respective set methods. This operation sets values in the Java fields in the EmployeeBeanBMP class. EmployeeBeanBMP's ejbCreate method then checks whether the primary key for the employee, which is the employee number—emplNumber—already exists in the database. If it does, the method throws DuplicateKeyException to indicate to the client that an application-level error has occurred. If the employee number does not exist, the ejbCreate method creates a row for the employee in the database by calling the createRow helper method. Finally, the ejbCreate method returns the new bean instance's primary key, as required for BMP entity beans. The container converts this primary key to an Employee reference and returns it to the client.

Two additional entity bean life-cycle methods are in the EmployeeBeanBMP class: setEntityContext and unsetEntityContext. Code Example 8.29 shows the code for these methods:

```
public void setEntityContext(EntityContext c) {
    super.setEntityContext(c);
    String dataSourceName = "java:comp/env/jdbc/EmployeeDatabase";
    try {
        Context ctx = new InitialContext();
        dataSource = (DataSource)ctx.lookup(dataSourceName);
    } catch ( Exception ex ) {
        throw new EJBException("Unable to look up dataSource "
                + dataSourceName);
    }
}

public void unsetEntityContext() {
    dataSource = null;
```

```
        super.unsetEntityContext();
    }
```

Code Example 8.29 The setEntityContext and unsetEntityContext Methods

The setEntityContext method is called immediately after the EmployeeBean-BMP class is instantiated. The method first calls the EmployeeBeanBMP superclass's setEntityContext method to allow the superclass to do any necessary initialization. The method then looks up the JDBC DataSource object for EmployeeDatabase from the JNDI environment.

The unsetEntityContext is the last method called before the EmployeeBean-BMP instance is destroyed. This method clears the value of the DataSource field and calls the superclass's unsetEntityContext method to allow the superclass to perform any required cleanup.

Database Access Methods

The EmployeeBeanBMP class implements the ejbFindByPrimaryKey method (Code Example 8.30):

```
public Integer ejbFindByPrimaryKey(Integer emplNum)
        throws FinderException {
    // Try to load the row for this primary key
    if ( !primaryKeyExists(emplNum.intValue()) ) {
        throw new ObjectNotFoundException("Primary key " + primaryKey
                + " not found");
    }
    return emplNum;
}
```

Code Example 8.30 The EmployeeBeanBMP Class ejbFindByPrimaryKey Method

The ejbFindByPrimaryKey method checks whether the emplNum argument—the primary key for the EmployeeEJB bean—exists in the database, doing so by calling the helper method primaryKeyExists. If the employee number does not exist, the method throws ObjectNotFoundException to inform the client. If the employee number does exist, the method returns the primary key. The container converts this primary key to an Employee reference and returns it to the client.

The EmployeeBeanBMP class also implements the ejbRemove method, as shown in Code Example 8.31:

```
public void ejbRemove() throws RemoveException {
    super.ejbRemove();

    // remove the row for this primary key
    removeRow();

    // clear all CMP fields
    employeeNumber = null;
    firstName = null;
    lastName = null;
    birthDate = null;
}
```

Code Example 8.31 The ejbRemove Method in EmployeeBeanBMP

The ejbRemove method first calls the ejbRemove method of the superclass EmployeeBean. This allows the superclass's ejbRemove implementation to do any needed work. Then EmployeeBeanBMP's ejbRemove method calls the helper method removeRow to remove the row for this bean instance from the database. After this, the ejbRemove method clears all employee-specific fields. This is an important step because the bean instance goes into the container's pool after removal and can be used for another employee with a different identity and different fields. The ejbRemove method needs to clean up all fields that are specific to the particular employee. Note that ejbRemove does not need to clear the dataSource field, because that field's value does not depend on any particular employee.

Now let's examine the ejbLoad and ejbStore methods, which are used to synchronize the state of the bean with the persistent state in the database. The ejbLoad method is usually called at the beginning of a transaction, before any business methods are called. The ejbStore method is usually called at the end of a transaction, when a transaction is committed. Code Example 8.32 shows the code for these methods:

```
public void ejbLoad() {
    try {
        loadRow();
    } catch ( Exception ex ) {
        throw new NoSuchEntityException(
            "Exception caught in ejbLoad: "+ex);
    }
    super.ejbLoad();
}

public void ejbStore() {
    super.ejbStore();
    try {
        storeRow();
    } catch ( Exception ex ) {
        throw new EJBException("Exception caught in ejbStore ", ex);
    }
}
```

Code Example 8.32 EmployeeBeanBMP's ejbLoad and ejbStore Methods

The ejbLoad method calls the loadRow helper method to load the state of the bean. The loadRow helper method does a database read, using the employee number primary key; retrieves the row for the employee; and sets the CMP fields in the EmployeeBeanBMP class. After the loadRow method completes successfully, the ejbLoad method calls the superclass EmployeeBean's ejbLoad method to allow the superclass to initialize any cached transient variables from the CMP fields.

The ejbStore method first calls the superclass EmployeeBean's ejbStore method. This allows the superclass to save any cached data to the CMP fields. After this, the ejbStore method stores the state of EmployeeBeanBMP by calling the storeRow helper method, which writes all the CMP fields to the database row representing the employee. For better performance, EmployeeBeanBMP should perform this database write only if the bean's CMP fields have been modified since the last time they were loaded. This optimization can be done by maintaining a flag in the EmployeeBeanBMP's instance variable that indicates whether the bean's state is "dirty"—that is, changed. The flag needs to be set in every set method that modifies the bean's state.

An entity bean with bean-managed persistence must also implement the ejb-Passivate and ejbActivate methods. Code Example 8.33 shows how Employee-BeanBMP implemented these two methods:

```
public void ejbActivate() {
    employeeNumber = (Integer)entityContext.getPrimaryKey();
}

public void ejbPassivate() {
    // clear all CMP fields
    employeeNumber = null;
    firstName = null;
    lastName = null;
    birthDate = null;
}
```

Code Example 8.33 EmployeeBeanBMP ejbActivate and ejbPassivate Methods

The ejbActivate method is called when an entity bean instance is being associated with a specific primary key value. The EmployeeBeanBMP's ejbActivate method initializes the employeeNumber field to the instance's primary key value. This association step is very important because it allows subsequent methods, such as ejbLoad, to operate on the correct primary key. In fact, ejbActivate is typically called immediately before ejbLoad at the beginning of a transaction.

The ejbPassivate method is called when the container wants to reclaim the memory associated with a bean instance and return the bean instance to its pool. The ejbPassivate method clears the values of all employee-specific fields—that is, the CMP fields. After the ejbPassivate method completes, the bean instance is no longer associated with an identity and, by calling ejbActivate, can be used to service a request on behalf of a different employee.

8.3.3   Payroll System

Prior to the deployment of Wombat's benefits application, Star Enterprise's payroll department developed a payroll application to give its enterprise applications access to payroll information. The payroll application consists of the PayrollEJB stateless session bean, described in Section 4.5, PayrollEJB Stateless Session Bean, on page

110. The payroll information is stored in `PayrollDatabase`, whose schema is described in Section 4.6.3, The Payroll Database, on page 123.

To integrate the PayrollEJB with the Benefits Enrollment application developed by Wombat, Star Enterprise's IT department develops an implementation of the `DeductionUpdateBean` command bean interface provided by Wombat. The deployer then sets the class name of this interface in the EnrollmentEJB's environment. This allows EnrollmentEJB to instantiate the `DeductionUpdateBean` implementation and use it to update the benefits deduction in Star Enterprise's payroll system.

8.4   Conclusion

We have now completed our examination of entity beans. This chapter presented an employee Benefits Enrollment application that was similar to the example presented earlier. However, this example was built and deployed using entity beans when appropriate rather than relying completely on session beans.

The example application clearly illustrated the differences, from a developer's point of view, of using entity beans. The application focused on the various techniques for working with entity beans, such as using container-managed persistence and container-managed relationships, caching persistent state, subclassing techniques, and so forth, and how best to use the features of these types of beans.

The example application also illustrated how to use the EJB timer service and the JavaMail APIs to provide plan administrators with statistics about the application by e-mail on a regular basis.

This chapter showed how entity beans are more appropriate for applications that must be easily adapted for different customers with different operational environments. Typically, these are applications built by ISVs rather than by an enterprise's in-house IT department.

CHAPTER 9

Using Enterprise JavaBeans in Web Services

WEB services today play an increasingly important role for enterprise applications. In particular, Web services enable an open, interoperable means of communicating between businesses over the Internet. Web services technology represents a new paradigm for enterprise applications to integrate with other applications within an enterprise, as well as at customer, supplier, and partner sites.

This chapter presents concepts, techniques, and code examples for applying Enterprise JavaBeans technology toward Web services applications. The chapter

- Introduces Web services technologies and shows how to use them for application integration

- Explains how to expose an existing EJB-based enterprise application as a Web service

- Shows how to develop a new Web service using enterprise beans

- Shows how to use Java API for XML-based RPC (JAX-RPC) to access a Web service application from an enterprise bean

- Illustrates how to integrate an enterprise application with external systems, using Web services from entity beans with bean-managed persistence

The same Benefits Enrollment application example discussed in the previous chapters forms the basis for the examples illustrating these Web services topics. Star Enterprise must integrate the Benefits Enrollment application with health plan applications provided by external companies. We show how to use Web services technology to integrate the Star Enterprise's Benefits Enrollment application with these insurance companies' health plan administration applications.

9.1   Introduction to Web Services

Web services technology represents an important step toward fulfilling the vision of the Internet as an open, interoperable environment in which customers and businesses can interact in ways that were not possible before. The technology is based on fundamental Internet technologies developed during the last few years by a variety of standards bodies, including the World Wide Web Consortium (W3C) and the Internet Engineering Task Force (IETF). These Internet technologies allow software applications developed by various vendors or individuals to interoperate, regardless of the software or hardware systems used to implement the applications.

9.1.1   Web Services Technologies

The building blocks of Web services technology are Extensible Markup Language (XML) and HyperText Transfer Protocol (HTTP), which together provide a way to flexibly represent structured information and exchange it over networks. Other standards contribute to making Web services possible, including standards for describing, accessing, and publishing the service:

- **Service description**—A software application that provides Web services must have a standard way of describing its services so that other applications can use them. The Web Services Description Language (WSDL) is the standard for describing a service.

  WSDL consists of a specific set of XML elements. Developed by the W3C, this standard allows a service to be described as a collection of *port types* that in turn consist of a set of *operations*. Operations can be either synchronous—a request followed by a response—or asynchronous—the sender sends the message and continues processing without expecting a response. Each operation contains a description of the input and output *messages* describing the information that is expected and returned by an operation. Messages can be procedural in nature—describing parameters to the operation—or document oriented—containing an XML document, such as a purchase order. Port types are bound to *ports*. Ports can be accessed over a specific protocol and data format at a network endpoint consisting of a host name and TCP/IP port number, all of which are specified through a *binding*. Thus, a WSDL document has all the elements necessary to provide a complete description of a Web service in a platform-independent manner.

- **Service access**—It is essential for interoperable Web services to have a standard network protocol and data format for exchanging information. The Simple Object Access Protocol (SOAP), along with the data formats and type system described by the XML Schema standard, provide the technology for a standard network protocol and data format. (Both SOAP and XML are defined by the W3C.)

    SOAP messages are XML documents containing the necessary header information to allow a message to be properly transmitted from sender to receiver, as well as a body containing the service request or response message. The SOAP standard includes a standard binding to HTTP, which allows SOAP messages to be exchanged over the ubiquitous HTTP.

- **Service publishing and discovery**—For Web services to initiate interactions with other Web services, there must be a standard way for a service to advertise its existence in a domain and for other services to search for and discover its contact information, such as network endpoint, protocol, and so forth, and the operations it supports. The Universal Description, Discovery, and Integration (UDDI) standard makes service publishing and discovery possible.

    The UDDI standard, developed by the UDDI Project, defines how to publish and discover Web services through a public registry, or directory. Information in an UDDI registry divides into three categories: "white pages," which include information such as contact addresses; "yellow pages," which organize businesses into categories; and "green pages," which provide technical information on how to access a service. Using this information, services can begin interacting with one another in a standard manner.

The WSDL, SOAP, and UDDI standards form the backbone of Web services technology. Enterprise applications use these technologies to interact with other applications at customer, supplier, and partner locations. Such interactions allow these applications to exchange business information and to conduct transactions rapidly. Enterprises in a variety of industries are becoming aware of the cost savings, along with productivity and efficiency gains, achieved by using Web services. As a result, businesses in diverse industries are making significant investments to enable their enterprises to use Web services.

9.1.2   J2EE and Web Services

Although Web services provide a new way for applications to interoperate over the Internet, an enterprise still must develop and implement a Web services application, or it must expose existing applications as Web services. To expeditiously implement or expose a Web service requires an application development and deployment platform that is powerful and full featured yet at the same time easy for developers and deployers to use. The J2EE platform leverages the strengths of the Java programming language and enterprise APIs, including the EJB technology, to provide an industry-leading Web services platform.

The strengths of the J2EE platform include a set of component models that allow developers to focus on writing the business logic in their applications and to delegate system-level details to infrastructure layers. In addition, the platform's range of business integration features for accessing relational databases, messaging systems, and enterprise information systems makes it easy to leverage existing enterprise information assets. These features are coupled with a powerful set of Web technologies, revolving around XML and HTTP, that simplify access to J2EE applications from customers and other business applications.

The J2EE 1.4 platform release includes an entire set of Web services technologies:

- **Java API for XML-based RPC (JAX-RPC)**—Major enterprise vendors, through the Java Community Process (JCP), worked together to develop the JAX-RPC standard. JAX-RPC defines Java APIs for accessing Web services from Java applications: how to map a WSDL description of a Web service to a Java interface, called the *service endpoint interface*. JAX-RPC also defines how to map existing Java application interfaces to WSDL descriptions. As a result, applications using JAX-RPC program to familiar Java interfaces and data types and do not need to deal with low-level details, such as parsing or composing XML documents and extracting XML documents from SOAP messages.

  Furthermore, JAX-RPC implementations provide the client- and server-side libraries to send and receive Web services requests over SOAP. JAX-RPC thus provides the necessary support for Java applications to access Web services, implement Web services, and be transformed into Web services.

- **Java API for XML Registries (JAX-R)**—JAX-R provides APIs that Java developers use to access XML registries, including registries based on UDDI.

Similar to JAX-RPC, JAX-R is being developed through the JCP by a large number of enterprise vendors.

- **SOAP with Attachments API for Java (SAAJ)**—SAAJ defines APIs that allow Java applications to construct SOAP 1.1 messages and send them to peers on a network. It also defines APIs for consuming and manipulating SOAP messages that have been received by an application. SAAJ provides functionality to create SOAP messages and then add header, body, and fault elements to those messages.

- **Java API for XML Processing (JAX-P)**—JAX-P defines APIs that Java applications use to parse, manipulate, and transform XML documents. It includes the W3C standard programming APIs: Simple API for XML (SAX), Document Object Model (DOM), and Transformation API for XML (TrAX). JAX-P provides a powerful set of APIs that applications use to produce and consume XML documents they have received from or intend to send to Web services.

- **Java API for XML Binding (JAX-B)**—JAX-B provides APIs and standards for representing XML documents and fragments as Java data structures. JAX-B defines how to map a document type definition (DTD) or schema for an XML document into a set of Java classes. This mapping allows instance documents that conform to the DTD or schema to be represented in memory as a set of Java objects that are instances of the corresponding Java classes. Thus, the Java programmer can use a high-level object-oriented view of the underlying XML document; the developer does not have to deal with details of the document structure and XML-specific APIs.

In addition, the EJB 2.1 architecture defines how to use an enterprise bean to implement a Web services endpoint. The Web Services for J2EE specification also describes how to develop and deploy Web services clients and servers in a J2EE environment.

9.1.3 Security and J2EE-Based Web Services

Enterprises that build Web services to expose their enterprise applications to customers, suppliers, or partners must be sure that such Web services are secure. Enterprise applications must be able to access and update business-critical data. The availability of enterprise applications is critical to the functioning of business processes in the enterprise. It is imperative that Web services not impair the consistency or availability of enterprise applications and data.

The technologies that predated Web services did not implement security uniformly. As a result, most enterprise organizations used different security standards, which made it difficult for organizations to interoperate securely, creating a problematic situation.

Web services technology provides solutions to such security concerns by providing standardization. Some of these solutions are based on established standards, such as the Secure Sockets Layer (SSL). Other standards, such as for security information in SOAP messages, are forthcoming. Standards bodies are giving the security area intense attention, and security standards for resolving security issues across enterprises using Web services are still evolving.

The EJB architecture and the J2EE platform provide an "enterprise-strength" security infrastructure that enables administrators to control who is allowed to access what applications and data. This security is achieved through

- Message protection, for ensuring the integrity and confidentiality of data as it is transmitted over the Internet

- Authentication, for verifying the identity of clients of Web services

- Authorization, for restricting access to only an allowed set of operations

Chapter 11, Managing Security, discusses the security infrastructure in detail. The important point for developers of EJB-based Web services is that there are no new APIs for Web services security. Instead, the container takes care of the security needs of the application, based on information provided in the deployment descriptor.

The Web services features of the EJB architecture also allow for modular, componentized, and incremental development of Web services. For example, an enterprise may expose just a small component of its large enterprise application as a Web service, keeping the remaining parts of the application unaffected. This permits the enterprise to tightly control the set of allowed operations that can be performed by external users. Furthermore, security for such external access is enforced at the entry point, which in this case is the EJB-based Web service hosted and administered by the enterprise. The administrators of the Web service use the familiar security administration tools provided by the J2EE product to modify the Web service and control who can access what parts of the service. Thus, an enterprise can build and administer the Web service with minimal incremental work.

The next sections discuss how to leverage the strengths of the EJB architecture, Web services technologies, and these Java APIs—JAX-RPC, JAX-R, JAX-P, and JAX-B—to develop Web services using enterprise beans.

9.2   Developing a Web Service Using Stateless Session Beans

Stateless session beans are particularly well suited for developing Web services. Web services and stateless session beans share significant features of statelessness, and they each have no specific instance identity. Because Web services endpoints that are described using WSDL are stateless—that is, they do not hold state on behalf of clients across client requests—they map nicely into stateless session beans.

Moreover, Web services do not have an instance-specific identity. This means that a request message from a client is not targeted at any particular instance of a Web service. Stateless session beans likewise do not have an instance-specific identity. As a result, each stateless session bean type can be mapped to a WSDL port type. Each operation within the port type maps to a business method of the stateless session bean.

The EJB 2.1 architecture, recently developed as part of the Java Community Process, explains how to develop a Web service using a stateless session bean. This chapter discusses how the EJB 2.1 architecture specifies implementing Web services with stateless session beans.

When developing a Web service using a stateless session bean, the developer should note some differences in the bean's usage. To begin with, the Web service developer does not use the stateless session bean's home interface, as the Web services model does not include the use of the factory pattern implied by the home interface. In addition, the developer models the stateless session bean's business logic interface as a JAX-RPC service endpoint interface.

A developer of a Web services interface needs to follow a few simple rules. The Web services interface extends `java.rmi.Remote`, and its methods throw the `java.rmi.RemoteException` exception.

Methods of the Web services interface use one of the following types: Java primitive types, Java classes that are JAX-RPC value types, Java mappings of MIME (Multipurpose Internet Mail Extensions) types—such as `java.awt.Image` for the MIME type `image/gif` and `javax.xml.transform.Source` for the MIME type `text/xml`—or arrays of any of those types. Web services interface methods are not allowed to use remote reference types.

JAX-RPC value types are Java classes that do not implement the `java.rmi.Remote` interface. To achieve the same semantics as Java serialization, the value type's class must also implement the `java.io.Serializable` interface, and the class should have only public, nontransient fields. This restriction is needed because the default mapping of JAX-RPC interfaces to WSDL maps only the `public`, nontransient fields.

9.2.1   Developing a New Web Service

There are two approaches for developing a new Web service using stateless session beans:

1. **Start with a Java interface for the Web service**—In this approach, you first create one or more Java service endpoint interfaces containing the business methods to be provided by the Web service. You then use a tool that implements the JAX-RPC standard to map the Java interfaces to a WSDL document describing the Web service. The tool generates the WSDL interface, and you program the code at the familiar level of Java interfaces, without dealing with the details of WSDL documents. Starting with a Java interface is the simplest approach for Java developers.

2. **Start with a WSDL description of the Web service**—In this approach, you first obtain a WSDL document for the Web service. This WSDL document might have been developed jointly with the users of the service, which might be another enterprise, or it might be a publicly available service specified by a standards body. Once you obtain the WSDL document, you use a tool that implements the JAX-RPC standard to generate the Java service endpoint interfaces—one for each port type in the WSDL.

With either approach, you ultimately obtain a set of service endpoint interfaces for the Web service that you are developing. The service endpoint interface contains the business methods that you need to implement in the stateless session bean class. There will be one stateless session bean for each service endpoint interface.

The stateless session bean implementation class is implemented using the same programming model as described in previous chapters. There is only one restriction: if the bean does not have home and component interfaces—local or remote—then the `getEJBObject`/`getEJBLocalObject` and `getEJBHome`/`getEJBLocalHome` methods of the `SessionContext` interface should not be invoked. Of course, in special cases, a stateless session bean may have a Web service endpoint interface as well as remote or local home and component interfaces, in which case this restriction does not apply. One new method on the `SessionContext` interface is the `getMessageContext` method. This method returns a JAX-RPC `SOAPMessage-Context` object, from which the bean can access the SOAP message that was sent by the client to get access to headers and other information not available from other method parameters.

For more advanced uses, a bean may also provide JAX-RPC `Handler` classes. Handlers are like interceptors that have access to the low-level SOAP messages. The handler's `handleRequest` method is invoked by the container after receiving the SOAP request message but before invoking the bean's business method. The handler's `handleResponse` method is invoked by the container after the bean's business method completes but before sending the SOAP response message back to the client. A handler may examine, modify, add, or remove SOAP headers in the request or response messages. Examples of handler use include getting security information such as principal names and credentials; encrypting or signing message bodies; specifying transaction context, and so forth. Handlers may set properties in the JAX-RPC `MessageContext`, and these properties can be obtained by the stateless session bean class. Refer to the JAX-RPC tutorial, which is part of the Java™ Web Services Tutorial, at `http:/java.sun.com/webservices` for more information on programming handlers.

The next step is to declare the service endpoint interface in the deployment descriptor of the stateless session bean. You do this by using the `service-end-point` element in the bean's XML deployment descriptor.

To deploy the Web service in an EJB container, you also need to include a special Web services deployment descriptor, which is defined by the Web Services for J2EE specification. The Web services deployment descriptor is in the form of a `webservices.xml` file that is included in the ejb-jar file. This deployment descriptor ties together the Web service components—the WSDL document describing the Web service, the stateless session bean, its Web service endpoint interface, any `Handler` classes, and a JAX-RPC mapping file—into a Web service port that can be deployed into a J2EE server. The JAX-RPC mapping file, which is itself an XML document, provides details of how the Java service endpoint interface was generated from the WSDL. The mapping file contains at a minimum the package name of the Java interfaces for each namespace declared in the WSDL. It may also contain details of the mapping for each XML type into the corresponding Java type. Fortunately, developers don't need to hand-code this mapping XML file; the JAX-RPC tool used to generate the Java service interface can usually be used to create the mapping file, too, in case it is necessary to provide the complete mapping for each type.

Finally, all the Java classes and interfaces—the bean implementation class, the Web service endpoint interface class, and the `Handler` classes—and the XML descriptors—WSDL document, JAX-RPC mapping file, EJB deployment descriptor `ejb-jar.xml`, and the Web services deployment descriptor `webservices.xml`—are packaged together into an ejb-jar file.

When this JAR file is deployed into a J2EE container supporting Web services, the container generates all the necessary implementation classes and code for translating Web service requests sent by clients using SOAP over HTTP into invocations on instances of the stateless session bean class. The container also updates the WSDL document with the address and TCP/IP port numbers at which the Web service can be accessed. The WSDL service may be published to a registry, such as an UDDI registry, or the container may simply make the WSDL document available as a file, which can then be provided by other means to users of the service.

Java clients of the Web service use the WSDL document provided by the Web service. The clients generate a Java interface from the WSDL document, using a JAX-RPC-compliant tool, and then they program to that Java interface.

Non-Java clients must start from the WSDL description of the Web service and use language-specific tools and mechanisms to access the Web service. Section 9.4, Accessing a Web Service from an Enterprise Bean, on page 312 discusses how to access a Web service from an enterprise bean.

When you develop a Web service using a stateless session bean, you typically expose large-grained operations through the bean's Web service interface. Then, clients of the Web service access these operations through the service's interface. You may implement these large-grained operations by using a set of finer-grained session or entity beans. The stateless session bean acts as an aggregator, or facade, to the internal enterprise beans implementing the application's functionality. The stateless session bean's function is to serve the Web services view of the application; this is usually a restricted and controlled view that administrators of the enterprise carefully decide to expose to other enterprises.

9.2.2   Exposing Existing Stateless Session Bean as Web Service

The EJB architecture gives you a way to expose existing stateless session bean implementations as Web services. You can expose a stateless session bean implementation as a Web service by creating a JAX-RPC service endpoint interface from the stateless session bean's remote interface.

The JAX-RPC service endpoint interface needs to follow the rules for service endpoint interfaces described in the preceding section. This means that the interface can include only those business methods of the stateless session bean's remote interface that follow the JAX-RPC rules for allowed types. If the application's existing beans do not follow the JAX-RPC rules, one way to enable the application for Web services is to develop "wrapper" beans that do follow the rules.

Using a JAX-RPC-compliant tool, the new service endpoint interface is used to generate the WSDL document for the Web service. Clients can then use this WSDL document to access the Web service. In addition, the deployment descriptor of the existing bean needs to be enhanced to declare the new service endpoint interface. After the service endpoint interface for the existing stateless session bean has been created, the interface should be packaged into the bean's JAR file, along with the bean's home, remote, and implementation classes; the EJB deployment descriptor; and the Web services deployment descriptor, as described in the preceding section.

9.3   Stateless Session Bean Web Service Example

This section describes an example application that illustrates how to put into practice the techniques just presented. This Web service example application builds on the Benefits Enrollment application discussed in previous chapters.

Star Enterprise decides to develop a more dynamic integration between its benefits enrollment system and the health care providers' medical and dental insurance plan systems. This enhanced integration is intended to dynamically and automatically update insurance plan information in the benefits enrollment system and will free Star Enterprise personnel from the time-consuming task of manually updating data about doctors and plan costs whenever an insurance provider changes its plan. The dynamic integration envisioned by Star Enterprise requires real-time communication between Star Enterprise's enrollment system and the insurance providers' systems. Thus, this is a good scenario for use of a Web service.

Star Enterprise works with Premium Health to develop a Web service for its insurance plan administration. Premium Health provides insurance plans to the employees of Star Enterprise, which hosts the Web service. Plan administrators at

Premium Health can modify plan information dynamically by "pushing" updates to Star Enterprise whenever a plan changes.

The insurance plan administration Web service consists of the Insurance-PlanAdminEJB stateless session bean. This bean implements the business logic of the Web service.

9.3.1 InsurancePlanAdminEJB Stateless Session Bean

The InsurancePlanAdminEJB stateless session bean contains business methods that allow plan administrators to obtain existing plan information, add doctors, and modify plan costs. The bean consists of the `InsurancePlanAdmin` service endpoint interface and the `InsurancePlanAdminBean` class. Note that there is no home interface and no remote interface.

`InsurancePlanAdmin` Service Interface

The InsurancePlanAdminEJB stateless session bean provides the `Insurance-PlanAdmin` Web service interface, which defines the bean's functionality. `InsurancePlanAdmin` is a JAX-RPC-compliant service endpoint interface. Code Example 9.1 shows the code for the interface:

```
public interface InsurancePlanAdmin extends Remote {
    void createInsurancePlan(String planId, String planName,
            int planType, double coverageFactor, double ageFactor,
            double smokerCost) throws RemoteException;
    PlanInfo getPlanInfo(String planId) throws RemoteException;
    void addDoctors(String planId, DoctorInfo[] doctors)
            throws RemoteException;
    void removeDoctors(String planId, DoctorInfo[] doctors)
            throws RemoteException;
    DoctorInfo[] getAllDoctors(String planId)
            throws RemoteException;
    void setSmokerCost(String planId, double cost)
            throws RemoteException;
    void setCoverageFactor(String planId, double s)
            throws RemoteException;
    void setAgeFactor(String planId, double s)
```

```
            throws RemoteException;
    }
```

Code Example 9.1   The `InsurancePlanAdmin` Service Endpoint Interface

The `InsurancePlanAdmin` interface follows the rules for a JAX-RPC service endpoint interface. Its methods' types are either Java primitive types or JAX-RPC value types. The two value types, `PlanInfo` and `DoctorInfo`, contain information about insurance plans and doctors (Code Example 9.2):

```java
public class DoctorInfo implements java.io.Serializable {
    public String firstName;
    public String lastName;
    public String specialty;
    public String[] hospitals;
    public int practiceSince;
}

public class PlanInfo implements java.io.Serializable {
    public String planId;
    public String planName;
    public int planType;
    public double coverageFactor;
    public double ageFactor;
    public double smokerCost;
}
```

Code Example 9.2   The `DoctorInfo` and `PlanInfo` Classes

The `DoctorInfo` and `PlanInfo` classes follow the JAX-RPC rules for value types. All their fields are `public`, and the types of the fields are Java primitives. An alternative way of designing JAX-RPC value types is to use the JavaBeans design pattern, whereby each private field `foo` needs to have a corresponding `getFoo` and `setFoo` method. When a value class follows the JAX-RPC rules, it can be mapped to XML schema types. In addition, instances of these classes can be serialized to XML elements in the SOAP messages that carry requests and responses between Web services.

InsurancePlanAdminBean Class

The InsurancePlanAdminEJB's business methods are implemented in the `Insur-ancePlanAdminBean` class. In addition to the bean's business methods, this class implements the usual set of methods required for a stateless session bean. See Code Example A.13 on page 420 for the complete code listing for this class.

The business methods of the `InsurancePlanAdminBean` class invoke methods on the PlanEJB bean through the `PlanHome` and `Plan` interfaces. (Section 8.2.5, PlanEJB Entity Bean, on page 266 describes the PlanEJB bean and its interfaces.) `InsurancePlanAdminBean` acts as a local client of PlanEJB. Code Example 9.3 shows the business method `addDoctors`, which accesses the PlanEJB bean:

```
public void addDoctors(String planId, DoctorInfo[] doctors)
{
    try {
        Plan plan = planHome.findByPrimaryKey(planId);
        for ( int i=0; i<doctors.length; i++ ) {
            // find or create a Doctor bean
            DoctorPkey pkey =
                new DoctorPkey(doctors[i].firstName,
                        doctors[i].lastName);
            Doctor doctor;
            try {
                doctor = doctorHome.findByPrimaryKey(pkey);
            } catch ( FinderException fe ) {
                doctor = doctorHome.create(doctors[i].firstName,
                        doctors[i].lastName,
                        doctors[i].specialty,
                        doctors[i].hospitals,
                        doctors[i].practiceSince);
            }
            plan.addDoctor(doctor);
        }
    } catch ( Exception ex ) {
        throw new EJBException(ex);
    }
}
```

Code Example 9.3   The addDoctors Method to Access PlanEJB

The state of the various insurance plan beans is stored in `BenefitsDatabase`. (See Section 8.2.9, The Benefits Database, on page 284.) Over the course of time, operations invoked by plan administrators from the insurance companies result in changes to the content of the insurance plans. These changes are saved as part of the persistent state of PlanEJB instances in `BenefitsDatabase`. Thus, the InsurancePlanAdminEJB bean and the InsurancePlanAdmin Web service provided by Star Enterprise serve to expose selected portions of its internal enterprise applications and data to Star Enterprise's partner insurance companies.

9.3.2   Developing and Packaging the Web Service

Star Enterprise followed the first approach described in Section 9.2.1, Developing a New Web Service, for developing the InsurancePlanAdmin Web service; Star Enterprise started with the Java service endpoint interface for the Web service and used a JAX-RPC-compliant tool to generate the WSDL for the Web service. (See Code Example A.14 on page 424 for a listing of the InsurancePlanAdminWeb WSDL document.) This WSDL document can be used as the basis for connecting to the InsurancePlanAdmin Web service from any insurance provider's enterprise. The important point to note here is that insurance providers may use any software technology, including non-Java infrastructures, to access the InsurancePlanAdmin Web service once they have the WSDL description of the Web service.

After developing the `InsurancePlanAdmin` interface and `InsurancePlan-AdminBean` stateless session bean class, Star Enterprise packages them into an ejb-jar file, `insurance-admin.jar`, which contains all classes referenced from the bean class and interface, such as the `DoctorInfo` and `PlanInfo` classes. It also contains the WSDL file, Web services deployment descriptor, and XML-Java mapping file. The stubs, skeletons, and serialization/deserialization code for translating SOAP requests into invocations on the bean class are not packaged with the ejb-jar file. Instead, they are generated by the JAX-RPC-compliant tools provided by the container at deployment time.

The `insurance-admin.jar` archive is then packaged along with the other Benefits Enrollment application components into the `benefits.ear` J2EE application archive. Packaging the application components into the same J2EE application archive is necessary because the InsurancePlanAdmin bean accesses PlanEJB through its local interfaces. Because they rely on local interfaces, they both need to be in the same application.

9.4   Accessing a Web Service from an Enterprise Bean

Enterprise beans can be used for both developing and accessing Web service applications. Enterprises can apply enterprise beans technology to access a Web service from an enterprise bean implementation class. This is necessary when an enterprise application needs to send information to or receive information from an external application, such as an application in another enterprise. Because the external application might not be written as an enterprise bean or as a Java application and might require communication across the Internet, it is advantageous to use Web services technology to access the external application.

Typically, an application client developer obtains a WSDL document describing the Web service and configures a service reference in an enterprise bean's environment. The EJB 2.1 architecture specifies how a bean developer can have the bean reference a Web service through a declaration in the bean's deployment descriptor. The deployer can then link the bean to a Web service installation. This implies that the Web service to be accessed is known at development time. However, the network endpoint (the host name and TCP/IP port number) may be provided by the deployer when deployment occurs. This mechanism is similar to the `ejb-ref` mechanism by which an enterprise bean can declare a reference to other enterprise beans.

For referencing Web services, the enterprise bean declares a `service-ref` element in its deployment descriptor. The `service-ref` element indicates the JNDI name—in the `java:comp/env` namespace—at which the lookup of the Web service endpoint is performed along with the expected Java type of the service interface for the Web service. This service interface has methods to return the proxy, or stub, object for each port type in the Web service. The proxy object implements the Java service endpoint interface to which the port type has been mapped. The Java service endpoint interface contains the methods for each operation in the port type. The EJB component can invoke these methods on the proxy object to send a request to the Web service.

The `service-ref` element also contains the location of the WSDL file from which the service interface was created and the location of the JAX-RPC mapping file. This mapping, which is itself an XML document, provides details of how the Java service interface was generated from the WSDL. Its format is the same as the mapping file provided by a stateful session bean that implements a Web service endpoint.

Finally, the `service-ref` element in an enterprise bean's deployment descriptor may also include a list of JAX-RPC `Handler` classes that are to be used during invocations on specific ports in the Web service. These handlers are invoked by the container before it sends the SOAP request message to the Web service and after it receives the SOAP response message from the Web service.

Let's look at an example that puts these techniques into practice.

9.4.1 Accessing a Web Service Example

This example illustrates the possibilities for further extending the integration of Star Enterprise's benefits enrollment system with its insurance providers' plan administration applications. Providence Health, a provider of health insurance plans, has installed in its enterprise a Web service that its clients use to access information about plan contents and costs. Star Enterprise decides to use this existing Web service and to "pull" information from Providence Health's Web service when an employee requests information about Providence Health's health plans.

Recall from the example in Chapter 8 that Star Enterprise uses a PlanEJB entity bean to store insurance plan information. This entity bean, which uses container-managed persistence, was developed by Wombat Inc. In that example, the PlanEJB bean stored its persistent state in `BenefitsDatabase`. We now develop an entity bean that delegates its business methods to Providence Health's Web service. This entity bean, ProvidencePlanEJB, is developed with bean-managed persistence. ProvidencePlanEJB extends PlanEJB and "wraps" the Web service from Providence Health. But first let us look at the Providence Health Web service itself.

9.4.2 Providence Health Web Service

Providence Health provides a description of its Web service to Star Enterprise, using a WSDL document (Code Example 9.4):

```
<?xml version="1.0" encoding="UTF-8"?>

<definitions name="Providence" targetNamespace="providence"
xmlns:tns="providence" xmlns="http://schemas.xmlsoap.org/wsdl/"
xmlns:soap="http://schemas.xmlsoap.org/wsdl/soap/" xmlns:xsd=
    "http://www.w3.org/2001/XMLSchema">

    <types>
```

```
<schema targetNamespace="providence" xmlns:xsi="http://
www.w3.org/2001/XMLSchema-instance" xmlns:tns="providence"
xmlns:soap-enc="http://schemas.xmlsoap.org/soap/encoding/"
xmlns:wsdl="http://schemas.xmlsoap.org/wsdl/" xmlns="http://
www.w3.org/2001/XMLSchema">
    <complexType name="DoctorInfo">
    <sequence>
        <element name="practiceSince" type="int"/>
        <element name="specialty" type="string"/>
        <element name="firstName" type="string"/>
        <element name="hospitals" type="tns:ArrayOfstring"/>
        <element name="lastName" type="string"/></sequence>
        </complexType>
    <complexType name="ArrayOfstring">
        <complexContent>
        <restriction base="soap-enc:Array">
        <attribute ref="soap-enc:arrayType"
            wsdl:arrayType="string[]"/></restriction>
        </complexContent></complexType>
    <complexType name="ArrayOfDoctorInfo">
        <complexContent>
        <restriction base="soap-enc:Array">
        <attribute ref="soap-enc:arrayType"
            wsdl:arrayType="tns:DoctorInfo[]"/>
            </restriction></complexContent></complexType>
    <complexType name="ArrayOfPlanInfo">
        <complexContent>
            <restriction base="soap-enc:Array">
            <attribute ref="soap-enc:arrayType"
                wsdl:arrayType="tns:PlanInfo[]"/>
            </restriction></complexContent></complexType>
    <complexType name="PlanInfo">
    <sequence>
        <element name="ageFactor" type="double"/>
        <element name="coverageFactor" type="double"/>
        <element name="planId" type="string"/>
        <element name="planName" type="string"/>
        <element name="planType" type="string"/>
        <element name="smokerCost" type="double"/></sequence>
```

```
        </complexType>
    </schema>
    </types>


<message name="getCost">
    <part name="planId" type="xsd:string"/>
    <part name="coverage" type="xsd:int"/>
    <part name="age" type="xsd:int"/>
    <part name="isSmoker" type="xsd:boolean"/></message>
<message name="getCostResponse">
    <part name="result" type="xsd:double"/></message>
<message name="getDoctorInfo">
    <part name="planId" type="xsd:string"/>
    <part name="doctorQuery" type="tns:DoctorInfo"/></message>
<message name="getDoctorInfoResponse">
    <part name="result" type="tns:ArrayOfDoctorInfo"/></message>
<message name="getPlanInfo">
    <part name="planId" type="xsd:string"/>
    <part name="planType" type="xsd:string"/>
    <part name="doctorQuery" type="tns:DoctorInfo"/></message>
<message name="getPlanInfoResponse">
    <part name="result" type="tns:ArrayOfPlanInfo"/></message>


<portType name="ProvidenceWebSvc">
    <operation name="getCost">
        <input message="tns:getCost"/>
        <output message="tns:getCostResponse"/></operation>
    <operation name="getDoctorInfo">
        <input message="tns:getDoctorInfo"/>
        <output message="tns:getDoctorInfoResponse"/></operation>
    <operation name="getPlanInfo">
        <input message="tns:getPlanInfo"/>
        <output message="tns:getPlanInfoResponse"/></operation>
</portType>


<binding name="ProvidenceWebSvcBinding"
        type="tns:ProvidenceWebSvc">
<operation name="getCost">
    <input>
```

```
        <soap:body encodingStyle="http://schemas.xmlsoap.org/soap/
          encoding/" use="encoded" namespace="providence"/></input>
      <output>
      <soap:body encodingStyle="http://schemas.xmlsoap.org/soap/
          encoding/" use="encoded" namespace="providence"/></output>
      <soap:operation soapAction=""/></operation>
  <operation name="getDoctorInfo">
      <input>
        <soap:body encodingStyle="http://schemas.xmlsoap.org/soap/
          encoding/" use="encoded" namespace="providence"/></input>
      <output>
        <soap:body encodingStyle="http://schemas.xmlsoap.org/soap/
          encoding/" use="encoded" namespace="providence"/></output>
      <soap:operation soapAction=""/></operation>
  <operation name="getPlanInfo">
      <input>
        <soap:body encodingStyle="http://schemas.xmlsoap.org/soap/
          encoding/" use="encoded" namespace="providence"/></input>
      <output>
        <soap:body encodingStyle="http://schemas.xmlsoap.org/soap/
          encoding/" use="encoded" namespace="providence"/></output>
      <soap:operation soapAction=""/></operation>
  <soap:binding transport="http://schemas.xmlsoap.org/soap/http"
      style="rpc"/>
  </binding>

  <service name="ProvidenceWebService">
    <port name="ProvidenceWebSvcPort"
        binding="tns:ProvidenceWebSvcBinding">
      <soap:address location="http://www.example.com/providence"/>
      </port>
  </service>
  </definitions>
```

Code Example 9.4   WSDL Description of the Providence Health Web Service

Star Enterprise's IT department uses this WSDL description as a starting point from which it maps the ProvidenceWebSvc port type to a Java service endpoint interface by using a tool that implements the JAX-RPC standard. The tool also generates a service class, `ProvidenceWebService`, from which a client can obtain a proxy, or stub, for the `ProvidenceWebSvcPort` port. In our example, the Web service has only one port. In general, the service class provides proxies for all ports declared in the Web service. Code Example 9.5 shows the code for the `ProvidenceWebSvcPort` interface:

```
public interface ProvidenceWebSvcPort extends java.rmi.Remote {
    public double getCost(String planId, int coverage, int age,
        boolean isSmoker) throws java.rmi.RemoteException;
    public com.star.plan.providence.DoctorInfo[] getDoctorInfo(
        String planId, com.star.plan.providence.DoctorInfo
        doctorQuery) throws java.rmi.RemoteException;
    public com.star.plan.providence.PlanInfo[] getPlanInfo(
        String planId, String planType,
        com.star.plan.providence.DoctorInfo doctorQuery)
        throws java.rmi.RemoteException;
}
```

Code Example 9.5   The `ProvidenceWebSvcPort` Service Endpoint Interface

The preceding service endpoint interface is a typical JAX-RPC service endpoint interface. Note that it contains business methods that use Java primitive types and the value types `PlanInfo` and `DoctorInfo`. The `getDoctorInfo` and `getPlanInfo` methods return an array of `PlanInfo` or `DoctorInfo` objects corresponding to the criteria specified by the respective method parameters. For example, the `doctorQuery` parameter provides a partial set of fields against which the Web service matches doctor records to choose the records to be returned. Comparing the WSDL document and the Java interfaces, it is obvious that the Java interface is simpler to understand and hides the complexity of the WSDL document.

9.4.3   ProvidencePlanEJB Entity Bean

The ProvidencePlanEJB entity bean integrates the Providence Health Web service with the Benefits Enrollment application developed by Wombat and deployed in Star Enterprise. The bean's home and component interfaces are `PlanHome` and `Plan`, which were described in Chapter 8. Because ProvidencePlanEJB uses PlanEJB's

PlanHome and Plan interfaces, all clients of PlanEJB can use ProvidencePlanEJB with no code changes or recompilation.

The bean implementation class for ProvidencePlanEJB, ProvidencePlanBean, uses bean-managed persistence. Instead of storing its state in BenefitsDatabase, ProvidencePlanEJB delegates all its operations to the Providence Health Web service. Thus, ProvidencePlanEJB does not itself load or store any persistent state. See Code Example A.15 on page 431 for the complete code listing for the ProvidencePlanBean class.

Code Example 9.6 shows the code for the setEntityContext method in ProvidencePlanBean for obtaining a reference to a service endpoint interface. The method obtains a reference to the ProvidenceWebSvcPort service endpoint interface, as well as the DoctorHome object:

```
public void setEntityContext(EntityContext ctx) {
    super.setEntityContext(ctx);
    try {
        InitialContext ic = new InitialContext();
        ProvidenceWebService service = (
                ProvidenceWebService)ic.lookup(
                "java:comp/env/service/ProvidenceWebService");
        providence = service.getProvidenceWebSvcPort();

        doctorHome = (DoctorHome)ic.lookup(
            "java:comp/env/ejb/ProvidenceDoctorEJB");
    }
    catch ( Exception ex ) {
        throw new EJBException(ex);
    }
}
```

Code Example 9.6   Obtaining a Web Service Reference

The service endpoint reference is declared in ProvidencePlanEJB's deployment descriptor, using a service-ref element. The deployer links this reference to an instance of ProvidenceWebService.

Code Example 9.7 shows the getDoctorsBySpecialty business method in the ProvidencePlanBean class. This method delegates to the getDoctorInfo operation in ProvidenceWebSvcPort:

```
public Collection getDoctorsBySpecialty(String specialty)
        throws FinderException, RemoteException {
    DoctorInfo doctorQuery = new DoctorInfo();
    doctorQuery.setSpecialty(specialty);
    DoctorInfo[] doctors = providence.getDoctorInfo(
            getPlanId(), doctorQuery);
    return convertToCollection(doctors);
}
```

Code Example 9.7   The `getDoctorsBySpecialty` Business Method

9.4.4 ProvidenceDoctorEJB Entity Bean

The ProvidenceDoctorEJB entity bean integrates the Providence Health Web service with the DoctorEJB interfaces in the Benefits Enrollment application deployed in Star Enterprise. The DoctorEJB bean's home and component interfaces are `DoctorHome` and `Doctor`, which are described in Section 8.2.6, DoctorEJB Entity Bean, on page 279. Because ProvidenceDoctorEJB uses DoctorEJB's `DoctorHome` and `Doctor` interfaces, all clients of DoctorEJB can use ProvidenceDoctorEJB with no code changes or recompilation.

The implementation class for ProvidenceDoctorEJB, `ProvidenceDoctorBean`, uses bean-managed persistence and delegates all its operations to the Providence Health Web service. See Code Example A.16 on page 439 for the complete code listing for the `ProvidenceDoctorBean` class.

9.4.5 Packaging

Star Enterprise packages the beans ProvidencePlanEJB and Providence-DoctorEJB—consisting of the bean classes and the home and component interfaces—the supporting `ProvidenceWebService` interface and referenced interfaces and classes, the WSDL file for Providence Health's Web service, the XML Java mapping file, and the EJB deployment descriptor (`ejb-jar.xml`) into an ejb-jar file called `providence.jar`. Note that Star Enterprise does not package in `providence.jar` the stub or proxy classes nor the classes for the serialization and deserialization of the XML schema elements that are described in the Providence Health Web service's WSDL description. Instead, the application server generates these classes at deployment. This JAR file is then packaged along with the other

JAR files in the Benefits Enrollment application and deployed in Star Enterprise's application server.

9.5   Document-Oriented Web Services

The preceding sections have shown how to develop a Web service using a stateless session bean and how to access a Web service given its WSDL description. The J2EE platform also supports a document-oriented programming model for EJB-based Web services. This document-oriented programming model is made possible because JAX-RPC supports passing parameters to Web service operations not only in the document mode defined by SOAP and WSDL, but also as attachments in messages. (For a more detailed treatment of these concepts, refer to the JAX-RPC section of the Java Web Services Tutorial, at `http://java.sun.com/webservices`.)

Today, enterprises prefer to interact by using paper or electronic documents. This document-oriented interaction style contrasts with the object-oriented RPC interaction style of the previous examples in this book. However, both interaction styles are useful in different scenarios. The document-oriented style is often best when it is necessary to build Web services that reflect traditional document-based business processes.

The document-oriented style of interaction is useful in the following circumstances:

- **A loosely coupled interaction is desired.** Loose coupling implies that the two communicating parties may be separated by geographical or temporal distances that make it difficult to interact in a tight request/response pattern. With loose coupling, the communicating parties need to agree only on the document formats to be exchanged.

- **The interaction may be asynchronous and involve complex interaction patterns.** The sender might not expect an immediate reply from the receiver. The sender thus continues with other processing after sending the request. The receiver receives the request and might process it at a later time or perhaps might need human intervention to process the request. The receiver might send multiple messages back to the sender while the receiver is processing the request. For example, the receiver might send an initial acknowledgment followed by status messages as the request moves through various stages of processing.

- **Large-grained operations are performed.** Each request involves a significant amount of work that might take days to complete.

- **The receiver processes the document as is.** The receiver does not convert the entire document into a programming language–native data structure, such as Java objects. Instead, the receiver extracts only the document elements of interest and passes the document to another component in the business workflow to complete other steps in the processing.

- **The content exchanged is considered "rich."** The documents exchanged have complex structures, including multiple types of elements, constraints on their values, and optional elements. Often the documents are self-describing, allowing the receiver to make sense of the content.

Document-oriented processing generally operates on XML documents. For such document-oriented styles of processing, the JAX-RPC and JAX-P standards provide techniques and APIs that allow application developers to create, send, receive, and consume XML documents.

The JAX-P specification, as well as the JAX-B specification and the allied W3C standards SAX, DOM, and TrAX, define APIs to create and process XML documents. An enterprise bean may use these APIs to directly create an XML document and populate it with its various elements before sending it to a Web service. An enterprise bean implementing a Web service may also use these same APIs to process a received XML document, using the APIs to extract the values associated with the received document's elements into Java objects and data types.

The following options exist for sending and receiving XML documents between partners in a Web service interaction:

- **Send the XML document as a text string over an HTTP request.** This may be done by using the J2SE URL APIs to open an HTTP URL connection to the Web service and then to post the XML document. The Web service side uses a servlet to receive the incoming text and to convert it to an XML document. The Web service then forwards the XML document to an enterprise bean for processing. Most Web and application server products today support this option, although it is low level and potentially more complex to program. However, this option may not be fully interoperable, because it does not use the Web services standards WSDL and SOAP.

- **Use the SOAP with Attachments protocol and the WSDL MIME data type bindings.** The WSDL and SOAP standards define how to send and receive documents—including XML documents, text documents, binary images, and so forth—in SOAP messages, using the MIME data type encodings. JAX-RPC defines corresponding Java APIs for document-oriented interactions based on these standards. An XML document is represented in the method signatures of the Web services endpoint interface, using the JAX-P type `javax.xml.transform.Source`. This makes it possible for a client to construct an XML document and provide it as a SAX, DOM, or stream source object to the method call on the Web services interface. Also, an enterprise bean can extract the XML document from the `Source` object that is passed in as a parameter to the business method call.

As you can see, the EJB architecture and allied J2EE APIs provide the necessary features to enable the development of Web services that use document-oriented styles of processing.

9.6   Conclusion

This chapter explored some new and upcoming technologies in the Web services area. The chapter briefly discussed Web services standards and the J2EE APIs that enable Java applications to use those standards and introduced the new features of the Enterprise JavaBeans architecture that pertain to Web services and that have been developed as part of the EJB 2.1 specification. These new features allow an enterprise bean to be used as the endpoint for a Web service, thus leveraging all the power and ease of use of the EJB architecture toward developing Web services.

The chapter also explored how an enterprise bean could use the JAX-RPC APIs to access a Web service based on a WSDL description of the service. Finally, the chapter presented an overview of document-oriented styles of interactions in Web services. Many of the new concepts were brought together with two example applications that used the new Web services features of the EJB and J2EE architectures.

CHAPTER 10

Understanding Transactions

THE EJB architecture provides for two kinds of transaction demarcation: container-managed transaction demarcation and bean-managed transaction demarcation. This chapter covers the essential aspects of transactions a typical application developer needs to know.

With the *container-managed transaction demarcation* approach, the EJB container does the bulk of the work of managing transactions for the programmer. This greatly simplifies the application developer's work when programming transactional applications. However, even though the container does the majority of the work, the bean provider or application assembler must still provide transaction-related instructions to the container. Part of this chapter explains how the example entity bean application described in Chapter 8 uses *transaction attributes,* which are special attributes set in the deployment descriptor to instruct the container on how to manage transactions for the benefits application.

This chapter also discusses *bean-managed transaction demarcation.* With this approach, the bean developer manages transaction boundaries programmatically from within the application code. The Benefits Enrollment application does not use bean-managed transaction demarcation. Instead, we discuss appropriate scenarios for using bean-managed transaction demarcation.

Application programmers benefit from developing their applications on platforms that support transactions. A transaction-based system simplifies application development because it frees the developer from the complex issues of failure recovery and multiuser programming. In addition, the EJB architecture does not limit transactions to single databases or single sites but rather supports distributed transactions that can simultaneously update multiple databases across multiple sites.

How is this accomplished? The EJB architecture permits the work of an application to, typically, be divided into a series of units. Each unit of work is a separate transaction. While the application progresses, the underlying system ensures that each unit of work—each transaction—fully completes without interference from other processes. If not, the system rolls back the transaction, completely undoing whatever work the transaction had performed.

The EJB architecture allows enterprise beans to use a declarative style of transaction management that differs from the traditional transaction management style. With declarative management, the enterprise bean application declares transaction attributes in the deployment descriptor. These transaction attributes explain how to partition the work of an application into separate, discrete units of work. The transaction attributes indicate to the container how it should apply transaction management to the execution of the bean's methods.

Using the traditional transaction management approach, the application was responsible for managing all aspects of a transaction. This entailed such operations as

- Explicitly starting the transaction

- Committing or rolling back the transaction

- Suspending and resuming the transaction association, particularly for applications that need more sophisticated transaction demarcation

A developer must have more programming expertise to write an application that is responsible for managing a transaction from start to finish. The code for such an application is more complex, and thus more difficult to write, and it is easy for "pilot error" to occur; for example, a programmer may forget to commit a transaction. Furthermore, it is difficult to reuse components that programmatically manage transaction boundaries as building blocks for applications with additional components.

With declarative transaction management, the container manages most, if not all, aspects of the transaction for the application. The container handles starting and ending the transaction and maintains its context throughout the life of the transaction. The container automatically propagates the transaction context into invoked enterprise beans and resource managers, based on the declarative instructions in the deployment descriptor. This greatly simplifies an application developer's responsibilities and tasks, especially for transactions in distributed environments. In addition, it means that the components are reusable as building blocks for other applications composed of multiple components.

10.1 Declarative Transaction Demarcation

Most applications are best off using the container-managed transaction demarcation feature, commonly referred to as *declarative transaction demarcation*, or *declarative transactions*. For this feature to work, application developers set up transaction attributes separate from their code: A transaction attribute is associated with each enterprise bean method. The EJB container uses these attributes to determine how it should handle transaction demarcation for that method. As a result, the application programmer does not need to include transaction demarcation code in the application.

10.1.1 Transaction Attributes

When a client uses an enterprise bean's home or component interface to invoke a method, the container interposes on the method invocation to inject the container services. One of the services that the container injects is transaction demarcation.

The bean developer or application assembler uses the deployment descriptor to specify how the container should manage transaction demarcation. Essentially, the deployment descriptor allows the bean developer or application assembler to specify a transaction attribute for each method of the component and home interfaces.

Keep in mind that there are some limitations on the methods to which transaction attributes may be assigned. The deployment descriptor may not assign a transaction attribute to some of the methods of the home and component interfaces. For example, a session bean may define a transaction attribute only for the business methods defined in the bean's component interface, not to the methods of the home interface. In addition, a session bean may not assign transaction attributes to the methods defined in the EJBObject or EJBLocalObject interface, because the container implements these methods. Therefore, it is meaningless to define a transaction attribute for them.

Like a session bean, an entity bean may define a transaction attribute for each of the business methods in the bean's component interface. In addition, an entity bean may define transaction attributes for the create, find, and home methods defined in the home interface and for the remove methods inherited from the EJBObject/EJBLocalObject and EJBHome/EJBLocalHome interfaces. However, an entity bean may not define transaction attributes for all other methods defined in the EJBObject/EJBLocalObject and EJBHome/EJBLocalHome interfaces. Because the container implements these other methods, it would be meaningless for the entity bean to define a transaction attribute for them.

It is important to note one implication of this rule. The create and remove methods of an entity bean have transaction attributes, but the create and remove methods of a session bean do not have transaction attributes. The container treats the create and remove methods of a session bean as if they had the NotSupported transaction attribute.

10.1.2   Transaction Attribute Values

A transaction attribute may have one of six values:

1. Required
2. RequiresNew
3. Supports
4. NotSupported
5. Mandatory
6. Never

The following sections explain how transaction attributes are used.

Required

The Required transaction attribute is typically used for the bean methods that update databases or other transaction-capable resource managers and hence is used for the methods of CMP entity beans. The Required transaction attribute ensures that all the updates from the method are performed atomically and that the updates done by the enterprise bean method can be included in a larger transaction. A transaction is required in such scenarios to achieve application correctness.

How does the container interpret and apply the Required transaction attribute? If a method is assigned the Required transaction attribute, the container executes the method with a transaction context so that one of two events occurs:

1. If the method caller is already associated with a transaction context, the container includes the execution of the method in the client's existing transaction context.

2. If the method caller is not associated with a transaction context, the container starts a transaction before the execution of the method and commits the transaction after the method has completed.

The `EnrollmentBean` in the application in Chapter 8 uses the `Required` transaction attribute for the `commitSelections` method. By using this attribute for this method, the application ensures that the updates to `BenefitsDatabase` and the payroll system are performed as a single transaction.

RequiresNew

The `RequiresNew` transaction attribute, like the `Required` attribute, is typically used for methods that update databases. However, methods that use the `RequiresNew` attribute should have the database updates committed regardless of the outcome of the caller's transaction.

The container applies the `RequiresNew` transaction attribute somewhat differently than the `Required` attribute does. The container always executes a method that is assigned the `RequiresNew` transaction attribute in a new transaction context. This means that the container starts a new transaction before executing the method and commits the transaction after the method completes. If the method caller is already associated with a transaction context when calling the method, the container suspends the association for the duration of the new transaction.

In what situations would the `RequiresNew` transaction attribute be useful? An application service provider may want to track, for marketing or billing purposes, the applications that each of its users has executed. Use of the `RequiresNew` attribute enables the application service provider to implement such tracking. The service provider uses the ApplicationStatistics enterprise bean for collecting the application use information. Each time a user invokes an application, it in turn invokes the `recordUsage` method on the ApplicationStatistics bean. The `recordUsage` method is assigned the `RequiresNew` transaction attribute to ensure that it records the use information even if the actual application rolls back its transaction. In contrast, if the `Required` attribute were used for the `recordUsage` method and the application rolled back its transaction, there would be no record that the user ran the application.

Supports

The `Supports` transaction attribute is used when a method does not absolutely require a transaction. When a method is assigned the `Supports` transaction attribute, the method's transaction context depends on the transaction context of the method caller. The container executes the method with or without a transaction context, depending on whether the method caller is associated with a transaction context.

If the caller is associated with a transaction context, the container includes the method execution in the caller's transaction. (In this case, the container's execution of the method is the same as if the method had been assigned the `Required` transaction attribute.)

If the caller is not associated with a transaction context, the container executes the method in a manner that transaction semantics are not defined by the EJB specification. (In this case, the container's execution of the method is the same as if the method had been assigned the `NotSupported` transaction attribute.)

When would you use the `Supports` transaction attribute? You typically use this attribute for those methods in which atomicity of multiple updates from within the method is not an issue. These cases include methods that make no updates—directly or indirectly via other enterprise beans—to data. Or, they perform only a single data-update operation that is guaranteed to be atomic by other mechanisms, such as atomicity of an SQL statement. The `Supports` attribute allows the container to avoid the overhead of using a transaction for executing a method when a transaction is not needed. At the same time, the attribute tells the container to include the work of the method into the client's transaction when this is required.

NotSupported

A method may also be assigned the `NotSupported` transaction attribute. In this situation, the container invokes the method in a manner that transaction semantics are not defined by the EJB specification. Normally, the EJB specification allows the container to invoke a method with no transaction context or in some container-specific local transaction context. When a caller invokes a method with the `Not-Supported` transaction attribute and the caller is associated with a transaction context defined by the EJB specification, the container suspends the caller's transaction association for the duration of the method.

When would you use the `NotSupported` transaction attribute? You typically use the `NotSupported` transaction attribute in two cases. You would assign this attribute to those methods of an enterprise bean that use resource managers not capable of interfacing with an external transaction coordinator or when the correct application semantics do not depend on performing resource manager access in a transaction.

When an enterprise bean uses resource managers incapable of interfacing with an external transaction coordinator, the container cannot propagate the transaction context into the resource managers. Using the `NotSupported` transaction attribute for the bean's methods instructs the container that the application developer has taken into consideration the dependency on the less capable transaction manager.

The example application in Chapter 9, Using Enterprise JavaBeans in Web Services, uses the `NotSupported` attribute for the methods of the WrapperPlan-Bean enterprise bean. WrapperPlanBean uses the Providence Health Web service. Because Web services do not support propagating a transaction, the assembler or bean developer assigned the `NotSupported` transaction attribute to all the methods of the WrapperPlanBean enterprise bean. The bean developer designed the WrapperPlanBean such that its communication with Providence Health's Web service does not require a transaction for its correctness.

Mandatory

When a method is assigned the `Mandatory` transaction attribute, the container first checks that the caller is associated with a transaction context. If the caller is not associated with a transaction context, the container throws the `javax.transaction.TransactionRequired` exception to the caller. If the client is associated with a transaction, the container performs the method invocation in the same way as for the `Required` attribute: The container includes the execution of the method in the client's existing transaction context.

When would you use the `Mandatory` transaction attribute? Use this attribute for a method for which an application assembly error would occur if the method were invoked by a caller without a transaction context.

Never

When a method is assigned the `Never` transaction attribute, the container first checks that the caller is associated with a transaction context. If the caller is associated with a transaction context, the container throws `java.rmi.RemoteException` to the client. If the caller is not associated with a transaction, the container invokes the method in the same way as the `NotSupported` attribute. You use the `Never` attribute when you want the container to ensure that a transactional client does not invoke an enterprise bean method that is not capable of transaction.

Summary of Transaction Attributes

Table 10.1 summarizes the transaction context that the EJB container passes to an invoked business method. The table also illustrates the transaction context that the container passes to the resource managers called by the invoked business method.

As illustrated, the transaction context passed by the container is a function of the transaction attribute and the client's transaction context.

In Table 10.1, *T1* represents a transaction passed with the client request; *T2* represents a transaction initiated by the container. Keep in mind that the enterprise bean's business method may invoke other enterprise beans via their home and component interfaces. When this occurs, the transaction indicated beneath the column *Transaction Associated with Business Method* is passed as part of the client context to the target enterprise bean.

Table 10.1 Summary of Transaction Attributes

Transaction Attribute	Client's Transaction	Transaction Associated with Business Method	Transaction Associated with Resource Managers
Required	None	T2	T2
	T1	T1	T1
RequiresNew	None	T2	T2
	T1	T2	T2
Supports	None	None	None
	T1	T1	T1
NotSupported	None	None	None
	T1	None	None
Mandatory	None	Error	NA
	T1	T1	T1
Never	None	None	None
	T1	Error	NA

Note on Transaction Attributes for Entity Beans

As explained in Section 7.2.4, Caching Entity Bean State, on page 219, a BMP entity bean may use the ejbLoad and ejbStore methods to perform caching of data. For this caching to work correctly, the container must combine the ejbLoad method, the business methods, and the ejbStore method into a single transaction. This means that if the bean depends on the ejbLoad and ejbStore methods to manage caching, it should not be using the NotSupported, Supports, and Never transaction attributes.

10.1.3 Transaction Attributes for Message-Driven Beans

Message-driven beans have only one method, `onMessage`, to which the container delivers messages. Because transaction context never flows over JMS messages, a message-driven bean can never perform work in the scope of the client's transaction. The transaction attributes of the `onMessage` method are hence restricted to `Required` and `NotSupported`.

If the `onMessage` method has a transaction attribute of `Required`, the container starts a transaction before invoking the method, and all work done by `onMessage`—such as database access, invocations on other beans, and so forth—are part of that new transaction. In addition, the message delivery itself is part of the transaction. This means that if the transaction aborts for any reason, such as a failed database update attempt by the bean, the message delivery is also aborted. The `Required` transaction attribute also ensures that the container redelivers the message at a later point.

If the `onMessage` method has the `NotSupported` transaction attribute, the container does not start a transaction before calling the message-driven bean. In other words, the message-driven bean runs without a transaction.

Message-driven beans may also use bean-managed transaction demarcation, as described in Section 10.2.2, Transaction Demarcation by a Session Bean, on page 338.

10.1.4 Transaction Attributes for Sample Application

Table 10.2 shows the transaction attributes used for methods of the entity bean sample application—the application discussed in Chapter 7, Understanding Entity Beans, and Chapter 9, Using Enterprise JavaBeans in Web Services. Following the table is an explanation of why these attributes were assigned in this manner.

Table 10.2 Method Transaction Attributes for Sample Application

Enterprise Bean Name	Method Name	Transaction Attribute
Enrollment	`getEmployeeInfo`, `getCoverageOptions`, `setCoverageOption`, `getMedicalOptions`, `setMedicalOption`, `getDentalOptions`, `setDentalOption`, `isSmoker`, `setSmoker`, `getSummary`	Supports
	`commitSelections`	Required
Selection	`getCopy`, `updateFromCopy`, `remove`	Required

Table 10.2 Method Transaction Attributes for Sample Application

Enterprise Bean Name	Method Name	Transaction Attribute
SelectionHome	`create, findByPrimaryKey, remove`	`Required`
Plan	`getPlanType, getPlanId, getPlanName, getAgeFactor, setAgeFactor, get-CoverageFactor, setCoverageFactor, getSmokerCost, setSmokerCost, add-Doctor, removeDoctor, getCost, getAllDoctors, getDoctorsByName, getDoctorsBySpecialty, remove`	`Required`
PlanHome	`create, findByPrimaryKey, findMedicalPlans, findDentalPlans, findByDoctor, updateSmokerCosts, get-MedicalPlanNames, getDentalPlanNames, remove`	`Required`
Doctor	`getFirstName, getLastName, get-Specialty, getHospitals, get-PracticeSince, remove`	`Required`
DoctorHome	`create, findByPrimaryKey, remove`	`Required`
Employee	`getEmployeeNumber, getFirstName, get-LastName, getBirthDate, remove`	`Required`
EmployeeHome	`create, findByPrimaryKey, remove`	`Required`
Payroll, PayrollLocal	`setSalary, getSalary, setBenefits-Deduction, getBenefitsDeduction`	`Supports`
PayrollMDB	`onMessage`	`Required`
Insurance-PlanAdmin	`createInsurancePlan, getPlanInfo, addDoctors, removeDoctors, getAll-Doctors, setSmokerCost, setAge-Factor, setCoverageFactor`	`Required`
WrapperPlanEJB	`all methods`	`NotSupported`
Wrapper-DoctorEJB	`all methods`	`NotSupported`

Wombat assigned the `Required` transaction attribute to the `commitSelections` method defined in the `Enrollment` remote interface. The `commitSelections` method updates multiple databases, and therefore Wombat uses a transaction to achieve atomicity of the multiple updates. Wombat assigned the `Supports` attribute to all other methods of the `Enrollment` remote interface because these methods do not require a transaction for their correctness. (The methods only read data from the database.)

Wombat assigned the `Required` transaction attribute to all the methods of all the entity beans. Using the `Required` attribute is typical for methods of an entity bean because it guarantees that the container includes the execution of the `ejbLoad` method, the business methods, and the `ejbStore` method in a single transaction. See Section 7.2.4, Caching Entity Bean State, on page 219.

Star Enterprise assigned the `Supports` transaction attribute to the methods on the PayrollEJB's local and remote interfaces. The `Supports` transaction attribute allows the work performed by those methods to be part of the client's transaction, if there is one. However, if there is no client transaction, the work performed by PayrollEJB is not part of a global transaction. Star Enterprise also assigned the `Required` attribute to the `onMessage` method of the PayrollMDB message-driven bean because the work it performs, as well as the message delivery, needs to be part of the same transaction. If the payroll update is aborted for any reason, the message delivery also needs to be aborted, and the message needs to be redelivered.

The `InsurancePlanAdmin` Web service interface has all its methods set to the `Required` attribute. This allows `InsurancePlanAdmin` to make multiple fine-grained calls on the PlanEJB and DoctorEJB entity beans through their local interfaces within the scope of one transaction. If `InsurancePlanAdmin` did not run in a transaction, each call on PlanEJB and DoctorEJB would result in a separate transaction starting and committing, and this would greatly increase performance overhead.

The WrapperPlanEJB and WrapperDoctorEJB beans have all their methods set to the `NotSupported` transaction attribute. They do this because they do not perform any transactional work by themselves. Instead, they delegate all transactional work to the Providence Health Web service.

10.2 Programmatic Transaction Demarcation

The preferred way to demarcate transactions in EJB applications is to use transaction attributes. By using transaction attributes, the bean developer does not have to manage transaction boundaries programmatically in the enterprise bean's code. However, although declarative transaction demarcation via transaction attributes works in most cases, the declarative demarcation does not provide the required functionality in some situations or is awkward to use, such as when it forces the application developer to partition the application unnaturally into multiple enterprise beans to achieve the required transaction demarcation.

This section discusses when and how the application developer should use programmatic transaction demarcation to control transaction boundaries programmatically. The application developer may control the transaction boundaries programmatically either in the client code for the enterprise bean or directly in the enterprise bean business methods.

10.2.1   Transaction Demarcation by a Client

Typically, an enterprise bean client, such as a Web application or a stand-alone Java client application, does not manage transaction boundaries. Instead, the client invokes methods on an enterprise bean, and the EJB container in which the target enterprise bean is deployed automatically manages transactions based on the values of the transaction attributes for the invoked method. This container-provided transaction demarcation is transparent to the client. The client either sees a successful completion of the invoked method or, if an error occurs, receives the `java.rmi.RemoteException` exception from the invoked method.

Certain situations require the client to demarcate transactions programmatically. Typically, in these situations, the client needs to combine the invocation of multiple methods into a single transaction. The methods can be on the same enterprise bean or on multiple beans. For this to work, the client needs to demarcate transactions programmatically, which the client accomplishes by using the `javax.transaction.UserTransaction` interface. (The `javax.transaction.UserTransaction` interface is part of the Java™ Transaction API [JTA]. More information about JTA is available at `http://java.sun.com/j2ee/docs.html`.) The client obtains the `javax.transaction.UserTransaction` interface from its environment, using the JNDI name `java:comp/UserTransaction`.

The MyServlet servlet, which transfers funds from one bank account to another, illustrates this. Figure 10.1 shows the OID for the interactions that occur during MyServlet's operation.

MyServlet executes the funds transfer in a single transaction by using the TransferFunds JavaBean component. (Note that TransferFunds is not an enterprise bean. However, as far as the discussion of transactions is concerned, the Transfer-Funds bean is considered part of the servlet.)

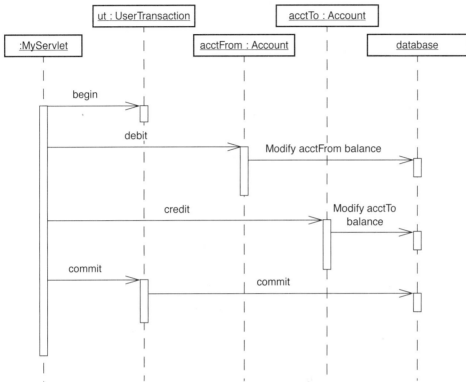

Figure 10.1 MyServlet OID

Code Example 10.1 shows the MyServlet code:

```
public class MyServlet extends HttpServlet {
    public void service(ServletRequest req, ServletResponse resp) {
        ...
        TransferFunds transferFunds = new TransferFunds();
        transferFunds.setAccountFrom(...);
        transferFunds.setAccountTo(...);
        transferFunds.setAmount(...);
        try {
            transferFunds.execute();
        } catch (TransferException ex) {
            ...
        }
```

```
            ...
        }
    }
```

Code Example 10.1 The MyServlet Class

Code Example 10.2 shows the code for the TransferFunds JavaBean:

```
import javax.transaction.*;
...

public class TransferFunds {
    String accountNumberFrom;
    String accountNumberTo;
    double amount;

    public void setAccountFrom(String accountNumber) {
        accountNumberFrom = accountNumber;
    }

    public void setAccountTo(String accountNumber) {
        accountNumberTo = accountNumber;
    }

    public void setAmount(double amt) {
        amount = amt;
    }

    public void execute() throws TransferException
    {
        UserTransaction ut = null;

        try {
            ...
            AccountHome h1 = ...;
            AccountHome h2 = ...;
            Account acctFrom = h1.findByPrimaryKey(
                                    accountNumberFrom);
```

```
      Account acctTo = h2.findByPrimaryKey(
                              accountNumberTo);

      // Obtain the UserTransaction interface.
      Context initCtx = new InitialContext();
      ut = (UserTransaction)initCtx.lookup(
          "java:comp/UserTransaction");

      // Perform the transfer.
      ut.begin();
      acctFrom.debit(amount);
      acctTo.credit(amount);
      ut.commit();
      // Transfer was completed.
    } catch (Exception ex) {
      try {
        if (ut != null)
          ut.rollback();
      } catch (Exception ex) {
      }
      // Transfer was not completed.
      throw new TransferException(ex);
    }
  }
}
```

Code Example 10.2 The TransferFunds JavaBean Class

Let's take a closer look at the implementation of the execute method of the TransferFunds JavaBean. The servlet client uses the execute method to accomplish a number of tasks. Assuming that it does not encounter any failures, the client code works as described in the next paragraph.

First, the client obtains the remote interfaces for the two accounts—acctFrom and acctTo—involved in the transaction. The client then uses the JNDI API to obtain a reference to the UserTransaction interface from the servlet's environment. Once it obtains the reference, the client starts a transaction, using the begin method of the UserTransaction interface. The client then debits the acctFrom account and credits the `acctTo` account. Finally, the client commits the transaction, using the `commit` method of the `UserTransaction` interface.

However, what is even more interesting is how the `execute` method deals with failures. Note that the `execute` method wraps all its statements in a `try` block. If the execution of the statements in the `try` block raises an exception, this executes the block of code in the `catch` clause. The block of code in the `catch` clause attempts to roll back the in-progress transaction started by the `execute` method and throws `TransferException` to the caller.

If the servlet container crashes before the transaction is committed, the transaction manager will automatically roll back all updates performed by the `execute` method. For example, if the `execute` method debited `acctFrom` before the servlet container crashed, the transaction manager instructs the database that stores `acctFrom` to roll back the changes caused by the `debit` operation.

10.2.2 Transaction Demarcation by a Session Bean

A session bean or a message-driven bean can use the `UserTransaction` interface to demarcate transactions programmatically. However, an entity bean cannot use the `UserTransaction` interface. In this section, we describe a typical scenario in which the session bean developer uses the `UserTransaction` interface to demarcate a transaction rather than relying on the declarative transaction demarcation via transaction attributes.

The J2EE platform does not allow a stand-alone Java application to use the `UserTransaction` interface. How can a stand-alone Java application perform multiple invocations to an enterprise bean within a single transaction if it cannot use the `UserTransaction` interface? The application can use the bean-managed transaction demarcation feature of the EJB specification to combine multiple client-invoked methods into a single transaction. It would be impossible for a stand-alone Java application to achieve this—combining multiple client-invoked methods into a single transaction—with declarative transaction demarcation.

We illustrate this by using the session bean example from Chapter 4. Let's assume that a stand-alone Java client application uses the EnrollmentEJB session bean in that example. Let's further assume, for the sake of this illustration, that the logic of the Benefits Enrollment application requires that all data access performed by the multiple steps of the entire enrollment business process be part of a single transaction. (This is not a very realistic example!)

In such a scenario, the application developer would design the EnrollmentEJB session bean as a bean with bean-managed transaction demarcation. The developer would modify the EnrollmentBean class—described in Section 4.4.2, EnrollmentBean Session Bean Class Details, on page 89—to obtain and use the UserTransaction interface in the ejbCreate and commitSelections methods, as illustrated in Code Example 10.3:

```
public class EnrollmentBean implements SessionBean
{
    UserTransaction ut = null;
    ...
    public void ejbCreate(int emplNum) throws EnrollmentException
    {
        // Obtain the UserTransaction interface from the
        // session bean's environment.
        Context initCtx = new InitialContext();
        ut = (UserTransaction)initCtx.lookup(
                "java:comp/UserTransaction");

        // Start a transaction.
        ut.begin();

        // The rest of the ejbCreate method
        employeeNumber = emplNum;
            ...
    }
    ...
    public void commitSelections() {

        // Insert new or update existing benefits selection record.
        if (recordDoesNotExist) {
            benefitsDAO.insertSelection(selection);
            recordDoesNotExist = false;
        } else {
            benefitsDAO.updateSelection(selection);
        }

        // Update information in the payroll system.
        try {
            payroll.setBenefitsDeduction(employeeNumber,
                                         payrollDeduction);
```

```
        } catch (Exception ex) {
           throw new EJBException(ex);
        }

        // Commit the transaction started in ejbCreate.
        try {
           ut.commit();
        } catch (Exception ex) {
           // Handle exception from commit.
           ...
        }
     }
     ...
}
```

Code Example 10.3 EnrollmentBean Class with Bean-Managed Transaction
                    Demarcation

The ejbCreate method starts a transaction that then spans all the methods invoked by the client application. The commitSelections method commits the transaction after the client application has completed its work.

Figures 10.2 and 10.3 show the OIDs for these transaction operations. The OID diagrams illustrate the interactions between the Enrollment session object and the transaction manager that take place via the UserTransaction interface. They also illustrate the interactions between the transaction manager and the corporate databases.

The Enrollment session object starts the transaction by invoking the begin method on the UserTransaction interface, which causes the container to include the access to the corporate databases performed by the Enrollment object as part of the transaction. As the OID diagram illustrates, the container enlists the corporate databases with the transaction.

In addition, when the Enrollment object invokes the Payroll object, the container propagates the transaction context to the Payroll object to include the payroll-deduction update as part of the transaction. Finally, the Enrollment object commits the transaction by invoking the commit method on the UserTransaction interface. The transaction manager instructs the corporate databases to commit the changes made by the transaction. If the corporate databases are located on multiple servers, the transaction manager performs the two-phase commit protocol.

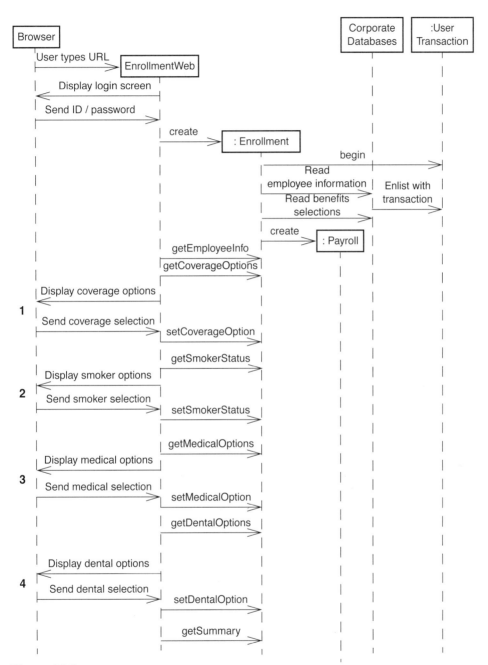

Figure 10.2 Transaction OID, Part 1

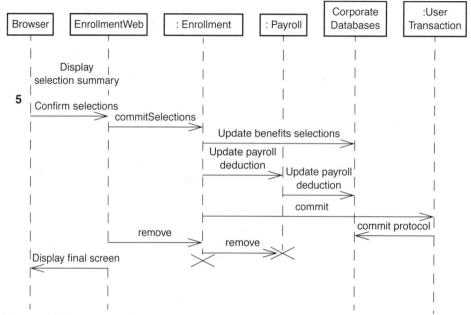

Figure 10.3 Transaction OID, Part 2

All the accesses to the corporate databases between the `UserTransaction.begin` method invoked in the `ejbCreate` method and the `UserTransaction.commit` method invoked at the end of the `commitSelections` method are part of a single transaction.

What are the pitfalls of using bean-managed transaction demarcation? As we stated earlier, bean-managed transaction demarcation is typically used to combine multiple client-invoked methods into a single transaction. This means that a transaction is "in progress" across a client's multiple interactions with the application. The transaction may block other transactions because a transaction causes the resource managers to hold locks on the data accessed by the transaction. If a user works slowly or leaves the application in the middle of the in-progress transaction, the transaction may block all other users' transactions that need access to the data now locked by the slow user's transaction.

Therefore, transactions that span multiple user interactions with an application should be used only in environments with a small population of well-behaved users. And just as important, such transactions should always be used with a great deal of care. For example, it would be very unusual if a Web-based application—

with its multitude of unregulated users—used transactions that span user interactions. For this reason, the benefits applications described in Chapters 4 and 8 do not use transactions that span interactions with the user.

10.2.3 Pitfalls of Using Programmatic Transaction Demarcation

The developer using programmatic transaction demarcation needs to be very careful in the placement of the `begin`, `commit`, and `rollback` calls in the application code.

- The programmer must ensure that `begin` is not called when the application is already associated with a transaction. J2EE does not support nested transactions.

- The programmer must ensure that the application will eventually commit or roll back the transaction. This may be nontrivial if the application code has many execution paths and Java exceptions are thrown. If the application does not commit or roll back a transaction, the transaction manager will eventually timeout the transaction and roll it back. Before the timeout expires, the locks held by the transaction may block other transactions from making progress.

Therefore, an application developer should use declarative transaction demarcation whenever possible and should apply programmatic transaction demarcation only for those cases for which declarative transaction demarcation does not work. The container implements declarative transaction demarcation and properly handles all the application execution paths.

10.3 Conclusion

This chapter explained the transaction attributes defined by the EJB architecture and showed how to apply them with declarative transaction demarcation. The chapter also explained and demonstrated how to do transaction demarcation by clients and by session beans.

From here, we move to the issues surrounding security. Chapter 11 describes how to handle security from the point of view of application developers and deployers.

CHAPTER 11

Managing Security

SECURITY is of paramount importance for an enterprise. The EJB architecture provides comprehensive support for security management. This support is particularly useful given the wide variety of protocols and security mechanisms that enterprises may use today.

This chapter describes the EJB security environment from the point of view of an application developer, focusing on how he or she handles security. The chapter also focuses on how the deployer maps this security view to the security management infrastructure of the enterprise.

In today's environment, it is commonplace for EJB applications to control important business functions in the enterprise. Enterprise beans routinely have access to confidential data in the enterprise. To ensure the continued integrity and confidentiality of this data, it is important that only authorized users be permitted to invoke enterprise bean methods. An authorized user is a one whose position or role in the enterprise necessitates that he or she perform the business function implemented by the method, or it may be someone whose managerial responsibilities necessitate access to these business functions. For example, in the case of our example entity bean application in Chapter 8, it is important to ensure that confidential employee information, such as an employee's payroll data, is accessible only to the users who are authorized to access the information, such as the payroll department.

The basic security management problem that confronts an application developer is the diversity of security management approaches. Different enterprises manage security in many different ways in their operational environments. Most often, the goal of an application developer is to develop an application that can be deployed in multiple operational environments. When each such operational environment uses different security mechanisms and policies, it becomes a real challenge to address the security needs of the application.

Because both the application developer and the deployer potentially share the responsibilities for security management, a fine line must be maintained between the two because there are trade-offs when one or the other takes responsibility for implementing security policies. On the one hand, when the application developer designs and codes the security policies into the application, it is easier for the deployer to deploy the application if the policies meet the needs of the operational environment. However, the same application is no longer reusable across multiple operational environments. On the other hand, if the application developer leaves the security of the application to the deployer, the deployer must be familiar with the intimate details of the application to secure it in the operational environment.

The EJB architecture is designed so that the deployer bears the most burden for securing an application. At the same time, the EJB architecture makes the deployer's job easier. The security support in the EJB architecture allows the application developer to pass certain security-related information to the deployer. This information frees the deployer from having to understand the intimate details of the application in order to secure it.

The EJB architecture carefully apportions the responsibility for the security of EJB applications across the multiple EJB roles. The following sections describe the security responsibilities of the individual EJB roles.

11.1   Responsibilities of the System Administrator

The system administrator is responsible for the overall security configuration of the enterprise's network environment. Although most of the system administrator's tasks are independent of specific applications deployed in the enterprise, these security administration tasks affect the deployment of EJB applications.

In this section, we describe the security administration procedures relevant to the discussion of EJB application security. Keep in mind that the EJB specification does not define or require these procedures; rather, they are typically used in enterprise environments.

The following system administration tasks are relevant to the deployment of an EJB application:

- **Administering security principals**—A security principal roughly corresponds to a user account. Administering security principals includes such tasks as adding and removing user accounts, adding a user account to the appropriate user groups, and so forth. A user group represents a group of users having a certain set of privileges. A user account may belong to multiple user groups.

- **Managing the necessary principal mappings on the enterprise's network**—Principal mapping is required in certain circumstances when related applications run in different security domains. For example, the system administrator must manage principal mapping when an application running in one security domain invokes an application or a database in a different security domain, and each security domain has its own set of security principals.

- **Integrating the EJB container into the enterprise's secure network environment**

Let's look at some of the tasks that a system administrator at Star Enterprise may perform that are relevant to the deployment of the benefits application described in Chapter 8.

11.1.1 Administering Users and Security Principals

To begin, the Star Enterprise system administrator manages the user accounts and user groups. The system administrator creates a user account for a new employee. Depending on the employee's role in the enterprise, the system administrator adds the user account to the appropriate user groups. For example, when Mary Smith joins the benefits administration department as the department director, the system administrator creates a user account for her and adds her user account to the *employees, payroll-department,* and *directors* user groups.

The user account information is used for *authentication* and *authorization* purposes. Authentication takes place when a user connects to the system. For example, when Mary Smith logs in to her computer, she first needs to authenticate herself—prove that she is indeed Mary Smith—to the enterprise network security manager.

After she authenticates herself, Mary's session is associated with a security token. The security token represents the information from her user account, including the user groups to which the user account belongs, and it allows applications and servers to check authorizations. When Mary invokes an application or a database on the enterprise's network, the security token is passed along with the request to the target application or database. The target application or database server uses the passed security token to check whether Mary Smith is authorized to access the requested application or data.

11.1.2 Managing Principal Mapping

Passing the security token works only if the target application or database system understands the security token. If it is in a different security domain, the target application or database system may not understand the token. Such a situation necessitates one of two solutions:

1. The user needs to log in to the target system. Mary Smith has to log in a second time, directly to the target application or database system.

2. The enterprise security infrastructure maps the security token associated with Mary Smith's original session with her computer to another security token that is usable on the target system.

This second technique, called *principal mapping*, is managed by the system administrator. Principal mapping allows Mary Smith to use a single password across the entire set of applications and database systems at Star Enterprise.

In our benefits application example, the payroll system is an application running on a mainframe. The payroll system does not understand the security token received from the network on which Mary Smith's computer resides. In order for the payroll system to recognize Mary Smith—or any other user from that network—as an authorized user, the Payroll App Server EJB container (see Figure 8.1 on page 246) needs to perform principal mapping on the calls coming to the mainframe payroll application.

For the EJB container to perform principal mapping, the system administrator must have already set it up. The principal mapping maps all clients of PayrollEJB to a single mainframe user. From the perspective of the mainframe, all instances of `PayrollBean` use the identity of a single mainframe user, which we'll call *payroll user*, to invoke the mainframe payroll system. Within the mainframe environment, the payroll user is authorized to access all the information needed by PayrollEJB. Figure 11.1 illustrates mapping of principals.

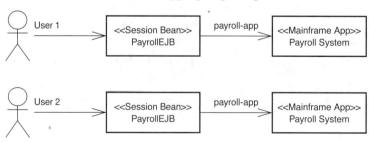

Figure 11.1 Principal Mapping

11.2 Responsibilities of the Container Provider

In EJB applications, the container bears most of the responsibility for enforcing application security at runtime. The EJB container is responsible for a number of tasks related to authentication and security principals. In addition, the container is responsible for tasks pertaining to the management of security in a multiapplication and multidomain environment.

The EJB container provider is responsible for providing the security mechanisms applicable to the target operational environment. Because it is typically an integral part of the security infrastructure of the operational environment, the EJB container interacts with the other parts of the operational environment to implement the security mechanisms.

11.2.1 Authentication and Authorization Tasks

The container handles authentication and authorization tasks in the following areas:

- **Authenticating principals**—Typically, the user accounts and the definitions of the user groups in the operational environment are stored in an external directory system rather than directly in the container. User accounts and groups are kept in an external directory from the container because all enterprise applications use this information, not just the EJB applications running in the container. Therefore, the container must be able to interface in a secure manner with the user account information. An enterprise may use either a proprietary protocol or standard protocol, such as the Kerberos protocol, for this purpose.

- **Enforcing method permissions**—The EJB container enforces the method permissions defined in the application's deployment descriptor. The EJB container dispatches a client-invoked method on an enterprise bean only if the client has been assigned a security role that has permission to invoke the target method. Otherwise, the container throws an exception to the client.

- **Controlling access to resource managers**—Many enterprise beans access resource managers, such as databases. The EJB container is responsible for managing the authentication protocol with the resource manager, based on the deployer's instructions.

11.2.2   Managing Multiple Applications and Domains

The container also has tasks related to managing security among multiple applications and multiple domains. Many enterprise environments run multiple applications, often across various security domains. To ensure that no security breaches occur among the various applications, the container is responsible for the following tasks:

- **Ensuring the integrity of concurrent applications**—The container may execute multiple applications at the same time, may handle invocations from multiple clients at the same time, and may cache sensitive data in memory. The container ensures that this concurrent activity does not result in a security breach. The container must isolate the running applications and users from one another so that information is not "leaked" via the container from one application to another. In addition, the container ensures that data access by one user is not exposed to another user. The container should be implemented to be safe from security attacks.

- **Mapping principals between domains**—When clients from one security domain invoke enterprise beans in a different security domain or when the beans invoke other enterprise beans or other types of applications that are in different security domains, the container participates in the protocol for mapping the principals between the domains.

- **Keeping an audit trail**—The container typically maintains an audit trail of detected attempts to breach security. This audit trail is intended for the system administrator to identify security threats.

11.3   Application Provider's View of Security

An EJB application provider has essentially two choices for managing security:

1. To perform security management in the application code.

2. To delegate most of the security management to the deployer. The deployer then uses the facilities of the EJB container and the security infrastructure of the target operational environment to secure the application.

We discuss these two options from the perspective of user authentication and authorization.

11.3.1 Client Authentication

We recommend that EJB applications *not* perform user authentication logic in the application code. Instead, developers of EJB applications should rely on the deployer to ensure that the caller of an enterprise bean method has been authenticated prior to invoking the method. At runtime, the EJB container authenticates the client before the container dispatches a business method. The container makes the identity of the method caller available to the invoked enterprise bean method via the getCallerPrincipal method of the EJBContext interface.

Why is it recommended that EJB applications not perform authentication logic? There are two reasons for this recommendation:

1. Developing bulletproof authentication logic is not a simple application programming task. A developer who is not a security expert may introduce a security hole in the application.

2. Hard-coding authentication logic makes the EJB application less reusable across multiple operational environments. For example, once authentication logic is embedded in the application code, it is impossible to deploy the enterprise bean in an operational environment that uses a single sign-on framework for all its applications.

11.3.2 Authorization

The guidelines for implementing authorization—the rules that specify which users can perform which business functions—are less straightforward than those for authentication. Ideally, authorization rules should be decoupled from the application code. This permits the rules to be set based on the operational environment and lets the container be responsible for their enforcement. When decoupled from the application code, the deployer can modify the authorization rules to meet the unique needs of the particular operational environment. Furthermore, decoupling the authentication logic from the application code enables the container to enforce the authentication rules rather than rely on the application to make the authorization checks itself. Because a vendor with expertise in security typically develops the container, the application overall is more secure when the container enforces the authentication rules.

In practice, however, many authorization rules are too fine grained or too application specific—that is, the rules may be a function of data passed by the client and data read from a database—to be decoupled from the application code. An example is a rule that states the following: An expense request larger than $5,000 must be approved by the division's vice president unless the requester is at least a director in the company, or the item to be expensed was purchased from a list of preapproved suppliers.

Consequently, developers must evaluate their own applications and decide whether to delegate an authorization rule to the container to enforce or to handle the rule as part of the application's business logic and thus code its treatment in the application. We recommend using the following guidelines for this decision:

- Authorization rules that restrict access to the enterprise beans' methods to a group (or groups) of users should *not* be coded into the application. An example of such a rule is the following: Only users belonging to this department can invoke this method. Instead, use the EJB declarative security mechanism to define these authorization rules. When this mechanism is used, the EJB container enforces these authorization rules at runtime.

- Authorization rules that are too fine grained or that use application-specific data do not typically fit the EJB declarative security mechanism. The application developer should treat these rules as application logic and implement them in the application code. For these cases, however, the application developer should use good programming practices to separate the code implementing the authorization logic from the code implementing the rest of the business logic. This facilitates configuring, modifying, or replacing the authorization logic, if necessary, at application deployment. (Note that this is similar to separating the code implementing data access from the code implementing business logic.)

11.3.3 Declarative Security Mechanism

As mentioned previously, the EJB declarative security mechanism allows decoupling of a certain type of authentication rules from the business logic of the application. The application provider uses the deployment descriptor to define a set of security roles and their associated method permissions for the enterprise beans. This information represents the client authorization rules intended by the application provider. The deployer uses this information as input when securing the application in a specific operational environment (Figure 11.2).

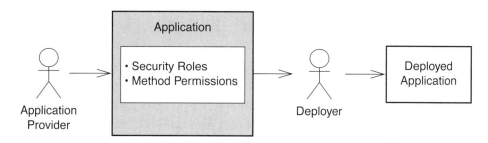

Figure 11.2 Declarative Security Mechanisms

The definitions of the security roles and their associated method permissions simplify the deployer's task. The definitions of the security roles free the deployer from having to learn each enterprise bean method's function to determine who should be allowed to invoke that method. Instead, the deployer needs to understand a much smaller set of security roles to secure the application.

11.3.4 Security Roles

The definitions of the security roles advise the deployer on how the application provider envisioned the application would be used from a security perspective. Each security role represents an actor—a type of user—for the application. Each actor performs one or more use cases.

For example, Wombat, which developed the Benefits Enrollment application, may define two security roles in the `benefits_ejb.jar` file deployment descriptor:

1. **The *employees* security role.** This security role represents enterprise employees who access the benefits application to manage their benefits choices.

2. **The *plan-admin* security role.** This security role represents enterprise plan administration staff who manage the health and dental insurance plans.

11.3.5 Method Permissions

In the deployment descriptor, a method permission is a declaration pertaining to security roles. You can think of a method permission as stating that a given security role invokes a given enterprise bean method when running the application. A method permission declaration instructs the tools used by the deployer to ensure that the users with the specified security role be allowed to invoke the method. In addition, the developer or assembler may mark a method as being *unchecked* or *uncall-*

able. For a method marked *unchecked*, no authorization checks are performed prior to invoking the method. A method marked *uncallable* is a method that may never be called.

For example, Wombat uses the method permission mechanism in the deployment descriptor to declare the following:

- The security role *employee* should have access to all methods of the Enrollment and Selection beans and to read-only methods of the Employee, Plan, and Doctor beans. Employees with this security role are not allowed to invoke the `create` and `remove` methods nor any methods that modify the state of the employee and insurance plan entity beans.

- The security role *benefits-admin* needs access to the methods that modify the state of insurance plans, so it is allowed to invoke all methods of the Plan and Doctor beans, including `create` and `remove`.

How do security roles and method permissions simplify the deployer's task? When deploying the `premiumhealth_ejb.jar` file, the deployer is concerned only with the two security roles: *employee* and *benefits-admin*. The deployer does not have to study each individual enterprise bean method's function.

Typically, the deployment tools display the security roles and prompt the deployer to assign individual users or user groups, to each security role. The tools and the EJB container automatically ensure that assigned users or user groups have access to the methods specified in the method permissions.

11.3.6 Using the RunAs Principal

Normally, an enterprise bean executes in the security context of the caller. This implies that by default, any resources or other beans used by the first bean are also accessed under the client's security context—or without a security context, if the client's request was not secured.

The application developer or assembler can change the principal under which resources and other beans are accessed by a bean by setting a *RunAs* principal for the bean. This is done by specifying a `run-as` security role in the deployment descriptor. The deployer then chooses a user from the execution environment under whose security principal the bean executes.

The RunAs mechanism is usually necessary for a message-driven bean because the client's message does not carry a security principal.

11.3.7 Programmatic Security API

The EJB specification defines in the `EJBContext` interface two methods that allow an invoked enterprise bean method to obtain security information about the method's caller:

1. `getCallerPrincipal`—This method returns the `java.security.Principal` object representing the current caller. The enterprise bean can use this method to determine the current caller.

2. `isCallerInRole`—This method allows the enterprise bean method to test whether the current caller is assigned to a given security role defined in the deployment descriptor.

The application developer or deployer can use these two security methods in the enterprise bean application logic to perform programmatically the authorization checks that are not easily done using the declarative security mechanism. For example, let's assume that the deployer of the PayrollEJB bean wants to allow each employee to access only his or her personal salary information via the `get-Salary` method. In addition, the deployer wants to allow the entire payroll staff to access the salaries of all employees. Note that this authentication rule cannot be expressed using the declarative security mechanism.

One possible way for the deployer to implement this authentication rule is to subclass the generic `PayrollBean` class, which has no security checks, and produce a `StarPayrollBean` class that includes the desired authentication check (Code Example 11.1):

```
public class StarPayrollBean extends PayrollBean {
    Session sessionCtx;

    public double getSalary(int emplNumber) {
        Principal callerPrincipal = sessionCtx.getCallerPrincipal();
        int callerEmplNumber =
            Integer.parseInt(callerPrincipal.getName());

        if (sessionCtx.isCallerInRole("employee") &&
                emplNumber == callerEmplNumber) ||
            sessionCtx.isCallerInRole("payroll-dept")) {
          // Allow access.
          return super.getSalary(emplNumber);
        } else {
```

```
                    throw new SecurityException("access to salary denied");
                }
            }

        public void setSessionContext(SessionContext sc) {
            sessionCtx = sc;
            super.setSessionContext(sc);
        }
    }
```

Code Example 11.1 Adding Authentication Checks to a Bean

Note that StarPayrollBean uses the getCallerPrincipal method to obtain
the caller's principal and then invokes the isCallerInRole method to check the
caller's role before allowing access to the salary data. If the caller's role is that of
an *employee*—and the caller's employee number matches that of the salary
record—or the caller is part of the payroll department, the method permits access
to the salary data; otherwise, it throws a security exception.

In our example, we illustrated how a deployer can use subclassing to add a
fine-grained authorization rule to a method. Of course, the developer of the PayrollBean bean could implement this authorization rule directly in the PayrollBean
class, but the PayrollBean bean would become less reusable as a result because
the format of the caller's principal returned by the getCallerPrincipal method
depends on the application server and security mechanisms used in an enterprise.

11.3.8 Example Security Application

The example application from Chapter 8 uses the declarative security mechanism.
In this section, we discuss the security views of each of the providers of the application's parts—the Wombat ISV and Star Enterprise.

Wombat Developer's View of Security

The Wombat application developer has no knowledge of the security environment at
the customer site: Star Enterprise. For example, the developer does not know the
user accounts or user groups defined by the system administrator at Star Enterprise.

To handle this situation, an ISV analyzes its application from a security point
of view, defining intended use cases of the various application parts and defining

security roles for each case. Essentially, the developer details the functions that application users will perform and then defines distinct roles permitted to perform particular sets of functions.

Wombat defines two security roles that summarize the intended use cases of the Wombat application's parts from the security point of view:

1. **The *employee* security role**—This role represents the end user of the application: an employee who uses the benefits self-service application. The *employee* security role is intended to perform only the benefits enrollment business process. It is not allowed, for example, to modify the benefits plans offered to employees.

2. **The *benefits-admin* security role**—This role represents the staff of the benefits department. The *benefits-admin* security role administers the benefits plans offered to employees.

After identifying the security roles for the enterprise beans, the Wombat developer defines the method permissions that each security role must have to perform its application use cases. The method permissions are depicted in Table 11.1.

The *employee* security role needs to have access to all the methods of EnrollmentEJB, which in turn needs to have access to the methods of SelectionEJB, WrapperPlanEJB, and EmployeeEJB. The reason is that the implementation of EnrollmentEJB calls these methods—that is, these methods are called from the `EnrollmentBean` class.

Some enterprise bean methods, such as the create and `remove` methods of the EmployeeEJB's local home interface, are not associated with a security role. What does this mean? Wombat designed the interfaces of its enterprise beans to be used by other applications, not just by the enrollment application. The enrollment application does not use some of the methods, and these methods are not associated with a security role.

How should the deployer treat these methods? Unless the deployer wants to enable other applications to access to these methods, the deployer should simply disallow access to these methods by marking them as *uncallable*.

Table 11.1 Security Roles for Beans Developed by Wombat

Enterprise Bean Name	Method Name	Security Roles
Enrollment	getEmployeeInfo, getCoverageOptions, setCoverageOption, getMedicalOptions, setMedicalOption, getDentalOptions, setDentalOption, isSmoker, setSmoker, getSummary, commitSelections	employee
Selection	getCopy, updateFromCopy, remove	employee
SelectionHome	create, findByPrimaryKey, remove	employee
Plan	getPlanType, getPlanId, getPlanName, getAgeFactor, getCoverageFactor, getSmokerCost, getCost, getAllDoctors, getDoctorsByName, getDoctorsBySpecialty	employee, benefits-admin
	setAgeFactor, setCoverageFactor, setSmokerCost, addDoctor, removeDoctor, remove	benefits-admin
PlanHome	findByPrimaryKey, findMedicalPlans, findDentalPlans, findByDoctor, getMedicalPlanNames, getDentalPlanNames	employee, benefits-admin
	create, updateSmokerCosts, remove	benefits-admin
Doctor	getFirstName, getLastName, getSpecialty, getHospitals, getPracticeSince	employee, benefits-admin
	remove	benefits-admin
DoctorHome	findByPrimaryKey	employee, benefits-admin
	create, remove	benefits-admin
Employee	getEmployeeNumber, getFirstName, getLastName, getBirthDate	employee
EmployeeHome	findByPrimaryKey	employee

Star Enterprise's View of Security Roles

Star Enterprise's IT department developed some enterprise beans and integrated them with Wombat's Benefits Enrollment application. The security settings for the beans developed by Star Enterprise are as follows:

- **PayrollEJB**—The PayrollEJB bean defines the security roles *employee* and *payroll-dept*. Although both roles are allowed to invoke the `setBenefitsDeduction`, `getBenefitsDeduction`, and `getSalary` methods, only the *payroll-dept* role can invoke the `setSalary` method.

- **WrapperPlanEJB and WrapperDoctorEJB**—These two beans were developed by Star Enterprise as an integration point for accessing the Web service from Providence Health. These beans simply delegate their functions to the Providence Health Web service; hence their methods are marked as *unchecked*. This allows the Benefits Enrollment application to invoke them with no security restrictions.

- **InsurancePlanAdminEJB**—This bean has a Web service interface, providing the plan administration Web service used by health plan providers to update their plan information remotely. InsurancePlanAdminEJB uses the security role *benefits-admin*. Only users belonging to this role are allowed to invoke InsurancePlanAdminEJB's methods. As a result, when the Web service is used from an insurance provider's enterprise, the insurance provider needs to authenticate itself to the Web service.

11.4 Deployer's Responsibility

Security deployment tasks, like all other application deployment tasks, are specific to the facilities provided by the EJB container and to the overall operational environment. Therefore, we can explain only at a high level how the deployer addresses the security requirements when deploying the benefits application at Star Enterprise.

11.4.1 Deploying Wombat's Enterprise Beans

The deployer assigns the user group *all-employees*, which represents all Star Enterprise employees, to the security role *employee* defined by the Wombat application. This ensures that all employees can use the application for benefits enrollment.

The deployer assigns the user group *benefits-department* to the *benefits-admin* security role defined by the Wombat application. This allows the members of Star Enterprise's benefits department to administer the benefits plans.

11.4.2 Deploying Star Enterprise's Beans

The PayrollEJB bean developed by Star Enterprise's IT department is deployed on the payroll application server. The security roles it declares are *employee* and *payroll-dept*. The deployer assigns the user group *all-employees* to the role *employee* and assigns the user group *payroll-department*, consisting of payroll administrators, to the *payroll-dept* security role.

While deploying the InsurancePlanAdmin Web service, the deployer creates user accounts for the insurance plan administrators who will use the Web service from a different enterprise. These users are added to the *benefits-admin* security role. At runtime, the users need to authenticate themselves to Star Enterprise's Web server hosting the Web service. The EJB container's authorization checks ensure that the users belong to the *benefits-admin* role before they are allowed to use the Web service.

11.5 Conclusion

This chapter explained key security concepts and showed how security is handled within an EJB container. The EJB architecture shifts the responsibility for securing an application from the application developer to qualified vendors, such as EJB container and server vendors, who are experts in the security domain.

Configuring an application's security is also done outside the application code, principally by mapping the security roles and method permissions defined in the deployment descriptor to the users and user groups in the target operational environment. These tasks are declarative in nature and typically are carried out by the system administrator and deployer.

This chapter concludes the main portion of the book. It is followed by Appendix A, which lists some of the supporting code examples that are less central to the example applications.

Code Samples

THIS appendix contains the complete class implementations for a number of the classes that are used to illustrate the benefits application. In particular, this section contains the classes with lengthy implementations, helper classes, and other classes that serve a more peripheral function to the example.

A.1 Session Bean Helper Classes

The following four code samples show the helper classes defined for the Enrollment session bean.

Code Example A.1   Definition of Helper Classes

```java
package com.star.benefits;

public class EmployeeInfo implements java.io.Serializable {
    int employeeNumber;
    String firstName;
    String lastName;

    public EmployeeInfo() { }
    public EmployeeInfo(int emplnum, String fname, String lname) {
        employeeNumber = emplnum;
        firstName = fname;
        lastName = lname;
    }
    public int getEmployeeNumber() { return employeeNumber; }
    public String getFirstName() { return firstName; }
    public String getLastName() { return lastName; }
```

```java
   public void setEmployeeNumber(int val) { employeeNumber = val; }
   public void setFirstName(String val) { firstName = val; }
   public void setLastName(String val) { lastName = val; }
}

package com.star.benefits;

public class Options implements java.io.Serializable {
   String[] optionDescription;
   double[] optionCost;
   int selectedOption;
   int size;

   public Options() {
      size = 0;
      selectedOption = -1;
   }

   public Options(int size) {
      this.size = size;
      optionDescription = new String[size];
      optionCost = new double[size];
      selectedOption = -1;
   }

   public String getOptionDescription(int i) {
      return optionDescription[i];
   }
   public void setOptionDescription(int i, String val) {
      optionDescription[i] = val;
   }
   public String[] getOptionDescription() {
      return optionDescription;
   }
   public void setOptionDescription(String[] vals) {
      optionDescription = vals;
   }

   public double getOptionCost(int i) {
```

```
        return optionCost[i];
    }
    public void setOptionCost(int i, double val) {
        optionCost[i] = val;
    }
    public double[] getOptionCost() {
        return optionCost;
    }

    public int getSelectedOption() {
        return selectedOption;
    }
    public void setSelectedOption(int val) {
        selectedOption = val;
    }

    public int getSize() {
        return size;
    }
}


package com.star.benefits;

public class Summary implements java.io.Serializable {
    String coverageOption;
    String medicalOption;
    String dentalOption;
    double medicalOptionCost;
    double dentalOptionCost;
    double totalCost;
    double payrollDeduction;
    boolean smokerStatus;

    public Summary() { }

    public String getCoverageDescription() {
        return coverageOption;
    }
    public void setCoverageDescription(String s) {
```

```
        coverageOption = s;
    }

    public String getMedicalDescription() {
        return medicalOption;
    }
    public void setMedicalDescription(String s) {
        medicalOption = s;
    }

    public String getDentalDescription() {
        return dentalOption;
    }
    public void setDentalDescription(String s) {
        dentalOption = s;
    }

    public double getMedicalCost() {
        return medicalOptionCost;
    }
    public void setMedicalCost(double c) {
        medicalOptionCost = c;
    }

    public double getDentalCost() {
        return dentalOptionCost;
    }
    public void setDentalCost(double c) {
        dentalOptionCost = c;
    }

    public double getTotalCost() {
        return totalCost;
    }
    public void setTotalCost(double c) {
        totalCost = c;
    }

    public void setPayrollDeduction(double c) {
```

```
        payrollDeduction = c;
    }
    public double getPayrollDeduction() {
        return payrollDeduction;
    }

    public boolean getSmokerStatus() {
        return smokerStatus;
    }
    public void setSmokerStatus(boolean s) {
        smokerStatus  = s;
    }
}

package com.star.benefits;

public class EnrollmentException extends Exception {
    // error codes
    public static int UNKNOWN = 0;
    public static int INVAL_PARAM = 1;

    static String[] defaultMessage = {
        "unknown error code",
        "invalid value of input parameter"
    };

    private int errorCode;

    public EnrollmentException() {
        super();
    }

    public EnrollmentException(String s) {
        super(s);
    }

    public EnrollmentException(int errorCode, String s) {
        super(s);
        this.errorCode = errorCode;
```

```
        }

        public EnrollmentException(int errorCode) {
            super(errorCode >= 0 && errorCode < defaultMessage.length ?
                defaultMessage[errorCode] : "");
            this.errorCode = errorCode;
        }
    }
}
```

A.2   EnrollmentBean Source Code

Here is the complete class implementation for the EnrollmentBean session bean
coded for the session bean application example in Chapter 4.

Code Example A.2   EnrollmentBean Source Code

```
package com.star.benefits;

import javax.ejb.*;

import java.util.Date;
import java.io.Serializable;
import javax.naming.Context;
import javax.naming.InitialContext;
import javax.sql.DataSource;
import java.sql.SQLException;

import com.star.benefits.db.DBQueryEmployee;
import com.star.benefits.db.DBQuerySelection;
import com.star.benefits.db.DBInsertSelection;
import com.star.benefits.db.DBUpdateSelection;

// The Employee class is used internally to represent the employee
// information in the instance's conversational state.
//
class Employee implements Serializable {
    int emplNumber;
    String firstName;
    String lastName;
```

```java
    Date birthDate;
    Date startDate;
}


// The Selection class is used internally to represent the benefits
// selections in the instance's conversational state.
//
class Selection implements Serializable {
    int emplNumber;
    int coverage;
    String medicalPlanId;
    String dentalPlanId;
    boolean smokerStatus;
}


// EnrollmentBean is a stateful session bean that implements
// the benefits enrollment business process.
//
public class EnrollmentBean implements SessionBean
{
    private final static String[] coverageDescriptions = {
        "Employee Only",
        "Employee and Spouse",
        "Employee, Spouse, and Children"
    };

    // Tables of Java classes that are used for calculation of
    // of cost of medical and dental benefits
    private HealthPlan[] medicalPlans;
    private HealthPlan[] dentalPlans;

    // Portion of the benefits cost paid by the employee (A
    // real-life application would read this value from the
    // database.)
    private double employeeCostFactor = 0.10;

    // Employee number that uniquely identifies an employee
    private int employeeNumber;
```

```
// Employee information read from database
private Employee employee;

// Employee's current benefits selections
private Selection selection;

// Indication if beans need to create selection record
private boolean createSelection;

// The following variables are calculated values and are
// used for programming convenience.
private int age;                // employee's age
private int medicalSelection = -1;    // index to medicalPlans
private int dentalSelection = -1;    // index to dentalPlans
private double totalCost;        // total benefits cost
private double payrollDeduction;    // payroll deduction

// JDBC data sources
private DataSource employeeDS;        // Employee database
private DataSource benefitsDS;        // Benefits database


// public no-arg constructor
public EnrollmentBean() { }

// business methods

// Get employee information.
public EmployeeInfo getEmployeeInfo() {
    return new EmployeeInfo(employeeNumber,
        employee.firstName, employee.lastName);
}

// Get coverage options.
public Options getCoverageOptions() {
    Options opt = new Options(coverageDescriptions.length);
    opt.setOptionDescription(coverageDescriptions);
    opt.setSelectedOption(selection.coverage);
    return opt;
```

```
        }

        // Set selected coverage option.
        public void setCoverageOption(int choice)
                throws EnrollmentException {

            if (choice >= 0 && choice < coverageDescriptions.length) {
                selection.coverage = choice;
            } else {
                throw new EnrollmentException(
                    EnrollmentException.INVAL_PARAM);
            }
        }

        // Get list of available medical options.
        public Options getMedicalOptions() {
            Options opt = new Options(medicalPlans.length);
            for (int i = 0; i < medicalPlans.length; i++) {
                HealthPlan plan = medicalPlans[i];
                opt.setOptionDescription(i, plan.getDescription());
                opt.setOptionCost(i,
                    plan.getCost(selection.coverage,
                        age, selection.smokerStatus));
            }
            opt.setSelectedOption(medicalSelection);
            return opt;
        }

        // Set selected medical option.
        public void setMedicalOption(int choice)
                throws EnrollmentException {

            if (choice >= 0 && choice < medicalPlans.length) {
                medicalSelection = choice;
                selection.medicalPlanId =
                    medicalPlans[choice].getPlanId();
            } else {
                throw new EnrollmentException(
                    EnrollmentException.INVAL_PARAM);
```

```
        }
    }

    // Get list of available dental options.
    public Options getDentalOptions() {
        Options opt = new Options(dentalPlans.length);
        for (int i = 0; i < dentalPlans.length; i++) {
            HealthPlan plan = dentalPlans[i];
            opt.setOptionDescription(i, plan.getDescription());
            opt.setOptionCost(i,
                plan.getCost(selection.coverage,
                    age, selection.smokerStatus));
        }
        opt.setSelectedOption(dentalSelection);
        return opt;
    }

    // Set selected dental option.
    public void setDentalOption(int choice)
            throws EnrollmentException {

        if (choice >= 0 && choice < dentalPlans.length) {
            dentalSelection = choice;
            selection.dentalPlanId =
                dentalPlans[choice].getPlanId();
        } else {
            throw new EnrollmentException(
                EnrollmentException.INVAL_PARAM);
        }
    }

    // Get smoker status.
    public boolean getSmokerStatus() {
        return selection.smokerStatus;
    }

    // Set smoker status.
    public void setSmokerStatus(boolean status) {
        selection.smokerStatus = status;
```

```
    }

    // Get summary of selected options and their cost.
    public Summary getSummary() {
        calculateTotalCostAndPayrollDeduction();
        Summary s = new Summary();
        s.setCoverageDescription(
            coverageDescriptions[selection.coverage]);

        s.setSmokerStatus(selection.smokerStatus);

        s.setMedicalDescription(
            medicalPlans[medicalSelection].getDescription());
        s.setMedicalCost(
            medicalPlans[medicalSelection].getCost(
                selection.coverage, age,
                selection.smokerStatus));

        s.setDentalDescription(
            dentalPlans[dentalSelection].getDescription());
        s.setDentalCost(
            dentalPlans[dentalSelection].getCost(
                selection.coverage, age,
                selection.smokerStatus));

        s.setTotalCost(totalCost);
        s.setPayrollDeduction(payrollDeduction);

        return s;
    }

    // Update corporate databases with the new selections.
    public void commitSelections() {

        // Insert new or update existing benefits selection record.
        if (createSelection) {
            DBInsertSelection cmd1 = null;
            try {
                cmd1 = new DBInsertSelection(benefitsDS);
```

```
                cmd1.setEmplNumber(employeeNumber);
                cmd1.setCoverage(selection.coverage);
                cmd1.setMedicalPlanId(selection.medicalPlanId);
                cmd1.setDentalPlanId(selection.dentalPlanId);
                cmd1.setSmokerStatus(selection.smokerStatus);
                cmd1.execute();
                createSelection = false;
            } catch (SQLException ex) {
                throw new EJBException(ex);
            } finally {
                if (cmd1 != null)
                    cmd1.release();
            }
        } else {
            DBUpdateSelection cmd2 = null;
            try {
                cmd2 = new DBUpdateSelection(benefitsDS);
                cmd2.setEmplNumber(employeeNumber);
                cmd2.setCoverage(selection.coverage);
                cmd2.setMedicalPlanId(selection.medicalPlanId);
                cmd2.setDentalPlanId(selection.dentalPlanId);
                cmd2.setSmokerStatus(selection.smokerStatus);
                cmd2.execute();
            } catch (SQLException ex) {
                throw new EJBException(ex);
            } finally {
                if (cmd2 != null)
                    cmd2.release();
            }
        }

        // Update information in the payroll system.
        DeductionUpdateBean deductionBean = null;
        try {
            deductionBean = new DeductionUpdateBean();
            deductionBean.setBenefitsDeduction(employeeNumber,
                            payrollDeduction);
            deductionBean.execute();
        } finally {
```

```
        if (deductionBean != null)
            deductionBean.release();
    }


}


// Initialize the state of the EmployeeBean instance.
public void ejbCreate(int emplNum) throws EnrollmentException {
    employeeNumber = emplNum;

    // Obtain values from bean's environment.
    readEnvironmentEntries();

    // Obtain JDBC data sources from environment.
    getDataSources();

    // Read employee information.
    DBQueryEmployee cmd1 = null;
    try {
        cmd1 = new DBQueryEmployee(employeeDS);
        cmd1.setEmployeeNumber(emplNum);
        cmd1.execute();
        if (cmd1.next()) {
            employee = new Employee();
            employee.emplNumber = emplNum;
            employee.firstName = cmd1.getFirstName();
            employee.lastName = cmd1.getLastName();
            employee.startDate = cmd1.getStartDate();
            employee.birthDate = cmd1.getBirthDate();
        } else {
            throw new EnrollmentException(
                "no employee record");
        }
    } catch (SQLException ex) {
        throw new EJBException(ex);
    } finally {
        if (cmd1 != null)
            cmd1.release();
    }
```

```
// Read the previous benefits selections.
DBQuerySelection cmd2 = null;
try {
    cmd2 = new DBQuerySelection(benefitsDS);
    cmd2.setEmployeeNumber(emplNum);
    cmd2.execute();
    if (cmd2.next()) {
        selection = new Selection();
        selection.emplNumber = emplNum;
        selection.coverage = cmd2.getCoverage();
        selection.medicalPlanId =
            cmd2.getMedicalPlanId();
        selection.dentalPlanId =
            cmd2.getDentalPlanId();
        selection.smokerStatus =
            cmd2.getSmokerStatus();
        createSelection = false;
    } else {
        // No previous selections exist in
        // the database. Initial selections to
        // default values.
        selection = new Selection();
        selection.emplNumber = emplNum;
        selection.coverage = 0;
        selection.medicalPlanId =
            medicalPlans[0].getPlanId();
        selection.dentalPlanId =
            dentalPlans[0].getPlanId();
        selection.smokerStatus = false;
        createSelection = true;
    }
} catch (SQLException ex) {
    throw new EJBException(ex);
} finally {
    if (cmd2 != null)
        cmd2.release();
}
```

```
    // Calculate employee's age.
    java.util.Date today = new java.util.Date();
    age = (int)((today.getTime() -
            employee.birthDate.getTime()) /
        ((long)365 * 24 * 60 * 60 * 1000));

    // Translate the medical plan ID to an index
    // into the medicalPlans table.
    for (int i = 0; i < medicalPlans.length; i++) {
        if (medicalPlans[i].getPlanId().equals(
            selection.medicalPlanId)) {
            medicalSelection = i;
            break;
        }
    }

    // Translate the dental plan ID to an index
    // into the dentalPlans table.
    for (int i = 0; i < dentalPlans.length; i++) {
        if (dentalPlans[i].getPlanId().equals(
            selection.dentalPlanId)) {
            dentalSelection = i;
            break;
        }
    }
}

// Clean up any resource held by the instance.
public void ejbRemove() {
}

// Release state that cannot be preserved across passivation.
public void ejbPassivate() {
  // All instance variables are either Serializable or one of the
    // special objects that are managed by the container
    // (e.g., DataSource).
}

// Reacquire state released before passivation.
```

```java
    public void ejbActivate() {
    }

    public void setSessionContext(SessionContext sc) {}

    // Helper methods follow

    // Calculate total benefits cost and payroll deduction.
    private void calculateTotalCostAndPayrollDeduction() {
        double medicalCost =
            medicalPlans[medicalSelection].getCost(
                selection.coverage,
                age, selection.smokerStatus);
        double dentalCost =
            dentalPlans[dentalSelection].getCost(
                selection.coverage,
                age, selection.smokerStatus);
        totalCost = medicalCost + dentalCost;
        payrollDeduction = totalCost * employeeCostFactor;
    }

    // Read and process enterprise bean's environment entries.
    private void readEnvironmentEntries() {
        try {
            Context ictx = new InitialContext();

            String medicalPlanList = (String)
                ictx.lookup("java:comp/env/medicalPlans");
            String[] medicalPlanClassNames =
                parseClassNames(medicalPlanList);
            medicalPlans =
                new HealthPlan[medicalPlanClassNames.length];
            for (int i = 0; i < medicalPlanClassNames.length; i++) {
                medicalPlans[i] = (HealthPlan)Class.forName(
                    medicalPlanClassNames[i]).newInstance();
            }

            String dentalPlanList = (String)
                ictx.lookup("java:comp/env/dentalPlans");
```

```
            String[] dentalPlanClassNames =
                parseClassNames(dentalPlanList);
            dentalPlans =
                new HealthPlan[dentalPlanClassNames.length];
            for (int i = 0; i < dentalPlanClassNames.length; i++) {
                dentalPlans[i] = (HealthPlan)Class.forName(
                    dentalPlanClassNames[i]).newInstance();
            }

        } catch (Exception ex) {
            ex.printStackTrace();
            throw new EJBException(ex);
        }
    }


    private void getDataSources() {
        try {
            Context ictx = new InitialContext();
            employeeDS = (DataSource)ictx.lookup(
                    "java:comp/env/jdbc/EmployeeDB");
            benefitsDS = (DataSource)ictx.lookup(
                    "java:comp/env/jdbc/BenefitsDB");
        } catch (Exception ex) {
            ex.printStackTrace();
            throw new EJBException(ex);
        }
    }


    // Parse ':' separated class names.
    //
    private static String[] parseClassNames(String list) {
        String[] rv = new String[0];

        while (list.length() != 0) {
            int x = list.indexOf(':');
            String name;

            if (x < 0) {
                name = list;
```

```
                    list = "";
            } else {
                name = list.substring(0, x);
                list = list.substring(x + 1);
            }
            if (name.length() == 0) {
                continue;
            }

            String[] orv = rv;
            rv = new String[rv.length + 1];
            for (int i = 0; i < orv.length; i++)
                rv[i] = orv[i];
            rv[rv.length - 1] = name;
        }
        return rv;
    }
}
```

A.3   PayrollEJB Session Bean Class

Here is the implementation of the PayrollEJB session bean class used in the session bean Benefits Enrollment application.

Code Example A.3   PayrollEJB Session Bean Source Code

```
package com.star.payroll;

import javax.ejb.*;

import javax.naming.*;
import java.sql.*;
import javax.sql.*;


// Payroll is a stateless session bean that provides
// access to the payroll system.
//
public class PayrollBean implements SessionBean
```

```
{

    private DataSource ds;

    public void setBenefitsDeduction(int emplNumber,
            double deduction) throws PayrollException
    {
        try {
            Connection con = getConnection();
            PreparedStatement pstmt = con.prepareStatement(
                "UPDATE Paychecks SET " +
                "pay_ded_benefits = ? " +
                "WHERE pay_empl = ?"
            );
            pstmt.setDouble(1, deduction);
            pstmt.setInt(2, emplNumber);
            if (pstmt.executeUpdate() == 0) {
                con.close();
                throw new PayrollException(
                    PayrollException.INVAL_EMPL_NUMBER);
            }
            con.close();
        } catch (Exception ex) {
            throw new EJBException(ex);
        }
    }

    public double getBenefitsDeduction(int emplNumber)
        throws PayrollException
    {
        try {
            Connection con = getConnection();
            Statement stmt = con.createStatement();
            PreparedStatement pstmt = con.prepareStatement(
                "SELECT pay_ded_benefits " +
                "FROM Paychecks " +
                "WHERE pay_emp = ?"
            );
            pstmt.setInt(1, emplNumber);
            ResultSet rs = pstmt.executeQuery();
```

```
                if (rs.next()) {
                    double deduction = rs.getDouble(1);
                    con.close();
                    return deduction;
                } else {
                    con.close();
                    throw new PayrollException(
                        PayrollException.INVAL_EMPL_NUMBER);
                }
            } catch (SQLException ex) {
                throw new EJBException(ex);
            }
        }


    public double getSalary(int emplNumber)
        throws PayrollException
    {
        try {
            Connection con = getConnection();
            Statement stmt = con.createStatement();
            PreparedStatement pstmt = con.prepareStatement(
                "SELECT pay_salary " +
                "FROM Paychecks " +
                "WHERE pay_emp = ?"
            );
            pstmt.setInt(1, emplNumber);
            ResultSet rs = pstmt.executeQuery();
            if (rs.next()) {
                double salary = rs.getDouble(1);
                con.close();
                return salary;
            } else {
                con.close();
                throw new PayrollException(
                    PayrollException.INVAL_EMPL_NUMBER);
            }
        } catch (SQLException ex) {
            throw new EJBException(ex);
        }
```

```
    }

    public void setSalary(int emplNumber, double salary)
        throws PayrollException
    {
        try {
            Connection con = getConnection();
            PreparedStatement pstmt = con.prepareStatement(
                "UPDATE Paychecks SET " +
                "pay_salary = ? " +
                "WHERE pay_empl = ?"
            );
            pstmt.setDouble(1, salary);
            pstmt.setInt(2, emplNumber);
            if (pstmt.executeUpdate() == 0) {
                con.close();
                throw new PayrollException(
                    PayrollException.INVAL_EMPL_NUMBER);
            }
            con.close();
        } catch (Exception ex) {
            throw new EJBException(ex);
        }
    }

    public void setSessionContext(SessionContext sc) {
        readEnvironment();
    }
    public void ejbCreate() {}
    public void ejbRemove() {}
    public void ejbPassivate() { /* never called */ }
    public void ejbActivate() { /* never called */ }

    private Connection getConnection() {
        try {
            return ds.getConnection();
        } catch (Exception ex) {
            throw new EJBException(ex);
        }
```

```
        }

        private void readEnvironment() {
            try {
                Context ictx = new InitialContext();
                ds = (DataSource)ictx.lookup(
                    "java:comp/env/jdbc/PayrollDB");
            } catch (Exception ex) {
                throw new EJBException(ex);
            }
        }
    }
```

A.4   Entity Application `EnrollmentBean` Implementation

Here is the complete implementation of the `EnrollmentBean` session bean class for the entity application example in Chapter 8.

Code Example A.4   `EnrollmentBean` Implementation for Entity Application

```
    package com.wombat.benefits;

    import java.util.Collection;

    import javax.ejb.*;
    import javax.naming.Context;
    import javax.naming.InitialContext;

    import com.wombat.plan.Plan;
    import com.wombat.plan.PlanHome;
    import com.wombat.plan.PlanException;


    // EnrollmentBean implements the benefits enrollment
    // business process.
    public class EnrollmentBean implements SessionBean
    {
        private final static String[] coverageDescriptions = {
            "Employee Only",
```

```
        "Employee and Spouse",
        "Employee, Spouse, and Children"
};

// Employee number that uniquely identifies an employee
private int employeeNumber;

private EmployeeHome employeeHome;
private Employee employee;

private SelectionHome selectionHome;
private Selection selection;
private SelectionCopy selCopy;

// Portion of the benefits cost paid by the employee
// (A real-life application would read this value from
// a benefits plan configuration database.)
private double employeeCostFactor = 0.10;

// Indication if a selection record exists for an employee
private boolean recordDoesNotExist = false;

// The following variables are calculated values and are
// used for programming convenience.
private int age;              // employee's age
private int medicalSelection = -1;    // index to medicalPlans
private int dentalSelection = -1;    // index to dentalPlans
private double totalCost;          // total benefits cost
private double payrollDeduction;    // payroll deduction

private PlanHome planHome;
// Arrays of local references to PlanEJB objects
private Plan[] medicalPlans;
private Plan[] dentalPlans;

private Class deductionBeanClass;


// public no-arg constructor
```

```
        public EnrollmentBean() { }



/*******************************************************************
/
/* business methods *
/
/*******************************************************************
/

    // Get employee information.
    public EmployeeInfo getEmployeeInfo() {
    return new EmployeeInfo(employeeNumber,
                employee.getFirstName(),
                employee.getLastName());
    }

    // Get coverage options.
    public Options getCoverageOptions() {
        Options opt = new Options(coverageDescriptions.length);
        opt.setOptionDescription(coverageDescriptions);
        opt.setSelectedOption(selCopy.getCoverage());
        return opt;
    }

    // Set selected coverage option.
    public void setCoverageOption(int choice)
            throws EnrollmentException {
        if (choice >= 0 && choice < coverageDescriptions.length) {
            selCopy.setCoverage(choice);
        } else {
            throw new EnrollmentException(
                EnrollmentException.INVAL_PARAM);
        }
    }

    // Get list of available medical options.
    public Options getMedicalOptions() throws EnrollmentException {
        Options opt = new Options(medicalPlans.length);
```

```java
    for (int i = 0; i < medicalPlans.length; i++) {
        Plan plan = medicalPlans[i];
        try {
            opt.setOptionDescription(i, plan.getPlanName());
            opt.setOptionCost(i, plan.getCost(
                selCopy.getCoverage(),
                age, selCopy.isSmoker()));
        } catch ( PlanException ex ) {
            throw new EnrollmentException(
              "Error obtaining cost for plan "
              + plan.getPlanName());
        }
    }
    opt.setSelectedOption(medicalSelection);
    return opt;
}


// Set selected medical option.
public void setMedicalOption(int choice)
        throws EnrollmentException
{
    if (choice >= 0 && choice < medicalPlans.length) {
        medicalSelection = choice;
        selCopy.setMedicalPlan(medicalPlans[choice]);
    } else {
        throw new EnrollmentException(
            EnrollmentException.INVAL_PARAM);
    }
}


// Get list of available dental options.
public Options getDentalOptions() throws EnrollmentException {
    Options opt = new Options(dentalPlans.length);
    for (int i = 0; i < dentalPlans.length; i++) {
        Plan plan = dentalPlans[i];
        try {
            opt.setOptionDescription(i, plan.getPlanName());
            opt.setOptionCost(i, plan.getCost(
                selCopy.getCoverage(),
```

```
                        age, selCopy.isSmoker()));
            } catch ( PlanException ex ) {
                throw new EnrollmentException(
                    "Error obtaining cost for plan "
                    + plan.getPlanName());
            }
        }
    opt.setSelectedOption(dentalSelection);
    return opt;
}


// Set selected dental option.
public void setDentalOption(int choice)
        throws EnrollmentException
{
    if (choice >= 0 && choice < dentalPlans.length) {
        dentalSelection = choice;
        selCopy.setDentalPlan(dentalPlans[choice]);
    } else {
        throw new EnrollmentException(
            EnrollmentException.INVAL_PARAM);
    }
}


// Get smoker status.
public boolean isSmoker() {
    return selCopy.isSmoker();
}


// Set smoker status.
public void setSmoker(boolean status) {
    selCopy.setSmoker(status);
}


// Get summary of selected options and their cost.
public Summary getSummary() {
    calculateTotalCostAndPayrollDeduction();
try {
    Summary s = new Summary();
```

```
    s.setCoverageDescription(
        coverageDescriptions[selCopy.getCoverage()]);
    s.setSmoker(selCopy.isSmoker());
    s.setMedicalDescription(
        medicalPlans[medicalSelection].getPlanName());
    s.setMedicalCost(
        medicalPlans[medicalSelection].getCost(
            selCopy.getCoverage(),
            age, selCopy.isSmoker()));
    s.setDentalDescription(
        dentalPlans[dentalSelection].getPlanName());
    s.setDentalCost(
        dentalPlans[dentalSelection].getCost(
            selCopy.getCoverage(),
            age, selCopy.isSmoker()));
    s.setTotalCost(totalCost);
    s.setPayrollDeduction(payrollDeduction);
    return s;
} catch (Exception ex) {
    throw new EJBException(ex);
}
}



// Update corporate databases with the new selections.
public void commitSelections() {
    try {
        if (recordDoesNotExist) {
            selection = selectionHome.create(selCopy);
            recordDoesNotExist = false;
        } else {
            selection.updateFromCopy(selCopy);
        }

    DeductionUpdateBean deductionBean = null;
    try {
    deductionBean = (DeductionUpdateBean)
            deductionBeanClass.newInstance();
    deductionBean.setBenefitsDeduction(employeeNumber,
```

```
                          payrollDeduction);
          deductionBean.execute();
           } finally {
          if (deductionBean != null)
             deductionBean.release();
           }
           } catch (Exception ex) {
              throw new EJBException(ex);
           }
      }




/
******************************************************************
/
/* EJB life-cycle methods */
/******************************************************************
/

     // Initialize the state of the EmployeeBean instance.
     public void ejbCreate(int emplNum) throws EnrollmentException {
         employeeNumber = emplNum;

         // Obtain values from bean's environment.
         readEnvironmentEntries();

         try {
             Collection coll = planHome.findMedicalPlans();
             medicalPlans = new Plan[coll.size()];
             medicalPlans = (Plan[])coll.toArray(medicalPlans);

             coll = planHome.findDentalPlans();
             dentalPlans = new Plan[coll.size()];
             dentalPlans = (Plan[])coll.toArray(dentalPlans);

             try {
                 employee = employeeHome.findByPrimaryKey(
                        new Integer(emplNum));
```

```
        } catch (ObjectNotFoundException ex) {
            throw new EnrollmentException(
                "employee not found");
        }

    try {
    selection = selectionHome.findByPrimaryKey(
                    new Integer(emplNum));
    } catch ( FinderException ex ) {}
        if (selection == null) {
            // This is the first time that the employee
            // runs this application. Use default values
            // for the selections.
            selCopy = new SelectionCopy();
            selCopy.setEmployee(employee);
            selCopy.setCoverage(0);
            selCopy.setMedicalPlan(medicalPlans[0]);
            selCopy.setDentalPlan(dentalPlans[0]);
            selCopy.setSmoker(false);
            recordDoesNotExist = true;
        } else {
            selCopy = selection.getCopy();
        }

        // Calculate employee's age.
        java.util.Date today = new java.util.Date();
        age = (int)((today.getTime() -
            employee.getBirthDate().getTime()) /
            ((long)365 * 24 * 60 * 60 * 1000));

        // Translate the medical plan ID to an index
        // into the medicalPlans table.
        String medicalPlanId = (String)
            selCopy.getMedicalPlan().getPrimaryKey();
        for (int i = 0; i < medicalPlans.length; i++) {
            if (medicalPlans[i].getPlanId().
                    equals(medicalPlanId)) {
                medicalSelection = i;
                break;
```

```
                }
            }

            // Translate the dental plan ID to an index
            // into the dentalPlans table.
            String dentalPlanId = (String)
                selCopy.getDentalPlan().getPrimaryKey();
            for (int i = 0; i < dentalPlans.length; i++) {
                if (dentalPlans[i].getPlanId().
                        equals(dentalPlanId)) {
                    dentalSelection = i;
                    break;
                }
            }

        } catch (Exception ex) {
            throw new EJBException(ex);
        }
    }

    // Clean up any resource held by the instance.
    public void ejbRemove() {}

    public void ejbPassivate() {}
    public void ejbActivate() {}
    public void setSessionContext(SessionContext sc) {}

/
********************************************************************
/
/* Helper methods */
/
********************************************************************
/

    // Calculate total benefits cost and payroll deduction.
    private void calculateTotalCostAndPayrollDeduction() {
        try {
            double medicalCost =
```

```
            medicalPlans[medicalSelection].getCost(
                selCopy.getCoverage(),
                age, selCopy.isSmoker());

        double dentalCost =
            dentalPlans[dentalSelection].getCost(
                selCopy.getCoverage(),
                age, selCopy.isSmoker());

        totalCost = medicalCost + dentalCost;
        payrollDeduction = totalCost * employeeCostFactor;
    } catch (Exception ex) {
        throw new EJBException(ex);
    }
}


// Read and process enterprise bean's environment entries.
private void readEnvironmentEntries() {
    try {
        Context ictx = new InitialContext();
        planHome = (PlanHome)ictx.lookup(
                "java:comp/env/ejb/PlanEJB");
        employeeHome = (EmployeeHome)ictx.lookup(
                "java:comp/env/ejb/EmployeeEJB");
        selectionHome = (SelectionHome)ictx.lookup(
                "java:comp/env/ejb/SelectionEJB");
        String deductionBeanName = (String)ictx.lookup(
                "java:comp/env/DeductionBeanClass");
    deductionBeanClass = Class.forName(deductionBeanName);
    } catch (Exception ex) {
        throw new EJBException(ex);
    }
}
}
```

A.5   SelectionBean Implementation

Here is the complete implementation of the SelectionBean entity bean class used
in the entity application example in Chapter 8. This class illustrates the EJB 2.0
container-managed persistence approach.

Code Example A.5   Abstract Schema for SelectionBean Entity Bean Class

```
package com.wombat.benefits;

import javax.ejb.*;

import javax.naming.Context;
import javax.naming.InitialContext;

import com.wombat.AbstractEntityBean;
import com.wombat.plan.Plan;

public abstract class SelectionBean extends AbstractEntityBean
{
    // container-managed persistence fields
    // primary key field
    public abstract Integer getEmployeeNumber();
    public abstract void setEmployeeNumber(Integer n);

    public abstract int getCoverage();
    public abstract void setCoverage(int c);

    public abstract boolean getSmokerStatus();
    public abstract void setSmokerStatus(boolean s);

    // container-managed relationship fields
    public abstract Plan getMedicalPlan();
    public abstract void setMedicalPlan(Plan p);

    public abstract Plan getDentalPlan();
    public abstract void setDentalPlan(Plan p);

    // values obtained from environment
    private boolean checkPlanType;
```

```
    private EmployeeHome employeeHome;



/
*****************************************************************
/
/* business methods from local interface
/
*****************************************************************
/

    public SelectionCopy getCopy() {
        SelectionCopy copy = new SelectionCopy();
        Employee emp=null;
    try {
        emp = employeeHome.findByPrimaryKey(getEmployeeNumber());
    } catch ( FinderException ex ) {
        throw new EJBException(ex);
    }
        copy.setEmployee(emp);
        copy.setCoverage(getCoverage());
        copy.setMedicalPlan(getMedicalPlan());
        copy.setDentalPlan(getDentalPlan());
        copy.setSmoker(getSmokerStatus());
        return copy;
    }

    public void updateFromCopy(SelectionCopy copy)
        throws SelectionException
    {
    if (!getEmployeeNumber().equals(
        copy.getEmployee().getEmployeeNumber()))
        throw new SelectionException(
            "can't change employee in selection");
        updateMedicalPlan(copy.getMedicalPlan());
        updateDentalPlan(copy.getDentalPlan());
        setSmokerStatus(copy.isSmoker());
        updateCoverage(copy.getCoverage());
    }
```

```
/
******************************************************************
/
/* Helper methods to validate new CMP field values before setting
/* them
/
******************************************************************
/

    private void updateCoverage(int v) throws SelectionException {
        switch (v) {
        case Plan.EMPLOYEE_ONLY:
        case Plan.EMPLOYEE_SPOUSE:
        case Plan.EMPLOYEE_SPOUSE_CHILDREN:
            setCoverage(v);
            break;
        default:
            throw new SelectionException(
                SelectionException.INVAL_COVERAGE);
        }
    }

    private void updateMedicalPlan(Plan p) throws SelectionException
{
        if (checkPlanType) {
            int type = p.getPlanType();
            if (type != Plan.MEDICAL_PLAN)
                throw new SelectionException(
                    SelectionException.INVAL_PLAN_TYPE);
        }
        setMedicalPlan(p);
    }

    private void updateDentalPlan(Plan p) throws SelectionException {
        if (checkPlanType) {
            int type = p.getPlanType();
            if (type != Plan.DENTAL_PLAN)
```

```
                throw new SelectionException(
                    SelectionException.INVAL_PLAN_TYPE);
        }
        setDentalPlan(p);
    }




/*******************************************************************
/
/* EntityBean life-cycle methods      */
/*******************************************************************
/

    public Integer ejbCreate(SelectionCopy copy)
        throws SelectionException, CreateException
    {
    setEmployeeNumber(copy.getEmployee().getEmployeeNumber());
        setSmokerStatus(copy.isSmoker());
        updateCoverage(copy.getCoverage());

        return null; // ejbCreate returns null in CMP beans
    }

    public void ejbPostCreate(SelectionCopy copy)
    throws SelectionException, CreateException
    {
    // set relationships (cannot be set in ejbCreate)
        updateMedicalPlan(copy.getMedicalPlan());
        updateDentalPlan(copy.getDentalPlan());
    }

    public void setEntityContext(EntityContext ctx) {
        super.setEntityContext(ctx);
        readEnvironment();
    }

    private void readEnvironment() {
        try {
```

```
            Context ictx = new InitialContext();
            Boolean val = (Boolean)ictx.lookup(
                    "java:comp/env/checkPlanType");
            checkPlanType = val.booleanValue();
            employeeHome = (EmployeeHome)ictx.lookup(
                    "java:comp/env/ejb/EmployeeEJB");
        } catch (Exception ex) {
            throw new EJBException(ex);
        }
    }
}
```

A.6   PlanBean Implementation Class

Here is the complete implementation of the PlanBean entity bean class.

Code Example A.6   PlanBean Abstract Entity Bean Class

```
package com.wombat.plan;

import javax.ejb.*;
import javax.mail.*;
import javax.mail.internet.*;
import javax.naming.*;
import java.util.*;

import com.wombat.AbstractEntityBean;

public abstract class PlanBean extends AbstractEntityBean
            implements TimedObject
{

    // container-managed persistence (CMP) fields
    // primary key field
    public abstract String getPlanId();
    public abstract void setPlanId(String s);

    public abstract String getPlanName();
    public abstract void setPlanName(String s);
```

```
        public abstract int getPlanType();
        public abstract void setPlanType(int s);

        public abstract double getCoverageFactor();
        public abstract void setCoverageFactor(double s);

        public abstract double getAgeFactor();
        public abstract void setAgeFactor(double s);

        public abstract double getSmokerCost();
        public abstract void setSmokerCost(double s);

        // container-managed relationship (CMR) fields
        public abstract Collection getDoctors();
        public abstract void setDoctors(Collection doctors);


/
********************************************************************
/
/* business methods from local interface
*/
/
********************************************************************
/

        public double getCost(int coverage, int age, boolean isSmoker)
            throws PlanException
        {
            double cost = getCoverageFactor() * coverage
                    + getAgeFactor() * age;
            if ( isSmoker )
                cost += getSmokerCost();

            return cost;
        }

        public void addDoctor(Doctor doctor) throws PlanException {
```

```
            getDoctors().add(doctor);
        }

    public boolean removeDoctor(Doctor doctor) throws PlanException {
        return getDoctors().remove(doctor);
    }

    public Collection getAllDoctors() throws FinderException {
        Collection doctors = getDoctors();
        Collection doctorsCopy = new ArrayList(doctors);
        return doctorsCopy;
    }

    public Collection getDoctorsByName(String fname, String lname)
            throws FinderException {
        return ejbSelectDoctorsByName(getPlanId(), fname, lname);
    }

    public Collection getDoctorsBySpecialty(String specialty)
            throws FinderException {
        return ejbSelectDoctorsBySpecialty(getPlanId(), specialty);
    }

/
********************************************************************
/
/* home business methods from local home interface */
/
********************************************************************
/

    // Update smoker costs for all plans.
    public void ejbHomeUpdateSmokerCosts(double cost)
            throws FinderException {
        Collection allPlans = ejbSelectAllPlans();
        Iterator itr = allPlans.iterator();
        while ( itr.hasNext() ) {
            Plan plan = (Plan)itr.next();
            plan.setSmokerCost(cost);
```

```
        }
    }

    // Get all medical plan names.
    public String[] ejbHomeGetMedicalPlanNames()
            throws FinderException {
        Collection names = ejbSelectPlanNames(Plan.MEDICAL_PLAN);
        return (String[])names.toArray(new String[names.size()]);
    }

    // Get all dental plan names.
    public String[] ejbHomeGetDentalPlanNames()
            throws FinderException {
        Collection names = ejbSelectPlanNames(Plan.DENTAL_PLAN);
        return (String[])names.toArray(new String[names.size()]);
    }

/
*****************************************************************
/
/* ejbSelect method declarations */
/
*****************************************************************
/

    public abstract Collection ejbSelectAllPlans()
        throws FinderException;

    public abstract Collection ejbSelectPlanNames(int planType)
        throws FinderException;

    public abstract Collection ejbSelectDoctorsByName
            (String planId, String fname, String lname)
        throws FinderException;

    public abstract Collection ejbSelectDoctorsBySpecialty
            (String planId, String specialty)
        throws FinderException;
```

```
        public abstract long ejbSelectNumEmployeesInPlan(Plan plan)
                throws FinderException;


/
********************************************************************
/
/* create method */
/
********************************************************************
/

        public String ejbCreate(String planId, String planName,
                int planType, double coverageFactor, double ageFactor,
                double smokerCost) throws CreateException
        {
            setPlanId(planId);
            setPlanName(planName);
            setPlanType(planType);
            setCoverageFactor(coverageFactor);
            setAgeFactor(ageFactor);
            setSmokerCost(smokerCost);
            return null;
        }

        public void ejbPostCreate(String planId, String planName,
                int planType, double coverageFactor, double ageFactor,
                double smokerCost) throws CreateException
        {
            // Start timer for daily statistics to be e-mailed at
            // midnight.
            // First get a Date object for midnight starting
            // from the next day.
            GregorianCalendar cal = new GregorianCalendar();
            int dayOfYear = cal.get(Calendar.DAY_OF_YEAR);
            cal.set(Calendar.DAY_OF_YEAR, (dayOfYear+1)%365);
            cal.set(Calendar.HOUR_OF_DAY, 0);
            cal.set(Calendar.MINUTE, 0);
            cal.set(Calendar.SECOND, 0);
            Date midnight = cal.getTime();
```

```
        long interval = 1000 * 3600 * 24; // milliseconds in 1 day

      TimerService timerService = entityContext.getTimerService();
       timerService.createTimer(midnight, interval, null);
    }

/
*****************************************************************
/
/* timeout method */
/
*****************************************************************
/

    public void ejbTimeout(javax.ejb.Timer timer) {
        try {
          // Get the number of employees who have subscribed
          // to this plan.
          long numEmployeesInThisPlan = ejbSelectNumEmployeesInPlan(
                        (Plan)entityContext.getEJBLocalObject());

            String emailText = "Plan " + getPlanName() + " has "
                        + numEmployeesInThisPlan + " employees.";

            // e-mail the text.
            InitialContext ic = new InitialContext();
            Session session = (Session)ic.lookup(
                  "java:comp/env/MailSession");
            String toAddress = (String)ic.lookup(
                  "java:comp/env/toAddress");
            String fromAddress = (String)ic.lookup("
                  java:comp/env/fromAddress");

            Message msg = new MimeMessage(session);
            msg.setFrom(new InternetAddress(fromAddress));
            msg.addRecipient(Message.RecipientType.TO,
                        new InternetAddress(toAddress));
            msg.setSubject("Statistics");
```

```
                    msg.setText(emailText);

                    Transport.send(msg);
               } catch ( Exception ex ) {
                    throw new EJBException(ex);
               }
          }
     }
```

A.7   EmployeeBeanBMP Class

This is the source code for the EmployeeBeanBMP class.

Code Example A.7   EmployeeBeanBMP Source Code

```
package com.star.benefits;

import java.util.Date;
import java.sql.*;
import javax.sql.*;
import javax.naming.*;
import javax.ejb.*;

import com.wombat.benefits.EmployeeBean;

public class EmployeeBeanBMP extends EmployeeBean {

     private DataSource dataSource;

     private Integer employeeNumber;
     private String firstName;
     private String lastName;
     private Date birthDate;

     // Implementations of CMP field get/set methods
     public Integer getEmployeeNumber() {
     return employeeNumber;
     }
```

```
public void setEmployeeNumber(Integer n) {
employeeNumber = n;
}

public String getFirstName() {
return firstName;
}

public void setFirstName(String s) {
firstName = s;
}

public String getLastName() {
return lastName;
}

public void setLastName(String s) {
lastName = s;
}

public Date getBirthDate() {
return birthDate;
}

public void setBirthDate(Date d) {
birthDate = d;
}


// EntityBean life-cycle methods
public void setEntityContext(EntityContext c)
{
    super.setEntityContext(c);

String dataSourceName = "java:comp/env/jdbc/EmployeeDatabase";
    try {
        Context ctx = new InitialContext();
        dataSource = (DataSource)ctx.lookup(dataSourceName);
    } catch ( Exception ex ) {
```

```java
            throw new EJBException("Unable to look up dataSource "
                + dataSourceName);
        }
    }

    public void unsetEntityContext()
    {
dataSource = null;
super.unsetEntityContext();
    }

    public Integer ejbCreate(int emplNumber, String fname,
            String lname, Date birthDate)
            throws CreateException
    {
// This sets all the CMP fields.
super.ejbCreate(emplNumber, fname, lname, birthDate);

// Check if the primary key exists.
if ( primaryKeyExists(emplNumber) ) {
    throw new DuplicateKeyException(
            "Employee number " + emplNumber +
            " already exists in database");
}

// C.reate a row for this bean instance
createRow();

// Return the primary key.
return new Integer(emplNumber);
    }

    public void ejbPostCreate(int emplNumber, String fname,
            String lname, Date birthDate)
            throws CreateException
    {}

    public Integer ejbFindByPrimaryKey(Integer primaryKey)
        throws FinderException
```

```
{
    // Try to load the row for this primary key.
    if ( !primaryKeyExists(primaryKey.intValue()) ) {
        throw new ObjectNotFoundException(
            "Primary key " + primaryKey
            + " not found");
}

    return primaryKey;
}

public void ejbRemove() throws RemoveException
{
super.ejbRemove();

    // Remove the row for this primary key.
    removeRow();

// Clear all CMP fields.
employeeNumber = null;
firstName = null;
lastName = null;
birthDate = null;
}

public void ejbLoad()
{
    try {
        loadRow();
    } catch ( Exception ex ) {
        throw new NoSuchEntityException(
            "Exception caught in ejbLoad: " + ex);
    }
super.ejbLoad();
}

public void ejbStore()
{
super.ejbStore();
```

```
        try {
            storeRow();
        } catch ( Exception ex ) {
            throw new EJBException("Exception caught in ejbStore ",
                ex);
        }
    }


    public void ejbActivate()
    {
        employeeNumber = (Integer)entityContext.getPrimaryKey();
    }


    public void ejbPassivate()
    {
// Clear all CMP fields.
employeeNumber = null;
firstName = null;
lastName = null;
birthDate = null;
    }


/****************************************************************/
/* Below is all the database access code
**********************************/
/
    private void createRow()
    {
        // Create row for this accountId.
Connection con=null;
PreparedStatement stmt=null;
int resultCount;
try {
    con = dataSource.getConnection();
    String query = "INSERT INTO employees
        (empl_id, empl_first_name, empl_last_name,
        empl_birth_date) VALUES (?, ?, ?, ?)";
    stmt = con.prepareStatement(query);
    stmt.setInt(1, employeeNumber.intValue());
```

```
        stmt.setString(2, firstName);
        stmt.setString(3, lastName);
        stmt.setDate(4, new java.sql.Date(birthDate.getTime()));
        resultCount = stmt.executeUpdate();
    } catch ( Exception ex ) {
        throw new EJBException(ex);
    } finally {
        try {
        if ( con != null ) con.close();
        if ( stmt != null ) stmt.close();
        } catch ( Exception ex ) {}
    }

        if ( resultCount != 1 )
            throw new EJBException("Unable to insert row");
    }


    private void removeRow()
    {
    Connection con=null;
    Statement stmt=null;
    int resultCount;
    try {
        con = dataSource.getConnection();
        stmt = con.createStatement();
        String query =
        "DELETE FROM employees WHERE empl_id = " + employeeNumber;
        resultCount = stmt.executeUpdate(query);
    } catch ( Exception ex ) {
        throw new EJBException(ex);
    } finally {
        try {
        if ( con != null ) con.close();
        if ( stmt != null ) stmt.close();
        } catch ( Exception ex ) {}
    }

        if ( resultCount != 1 )
            throw new EJBException("Unable to delete row");
    }
```

```
    private boolean primaryKeyExists(int emplNum)
    {
Connection con=null;
Statement stmt=null;
try {
    con = dataSource.getConnection();
    stmt = con.createStatement();
    String query = "SELECT empl_id"
        + " FROM employees WHERE empl_id = " + emplNum;
    ResultSet result = stmt.executeQuery(query);
    if ( !result.next() )
    return false;
    return true;
} catch ( Exception ex ) {
    throw new EJBException(ex);
} finally {
    try {
    if ( con != null ) con.close();
    if ( stmt != null ) stmt.close();
    } catch ( Exception ex ) {}
}
}

    private void loadRow()
    {
Connection con=null;
Statement stmt=null;
try {
    con = dataSource.getConnection();
    stmt = con.createStatement();
    String query = "SELECT empl_first_name, empl_last_name,
            empl_birth_date"
        + " FROM employees WHERE empl_id = " + employeeNumber;
    ResultSet result = stmt.executeQuery(query);
    if ( !result.next() )
    throw new NoSuchEntityException(
            "No database row for primary key: " + employeeNumber);
    firstName = result.getString(1);
    lastName = result.getString(2);
```

```
      birthDate = result.getDate(3);
  } catch ( Exception ex ) {
      throw new EJBException(ex);
  } finally {
      try {
      if ( con != null ) con.close();
      if ( stmt != null ) stmt.close();
      } catch ( Exception ex ) {}
  }
  }

  private void storeRow()
  {
Connection con=null;
      PreparedStatement stmt=null;
  int resultCount;
  try {
      con = dataSource.getConnection();
      String query =  "UPDATE employees SET empl_first_name = ?,
          empl_last_name = ?, empl_birth_date = ?
          WHERE empl_id = ?";
      stmt = con.prepareStatement(query);
      stmt.setString(1, firstName);
      stmt.setString(2, lastName);
      stmt.setDate(3, new java.sql.Date(birthDate.getTime()));
      stmt.setInt(4, employeeNumber.intValue());
      resultCount = stmt.executeUpdate();
  } catch ( Exception ex ) {
      throw new EJBException(ex);
  } finally {
      try {
      if ( con != null ) con.close();
      if ( stmt != null ) stmt.close();
      } catch ( Exception ex ) {}
  }
      if ( resultCount != 1 )
          throw new EJBException("Unable to store row");
  }
}
```

A.8   PayrollBean Implementation Class Using Connectors

Here is the source code for the PayrollBean class, which illustrates using the
J2EE Connector architecture to access the mainframe-based payroll system, as
described in Chapter 6.

Code Example A.8   PayrollBean Class

```
package com.aardvark.payroll.impl;

import javax.ejb.*;

import javax.naming.Context;
import javax.naming.InitialContext;
import javax.naming.NamingException;

import javax.resource.cci.ConnectionFactory;
import javax.resource.cci.Connection;
import javax.resource.cci.MappedRecord;
import javax.resource.cci.RecordFactory;
import javax.resource.cci.InteractionSpec;
import javax.resource.cci.Interaction;

import javax.resource.ResourceException;

import com.aardvark.payroll.PayrollException;

public class PayrollBean implements SessionBean {
    // Mainframe connection factory
    private ConnectionFactory connectionFactory;

    public void setBenefitsDeduction(int emplNumber,
        double deduction) throws PayrollException
    {
        Connection cx = null;
        try {
            // Obtain connection to mainframe.
            cx = getConnection();

            // Create an interaction object.
```

```
      Interaction ix = cx.createInteraction();

      InteractionSpecImpl ixSpec = new InteractionSpecImpl();

      // Set the name of the TP program to be invoked.
      ixSpec.setFunctionName("SETPAYROLL_DEDUCTION");

      // Specify that we will be sending input parameters
      // to the TP program but are expecting to receive
      // no output parameters.
      ixSpec.setInteractionVerb(InteractionSpec.SYNC_SEND);

      RecordFactory rf = ix.getRecordFactory();

      // Create an object that knows how to
      // format the input parameters.
      MappedRecord input =
         rf.createMappedRecord("PAYROLLINFO_DEDUCTION");
      input.put("EMPLOYEENUMBER", new Integer(emplNumber));
      input.put("DEDUCTION", new Double(deduction));

      // Execute invokes the TP program, passing it
      // the input parameters.
      ix.execute(ixSpec, input);
   } catch (ResourceException ex) {
      throw new EJBException(ex);
   } finally {
      try {
         if (cx != null) cx.close();
      } catch (ResourceException ex) {
      }
   }
}

public double getBenefitsDeduction(int emplNumber)
   throws PayrollException
{
   Connection cx = null;
   try {
```

```
        cx = getConnection();
        Interaction ix = cx.createInteraction();

        InteractionSpecImpl ixSpec = new InteractionSpecImpl();
        ixSpec.setFunctionName("GETPAYROLLDATA");
        ixSpec.setInteractionVerb(
           InteractionSpec.SYNC_SEND_RECEIVE);

        RecordFactory rf = ix.getRecordFactory();

        MappedRecord input =
           rf.createMappedRecord("EMPLOYEEINFO");
        input.put("EMPLOYEENUMBER", new Integer(emplNumber));

        EmployeeRecord employee = new EmployeeRecordImpl();

        if (ix.execute(ixSpec, input, employee))
           return employee.getBenefitsDeduction();
        else
           throw new PayrollException(
              PayrollException.INVAL_EMPL_NUMBER);
     } catch (ResourceException ex) {
        throw new EJBException(ex);
     } finally {
        try {
           if (cx != null) cx.close();
        } catch (ResourceException ex) {
        }
     }
  }

  public void setSalary(int emplNumber, double salary)
     throws PayrollException
  {
     Connection cx = null;
     try {
        cx = getConnection();
        Interaction ix = cx.createInteraction();
```

```java
        InteractionSpecImpl ixSpec = new InteractionSpecImpl();
        ixSpec.setFunctionName("SETPAYROLL_SALARY");
        ixSpec.setInteractionVerb(InteractionSpec.SYNC_SEND);

        RecordFactory rf = ix.getRecordFactory();

        MappedRecord input =
            rf.createMappedRecord("PAYROLLINFO_SALARY");
        input.put("EMPLOYEENUMBER", new Integer(emplNumber));
        input.put("SALARY", new Double(salary));

        ix.execute(ixSpec, input);
    } catch (ResourceException ex) {
        throw new EJBException(ex);
    } finally {
        try {
            if (cx != null) cx.close();
        } catch (ResourceException ex) {
        }
    }
}

public double getSalary(int emplNumber)
    throws PayrollException
{
    Connection cx = null;
    try {
        cx = getConnection();
        Interaction ix = cx.createInteraction();

        InteractionSpecImpl ixSpec = new InteractionSpecImpl();
        ixSpec.setFunctionName("GETPAYROLLDATA");
        ixSpec.setInteractionVerb(
            InteractionSpec.SYNC_SEND_RECEIVE);

        RecordFactory rf = ix.getRecordFactory();

        MappedRecord input =
            rf.createMappedRecord("EMPLOYEEINFO");
```

```
            input.put("EMPLOYEENUMBER", new Integer(emplNumber));

            EmployeeRecord employee = new EmployeeRecordImpl();

            if (ix.execute(ixSpec, input, employee))
               return employee.getSalary();
            else
               throw new PayrollException(
                  PayrollException.INVAL_EMPL_NUMBER);
         } catch (ResourceException ex) {
            throw new EJBException(ex);
         } finally {
            try {
               if (cx != null) cx.close();
            } catch (ResourceException ex) {
            }
         }
      }


      public void ejbCreate() {}
      public void ejbRemove() {}
      public void ejbPassivate() {}
      public void ejbActivate() {}
      public void setSessionContext(SessionContext sc) {}

      private Connection getConnection() {
         try {
            Connection cx = connectionFactory.getConnection();
            return cx;
         } catch (ResourceException ex) {
            throw new EJBException(ex);
         }
      }

      private void readEnvironment() {
         try {
            Context nc = new InitialContext();

            connectionFactory = (ConnectionFactory)nc.lookup(
```

```
            "java:comp/env/eis/ConnectionFactory");
        } catch (NamingException ex) {
            throw new EJBException(ex);
        }
    }
}
```

A.9   CCI Interface Classes

Following is a brief description of the classes that implement the CCI interface.
Tools normally generate these classes from the definition of the mainframe program external interface, such as, for example, from the COBOL Common Area
format of a TP program.

The InteractionSpecImpl class implements the InteractionSpec CCI interface. The InteractionSpecImpl class is used for specifying the name of the target
TP program and the direction of argument passing (Code Example A.9).

Code Example A.9 InteractionSpecImpl Class

```
    package com.aardvark.payroll.impl;

    import javax.resource.cci.InteractionSpec;

    public class InteractionSpecImpl implements InteractionSpec {
        private String functionName;
        private int interactionVerb;

        // String with the name of TP program
        public void setFunctionName(String functionName) {
            this.functionName = functionName;
        }
        public String getFunctionName() {
            return this.functionName;
        }

        // Interaction verb indicates the direction
        // of parameter passing. It is one of
        // SYNC_SEND, SYNC_SEND_RECEIVE, and SYNC_RECEIVE.
        public void setInteractionVerb(int verb) {
```

```
                this.interactionVerb = verb;
        }
        public int getInteractionVerb() {
           return this.interactionVerb;
        }
    }
```

The `RecordImpl` class implements the CCI `Record` interface. Its implementation, shown in Code Example A.10, is used as the superclass for application-specific record classes.

Code Example A.10 `RecordImpl` Class

```
    package com.aardvark.payroll.impl;

    import javax.resource.cci.Streamable;
    import javax.resource.cci.Record;

    import java.io.Serializable;
    import java.io.IOException;
    import java.io.InputStream;
    import java.io.OutputStream;

    public class RecordImpl implements Record, Serializable, Streamable
    {
        String  name;
        String  desc;

        public RecordImpl() {}

        // Name of the record
        public void setRecordName(String name) {
           this.name = name;
        }
        public String getRecordName() {
           return name;
        }

        // Short description string for this record
        public void setRecordShortDescription(String description) {
```

```
         this.desc = description;
      }
      public String getRecordShortDescription() {
         return desc;
      }

      // Check if this instance is equal to another record.
      public boolean equals(Object other) {
         // ...
      }

      // Read data from InputStream, and initialize fields.
      public void read(InputStream istream) throws IOException {
         //....
      }

      // Write fields of a streamable object to OutputStream.
      public void write(OutputStream ostream) throws IOException {
         //...
      }

      public Object clone() throws CloneNotSupportedException {
         return this;
      }
   }
```

The `EmployeeRecord` class defines the interface that a Java application uses to get and set the values of input arguments for communication with the TP programs (Code Example A.11).

Code Example A.11 `EmployeeRecord` Class

```
   package com.aardvark.payroll.impl;

   import javax.resource.cci.Record;

   public interface EmployeeRecord extends Record  {
      void setName(String name);
      void setId(int id);
      void setSalary(double salary);
```

```
    void setBenefitsDeduction(double deduction);

    String getName();
    int getId();
    double getSalary();
    double getBenefitsDeduction();
}
```

The `EmployeeRecordImpl` class implements the `EmployeeRecord` interface and is responsible for the conversion between the Java representation of the values of arguments and the representation understood by the mainframe program. The data in the mainframe representation is passed to a mainframe resource adaptor through the `InputStream` and `OutputStream` interfaces (Code Example A.12).

Code Example A.12 `EmployeeRecordImpl` Class

```
package com.aardvark.payroll.impl;

import javax.resource.cci.Streamable;

import java.io.Serializable;
import java.io.IOException;
import java.io.InputStream;
import java.io.OutputStream;

public class EmployeeRecordImpl extends RecordImpl
        implements EmployeeRecord, Serializable, Streamable {

    private String name;
    private int id;
    private double deduction;
    private double salary;

    public EmployeeRecordImpl() {}

    public void setName(String name) {
        this.name = name;
    }
    public void setId(int id) {
        this.id = id;
```

```
        }
        public void setSalary(double salary) {
            this.salary = salary;
        }
        public void setBenefitsDeduction(double deduction) {
            this.deduction = deduction;
        }

        public String getName() {
            return name;
        }
        public int getId() {
            return id;
        }
        public double getSalary() {
            return this.salary;
        }
        public double getBenefitsDeduction() {
            return this.deduction;
        }

        // Read data from a stream, and set the values of fields.
        public void read(InputStream istream) throws IOException {
            super.read(istream);
            //....
        }

        // Write the values of fields to a stream.
        public void write(OutputStream ostream) throws IOException {
            super.write(ostream);
            //...
        }
    }
```

A.10 InsurancePlanAdminBean Class

Code Example A.13 shows the source code for the InsurancePlanAdminBean class described in Chapter 9.

Code Example A.13 InsurancePlanAdminBean Class Source Code

```java
package com.star.admin;

import javax.ejb.*;
import javax.naming.InitialContext;
import java.util.Collection;

import com.wombat.plan.*;

public class InsurancePlanAdminBean implements SessionBean {
    private SessionContext sessionContext;
    private PlanHome planHome;
    private DoctorHome doctorHome;

    public InsurancePlanAdminBean(){}

    public void createInsurancePlan(String planId, String planName,
        int planType, double coverageFactor, double ageFactor,
                double smokerCost)
    {
    try {
        Plan newPlan = planHome.create(planId, planName, planType,
                    coverageFactor, ageFactor, smokerCost);
    } catch ( CreateException ex ) {
        throw new EJBException(ex);
    }
    }

    public PlanInfo getPlanInfo(String planId)
    {
    try {
        Plan plan = planHome.findByPrimaryKey(planId);
        PlanInfo planInfo = new PlanInfo();
        planInfo.planId = plan.getPlanId();
        planInfo.planName = plan.getPlanName();
        planInfo.planType = plan.getPlanType();
        planInfo.coverageFactor = plan.getCoverageFactor();
        planInfo.ageFactor = plan.getAgeFactor();
        planInfo.smokerCost = plan.getSmokerCost();
```

```
    return planInfo;
} catch ( Exception ex ) {
    throw new EJBException(ex);
}
}


public void addDoctors(String planId, DoctorInfo[] doctors)
{
try {
    Plan plan = planHome.findByPrimaryKey(planId);
    for ( int i=0; i<doctors.length; i++ ) {
    // Find or create a Doctor bean.
    DoctorPkey pkey = new DoctorPkey(doctors[i].firstName,
                 doctors[i].lastName);
    Doctor doctor;
    try {
        doctor = doctorHome.findByPrimaryKey(pkey);
    } catch ( FinderException fe ) {
        doctor = doctorHome.create(doctors[i].firstName,
                     doctors[i].lastName,
                     doctors[i].specialty,
                     doctors[i].hospitals,
                     doctors[i].practiceSince);
    }
    plan.addDoctor(doctor);
    }
} catch ( Exception ex ) {
    throw new EJBException(ex);
}
}

public void removeDoctors(String planId, DoctorInfo[] doctors)
{
try {
    Plan plan = planHome.findByPrimaryKey(planId);
    for ( int i=0; i<doctors.length; i++ ) {
    // Find a Doctor bean.
    DoctorPkey pkey = new DoctorPkey(doctors[i].firstName,
```

```
                            doctors[i].lastName);
        Doctor doctor;
        try {
            doctor = doctorHome.findByPrimaryKey(pkey);
        } catch ( FinderException ex ) {
            throw new EJBException(ex);
        }

        plan.removeDoctor(doctor);
        }
    } catch ( Exception ex ) {
        throw new EJBException(ex);
    }
    }

    public DoctorInfo[] getAllDoctors(String planId)
    {
    try {
        Plan plan = planHome.findByPrimaryKey(planId);
        Collection doctors = plan.getAllDoctors();
        return (DoctorInfo[])doctors.toArray(
                new Doctor[doctors.size()]);
    } catch ( Exception ex ) {
        throw new EJBException(ex);
    }
    }

    public void setSmokerCost(String planId, double cost)
    {
    try {
        Plan plan = planHome.findByPrimaryKey(planId);
        plan.setSmokerCost(cost);
    } catch ( Exception ex ) {
        throw new EJBException(ex);
    }
    }

    public void setCoverageFactor(String planId, double s)
    {
```

```
try {
    Plan plan = planHome.findByPrimaryKey(planId);
    plan.setCoverageFactor(s);
} catch ( Exception ex ) {
    throw new EJBException(ex);
}
 }

 public void setAgeFactor(String planId, double s)
 {
try {
    Plan plan = planHome.findByPrimaryKey(planId);
    plan.setAgeFactor(s);
} catch ( Exception ex ) {
    throw new EJBException(ex);
}
 }


 /* Life-cycle methods */

 public void setSessionContext(SessionContext sessionContext) {
    this.sessionContext = sessionContext;

try {
    // Look up local home object for PlanEJB using JNDI.
    InitialContext initialContext = new InitialContext();
    planHome = (PlanHome)initialContext.lookup(
                "java:comp/env/ejb/PlanEJB");
    doctorHome = (DoctorHome)initialContext.lookup(
                "java:comp/env/ejb/DoctorEJB");
} catch ( Exception ex ) {
    throw new EJBException(ex);
}
 }

public void ejbCreate() {}

public void ejbRemove() {}
```

```
    public void ejbActivate() {}

    public void ejbPassivate() {}
}
```

A.11 InsurancePlanAdmin WSDL Description

Code Example A.14 shows the WSDL description of the InsurancePlanAdmin
Web service provided by Star Enterprise, as described in Chapter 9.

Code Example A.14 InsurancePlanAdmin Web Service Description

```xml
<?xml version="1.0" encoding="UTF-8"?>

<definitions name="InsurancePlanAdminService"
targetNamespace="http://example.com/InsurancePlanAdmin"
xmlns:tns="http://example.com/InsurancePlanAdmin"
xmlns="http://schemas.xmlsoap.org/wsdl/"
xmlns:soap="http://schemas.xmlsoap.org/wsdl/soap/"
xmlns:xsd="http://www.w3.org/2001/XMLSchema">
  <types>
    <schema targetNamespace="http://example.com/InsurancePlanAdmin"
xmlns:xsi="http://www.w3.org/2001/XMLSchema-instance"
xmlns:tns="http://example.com/InsurancePlanAdmin"
xmlns:soap-enc="http://schemas.xmlsoap.org/soap/encoding/"
xmlns:wsdl="http://schemas.xmlsoap.org/wsdl/"
xmlns="http://www.w3.org/2001/XMLSchema">
        <import namespace=
            "http://schemas.xmlsoap.org/soap/encoding/"/>
        <complexType name="ArrayOfDoctorInfo">
          <complexContent>
            <restriction base="soap-enc:Array">
              <attribute ref="soap-enc:arrayType"
            wsdl:arrayType="tns:DoctorInfo[]"/>
          </restriction></complexContent>
          </complexType>
        <complexType name="DoctorInfo">
          <sequence>
```

```
          <element name="firstName" type="string"/>
          <element name="hospitals" type="tns:ArrayOfstring"/>
          <element name="lastName" type="string"/>
          <element name="practiceSince" type="int"/>
          <element name="specialty" type="string"/></sequence>
      </complexType>
    <complexType name="ArrayOfstring">
      <complexContent>
        <restriction base="soap-enc:Array">
          <attribute ref="soap-enc:arrayType"
            wsdl:arrayType="string[]"/>
      </restriction></complexContent></complexType>
    <complexType name="PlanInfo">
      <sequence>
        <element name="ageFactor" type="double"/>
        <element name="coverageFactor" type="double"/>
        <element name="planId" type="string"/>
        <element name="planName" type="string"/>
        <element name="planType" type="int"/>
        <element name="smokerCost" type="double"/>
      </sequence></complexType></schema></types>
<message name="InsurancePlanAdmin_addDoctors">
  <part name="String_1" type="xsd:string"/>
  <part name="arrayOfDoctorInfo_2"
        type="tns:ArrayOfDoctorInfo"/>
  </message>
<message name="InsurancePlanAdmin_addDoctorsResponse"/>
<message name="InsurancePlanAdmin_createInsurancePlan">
  <part name="String_1" type="xsd:string"/>
  <part name="String_2" type="xsd:string"/>
  <part name="int_3" type="xsd:int"/>
  <part name="double_4" type="xsd:double"/>
  <part name="double_5" type="xsd:double"/>
  <part name="double_6" type="xsd:double"/></message>
<message name="InsurancePlanAdmin_createInsurancePlanResponse"/>
<message name="InsurancePlanAdmin_getAllDoctors">
  <part name="String_1" type="xsd:string"/></message>
<message name="InsurancePlanAdmin_getAllDoctorsResponse">
  <part name="result" type="tns:ArrayOfDoctorInfo"/></message>
```

```
<message name="InsurancePlanAdmin_getPlanInfo">
  <part name="String_1" type="xsd:string"/></message>
<message name="InsurancePlanAdmin_getPlanInfoResponse">
  <part name="result" type="tns:PlanInfo"/></message>
<message name="InsurancePlanAdmin_removeDoctors">
  <part name="String_1" type="xsd:string"/>
  <part name="arrayOfDoctorInfo_2"
        type="tns:ArrayOfDoctorInfo"/>
  </message>
<message name="InsurancePlanAdmin_removeDoctorsResponse"/>
<message name="InsurancePlanAdmin_setAgeFactor">
  <part name="String_1" type="xsd:string"/>
  <part name="double_2" type="xsd:double"/></message>
<message name="InsurancePlanAdmin_setAgeFactorResponse"/>
<message name="InsurancePlanAdmin_setCoverageFactor">
  <part name="String_1" type="xsd:string"/>
  <part name="double_2" type="xsd:double"/></message>
<message name="InsurancePlanAdmin_setCoverageFactorResponse"/>
<message name="InsurancePlanAdmin_setSmokerCost">
  <part name="String_1" type="xsd:string"/>
  <part name="double_2" type="xsd:double"/></message>
<message name="InsurancePlanAdmin_setSmokerCostResponse"/>
<portType name="InsurancePlanAdmin">
  <operation name="addDoctors" parameterOrder="String_1
          arrayOfDoctorInfo_2">
  <input message="tns:InsurancePlanAdmin_addDoctors"/>
  <output message="tns:InsurancePlanAdmin_addDoctorsResponse"/>
  </operation>
  <operation name="createInsurancePlan"
        parameterOrder="String_1 String_2 int_3 double_4
        double_5 double_6">
    <input message="tns:InsurancePlanAdmin_createInsurancePlan"/>
     <output message=
        "tns:InsurancePlanAdmin_createInsurancePlanResponse"/>
  </operation>
  <operation name="getAllDoctors" parameterOrder="String_1">
  <input message="tns:InsurancePlanAdmin_getAllDoctors"/>
    <output message=
        "tns:InsurancePlanAdmin_getAllDoctorsResponse"/>
```

```
      </operation>
      <operation name="getPlanInfo" parameterOrder="String_1">
        <input message="tns:InsurancePlanAdmin_getPlanInfo"/>
        <output message="tns:InsurancePlanAdmin_getPlanInfoResponse"/>
      </operation>
      <operation name="removeDoctors" parameterOrder="String_1
                   arrayOfDoctorInfo_2">
      <input message="tns:InsurancePlanAdmin_removeDoctors"/>
      <output message=
            "tns:InsurancePlanAdmin_removeDoctorsResponse"/>
      </operation>
      <operation name="setAgeFactor" parameterOrder="String_1
              double_2">
      <input message="tns:InsurancePlanAdmin_setAgeFactor"/>
      <output message="tns:InsurancePlanAdmin_setAgeFactorResponse"/>
      </operation>
      <operation name="setCoverageFactor"
            parameterOrder="String_1 double_2">
      <input message="tns:InsurancePlanAdmin_setCoverageFactor"/>
      <output message=
              "tns:InsurancePlanAdmin_setCoverageFactorResponse"/>
      </operation>
      <operation name="setSmokerCost"
              parameterOrder="String_1 double_2">
      <input message="tns:InsurancePlanAdmin_setSmokerCost"/>
      <output message=
              "tns:InsurancePlanAdmin_setSmokerCostResponse"/>
      </operation></portType>
<binding name="InsurancePlanAdminBinding"
          type="tns:InsurancePlanAdmin">
    <operation name="addDoctors">
      <input>
        <soap:body
        encodingStyle="http://schemas.xmlsoap.org/soap/encoding/"
        use="encoded"
        namespace="http://example.com/InsurancePlanAdmin"/>
        </input>
      <output>
        <soap:body
```

```
      encodingStyle="http://schemas.xmlsoap.org/soap/encoding/"
      use="encoded"
      namespace="http://example.com/InsurancePlanAdmin"/>
      </output>
    <soap:operation soapAction=""/></operation>
<operation name="createInsurancePlan">
    <input>
      <soap:body encodingStyle=
      "http://schemas.xmlsoap.org/soap/encoding/"
      use="encoded"
      namespace="http://example.com/ InsurancePlanAdmin"/>
      </input>
    <output>
      <soap:body
      encodingStyle="http://schemas.xmlsoap.org/soap/encoding/"
      use="encoded"
      namespace="http://example.com/InsurancePlanAdmin"/>
      </output>
    <soap:operation soapAction=""/></operation>
<operation name="getAllDoctors">
    <input>
      <soap:body
      encodingStyle="http://schemas.xmlsoap.org/soap/encoding/"
      use="encoded"
      namespace="http://example.com/InsurancePlanAdmin"/>
      </input>
    <output>
      <soap:body
      encodingStyle="http://schemas.xmlsoap.org/soap/encoding/"
      use="encoded"
      namespace="http://example.com/InsurancePlanAdmin"/>
      </output>
    <soap:operation soapAction=""/></operation>
<operation name="getPlanInfo">
    <input>
      <soap:body
      encodingStyle="http://schemas.xmlsoap.org/soap/encoding/"
      use="encoded"
      namespace="http://example.com/InsurancePlanAdmin"/>
```

```
    </input>
   <output>
     <soap:body
    encodingStyle="http://schemas.xmlsoap.org/soap/encoding/"
    use="encoded"
    namespace="http://example.com/InsurancePlanAdmin"/>
</output>
   <soap:operation soapAction=""/></operation>
 <operation name="removeDoctors">
   <input>
     <soap:body
    encodingStyle="http://schemas.xmlsoap.org/soap/encoding/"
    use="encoded"
    namespace="http://example.com/InsurancePlanAdmin"/>
</input>
   <output>
     <soap:body
    encodingStyle="http://schemas.xmlsoap.org/soap/encoding/"
    use="encoded"
    namespace="http://example.com/InsurancePlanAdmin"/>
    </output>
   <soap:operation soapAction=""/></operation>
 <operation name="setAgeFactor">
   <input>
     <soap:body
    encodingStyle="http://schemas.xmlsoap.org/soap/encoding/"
    use="encoded"
    namespace="http://example.com/InsurancePlanAdmin"/>
    </input>
   <output>
     <soap:body
    encodingStyle="http://schemas.xmlsoap.org/soap/encoding/"
    use="encoded"
    namespace="http://example.com/InsurancePlanAdmin"/>
    </output>
   <soap:operation soapAction=""/></operation>
 <operation name="setCoverageFactor">
   <input>
     <soap:body
```

```
            encodingStyle="http://schemas.xmlsoap.org/soap/encoding/"
            use="encoded"
            namespace="http://example.com/InsurancePlanAdmin"/>
          </input>
          <output>
            <soap:body
            encodingStyle="http://schemas.xmlsoap.org/soap/encoding/"
            use="encoded"
            namespace="http://example.com/InsurancePlanAdmin"/>
          </output>
          <soap:operation soapAction=""/></operation>
        <operation name="setSmokerCost">
          <input>
            <soap:body
            encodingStyle="http://schemas.xmlsoap.org/soap/encoding/"
            use="encoded"
            namespace="http://example.com/InsurancePlanAdmin"/>
          </input>
          <output>
            <soap:body
            encodingStyle="http://schemas.xmlsoap.org/soap/encoding/"
            use="encoded"
            namespace="http://example.com/InsurancePlanAdmin"/>
          </output>
          <soap:operation soapAction=""/></operation>
        <soap:binding transport="http://schemas.xmlsoap.org/soap/http"
              style="rpc"/></binding>
          <service name="InsurancePlanAdminService">
          <port name="InsurancePlanAdminPort"
          binding="tns:InsurancePlanAdminBinding">
          <soap:address location=
          "http://www.example.com/star/InsurancePlanAdmin"/></port>
      </service>
      </definitions>
```

A.12 **ProvidencePlanBean** Class

Code Example A.15 shows the source code for the `ProvidencePlanBean` class described in Chapter 9.

Code Example A.15 `ProvidencePlanBean` Class Source Code

```
package com.star.plan;

import javax.ejb.*;
import javax.naming.*;
import java.util.*;
import java.rmi.RemoteException;

import com.wombat.plan.*;
import com.wombat.AbstractEntityBean;
import com.star.plan.providence.*;

public class ProvidencePlanBean extends AbstractEntityBean {

    private PlanInfo planInfo;
    private ProvidenceWebPort providence;
    private DoctorHome doctorHome;

    private static final String MEDICAL_PLAN = "MEDICAL_PLAN";
    private static final String DENTAL_PLAN = "DENTAL_PLAN";

/
********************************************************************
/
/* business methods from local interface      */
/
********************************************************************
/

    public String getPlanId() {
    return (String)entityContext.getPrimaryKey();
    }

    public int getPlanType() {
```

```java
    String planType = getPlanInfo().getPlanType();
    if ( planType.equals(MEDICAL_PLAN) )
        return Plan.MEDICAL_PLAN;
    else
        return Plan.DENTAL_PLAN;
    }

    public String getPlanName() {
    return getPlanInfo().getPlanName();
    }

    public double getAgeFactor() {
    return getPlanInfo().getAgeFactor();
    }
    public void setAgeFactor(double a) {
        throw new EJBException(
                "Unsupported operation for Providence Health plan");
    }

    public double getCoverageFactor() {
    return getPlanInfo().getCoverageFactor();
    }
    public void setCoverageFactor(double c) {
        throw new EJBException(
            "Unsupported operation for Providence Health plan");
    }

    public double getSmokerCost() {
        return getPlanInfo().getSmokerCost();
    }
    public void setSmokerCost(double cost) {
        throw new EJBException(
            "Unsupported operation for Providence Health plan");
    }

    public double getCost(int coverage, int age, boolean isSmoker)
        throws PlanException, RemoteException
    {
        return providence.getCost(getPlanId(), coverage, age,
```

```
            isSmoker);
    }

    public void addDoctor(Doctor doctor) throws PlanException {
        throw new PlanException(
            "Unsupported operation for Providence Health plan");
    }

    public boolean removeDoctor(Doctor doctor) throws PlanException {
        throw new PlanException(
            "Unsupported operation for Providence Health plan");
    }

    public Collection getAllDoctors()
            throws FinderException, RemoteException {
DoctorInfo[] doctors =
        providence.getDoctorInfo(getPlanId(), null);
return convertToCollection(doctors);
    }

    public Collection getDoctorsByName(String fname, String lname)
        throws FinderException, RemoteException {

DoctorInfo doctorQuery = new DoctorInfo();
doctorQuery.setFirstName(fname);
doctorQuery.setLastName(lname);
DoctorInfo[] doctors =
        providence.getDoctorInfo(getPlanId(), doctorQuery);
return convertToCollection(doctors);
    }

    public Collection getDoctorsBySpecialty(String specialty)
            throws FinderException, RemoteException {

DoctorInfo doctorQuery = new DoctorInfo();
doctorQuery.setSpecialty(specialty);
DoctorInfo[] doctors =
        providence.getDoctorInfo(getPlanId(), doctorQuery);
return convertToCollection(doctors);
```

```
        }


/
**********************************************************************
/
/* home business methods from local home interface      */
/
**********************************************************************
/

    // Update smoker costs for all plans.
    public void ejbHomeUpdateSmokerCosts(double cost)
          throws FinderException {
       throw new EJBException(
             "Unsupported operation for Providence Health plan");
    }

    // Get all medical plan names.
    public String[] ejbHomeGetMedicalPlanNames()
          throws FinderException, RemoteException {
    PlanInfo[] plans =
          providence.getPlanInfo(null, MEDICAL_PLAN, null);
    String[] planNames = new String[plans.length];
    for ( int i=0; i<plans.length; i++ ) {
        planNames[i] = plans[i].getPlanName();
    }
    return planNames;
    }

    // Get all dental plan names.
    public String[] ejbHomeGetDentalPlanNames()
          throws FinderException, RemoteException {
    PlanInfo[] plans =
          providence.getPlanInfo(null, DENTAL_PLAN, null);
    String[] planNames = new String[plans.length];
    for ( int i=0; i<plans.length; i++ ) {
        planNames[i] = plans[i].getPlanName();
    }
```

```
        return planNames;
    }



/
********************************************************************
/
/* find methods            */
/
********************************************************************
/

    public String ejbFindByPrimaryKey(String planId)
            throws FinderException, RemoteException {
        try {
            PlanInfo[] plans =
                providence.getPlanInfo(planId, null, null);
        } catch ( Exception ex ) {
            throw new ObjectNotFoundException();
        }
    return planId;
    }

    public Collection ejbFindMedicalPlans()
            throws FinderException, RemoteException {
        PlanInfo[] plans =
            providence.getPlanInfo(null, MEDICAL_PLAN, null);
        ArrayList planIds = new ArrayList();
        for ( int i=0; i<plans.length; i++ ) {
            planIds.add(plans[i].getPlanId());
        }
        return planIds;
    }

    public Collection ejbFindDentalPlans()
            throws FinderException, RemoteException {
        PlanInfo[] plans =
            providence.getPlanInfo(null, DENTAL_PLAN, null);
        ArrayList planIds = new ArrayList();
```

```
        for ( int i=0; i<plans.length; i++ ) {
            planIds.add(plans[i].getPlanId());
        }
        return planIds;
    }

    public Collection ejbFindByDoctor(String firstName,
            String lastName)
            throws FinderException, RemoteException {

        DoctorInfo doctorQuery = new DoctorInfo();
        doctorQuery.setFirstName(firstName);
        doctorQuery.setLastName(lastName);
        PlanInfo[] plans =
                providence.getPlanInfo(null, null, doctorQuery);
        ArrayList planIds = new ArrayList();
        for ( int i=0; i<plans.length; i++ ) {
            planIds.add(plans[i].getPlanId());
        }
        return planIds;
    }

/
********************************************************************
/
/* create methods          */
/
********************************************************************
/

    public String ejbCreate(String planId, String planName,
            int planType, double coverageFactor, double ageFactor,
            double smokerCost) throws CreateException
    {
        throw new CreateException(
            "Create not supported for Providence Health plan");
    }

    public void ejbPostCreate(String planId, String planName,
```

```
            int planType, double coverageFactor, double ageFactor,
            double smokerCost) throws CreateException
    {}


/
*******************************************************************
/
/* miscellaneous methods      */
/
*******************************************************************
/

    public void setEntityContext(EntityContext ctx) {
        super.setEntityContext(ctx);

        try {
            InitialContext ic = new InitialContext();
            ProvidenceWebService service =
                (ProvidenceWebService)ic.lookup(
                "java:comp/env/service/ProvidenceWebService");
            providence = service.getProvidenceWebSvcPort();

            doctorHome = (DoctorHome)ic.lookup(
                    "java:comp/env/ejb/ProvidenceDoctorEJB");
        }
        catch ( Exception ex ) {
            throw new EJBException(ex);
        }
    }

    public void ejbRemove() throws RemoveException {
        throw new RemoveException(
            "Remove not supported for Providence Health plan");
    }

    public void ejbPassivate() {
        planInfo = null;
    }
```

```
            public void ejbActivate() {
            }

            private Collection convertToCollection(DoctorInfo[] doctors) {
                Collection doctorsColl = new ArrayList();
                for ( int i=0; i<doctors.length; i++ ) {
                    doctorsColl.add(getDoctor(doctors[i]));
                }
                    return doctorsColl;
            }

            private Doctor getDoctor(DoctorInfo doctorInfo) {
            try {
                return doctorHome.findByPrimaryKey(
                        new DoctorPkey(doctorInfo.getFirstName(),
                                doctorInfo.getLastName()));
            } catch ( Exception ex ) {
                throw new EJBException(ex);
            }
            }

            private PlanInfo getPlanInfo() {
            if ( planInfo == null ) {
                try {
                planInfo =
                    providence.getPlanInfo(getPlanId(), null, null)[0];
                } catch ( Exception ex ) {
                throw new EJBException(ex);
                }
            }
            return planInfo;
            }
        }
```

A.13 ProvidenceDoctorBean Class

Code Example A.16 shows the source code for the `ProvidenceDoctorBean` class described in Chapter 9.

Code Example A.16 ProvidenceDoctorBean Class Source Code

```
package com.star.plan;

import javax.ejb.*;
import javax.naming.*;
import java.util.*;

import com.wombat.plan.*;
import com.wombat.AbstractEntityBean;
import com.star.plan.providence.*;

public class ProvidenceDoctorBean extends AbstractEntityBean {

    private DoctorInfo doctorInfo;
    private ProvidenceWebPort providence;

/
**********************************************************************
/
/* business methods             */
/
**********************************************************************
/

    public String getFirstName() {
    return getDoctorInfo().getFirstName();
    }

    public String getLastName() {
    return getDoctorInfo().getLastName();
    }

    public String getSpecialty() {
    return getDoctorInfo().getSpecialty();
    }

    public String[] getHospitals() {
    return getDoctorInfo().getHospitals();
    }
```

```
    public int getPracticeSince() {
    return getDoctorInfo().getPracticeSince();
    }



/
*****************************************************************
/
/* create, find methods      */
/
*****************************************************************
/

    public DoctorPkey ejbCreate(String firstName, String lastName,
                  String specialty, String[] hospitals,
                  int practiceSince) throws CreateException
    {
       throw new CreateException(
            "Create not supported for Providence Health plan");
    }

    public void ejbPostCreate(String firstName, String lastName,
                  String specialty, String[] hospitals,
                  int practiceSince) throws CreateException
    {}

    public DoctorPkey ejbFindByPrimaryKey(DoctorPkey pkey)
       throws FinderException
    {
    try {
       DoctorInfo doctorQuery = new DoctorInfo();
       doctorQuery.setFirstName(pkey.firstName);
       doctorQuery.setLastName(pkey.lastName);
       doctorInfo = providence.getDoctorInfo(null, doctorQuery)[0];
    } catch ( Exception ex ) {
       throw new ObjectNotFoundException();
    }
    return pkey;
```

```
    }

/
*******************************************************************
/
/* miscellaneous methods    */
/
*******************************************************************
/

    public void setEntityContext(EntityContext ctx) {
    super.setEntityContext(ctx);

    try {
        InitialContext ic = new InitialContext();
        ProvidenceWebService service =
            (ProvidenceWebService)ic.lookup(
            "java:comp/env/service/ProvidenceWebService");
        providence = service.getProvidenceWebSvcPort();
    }
    catch ( Exception ex ) {
        throw new EJBException(ex);
    }
    }

    public void ejbRemove() {
    doctorInfo = null;
    }

    public void ejbPassivate() {
    doctorInfo = null;
    }

    private DoctorInfo getDoctorInfo() {
    if ( doctorInfo == null ) {
        DoctorPkey pkey = (DoctorPkey)entityContext.getPrimaryKey();
        try {
            DoctorInfo doctorQuery = new DoctorInfo();
            doctorQuery.setFirstName(pkey.firstName);
```

```
                    doctorQuery.setLastName(pkey.lastName);
                    doctorInfo =
                        providence.getDoctorInfo(null, doctorQuery)[0];
                } catch ( Exception ex ) {
                    throw new EJBException(ex);
                }
            }
            return doctorInfo;
        }
    }
```

A.14 Command Beans

The following code examples show the command beans discussed in Section 4.4.2. The DBQueryEmployee command bean (Code Example A.17) reads employee information for an employee with a given employee number from a database.

Code Example A.17 DBQueryEmployee Command Bean

```
package com.star.benefits.db;

import java.sql.SQLException;
import java.util.Date;
import javax.sql.DataSource;

public class DBQueryEmployee extends DBQueryBean {
    static String statement =
        "SELECT empl_first_name, empl_last_name, empl_birth_date " +
            "empl_start_date, empl_dept_id " +
        "FROM employees WHERE empl_id = ?";

    public DBQueryEmployee(DataSource ds) throws SQLException {
        super(ds, statement);
    }

    public void setEmployeeNumber(int emplNum) throws SQLException {
        pstmt.setInt(1, emplNum);
    }
```

```
    public String getFirstName() throws SQLException {
        return resultSet.getString(1);
    }
    public String getLastName() throws SQLException {
        return resultSet.getString(2);
    }
    public Date getBirthDate() throws SQLException {
        return resultSet.getDate(3);
    }
    public Date getStartDate() throws SQLException {
        return resultSet.getDate(4);
    }
    public int getDepartmentNumber() throws SQLException {
        return resultSet.getInt(5);
    }
}
```

The DBQuerySelection command bean (Code Example A.18) reads the benefits selections for an employee with a given employee number from a database.

Code Example A.18 DBQuerySelection Command Bean

```
package com.star.benefits.db;

import java.sql.SQLException;
import javax.sql.DataSource;

public class DBQuerySelection extends DBQueryBean {
    static String statement =
        "SELECT sel_coverage, sel_smoker, " +
            "sel_medical_plan,  sel_dental_plan" +
        "FROM Selections WHERE sel_empl = ?";

    public DBQuerySelection(DataSource ds) throws SQLException {
        super(ds, statement);
    }

    public void setEmployeeNumber(int emplNum) throws SQLException {
        pstmt.setInt(1, emplNum);
```

```
      }

      public int getCoverage() throws SQLException {
         return resultSet.getInt(1);
      }
      public boolean getSmokerStatus() throws SQLException {
         return resultSet.getString(2).equals("Y");
      }
      public String getMedicalPlanId() throws SQLException {
         return resultSet.getString(3);
      }
      public String getDentalPlanId() throws SQLException {
         return resultSet.getString(4);
      }
   }
```

The DBInsertSelection command bean (Code Example A.19) inserts benefits selections into the database.

Code Example A.19 DBQInsertSelection Command Bean

```
      package com.star.benefits.db;

      import java.sql.SQLException;
      import javax.sql.DataSource;

      public class DBInsertSelection extends DBUpdateBean {
         static String statement =
            "INSERT INTO Selections VALUES (?, ?, ?, ?, ?)";

         public DBInsertSelection(DataSource ds) throws SQLException {
            super(ds, statement);
         }

         public void setEmplNumber(int emplNum) throws SQLException {
            pstmt.setInt(1, emplNum);
         }
         public void setCoverage(int cov) throws SQLException {
            pstmt.setInt(2, cov);
         }
```

```
      public void setMedicalPlanId(String id) throws SQLException {
         pstmt.setString(3, id);
      }
      public void setDentalPlanId(String id) throws SQLException {
         pstmt.setString(4, id);
      }
      public void setSmokerStatus(boolean st) throws SQLException {
         pstmt.setString(5, st ? "Y" : "N");
      }
   }
```

The DBUpdateSelection command bean (Code Example A.20) updates benefits selections in the database.

Code Example A.20 DBQUpdateSelection Command Bean

```
   package com.star.benefits.db;

   import java.sql.SQLException;
   import javax.sql.DataSource;

   public class DBUpdateSelection extends DBUpdateBean {
      static String statement =
         "UPDATE Selections SET " +
            "sel_coverage = ?, " +
            "sel_medical_plan = ?, " +
            "sel_dental_plan = ?, " +
            "sel_smoker = ? " +
         "WHERE sel_empl = ?";

      public DBUpdateSelection(DataSource ds) throws SQLException {
         super(ds, statement);
      }

      public void setEmplNumber(int emplNum) throws SQLException {
         pstmt.setInt(5, emplNum);
      }
      public void setCoverage(int cov) throws SQLException {
         pstmt.setInt(1, cov);
      }
```

```
   public void setMedicalPlanId(String id) throws SQLException {
      pstmt.setString(2, id);
   }
   public void setDentalPlanId(String id) throws SQLException {
      pstmt.setString(3, id);
   }
   public void setSmokerStatus(boolean st) throws SQLException {
      pstmt.setString(4, st ? "Y" : "N");
   }
}
```

Code Example A.21 illustrates the database-related command beans' super-classes.

Code Example A.21 Command Bean Superclasses

```
package com.star.benefits.db;

import java.sql.Connection;
import java.sql.PreparedStatement;
import java.sql.ResultSet;
import java.sql.SQLException;
import javax.sql.DataSource;

public class DBQueryBean {
   protected PreparedStatement pstmt;
   protected ResultSet resultSet = null;
   private Connection con;

   protected DBQueryBean(DataSource ds, String statement)
     throws SQLException
   {
     con = ds.getConnection();
     pstmt = con.prepareStatement(statement);
   }

   public void execute() throws SQLException {
      resultSet = pstmt.executeQuery();
   }
```

```java
    public boolean next() throws SQLException {
        return resultSet.next();
    }

    public void release() {
        try {
            if (resultSet != null)
                resultSet.close();
            if (pstmt != null)
                pstmt.close();
            if (con != null)
                con.close();
        } catch (SQLException ex) {
        }
    }
}

package com.star.benefits.db;

import java.sql.Connection;
import java.sql.PreparedStatement;
import java.sql.SQLException;
import javax.sql.DataSource;

public class DBUpdateBean {
    protected PreparedStatement pstmt;
    private Connection con;

    public int execute() throws SQLException {
        int rowCount = pstmt.executeUpdate();
        pstmt.close();
        con.close();
        return rowCount;
    }

    protected DBUpdateBean(DataSource ds, String statement)
        throws SQLException
    {
        con = ds.getConnection();
```

```
        pstmt = con.prepareStatement(statement);
    }

    public void release() { }
}
```

Glossary

ACID The acronym for the four properties guaranteed by transactions: atomicity, consistency, isolation, and durability.

activation The process of associating an enterprise bean object with an instance of an enterprise bean class. For a stateful session bean, activation results in restoring a session object's state from secondary memory.

actor A user or another program that interacts with an enterprise bean application.

application assembler An individual who combines enterprise beans, and possibly other application components, into larger, deployable application units.

application client A first-tier client component that executes in its own JVM. Application clients have access to some J2EE platform APIs (JNDI, JDBC, RMI-IIOP, JMS).

authentication Occurring as part of the security process, a step during which a user proves his or her identity to the enterprise network security manager.

authorization Occurring as part of the security process, a step during which the target application or database server verifies whether the user has the authority to access the requested application or data.

bean developer The programmer who writes the enterprise bean code implementing the business logic and produces enterprise beans.

bean-managed persistence (BMP) An approach to managing entity object state persistence whereby the entity bean itself manages the access to the underlying state in a resource manager.

bean-managed transaction demarcation   An approach to managing transactions whereby the bean developer manages transaction boundaries programmatically from within the application code.

business entity   A business object representing some information maintained by an enterprise.

business process   A business object that typically encapsulates an interaction of a user with business entities.

client-view API   The enterprise bean home interface and enterprise bean component interface.

collaborative business process   A business process with multiple actors.

command bean   A JavaBean used by an application to encapsulate a call to another application or a database call. Enterprise applications frequently use this design pattern.

commit   The point in a transaction when all updates to any resources involved in the transaction are made permanent.

Common Gateway Interface (CGI)   One of the interfaces for developing Dynamic HTML pages and Web applications.

Common Object Request Broker Architecture (CORBA)   A language-independent, distributed object model specified by the Object Management Group (OMG).

connection factory   An object that produces connections.

connector   A standard extension mechanism for containers to provide connectivity to enterprise information systems. A connector is specific to an enterprise information system and consists of a resource adapter and application development tools for enterprise information systems.

Connector architecture   An architecture for the integration of J2EE products with enterprise information systems. The two parts to this architecture are a resource adapter provided by an enterprise information system vendor and the J2EE product that allows this resource adapter to plug in. This architecture defines a set of contracts that a resource adapter has to support to plug in to a J2EE product—for example, transactions, security, and resource management.

container artifacts   Classes generated by the EJB container–provided deployment tools that bind the enterprise beans with the container at runtime. The container artifacts allow the container to interpose on the client calls to the enterprise beans and to inject its services into the application.

container-managed persistence (CMP) An approach to managing entity object state persistence whereby the container manages the transfer of data between the entity bean instance and the underlying resource manager.

container-managed transaction demarcation An approach to managing transactions whereby the EJB container defines the transaction boundaries by using the transaction attributes provided in the deployment descriptor.

conversational business process A business process with a single actor who engages in a conversation with the application. An example of a conversational business process is an application that displays a sequence of forms to the user and validates the data input by the user.

conversational state State retained in a session object during the conversation between the client of the application and the application itself. The state consists of the session bean instance fields and the transitive closure of the objects that are reachable from the bean's fields.

create method A method defined in the home interface and invoked by a client to create an enterprise bean.

declarative transaction demarcation Container-managed transaction demarcation. Also referred to as *declarative transactions*.

dependent object A business entity that is not directly exposed to a multitude of applications. External clients can access dependent objects only through a specific entity bean that uses the dependent object.

deployer In the target operational environment, an expert who installs enterprise beans in an EJB container. The deployer may also customize the enterprise beans for the target operational environment.

Deployment descriptor An XML document that contains the declarative information about the enterprise bean. The deployment descriptor directs a deployment tool to deploy enterprise beans with specific container options and describes configuration requirements that the deployer must resolve.

.ear file An enterprise application archive file that contains a J2EE application.

EJB container A programming environment for the development, deployment, and runtime management of enterprise beans.

EJB container provider A vendor that provides the EJB container.

ejb-jar file A Java archive (JAR) file that contains one or more enterprise beans with their deployment descriptor.

EJB server   Software that provides services to an EJB container. For example, an EJB container typically relies on a transaction manager that is part of the EJB server to perform the two-phase commit across all participating resource managers. The J2EE architecture assumes that an EJB container is hosted by an EJB server from the same vendor, so it does not specify the contract between these two entities. An EJB server may host one or more EJB containers.

EJB server provider   A vendor that supplies an EJB server.

EJB timer service   A container-provided service that allows enterprise beans to register for timer callbacks. Timer callbacks can occur at a specified time, after an elapsed period of time, or at specified intervals.

enterprise bean   A component that is part of a distributed enterprise application and that implements a business process or business entity. The types of enterprise beans are session beans, entity beans, and message-driven beans.

enterprise bean class   A Java class that implements the business methods and the enterprise bean object life-cycle methods.

enterprise bean deployment   The process of installing an enterprise bean in an EJB container.

enterprise bean home objects   Objects that implement the enterprise bean home interface. The EJB container implements these objects.

enterprise bean objects   Objects that implement the enterprise bean's component interface. The EJB container implements these objects.

entity bean   A type of enterprise bean that can be shared by multiple clients and the state of which is maintained in a resource manager. An entity bean can implement a business entity or a business process.

entity bean home objects   Objects that implement an entity bean's home interface.

entity object   Objects that implement an entity bean's component interface. These objects are object-oriented representations of real-life business entities and business processes.

Extensible Markup Language (XML)   A markup language that allows you to define the tags, or markup, needed to identify data and text in XML documents. The deployment descriptors are expressed in XML.

find method   A method defined in the home interface and invoked by a client to locate an entity bean.

handle   An object that identifies an enterprise bean. A client may serialize the handle and then later deserialize it to obtain a reference to the enterprise bean.

home handle   An object that can be used to obtain a reference to the home interface. A home interface can be serialized and written to stable storage and deserialized to obtain the reference.

home interface   One of two interfaces for an enterprise bean. The home interface defines zero or more methods for creating and removing an enterprise bean. For session beans, the home interface defines create and remove methods, whereas for entity beans, the home interface defines create, find, and remove methods.

Hypertext Markup Language (HTML)   A markup language for hypertext documents on the Internet. HTML enables the embedding of images, sounds, video streams, form fields, references to other objects with URLs, and basic text formatting.

HyperText Transfer Protocol (HTTP)   The Internet protocol used to fetch hypertext objects from remote hosts. HTTP messages consist of requests from client to server and responses from server to client.

ISV   Abbreviation for *independent software vendor.*

Java™ 2 Platform, Enterprise Edition (J2EE)   An environment for developing and deploying enterprise applications. The J2EE platform consists of a set of services, APIs, and protocols that provide functionality for developing multitiered, Web-based applications.

Java™ 2 Platform, Standard Edition (J2SE)   The core Java technology platform.

JavaServer Pages™ (JSP)   An extensible Web technology that uses template data, custom elements, scripting languages, and server-side Java objects to return dynamic content to a client. Typically, the template data is an HTML or XML element, and in many cases the client is a Web browser.

local interface   One of the business interfaces for an enterprise bean. The enterprise bean local interface defines the business methods that can be called by a client colocated on the same JVM as the bean.

message-driven bean   A type of enterprise bean that supports asynchronous communication.

method permission   A permission to invoke a specified group of methods of an enterprise bean's home and component interfaces.

passivation   The process of disassociating an enterprise bean object from an instance of the enterprise bean class. For a stateful session bean, passivation typically results in moving a session object's state to secondary memory.

persistence   The protocol for making an object's state durable.

primary key   An object that uniquely identifies an entity bean within a home.

remote interface   One of the business interfaces for an enterprise bean. The enterprise bean remote interface, which allows for distribution between a client and a bean, defines the business methods that can be called by a client.

remote method invocation (RMI)   A technology that allows an object running in one JVM to invoke methods on an object running in a different JVM.

resource manager   Provides access to a set of shared resources. A resource manager participates in a transaction. An example of a resource manager is a relational database management system (RDBMS).

resource manager connection   An object that represents a session with a resource manager.

resource manager connection factory   An object used for creating a resource manager connection.

RMI-IIOP   A version of RMI implemented to use CORBA IIOP. RMI-IIOP provides interoperability with CORBA objects implemented in any language, if all the remote interfaces are originally defined as RMI interfaces.

rollback   The point in a transaction when all updates to any resources involved in the transaction are reversed.

Secure Sockets Layer (SSL)   A security protocol that provides privacy over the Internet. The protocol allows client/server applications to communicate in a tamper-free way that cannot be eavesdropped. Servers are always authenticated, and clients are optionally authenticated.

servlet   A Java program that extends the functionality of a Web server. Servlets generate dynamic content and interact with Web clients by using a request/ response paradigm.

session bean   A type of enterprise bean that implements a conversational business process. A session bean may be stateful or stateless.

session bean home objects   Objects that implement a session bean's home interface.

session bean objects   Objects that implement a session bean's remote interface.

stateful session bean   A type of a session bean class that retains state on behalf of its client across multiple method invocations by the client. The state of a session bean is maintained by the container and is not externalized to a resource manager.

stateless session bean   A type of a session bean class that does not retain any client-specific state between client-invoked methods. All instances of a stateless session bean are identical.

system administrator   The person who configures and administers the enterprise computing and networking infrastructure, which includes the EJB server and container. The system administrator is also responsible for most security-related administration responsibilities.

transaction   An atomic unit of work that modifies data. A transaction encloses one or more program statements, all of which either complete or roll back. Transactions enable multiple users to access the same data concurrently.

transaction attribute   Specified in an enterprise bean's deployment descriptor, a value used by the EJB container to control the transaction scope when the enterprise bean's methods are invoked. A transaction attribute can have the following values: `Required`, `RequiresNew`, `Supports`, `NotSupported`, `Mandatory`, and `Never`.

transaction manager   Provides the services and management functions required to support transaction demarcation, transactional resource management, synchronization, and transaction context propagation.

transaction service   The same as the *transaction manager.*

.war file   A Web archive file containing the class files for servlets and JSPs.

Web application   An application built for the Internet with Java technologies, such as JSP and servlets, as well as with non-Java technologies, such as CGI and Perl.

Web component   A component, such as a servlet or JSP, that provides services in response to HTTP requests.

Web container   A programming environment for the development, deployment, and runtime management of servlets and JSP.

Web services   Services offered via the Web. In a typical Web services scenario, a business application sends a request to a service at a given URL using the SOAP protocol over HTTP. The service receives the request, processes it, and may return a response.

Index

The Java™ Series

The Java™ Web Services Tutorial

ISBN 0-201-63456-2

The Java™ Programming Language Third Edition

ISBN 0-201-70433-1

Effective Java™ Programming Language Guide

ISBN 0-201-31005-8

The J2EE™ Tutorial

ISBN 0-201-79168-4

The Java™ Tutorial, Third Edition
A Short Course on the Basics

ISBN 0-201-70393-9

The Java™ Tutorial Continued
The Rest of the JDK™

ISBN 0-201-48558-3

J2EE™ Technology in Practice
Building Business Applications with the Java™ 2 Platform, Enterprise Edition

ISBN 0-201-74622-0

The Java™ Developers ALMANAC 1.4, Volume 1
Examples and Quick Reference

ISBN 0-201-75280-8

The Java™ Developers ALMANAC 1.4, Volume 2
Examples and Quick Reference

ISBN 0-201-76810-0

The Java™ Class Libraries Second Edition, Volume 1
java.io java.lang java.math java.net java.text java.util

ISBN 0-201-31002-3

The Java™ Class Libraries Second Edition, Volume 2
java.applet java.awt java.beans

ISBN 0-201-31003-1

The Java™ Class Libraries Second Edition, Volume 1
Supplement for the Java™ 2 Platform Standard Edition, v1.2

ISBN 0-201-48552-4

Programming Open Service Gateways with Java Embedded Server™ Technology

ISBN 0-201-71102-8

Java Card™ Technology for Smart Cards
Architecture and Programmer's Guide

ISBN 0-201-70329-7

JavaSpaces™ Principles, Patterns, and Practice

ISBN 0-201-30955-6

The Java™ Language Specification Second Edition

ISBN 0-201-31008-2

Java™ Message Service API Tutorial and Reference
Messaging for the J2EE™ Platform

ISBN 0-201-78472-6

Inside Java™ 2 Platform Security, Second Edition
Architecture, API Design, and Implementation

ISBN 0-201-78791-1

Concurrent Programming in Java™ Second Edition
Design Principles and Patterns

ISBN 0-201-31009-0

JNDI API Tutorial and Reference
Building Directory-Enabled Java™ Applications

ISBN 0-201-70502-8

The Java™ Native Interface
Programmer's Guide and Specification

ISBN 0-201-32577-2

The Java™ Virtual Machine Specification Second Edition

ISBN 0-201-43294-3

Applying Enterprise JavaBeans™ 2.1 Second Edition
Component-Based Development for the J2EE™ Platform

ISBN 0-201-91466-2

Programming Wireless Devices with the Java™ 2 Platform, Micro Edition

ISBN 0-201-74627-1

Java™ 2 Platform, Enterprise Edition
Platform and Component Specifications

ISBN 0-201-70456-0

J2EE™ Connector Architecture and Enterprise Application Integration

ISBN 0-201-77580-8

Designing Enterprise Applications with the J2EE™ Platform, Second Edition

ISBN 0-201-78790-3

The Java 3D™ API Specification, Second Edition

ISBN 0-201-71041-2

Java™ Look and Feel Design Guidelines: Advanced Topics

ISBN 0-201-77582-4

The JFC Swing Tutorial
A Guide to Constructing GUIs

ISBN 0-201-43321-4

JDBC™ API Tutorial and Reference, Second Edition
Universal Data Access for the Java™ 2 Platform

ISBN 0-201-43328-1

Java™ Platform Performance
Strategies and Tactics

ISBN 0-201-70969-4

JDBC™ API Tutorial and Reference, Third Edition

ISBN 0-321-17384-8

Please see our Web site (http://www.awprofessional.com/javaseries)
for more information on these titles.